MW01006991

PUBLICATIONS OF THE
PERRY FOUNDATION FOR BIBLICAL RESEARCH
IN THE HEBREW UNIVERSITY OF JERUSALEM

A COMMENTARY ON THE BOOK OF GENESIS

by

U. CASSUTO

Late Professor of Bible at the Hebrew University of Jerusalem

Translated from the Hebrew by

ISRAEL ABRAHAMS

Professor of Hebrew, University of Cape Towr

PART II

FROM NOAH TO ABRAHAM

GENESIS VI 9 — XI 32

WITH AN APPENDIX: A FRAGMENT OF PART III

JERUSALEM

THE MAGNES PRESS, THE HEBREW UNIVERSITY

PART TWO

FROM NOAH TO ABRAHAM
A Commentary on Genesis VI 9—XI 32

מ.ד. קאסוטו: מנח עד אברהם

First published in Hebrew, Jerusalem 1949
and reprinted in 1953, 1959, 1965, 1969, 1974, 1978, 1983, 1986

First English Edition, Jerusalem 1964
Reprinted 1974, 1984, 1992, 1997

Distributed by The Magnes Press, P.O.B. 7695, Jerusalem 91076, Israel

©

All rights reserved by
The Magnes Press
The Hebrew University
Jerusalem 1997

ISBN 965–223–540–7

Typesetting: Central Press, Jerusalem
Printing: Ahva Cooperative Press, Jerusalem

TRANSLATOR'S FOREWORD

From Noah To Abraham is the second volume in a series of comprehensive commentaries on the Book of Genesis that the late Professor Umberto Cassuto had planned as part of a *magnum opus* embracing the whole Pentateuch and also the Book of Psalms.

The first volume bears a separate title, *From Adam To Noah,* but in the present book the author refers to it as Part I, in order to emphasize the relationship of the two volumes as an exegetical sequence. The nexus between the two commentaries is fully borne out by the style and techniques employed in the annotations. Above all the principles of interpretation are the same. These had previously been expounded by Professor Cassuto in his masterly Italian study *La Questione della Genesi* (1934), and summarized in his shorter Hebrew work, *The Documentary Hypothesis* (1942). Thereafter, elaborated in the light of the epoch-making archaeological discoveries of our time, especially in the field of Ugaritic literature, they formed the basis of his commentary on the opening chapters of Genesis. Now, by extending his method of exegesis in this volume to another section of the Torah, Cassuto indirectly buttressed his theories with new evidence of the inherent rightness of his approach. Just as in the realm of physics or chemistry every additional experiment that produces results consonant with a given hypothesis is regarded as added confirmation of its probability, so in the sphere of Biblical studies the successful extension of the area of exposition serves to validate the commentator's interpretative principles. These considerations apart, the present work is rich in original insights and scholarly illuminations that make it an invaluable guide to the Bible student — be he an erudite scholar or just a well-read lay enquirer — irrespective of the opinions he holds with regard to the Higher Critical doctrines.

The first Hebrew edition of *From Noah To Abraham* was confined to the *sidra* or pericope 'Noah' (Gen. vi 9–xi 32). Subsequent editions, however, included a fragment of the next pericope (*ibid.* xii 1–xvii 27) on which the author had started to work with the intention of producing a companion volume to his first two commentaries on Genesis; he named the new book, *Abraham And The Promised Land*. Man proposes . . . It was not, alas, Cassuto's destiny, to our infinite sorrow, to complete his plans. At the fifth verse of the thirteenth chapter of the first book of the Torah the pen fell from his strengthless hand.

The sudden and untimely passing of Cassuto, when he was at the height of his scholarly creativity, was an immeasurable loss to Jewish scholarship as a whole, and more specifically to Bible research and exposition. Even the fragment from the third volume of his commentary on Genesis is a brilliant example of exegetical writing. I shall, I believe, be voicing the views of many Biblical exegetes when I declare that we cannot but be grateful that this segment of his contemplated work was vouchsafed us, although the heart yearns for what the *maestro* still had in his mind but was not granted to bequeath to us in writing.

As in the case of the earlier volumes that I translated, I wish to acknowledge my debt of gratitude to all who assisted me in my labours. My heartfelt thanks go out in the first instance to Mr. Silas S. Perry, the munificent founder of 'The Perry Foundation for Biblical Research in the Hebrew University of Jerusalem' for his unfailing understanding, encouragement and inspiration. Dr. S. E. Loewenstamm came to my aid on all Ugaritic problems, and directly and indirectly helped me to unravel other baffling questions. Dr. Milka Cassuto-Salzmann prepared the Indexes and, as convener of the proof-readers, saw the book through the press with true filial devotion and zeal for correctness in every detail. The Printers had a major struggle in satisfying a fastidious and oft-times trying translator, but emerged triumphant. To all these, and others whom I cannot mention here, I wish to convey my sincere and grateful appreciation.

ISRAEL ABRAHAMS

Cape Town
December, 1962
Kislev, 5723

VIII

KEY TO THE TRANSLITERATION
HEBREW
(a) CONSONANTS

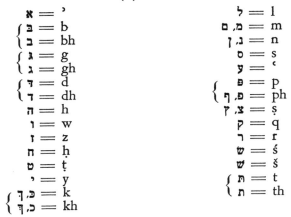

א	= ʾ		ל	= l
{ ב	= b		ם , מ	= m
{ ב	= bh		ן , נ	= n
{ ג	= g		ס	= s
{ ג	= gh		ע	= ʿ
{ ד	= d		ב	= p
{ ד	= dh		{ ף , פ	= ph
ה	= h		{ ץ , צ	= ṣ
ו	= w		ק	= q
ז	= z		ר	= r
ח	= ḥ		שׂ	= ś
ט	= ṭ		שׁ	= š
י	= y		{ ת	= t
{ ך , כ	= k		{ ת	= th
{ ך , כ	= kh			

Note: (1) Unsounded ה at the end of a word is not represented in the transcription;

(2) the customary English spelling is retained for Biblical names and rabbinic works and authorities.

(b) VOWELS

Long		Short	
ָ (Qāmeṣ gādhōl) = ā		ַ = a	
ִי (Ḥīreq gādhōl) = ī		ֶ = e	
= ē		ִ (Ḥīreq qāṭān) = i	
= ō		ָ (Qāmeṣ qāṭān) = o	
= ū		ֻ = u	

: (Šᵉwāʾ)	= ᵉ
ֱ	= ă
ֳ	= ŏ
ֳ	= ĕ

Note: Capital E represents ֶ , ֵ and ֵ ; thus אֱלֹהִים is transliterated ʾElōhīm, and אֵל is transcribed El.

ARABIC AND OTHER LANGUAGES

The method commonly used in scientific works was followed in the transliteration of Arabic, Akkadian, Egyptian and Ugaritic words.

CONTENTS

Part II: FROM NOAH TO ABRAHAM

SECTION ONE: The Flood (vi 9–ix 17)

CONTENTS

SECTION TWO: The Sons of Noah (ix 18–xi 9)

SECTION THREE: The History of the Sons of Shem (xi 10–32)

XII

APPENDIX

A Fragment of Part III: ABRAHAM AND THE PROMISED LAND

I REFER to the commentaries on the Book of Genesis only by the author's name (e.g., Dillmann, Gunkel, Jacob). Obvious abbreviations — for instance, *Forsch. u. Forthschr., Jew. Enc.* and the like — are not given here.

AJA	American Journal of Archaeology
ANET	J.B. Pritchard (ed.) *Ancient Near Eastern Texts relating to the Old Testament*, 2nd ed., Princeton 1955
ARW	Archiv für Religionswissenschaft
BASOR	Bulletin of the American Schools of Oriental Research
E	Elohist
E.V.	English Version of the O.T.
GSAI	Giornale della Società Asiatica Italiana
J	Jahwist
JAOS	Journal of the American Oriental Society
JBL	Journal of Biblical Literature
JNES	Journal of Near Eastern Studies
JPOS	Journal of the Palestine Oriental Society
K.	Kouyunjik Collection, British Museum
NThS	Nieuwe theologische Studiën
P	Priestly Code
Part I	U. Cassuto, *From Adam to Noah,* English translation, Jerusalem 1961 (A Commentary on the Book of Genesis, Part I)
Questione	U. Cassuto, *La Questione della Genesi,* Firenze 1934
RB	Revue Biblique
S	Seir
Studi	U. Cassuto, Studi sulla Genesi, *GSAI* N.S. I (1925–1926), pp. 193–239; 297–330
W.B.	H. Weld-Blundell Collection, Ashmolean Museum
ZDMG	Zeitschrift der deutschen morgenländischen Gesellschaft

FROM NOAH TO ABRAHAM

PREFACE

THIS VOLUME, which comprises an exposition of the pericope *Noah* (Gen. vi 9–xi 32), is a continuation of my Commentary on pericope *Bereshith* (Gen. i–vi 8), published several years ago under the title *From Adam to Noah* *. My observations in the Introduction to that study are equally applicable to the work that I now present to the reader.

It is my pleasant duty to express, from the deeps of the heart, my profound thanks and appreciation to Mr. Silas S. Perry, who established at the Hebrew University a Foundation for Biblical Research, and whose wish it was that this fund should be devoted, among other objects, to the continuation of my exposition of the Pentateuch. According to the plan decided upon, which I propose to follow, *Deo Volente,* in my remaining work in this series, the annotations to the Book of Genesis will take the detailed form that characterizes the two parts already in print, whilst the notes on the rest of the Torah will be briefer, one volume being allocated to each book. I shall not, however, delay the preparation of this shorter commentary until the completion of the longer one on Genesis. I hope that in the coming year I shall be privileged to publish my commentary on the Book of Exodus.

JERUSALEM, IYAR, 5709 (1949)

U. C.

---

* Referred to in this volume as Part I.

SECTION ONE

THE FLOOD

CHAPTER VI, VERSE 9 — CHAPTER IX, VERSE 17

INTRODUCTION

§ 1. THIS SECTION describes in detail the fulfilment of the Divine decision mentioned at the end of the preceding section. There it is briefly stated that the Lord resolved to bring general retribution upon mankind because of their evil deeds, and to blot them and all living creatures from the face of the ground; *But Noah found favour in the eyes of the Lord.* With this passing reference the section closes. Why Noah found grace in the Lord's eyes and how he was saved when the fearful punishment came is related in our section with epic elaboration. Noah, the man of perfect righteousness, was, on account of his righteousness, vouchsafed deliverance, together with his whole family and representatives of every species of animal, from the waters of the Flood, which the Lord had brought upon the earth in order to destroy all flesh. In this way there was a renewal of life on the face of the earth after the Deluge, and the blessing that was given to the First Man at the time of his creation was realized in Noah and his seed.

Here also, as in the story of Creation, the Torah controverts, in a number of respects, the tradition that was widespread among the neighbouring peoples concerning the Flood, and possibly, to some extent, even the stories that were current among the Israelites in early times. In this instance, too, the opposition of Scripture does not find expression in polemic or argument, but is merely implied in the modified account of the events. This new version inculcates important doctrines in conformity with the Torah's ideology. Primarily, it seeks to teach that the world is judged in accordance with righteousness, and that the Judge of the whole earth always acts justly towards both the wicked and the righteous. This is the basic teaching of the section; we shall revert to it later

3

on. Apart from this verity, the passage conveys incidentally other truths. For example, God's blessing to Noah and his sons after the Flood, which repeats the *ipsissima verba* of the benison bestowed on Adam and comes as the fulfilment of that ancient covenant, contains the thought that the word of the Lord endures for ever, under all conditions and in all circumstances. Similarly, certain aspects of the narrative emphasize, as we shall see in the continuation of our commentary, God's paternal love for his creatures, and also His attribute of mercy, which persists even when justice takes its course. So, too, we shall note how our passage points to the merit of doing God's bidding (vi 22, etc.); to the importance of being grateful for the good that comes to us from His hand (viii 20); to the unqualified prohibition of the shedding of human blood (ix 5–6); to the duty to respect the principle of life in other creatures (ix 4); to the need to honour the delicate relationship between man and other living beings (viii 9), and so forth.

§ 2.   Traditions relating to the Flood, or to a similar event, exist among different races throughout the world. Nearest to the Biblical account are those found among the peoples of Mesopotamia — the Sumerians and the Akkadians. From them these sagas passed on to the Hittites and the Hurrians, who adapted and translated the Mesopotamian texts on the subject; thereafter, apparently through the intermediacy of the Hittites, they were transmitted to the Greeks and from them, in turn, to the Hellenistic world, which possibly was also influenced by Jewish sources. The Romans, needless to say, are included in the ambit of Hellenistic culture. The legends of the Iranians, Indians and Chinese, on the other hand, are essentially different from the Biblical narrative, and have only a few indeterminate elements in common with it. A still greater divergence exists between the Biblical account and the Egyptian story that some scholars regard as a remote parallel to our section. This is likewise true of the myths found among some of the North European races. It has furthermore been suggested that evidence of a corresponding tradition among the Etruscans was to be seen in the model of a bronze boat, adorned with figures of various animals, that was discovered in one of the graves of Etruria. But it seems that in reality this vessel has a totally different significance

4

and is in no way related to Noah's ark. Stories about floods in general form part of the tribal folklore of distant countries, as far away as the southernmost regions of America, but these possibly preserve only memories of local happenings, or represent confused echoes of the Scriptural narratives, which the natives heard from Christian missionaries. But if we surmise, as several scholars have done, that a primitive tradition regarding the Flood passed from Asia to America with the migrations of the peoples in the paleo-lithic, or at the beginning of the mesolithic, age, this prototype would be so far removed in time as to make it quite impossible to determine its details and, *a fortiori*, to learn from its reconstruction ought that could shed light on the Bible story.

Only the Mesopotamian account of historical times could be of any help to us in elucidating our section. To this material we have to devote particular attention; and since the resemblance between the Mesopotamian and Biblical traditions is far more manifest in the narrative of the Deluge than in that of the preceding chapters, it is desirable at this stage to discuss the subject at somewhat greater length.

Great importance was attached in Mesopotamia to the story of the Flood, and already the ancient Sumerian writings make it (under the name A.MA.RU.) one of the their principal themes. It was a favourite subject with the poets, and on the basis of these epics, the 'historiographers' distinguished between the antediluvian and post-diluvian lists of kings. From the Sumerians the saga was handed down to the Akkadians, and the Deluge (in Akkadian, *abûbu*) also became a popular topic in Akkadian poetry from earliest time. Among the remains of the two literatures extant today are to be found documents containing descriptions of the Flood that differ in detail, and doubtless there also existed other texts on the subject at some time.

The earliest of those in our possession today is a Sumerian inscription belonging to the close of the third millenium B.C.E., which was discovered in Nippur and published in 1914 by A. Poebel. The main part of it recounts the story of the Flood and how Ziusudra, the hero of the narrative, was elevated to the rank of a deity (*Zi-u-sud-ra* appears to be the most correct form of the name, slight variations of which also occur). The tablet on which this document is recorded is mutilated and only a few fragments of the text have survived — about a third of each of its six columns. It would be impossible to understand these fragments fully without reference to another inscription of somewhat later date, which has reached us almost intact, namely, Tablet xi of the Gilgameš Epic; this text is in the Akkadian tongue and is undoubtedly based on the ancient Sumerian tradition. It is advisable, therefore, in order to facilitate the reader's understanding of the subject, that we should first glance at the account given in the Gilgameš Epic, and then proceed to the Sumerian version, and finally consider the remaining texts.

The Gilgameš Epic, which comprises in its tablets a mythological tale concerning the adventures and deeds of the hero Gilgameš, king of Erech, was, as S. N. Kramer has shown recently (1944) in a basic study of the subject, the work of the Babylonian poets, who gathered and arranged therein the material preserved in a number of separate Sumerian stories relating to this hero, and also in other Sumerian narratives that originally had no connection whatsoever with his career; they also augmented this store of legend with additions of their own.

The Babylonian epos was already in existence at the beginning of the second millenium B.C.E., and we possess fragments of it that were inscribed in the first half of that millenium. Subsequent to this recension in ancient Babylonian, an Assyrian copy was made of which we have larger fragments. An examination of the portions that have come down to us from both versions shows that although there are discrepancies between the two, on the whole they are in agreement. Hence, notwithstanding that the story of the Flood survives only in the Assyrian reproduction, it may be assumed that the narrative in the ancient Babylonian text was essentially similar to the account given in the Assyrian rendering.

The epic relates that the hero Gilgameš, greatly affected by the death of his friend Enkidu, and terrified by the darkness of the netherworld, yearned for eternal life such as the gods enjoyed; and in order to learn how this goal might be attained, he resolved to journey to the dwelling-place of Utnapištim (this is the Akkadian name of the hero, corresponding to the Sumerian *Ziusudra*), who was saved from the Flood and was raised to the status of

6

divinity; perchance he would be privileged to receive from him the desired information. After a harrowing journey through places full of alarming difficulties and terrifying perils, he succeeded in appearing before Utnapištim and asking his question. The latter, in order to demonstrate to him that his deification was due to special, non-recurrent circumstances, tells him the whole story of the Deluge.

I give here a detailed summary — for the most part, a literal translation from the Akkadian original — of the tale that Utnapištim unfolded to Gilgameš. I need hardly state that I have taken into account the results of the latest studies on the Gilgameš Epic up to that of A. L. Oppenheim (1948). I use round brackets ( ) to mark the words that have been inserted to complete the lacunae, and square brackets [ ] to indicate my explanatory insertions.

In his opening words, Utnapištim mentioned his city Šuruppak [or, Šurippak], which in his days already was ancient and inhabited by the gods. Now at the assembly of the great divinities, their hearts prompted them to bring the Flood upon the earth. [The plan was initiated and proposed, as will be explained further on, by the god Enlil; possibly it is on account of this that emphasis is given here, in the list of deities that participated in the assembly, to Enlil's title, 'their counsellor' (mālikšunu), although this is found in other places, too.] But Ea, another of the divinities that were present, [wished to rescue her beloved Utnapištim. Since, however, it is forbidden to reveal to any one what was decided in the assembly of the gods, Ea acted cunningly and] turned and spoke to the reed hut and to its wall [this may refer to the abode of Utnapištim and to the dream that he dreamt, as we shall see later. And thus Ea said:] 'O hut, hut, wall! Hear, O hut, give ear, O wall! Man of Šuruppak, son of Ubar-Tutu, pull down the house, build yourself a ship; abandon the possessions, preserve life; forsake the goods and save life! Aboard the ship let the seed of every living being come. The dimensions of the ship that you shall make shall be calculated; its width and its length shall be equal, and you shall cover it (a)s the deep' [possibly the meaning is: just as the waters of the deep cover the bottom of the sea; compare Isa. xi 9, Hab. ii 14; or: just as the waters

7

of the deep are covered and flow only through the springs, so shall the vessel be covered above, and in the cover there shall be one entrance, for going in and out].

'I [Utnapištim proceeds to reply] said to my lord Ea: "(I have heard), my lord, what thou hast thus commanded me; I shall honour and do it. But what shall I answer the city and the people and the elders [if they ask me for what purpose I build the boat]?"'. The god bade him reply: 'I flee before Enlil who hates me, and I turn to the Ocean to dwell there with Ea, my god, and he, Ea, shall bring down upon you rain of produce [the word *kibâti* has two meanings: it may signify *produce* and also *disaster,* calamity. The intention was therefore to mislead the inhabitants of the city by ambiguous talk].

Then Utnapištim described the construction of the ship in detail, its measurements, its division into compartments, the quantity of pitch [*kupru* in Akkadian; in Hebrew כֹּפֶר *kōpher*] that he used, and the large store of supplies that he laid in. He went on to relate that he took aboard the ship all his silver and gold, all the seed of living creatures that he had, all his household and relations, the cattle of the field and the beasts of the field, and all the craftsmen. Prior to this, the god Šamaš had set the time for him, saying: 'When the rain of disaster [see my note above] comes down in the evening, go on board the ship, and close its entrance.' When the appointed day arrived, the rain of calamity began to come down in the evening; then Utnapištim entered the ship and closed the door. He gave the boatman Puzur-Amurri charge of the piloting of the ship.

Morning came, and lo! a black cloud rose from the end of the sky, and the god Adad thundered therein . . . Irragal tore out the beams [dams]. Ninurta went and caused [the upper waters] to stream down upon the dams; the Anunnaki lifted up torches and illumined the whole earth with their light [expressions borrowed from the technical terminology of irrigation in the annual flooding of the rivers]. The fury of Adad reached the heavens, and he turned all the light into darkness . . . .

The gods were panic-stricken before the deluge; they fled and ascended to the heaven of Anu [that is, to the highest heaven]; they cowered like dogs and lay down at the extremity [of the world]. The goddess Ištar cried out like a woman in travail, the sweet-voiced head-goddess cried aloud . . . . The divinities, the Anunnaki, wept with her, the gods sat upon the ground and wept. . . . Six days and (six) nights the tempest blew, and the flood-waters deluged the land. When the seventh day came, the fury of the flood abated. The sea became calm, the wind was stilled and the flood ceased.

'Then I opened [Utnapištim continued] the window and the light fell upon my face [this appears to be the correct place of this sentence, which occurs further on in the tablet]; I gazed at the sea and behold there was silence: all the people had been turned to clay . . . I sat down on the bottom of the ship and I wept, and tears ran down my face. I looked to the bounds of the land, at the vast expanse of the sea, and behold, in the fourteen directions, the mountains of the regions had risen [above the face of the waters]. The ship came to a stop on Niṣir. Mount Niṣir stayed the ship and did not let her move. One day and a second, Mount Niṣir stayed the ship and did not let her move; a third day and a fourth, Mount Niṣir stayed the ship and did not let her move; a fifth day and a sixth, Mount Niṣir stayed the ship and did not let her move.

'When the seventh day arrived, I brought out the dove and sent her forth, and the dove went and turned back; there was no resting-place, so she returned. I brought out the swallow and sent her forth, and the swallow went and turned back; there was no resting-place for her, so she returned. I brought out the raven and sent it forth, and the raven went and, seeing that the waters had subsided, it ate and searched in the mud and cawed and did not return. I brought forth [everything] to the four corners of the world, and I offered a sacrifice and I burnt incense on the top of the mountain. Seven and seven bowls I set up, and beneath them [or: in them] I spread reeds, cedar-wood and myrtle. The gods smelled the odour, the gods smelled the sweet odour, and they gathered together like flies over the sacrificer' [possibly the meaning is that the deities were eager to eat of the oblations because during the deluge there was no one to offer sacrifices to them].

At this point Utnapištim tells of the disputes that broke out between the divinities around the offering. Ištar lifted up the great pendants that Anu had made for her, and cried: 'As truly as I shall not forget the lapis lazuli at my neck, so shall I never forget these days!' She proposed that Enlil should not be allowed to enjoy the sacrifice, since he acted unwisely in bringing catastrophe on the earth and destroying the children of men. Enlil, on the other hand, began to wax angry and to rage when he saw the ship and realized that several people had been saved from the waters of the deluge. Ninurta said: 'Who, but Ea, could do this thing? For behold, Ea knows every device' [that is, Ninurta disclosed that Ea was the cause of Utnapištim's deliverance]. Then Ea turned to Enlil and said to him: 'How didst thou bring the flood without consideration? Should not the sinner alone bear his sin? If it was thy wish to bring calamity upon mankind, thou couldst have sent against them a lion or a wolf or famine or pestilence, but thou shouldst not have killed all of them by flood.' As for himself, Ea asserted in self-defence: 'I did not reveal the secret of the great gods; I showed a dream to *Atraḫasis* [that is, the 'most wise', which is a title borne by Utnapištim, as we shall see later on], and then he heard the secret of the gods. And now [so Ea declares at the end of his narration] take counsel concerning him' [to wit, Utnapištim].

'Then Enlil boarded the ship [in view of the turn of events, he became reconciled to the existing position] and took hold of my hand [thus Utnapištim concluded his story] and brought me up [from the recesses of the ship to its covering] and he also brought up my wife, and caused her to kneel at my side, and he stood between us and touched our foreheads and blessed us [saying]: "Hitherto Utnapištim was a man, but now Utnapištim and his wife shall be like us, the gods, and Utnapištim shall dwell afar off, at the mouth of the rivers." So [the gods] took me, and afar off, at the mouth of the rivers, they caused me to dwell.'

This saga, it will be recalled, has its origin in Sumerian literature, and it helps up to understand the fragments of the earlier Sumerian Tablet (mentioned above) that was discovered in Nippur.

As I have already stated, only mutilated fragments of the

10

document have survived — a third approximately of each of its six columns. What remains of the first two columns of the Tablets refers to the creation of the world, the descent of kingship from heaven to earth, and the building of the five antediluvian Babylonian cities (Eridu, Badtibira, Larak, Sippar, Šuruppak), and the remnants of the other four columns contain fragments of the story of the Flood. The entire text was intended to be recited, it seems, as a magic incantation. The first surviving fragment appertaining to the Deluge (col. 3) takes up the story at a point after the deities' decision. The goddess Nintu or Innanna (that is, Ištar) cries aloud like a woman in travail for the bitter fate of mankind, and the god Enki (identical with Ea) devises a plan in his mind. King Ziusudra, who occupies himself with the administration of the temple in humility and reverence, dreams an amazing dream. In the next fragment (col. 4) we are told that he heard [in his dream] a voice that exhorted him to stand beside the wall and to hearken to the words that would be addressed to the wall; a flood would come upon the world, to destroy the seed of man in accordance with the resolve of the assembly of the gods and the command of Enlil. The segment left from col. 5 describes the storm of the deluge: the mighty winds blew violently and the flood swept down. The flood continued to pour down for seven days and seven nights, and the ship moved along over the face of the great waters, driven by the winds; then the sun reappeared and shed its light on the heavens and the earth. Thereupon Ziusudra opened the window of the ship, and the light of the sun entered therein. Ziusudra prostrated himself before the sun-god; he sacrificed a bull and offered up offerings of sheep. In the fragment from the last column (col. 6), it is stated that Ziusudra prostrated himself before Enlil, and that the latter endowed him with life like that of the gods and created for him an eternal godlike soul, and the divinities appointed his dwelling-place in the land where the sun rises.

This tablet is not the only extant document relating to the Sumerian tradition concerning the Flood. The following additional inscriptions, in particular, should be noted:

a) The first part of the Sumerian King List, which enumerates the kings who reigned before the Deluge in the five ancient cities that are named also in the aforementioned epic poem. At the beginning and the end of this section, when the descent of kingship from heaven and the Flood are referred to, there occur expressions similar to, and in some cases identical with, those in the epic — a clear indication, as Jacobsen has rightly pointed out in his monograph *The Sumerian King List,* of literary dependence.

b) The fragment K 11624 in the British Museum, which comprises the end of the list of antediluvian monarchs, followed by incomplete epic verses in the Sumerian language with an Akkadian rendering between the lines. These fractional sentences are actually, it seems, remnants of verses of the epic [in a late version] that had occurred in the mutilated portion of the Nippur Tablet between the fragmented texts of col. ii and col. iii (see Jacobsen, *op. cit.,* p. 60, note 113). They make mention also of the gathering and tumult (*ḫu-bur-šú[?]–[nu(?)]*) of people, from which it follows that also according to this recension, just as in the epic of *Atraḫasis* mentioned immediately below, the cause of the Flood was this tumult, which angered Enlil and did not permit him to sleep in peace.

c) Another Sumerian fragment (Nipp. 4611), in which one of the goddesses instructs Ziusudra (here we find one of the partial variants of the name) in the sacrificial rites and in his religious and ethical duties.

The Babylonian poets drew on the Sumerian material relating to the Flood not only in the Gilgameš Epic but also in other compositions. One of these is the poem that was called, in accordance with the practice of the ancient Orient, after its opening words, 'When the god the man', and which is usually referred to today as 'the Epic of Atraḫasis' (the by-name, as we have seen, of Utnapištim). Intact, this poem must have consisted of at least three tablets, and was intended, apparently, to serve as a kind of incantation for easing women's birth pangs. It was also originally written in the ancient Babylonian tongue, and subsequently an Assyrian version was made from it. There have survived only a few fragments of two tablets of the Babylonian recension, which were inscribed in the reign of one of the kings of the First Babylonian Dynasty (the first half of the second millenium B.C.E.), and a few fragments of two tablets belonging to the Assyrian version.

12

This poem relates that after the children of men had begun to multiply upon the face of the earth, their tumult disturbed the peace of Enlil and did not let him sleep. He therefore suggested to the other gods that calamities should be brought on mankind in order to reduce their numbers and their noise. The gods agreed to his proposal, and various disasters came upon humanity; these included seven years of famine, plague and other diseases, and the Flood. It is the latter that concerns us here. This text, also, tells of the dream that Ea showed in this connection to Atraḥasis, of the speech addressed to the hut and the wall, and of the building of the ship; and Ea's utterance here corresponds almost word for word with that in the Gilgameš Epic. In the first column of the second Babylonian fragment, we read: 'O wall, hearken unto me! O hut, take heed of my words! pull down the house, build yourself a ship; forsake possessions and save life; and the ship that you will make' .... From this point on almost the entire text as far as the end of the tablet is missing; but in the second column it is still possible to recognize the word *kupru* ('pitch'; Hebrew: כֹּפֶר *kōpher*). In one of the Assyrian fragments there is preserved part of the duologue between Ea and Atraḥasis (here I shall indicate in square brackets [ ] the words missing in the tablet) :... 'Go on board [the ship] and close the entrance thereof, [and bring int]o it your produce, your goods, and your household articles, [your wife], your family, your relatives and the craftsmen, [the cattle of] the field, the beasts of the field, all that eat grass; [I will se]nd them to you and they will guard your door.' [Atr]aḥasis opened his mouth [and sp]ake to Ea [his] lord: 'Never in my li[fe] have I made a ship [. . .]. Draw, pray, the pic[ture thereof] upon [the ea]rth, and I shall look at [the pict]ure [and I shall build] the ship [. . .] that which thou hast commanded me.'

There is still another fragment written in the ancient Babylonian tongue, which was discovered in Nippur. There are left on it only a few incomplete lines, apparently giving the words of Ea, who instructs Atraḥasis in regard to the making of the ship and its covering, and the bringing of the living creatures on board. It is impossible to tell to which text this fragment belongs; it may have formed part of the Epic of Atraḥasis, or of some other document. At all events, what is legible fits the subject-matter of this epic.

The Gilgameš Epic, and with it the story of the Flood incorporated therein, gained currency also in the land of the Hittites.
Among the texts found at Boğazköy, the site of the ancient capital
of the Hittites, there is a fragment of the saga in Babylonian, as
well as several fragments translated into the Hittite and Hurrian
languages. The fragments of the translations likewise contain references to the episode of the Deluge, which is proof of the dis-
semination of the Mesopotamian tradition on this topic in Asia
Minor.

A summary of this tradition in Greek is given in the work of the
Babylonian priest Berossus (third century B.C.E.). Although the
book was lost, its account of the Flood is known to us through
quotations from quotations, which are all based on Alexander Poly-
histor's excerpt from the narrative. Berossus altered several particulars of the story in order to make the subject more comprehensible to Greek readers; but, on the other hand, he preserved a
number of details of great antiquity, which hitherto had not been
found in the original sources. Following is the substance of his
account according to the fullest citation:

After the death of Ardates, his son Xisuthros (this name,
which is cited in other extracts as Sisuthros or Sisithros, seems
to have been formed from the Sumerian Ziusudra, whilst
Ardates was apparently intended for Ubar-Tutu) reigned for
eighteen šars (that is, 64,800 years). In his time a great flood
occurred (μέγας κατακλυσμός) the story of which is told as
follows: The god Kronos (here the Greek god is mentioned
instead of the Babylonian god Ea) appeared to him in a dream
and revealed to him that on the fifteenth day of the month
Daisios (corresponding to Sivan) mankind would be destroyed
by the waters of the flood. He therefore enjoined him to record
in a book the beginning and the middle and the end of all
things, and to bury these records in the city of the sun-god,
Sippara, (that is, the Babylonian city Sippar [another extract
reads: to bury there the books that he can find]); and also to
build for himself a ship, to go on board with his family and
his close friends, to take with him into it food and drink and
living creatures — birds and quadrupeds — and to sail when
all was ready. If he were asked whither he was sailing, he

should answer: 'To the gods, to beseech them to bestow pro-
sperity on humanity.'

He obeyed and built the vessel, five stadia in length and
two stadia in width. He did all that he had been commanded
and entered the boat with his wife and his sons and his close
friends. The flood came, and when the waters ceased to rain
down, Xisuthros sent forth several birds, and since the birds
found no food or resting-place, they returned to the ship. After
some days, he again sent out the birds, and they once more
returned to the vessel, their feet being muddied. When he let
them go a third time, they did not return to the boat. Then
Xisuthros understood that the land was already visible; he
loosened a little the seams of the ship and saw that it was
resting on one of the mountains. Together with his wife and
daughter and the boatman, he left the boat, prostrated himself
to the ground, and built an altar, and offered sacrifices to the
gods. Thereafter he disappeared together with those that left
the vessel with him. When those who remained in the ship
saw that he tarried, they, too, went out and sought him and
called him by his name. He did not appear to them, but a voice
was heard from heaven, which enjoined them ever to revere
the gods, for it was on account of his piety that he went to
dwell with the gods, and his wife and daughter and the boatman
were also granted this privilege. He further ordered them to
return to Babylon to recover, in accordance with the charge
put upon them, the writings that had been buried in Sippara,
and to transmit them to mankind. He likewise informed them
that the place where they were to be found was the land of
Armenia. On hearing all this, they offered up sacrifices to the
gods and journeyed on foot (or, by a circuitous route) to
Babylon). Parts of this ship, which had come to rest in
Armenia, still remain in the Kurdish mountains in Armenia,
and some people scrape off therefrom pitch and take it away
to use it for amulets. After reaching Babylon, they brought to
light the books at Sippara, built many cities, established temples,
and restored Babylon.

So far Berossus' account of the Flood, as it has come down to us.
Recently (1947) E.G. Kraeling advanced the theory that Beros-

15

sus had used a recension emanating from the Sumerian tradition, whose primary interest was not the rescue of Ziusudra but the rebuilding of Babylon and the revival of human culture due to the saving of the ancient books. He finds traces of this tradition also in the Torah, in Genesis xi, 1f. In our commentary to this passage, we shall revert to the subject.

§ 3. Comparison between the Biblical section on the Flood and the Mesopotamian stories on the same theme have often been made, the most recent attempt (1946) being in Heidel's work. The comparative studies published hitherto have not investigated the matter with all possible and necessary thoroughness; nor do they enter into an examination of the details of the narratives, although these are no less important than the broad parallels. It will not be superfluous, therefore, to devote further study to this comparison. In this subsection of the introduction, we shall deal with the general features of the saga and with its most important particulars; later on, in the notes on the text, we shall discuss additional details requisite to the exact elucidation of the passage. In the following subsections, we shall also have the opportunity of quoting material for collation from other parts of the Bible and from Rabbinic literature. The question of the *relationship* between the Mesopotamian and Israelite traditions we shall consider below, in § 4.

We shall begin with the parallels, and then proceed to the divergencies.

The essential narrative is identical in both traditions. The divine decision to destroy mankind and all other living creatures by the waters of the Flood; the salvation of one man with his relations and representatives of the animals by the divine injunction to build a structure (an ark or a ship), capable of floating on the water, and to enter it together with all who were destined to be saved; the coming down of the deluge; the grounding of the ark or ship on the top of a certain mountain; the sending forth of birds to ascertain if the waters had subsided from the face of the earth; the offering of sacrifices after the deliverance, their favourable acceptance and the divine blessing for the saved — all these elements are common both to the Israelite and to the Mesopotamian traditions.

Regarding details, the following points may be indicated as corresponding in the two traditions, the Biblical and the Mesopotamian:

16

(1)   The place of the hero of the Flood in the order of the generations. In the Pentateuchal version, he was the *tenth* in the genealogy of world-patriarchs; he likewise appears as the *tenth* in the list of antediluvian kings according to several recensions of the Mesopotamian tradition (see document W.B. 62, to which we referred earlier, in Pt. I, pp. 256 ff., and Berossus). But in other versions he is given as the ninth king: so the fragment K. 11624, and document W.B. 444 (see Pt.I, *loc. cit.*), which does not mention him explicitly but lists his father, Ubar-Tutu, eighth in the line of kings.

(2)   Possibly also the name of the hero of the Deluge. If the explanation, based on Ethiopic, of the name *Noah* as meaning *length,* which is advanced by several scholars, is correct, we may see in it a parallel to the name Ziusudra (probably signifying: 'he who lives long') and to that of Utnapištim (connoting possibly: 'found or saw life'). But all these interpretations are doubtful. On a parallel, found in the fragment of the Hurrian translation of the Gilgameš Epic, to the gloss on the name Noah in Gen. v 29 — 'this one shall bring us comfort' — which connects it with the stem נָחַם *nāḥam*, see Pt. I, p. 288.

(3)   The age of the hero of the Flood. The Torah gives Noah's age as 600 years at the time of the Flood; according to the afore-mentioned text W.B. 62, Ziusudra had reigned — before the Deluge, of course — ten šars, which came to 36,000 years, that is, 600 units of sixty years (on this unit see Pt. I, p. 258). Although Berossus states that Xisuthros had ruled 64,800 years, the witness of the original Sumerian document is sufficient to establish the ancient tradition.

(4)   The fixing of the measurements of the ark or ship by divine command (the dimensions vary; I shall discuss them later on in my commentary).

(5)   The division of the ark or ship into various storeys and rooms.

(6)   The specific mention of the covering, the entrance and the window of the boat or ark.

(7)   The use of pitch [כֹּפֶר *kōpher;* Akkadian *kupru*] in fitting out the ark or ship. The noun כֹּפֶר *kōpher* and the verb כָּפַר *kāphar* ['to cover with pitch'] are found nowhere else in Scripture.

17

(8)   The predetermination of the time of the commencement of the Flood.

(9)   Both in the Torah and in Berossus an exact date, month and day being mentioned, is given for the beginning of the Deluge (for the dates themselves see below, § 7, and my annotations to vii 11).

(10)   The Pentateuch clearly indicates that the animals came to Noah of their own accord, that is, as a result of an inner urge aroused in them by God (see my comments to vi 20); we are similarly told in the Epic of Atraḫasis that Ea promised Atraḫasis to send the animals to him.

(11)   Specific reference to the closing of the entrance of the ark or boat at the beginning of the Flood.

(12)   Specific mention of the opening of the window after the Deluge.

(13)   Express reference to the removal of the covering (or a part thereof) after the Flood.

(14)   The resting of the ark, according to the Torah, on the mountains of Ararat, that is, in the region subsequently called Armenia, and the grounding of the ship, according to Berossus, in Armenia (we shall discuss this matter, which is not so simple, in detail further on, in our commentary to viii 4; see also the end of this subsection).

(15)   The specification of the kinds of birds that were sent forth: raven and dove, though in different order.

(16)   In the Gilgameš Epic, the birds are sent out on the seventh day after the stranding of the vessel; similarly an interval of seven days elapses between one sending forth and another in the Penta- teuchal story (see my annotation on viii 8).

(17)   In the Torah narrative, too, if we follow the Septuagint version (viii 7), the raven did not return, just as in the Epic of Gilgameš.

(18)   Similarity of expressions in regard to the odour of the sacrifices: Gen. viii 21, *and the Lord smelled the pleasing odour;* in the Gilgameš Epic xi 159–160: 'The gods smelled the odour, the gods smelled the sweet odour.'

(19)   Other correspondences of expression: The word יִשְׁבֹּתוּ *yišbōthū* in Gen. viii 22 appears somewhat strange, for in all that

precedes there is no mention of any such cessation. Possibly we have here an echo of an ancient literary tradition, for in Akkadian the verb שָׁבַת *šābhath* signifies the action of the flood, which sweeps everything away, and this is the meaning of the synonymous verb *ùr* in the Sumerian.

In the Book of Genesis we find the phrase *to (in) His heart* both in connection with the Lord's decision to blot out man from off the earth (vi 6) and in regard to His ultimate resolve not to bring a flood again upon the world (viii 21); in the Epic of Gilgameš, xi 14 we are told that *their heart* prompted the gods to bring the Deluge. Likewise in the Sumerian Tablet of Nippur it is stated at the beginning of col. 3 that Enki (who is the same as Ea) devised a plan *in his heart*.

On the possible connection between the Hebrew word מַבּוּל *mabbūl* and the Akkadian *abûbu*, see below, my note on vi 17.

Having considered the parallels, let us now glance at the differences between the Mesopotamian stories and the Biblical narrative. In this instance, too, we shall first deal with the essential aspect of the subject and then with the details.

(1)   According to the Sumerian fragment K. 11624 and the Epic of Atraḫasis, Enlil wanted to destroy humanity because the noise of mankind disturbed him and did not let him sleep peacefully. It was for his own advantage and benefit that he put forward his proposal in the assembly of the gods, and induced them all to agree. In the Gilgameš Epic and in the summary of Berossus there is no mention of the reason for the decision taken at the assembly of the gods with regard to the Flood; it was an arbitrary resolution. Nor does the dispute that broke out between the gods after the Deluge, as described in the Gilgameš Epic, indicate that there was a motive for the decision. The questions that Ea asks Enlil are only hypothetical, and Ea does not imply that Enlil's decree had actually been intended as a punishment in any respect; on the contrary, Enlil does not attempt by a single word to justify his action.

In the Torah narrative, on the other hand, there is an ethical explanation. The Deluge is decreed purely as an act of justice; the Judge of the whole earth brings upon the sinners the retribution that they deserve, measure for measure. The moral corruption of humankind leads to their physical dissolution.

19

(2) The Mesopotamian texts depict even the deliverance of the hero of the Deluge as due to caprice. No reason is given for Ea's action for the benefit of Utnapištim. It was not on account of his uprightness or righteousness that Utnapištim was saved, but only because the god desired this. Even in the Sumerian fragment, which relates that Ziusudra devoted himself constantly to the Temple service, there is no reference to moral values, but only to Ea's intervention on behalf of one who watched over the cult. In the Gilgameš Epic we are told that Enlil was wroth when he saw that Utnapištim had been saved; in his view, all mankind were doomed to perish without any distinction being made between righteous and wicked. Only the late writer Berossus, living in the Hellenistic period, states that Xisuthros was deified because of his piety; but even he does not attribute Xisuthros' salvation from the Flood to his religious devotion.

In the Torah, on the contrary, the rescue of Noah is likewise an act of true justice; it is only right that the virtuous man should not be destroyed through the punishment of the sinners; therefore the Judge of the whole earth prepares for him a way of salvation.

(3) The Epic of Gilgameš portrays the gods as terrified and seeking refuge before the vast might of the elements of nature, which they themselves had let loose in order to bring a flood upon the world. In the Bible narrative God rules nature as He wills. He is outside nature and above it. He commands forces of nature to carry out their tasks and they obey Him. All that happens in the world does so in accordance with His desire; but to Him nothing happens.

(4) In the stories of the Mesopotamian peoples we are told of the differences of opinion among the divinities before the decision to bring the Deluge is taken, and of disputes, quarrels and recriminations between them after the Flood. In the Torah, needless to say, there is nothing corresponding to all this. No other will prevails in the world except that of the One God, and His will is absolute justice, leaving no room for, or possibility of, dispute.

(5) In the Gilgameš Epic it is related that when Utnapištim offers his sacrifices after the Deluge, the deities smell the sweet odour and gather like flies over the sacrificer. Even if we forgive the poet the unedifying simile, assuming that his intention, as

in the case of similar expressions in Homer's poems, was only to lessen somewhat the tension created by the narration of the terrifying events, nevertheless the picture of the gods scrambling for the pleasures of the sacrifice is based on an uncouth and primitive idea of the godhead, and reflects the notion current in Mesopotamia that the divinities actually ate and drank what human beings offered to them, and that they had need of oblations if they were not to suffer hunger and thirst. Now they were famished and parched, since throughout the period of the Flood no sacrifice had been offered to them. This conception is diametrically opposed to that of the Torah. In contrast to the whole of this portrayal, the Pentateuch merely contains the expression: *And the Lord smelled the pleasing odour;* only the odour — a thing without substance — is stated. The sacrifices, it should be mentioned, were *burnt offerings,* which were wholly consumed. To later generations the Biblical reference to the smelling of the pleasing odour may appear to smack of corporeality; but when we compare it with the parallel text in the Gilgameš Epic, we immediately realize how profound is the gulf between them. Generally speaking, it is not possible to understand Scriptural passages properly unless we pay attention to the ideas prevailing in their place and time of origin. Not only is there no thought of corporeality here, but, on the contrary, the verse is intended to negate the materialistic notions that characterized the concepts of that period. The precise sense in Hebrew of the expression under discussion we shall consider later on, in our annotations to viii 21.

(6)   The climax of the Mesopotamian stories is the exaltation of the hero of the Flood to divine status. In the Torah, Noah remains mortal after the Deluge just as he was before. The dividing-line between humanity and deity is not allowed to become blurred in the least.

(7)   The establishment of the Covenant for the good of mankind (Gen. ix 8–17) has no parallel in the Mesopotamian documents known to us so far.

Now let us pass on to the differences in the details of the accounts.

(1)   Ziusudra, even in his human state, was a king; whereas Noah was an ordinary person (on a similar distinction relative

to the patriarchs of the previous generations, see my observations above, Pt. I, pp. 262 f.).

(2)   Although the number of time-units comprised by Noah's life prior to the Deluge (600 years) corresponds, as we have noted, to the total units of time that Ziusudra lived before the Flood (10 šars, which come to 36,000 years, that is, 600 units of 60 years each), yet the units are different. The Torah set the measure of Noah's life at a minimum, in the same way as it dealt with the ages of the preceding generations (see Pt. I, pp. 252–264), and assigned to Noah's antediluvian life one sixtieth of the years recorded in the Mesopotamian tradition.

(3)   In the Mesopotamian inscriptions the refuge is the ship; in the Pentateuch it is the ark. We shall discuss the question of the ship and the ark below, in the commentary on vi 14, where we shall see how Scripture seeks to emphasize, by means of this detail, the Divine protection of Noah and all that were with him.

(4)   The measurements of the boat given by Berossus (in the Gilgameš Epic these are not quite clear, because the interpretation of the relevant sentences is in doubt) are highly exaggerated. Her length is almost a kilometre and her width is nearly half a kilometre. In this instance, too, the Bible reduces the figures to the minimum.

(5)   Ea instructs his loved one to mislead his fellow citizens, if they should ask for what purpose he is building the vessel. To this particular, which the Israelite ethic would not have tolerated, there is no parallel in the Torah.

(6)   The ship is closed before the Flood by Ziusudra or Utna-pištim; Noah's ark the Lord shuts in person (it has been suggested that vii 16 should read: 'and Noah shut himself in', but this conjecture is not well-founded; see my comment on the verse). Apparently the Torah wished to stress the Lord's paternal love and His providential care for all. Compare also my note to viii 1.

(7)   The Deluge continued, according to the Mesopotamians, seven days; according to the Torah, forty days. Here Scripture gives the higher figure, since it is the longer period that is the more credible; it is difficult to imagine so terrible a flood after a storm lasting no more than seven days.

(8)   The Mesopotamian narratives describe the Flood as a mighty

22

tempest accompanied by rain, lightning and thunder. The Pentateuch speaks only of rain and the waters of the deep. How this
divergency is to be explained, we shall see in our annotation to
vii 11.

(9)   The Gilgameš Epic relates that the ship stopped, when the
Deluge came to an end, on Mount Niṣir; this accords neither with
the Biblical account nor with that of Berossus. See above p. 18,
no. 14, and also further on, the commentary to viii 4.

§ 4.   Let us now endeavour to grapple with the question of the
relationship between the Mesopotamian tradition and the Pentateuchal narrative.

When fragments of the Gilgameš Epic referring to the Flood
were first discovered, many considered this text to be the source
from which the Biblical story emanated, possibly through the
mediation of the Canaanites. When other Mesopotamian fragments
on the same subject subsequently come to light, it immediately
became clear that the matter was not so simple. Clay propounded
the view that the original saga was 'Hebrew', that is, Amorite
(or, to use a term more in keeping with our present-day concepts,
West Semitic), from which the Mesopotamian legends evolved.
But neither view can readily be accepted. It is hard to imagine that
the Torah took over directly a pagan myth for inclusion in its
structure, even after editing it and making certain changes. Clay's
theory is still more difficult, since it is based on the supposed
existence of 'Amorite' texts, which actually we do not possess,
nor have we evidence of their existence. Today most scholars
(Heidel being the latest exponent of this view) are inclined to the
opinion that the Biblical and Mesopotamian narratives derive from
a common tradition. This is the third of three possibilities that can
be envisaged in an historical examination of literary works, when
there are two similar accounts, A and B: A may depend on B,
or B on A, or both may go back to a common source X. But sometimes the matter may be more complicated still. In this case, it is
certainly much more intricate. It will suffice to bear in mind that
the Sumerian and Akkadian inscriptions that have become available
to us were discovered by mere chance, and represent only an
exiguous residue of considerable material that has been lost. Since
even these are not few and vary considerably from one another, it

is likely that many more texts, differing from those in our possession, were once in existence. It is impossible, of course, to guess the contents of the inscriptions that have not survived.

The course of development of the tradition we may picture to ourselves as follows:

When the earliest ancestors of Israel dwelt in Ur of the Chaldees, they were undoubtedly well versed in the local Sumerian culture. As we have seen, the tradition regarding the Flood occupied an important place in that culture, and it is inconceivable that the circle in which the forefathers of the Israelites moved were not fully familiar with this tradition. It is impossible to tell its exact form, but undoubtedly it was in keeping with the idolatrous notions of the local inhabitants and not very different from the recensions that have come down to us. When the new religious ideas associated with the name of Abraham began to crystallize, there also developed, without doubt, a new conception of this tradition, which was subsequently brought over by the family of the Patriarchs to the land of Canaan. In that country, it seems, there existed no tradition concerning the Deluge (not only in the fragments of Ugaritic literature that are so far known to us, but even in the writings of Philo Byblius there is no mention of it); the progenitors of Israel, however, preserved the ancient memories, which were revised in accordance with their religious outlook, also in Canaan, and handed them down from generation to generation. To these was added, it appears, already at a very early period, an epic poem (possibly more than one), of the kind whose existence I discussed in my Hebrew essay on 'The Epic Poetry of Israel' (K*eneseth*, dedicated to H. N. Bialik, Vol. viii, pp. 121–142), and in my introductions to the account of Creation and the story of the Garden of Eden. There are many factors pointing to this, which merit detailing:

(1) First, we must note the poetic elements to be found in the section; these can well be explained as reflecting and continuing an older poetic tradition of the Israelites, and sometimes even as allusions to matters with which Israelite readers were already familiar. Such, for example, are the rhythmical verses marked by poetic expressions (vii 11: *all the fountains of the great deep burst forth / and the windows of the heavens were opened;* viii 2: *the fountains of the deep were closed / and the rain from the heavens*

was restrained; and so forth). To this category belongs also the reference to the bow of the Lord in the cloud, which seems to be a fragment of a theme that was more fully elaborated in the poem. Of this kind, too, are the poetic words, which are not to be found elsewhere in the Bible, like גֹּפֶר *gōpher* [name of tree], קִנִּים *qinnīm* (in the special sense of *rooms;* the usual meaning is 'nests'), כֹּפֶר *kōpher* ['pitch'] (this, as we have seen, is the word used in the Akkadian saga of the Flood), צֹהַר *ṣōhar* [see on vi 16], טָרָף *ṭārāph* ['fresh']; and other words like מַבּוּל *mabbūl* ['flood'] or יְקוּם *yeqūm* ['that which subsists', 'living things'], of which there are also not many examples in the Bible (see my commentary on all this). The verbal parallels to the Mesopotamian, poems, enumerated above in § 3 among the examples of corresponding details (Nos. 18, 19), likewise indicate a poetic tradition.

(2) In the Prophets and Hagiographa there are many allusions to the Flood. Some of them, like the mention of Noah, together with Daniel and Job (Ezek. xiv 14, 20), as an example of perfect righteousness, or expressions like *I will cut off mankind from the face of the earth* (Zeph. i 3), and similar phrases, may, it is true, be explained as simple echoes of the story of our section. Nevertheless, the fact that the verb כָּרַת *kārath* ['cut off'] describes in both these prophetic passages the principal Divine act, whilst in the Torah it occurs only incidentally at the end of the narrative, in the negative promises that God would not again bring a Deluge upon the world (ix 11), may possibly indicate the existence of an ancient literary tradition in which this verb was regularly used in connection with the Flood. From the prophet's statement that even Noah, Daniel and Job would deliver neither sons nor daughters if the Lord sent one of his four sore acts of judgment in order to punish a land that sinned against Him (Ezek. xiv 16, 18, 20), we cannot actually draw the conclusion that he had a different tradition from that of the Torah, which tells us that Noah's sons and wife and his sons' wives were also saved together with him; for it may well be that in the prophet's view our section assumes that all the members of Noah's household were righteous. However, in other parts of Scripture there occur definite allusions, especially in poetic form, to details that *are not found* in the Pentateuch, and apparently were known to the people from another

source. For instance, in Isa. liv 9, the Deluge is called *the waters
of Noah,* a phrase not used in the Torah; nevertheless, the prophet
uses it as a well established term. In the same verse there is also
mentioned, as an example of something known to all, the *oath*
that the Lord swore not to cause the waters of Noah to go over
the earth again. The Torah does, in truth, speak of a solemn
assurance, but not of an oath. The same applies to the reference
found in Jeremiah xxxiii 20–21, 25–26 (compare also *ibid.* xxxi
35–37), to the *covenant* of the Lord with the day and with the
night; our section does contain (viii 22) a promise that day and
night would not cease, but not an actual *covenant.* Also in Jeremiah
xxxiii 17–18, it is twice written לֹא יִכָּרֵת *lōʾ yikkārēth* ['there
shall not be cut off'], in keeping with the literary tradition concerning the Flood; and *ibid.* xxxi 36, the word יִשְׁבְּתוּ *yišbᵉthū* ['shall
cease'] occurs, corresponding to יִשְׁבֹּתוּ *yišbōthū* [pausal form] in
Gen. viii 22. In Psalms xxix 10 we find: *The Lord sits enthroned
over the flood; the Lord sits enthroned as King for ever;* if we
do not read as several expositors have suggested, לִמְלֹךְ *limlōkh*
['to reign'] instead of לַמַּבּוּל *lammabbūl* ['over the flood'], and
if we do not accept Epstein's explanation that the word מַבּוּל
mabbūl means *throne,* we may see in this verse an allusion to a
poetic saga concerning the Deluge that concluded with the acceptance of the *sovereignty of the Lord,* after the Flood, by all the
creatures of the world. The words of Ezekiel xxii 24, *a land . . .
nor rained upon in the day of indignation,* may possibly allude
to the fact that there was no flood in the land of Israel. This is
how some of the Talmudic sages (B. Zebaḥim 113a–b) understood the verse, and the point may also have been mentioned in
the poetic saga.

(3)   The details of the Deluge with which the Talmudic and
Midrashic literature embellishes the Torah account are in part
homiletical interpretations of Biblical texts or later legends, but
some of them correspond to what is narrated in the Mesopotamian
inscriptions and possibly belong to the ancient Israelite store of
tradition. Such, for instance, are the questions that the people of
the generation of the Flood asked Noah when he was occupied
with the building of the ark, and the answers he gave them (B.
Sanhedrin 108b, and the parallel passages). Also in the Epic

of Gilgameš and in the summary of Berossus reference is made to the questions and answers at the time of the construction of the boat. But the nature of the questions is wholly different, for whereas Utnapištim and Xisuthros reply to their contemporaries with guile in order to mislead them, Noah endeavours to reform them; nevertheless the parallel is unmistakable. Similarly, to quote another example, we find in Bereshith Rabba, xxxii 8 (see the variant reading in Theodor's edition, pp. 295–296) that the people who lived at the time of the Flood sought to overturn the ark, but the Holy one blessed be He surrounded it with lions to safeguard it; and in like vein the Epic of Atraḥasis relates: 'I shall send them (the animals) to you, and they shall guard your door (cf. Pritchard, *ANET*, p. 105 C l. 10). From the parallels to the Mesopotamian texts that occur in the late Midrashim like Pirke Rabbi Eliezer, the Book of Yashar and the Book of Noah, no evidence can be adduced relative to the Israelite tradition, since it is conceivable that they contain material that emanated at a late date, through some channel or series of channels, actually from a Mesopotamian source.

(4)   Traces of a poetic tradition may also be seen in certain words found in later literature, for example in the word חַלּוֹן *ḥallōn* ['window'] used, as in Ugaritic writings, for אֲרֻבֹּת הַשָּׁמַיִם *'arubbōth haššāmayim* ['windows (i.e. sluices) of heaven'] (in several MSS of Bereshith Rabba, xxxi 12, it is said of the giants: ['one of them . . .] would put his hand on the window [חַלּוֹן *ḥallōn*] and close it'; for the sources and variant readings see Theodor's edition, pp. 285–286).

The Torah could not very well pass over in silence the ancient poetic tradition regarding the Flood, which was already widely current among the Israelites. It was necessary to accept it for the sake of the continuity of the narrative of the history of man upon earth, and in order to provide a proper answer to the burning question that stirred every one who gave more than superficial thought to what this tradition related: Why did humanity suffer so terrible a calamity? Hence the Torah accepted the traditional story, purified and refined it, and harmonized it in all its aspects with its own doctrine.

It is impossible to determine precisely what innovations the

Israelite poets who lived in pre-Torah times introduced, and what changes the Torah made. But this is beyond doubt, that the Torah's aim was to remove from the story any residual heathen concepts and any detail that retained a semblance of idolatry about it.

On the hypothesis of such a course of development, it is possible to understand both the parallels and the differences between the Torah narrative and the Mesopotamian sagas. The acceptable elements were taken over, and those that were incongruous with the spirit of the Torah were silently ignored or were amended. Not only does the Torah exclude any reference to the will of the various gods or the natural forces, apart from the will of the Lord of the universe; not only does its concept of God transcend completely the world of nature; and not only is it free from any blurring of the boundaries between the human and the Divine; but also the more astonishing details, such as the exaggerated numbers, the incongruity between the duration of the Deluge and its results, the royal rank of the man who is saved, and the like, are absent or are reduced to a minimum; whilst the attributes of the divinity who acts arbitrarily and cunningly and gives deceitful counsel are changed to qualities of uprightness, of love for the creatures that are deserving of it, and of fatherly care for them. Thus the story that to begin with was amoral becomes a source of ethical instruction.

The primary lesson it inculcates, apart from the other teachings referred to in the first subsection of this introduction, is the answer it gives to the vexed question of the cause of the catastrophe, namely, that the universal disaster came on account of the universal wickedness of mankind, but the righteous were not destroyed together with the wicked. The answer, it is true, is only of a general character; it does not probe the problem of calamity deeply, paying no attention to exceptions, such as instances of the righteous suffering, or of good people who are overwhelmed along with the bad. But the narrative provided no opportunity for such profundity. It is content to instruct us in the broad principle of the matter, and to teach generally that justice prevails in the world. Subsequently, the prophets and thinkers of Israel gave deeper thought to the details of the subject and the exceptions, and tried to find an explanation of the problem of the catastrophes that annihilate the innocent equally with the guilty. Then we hear the answer based on the principle that the collective responsibility for the iniquities of a generation rests also on the one who has not sinned personally, in as much as he forms an integral part of the sinful society that did nothing to curb the wrongdoing; and the explanation that points to the spiritual consolation that 'God's nearness' brings to him who endures his suffering with love; and the view that stresses the limitations of the human mind, which is unable to grasp the mystery of Providence in its totality, whilst recognizing the general harmony prevailing in the world despite the disharmony discernible in any particular facet of it; and still other interpretations, diverse but not mutually exclusive, all of which perhaps contribute to man's endeavour to come as near as possible to the solution of the terrifying question.

It is not our task to deal with the development of the *post*-Torah tradition relative to the Flood, since our aim is to explain the Pentateuchal story. But a few words about the general features of· its later course will not be out of place. The ancient epic poetry continued to exist, and we found evidence of this in allusions in the books of the Prophets and the Hagiographa. We have also seen that even when the old epic poetry was forgotten, its subject-matter was preserved in the folk-memory in a manner that made it possible for it to be reflected in the Talmudic and Midrashic literature. In Hellenistic circles both the Jewish and Mesopotamian traditions assumed similar Graecized forms. Thus, for example, the word κατακλυσμός, which signified in classic Greek literature the flood of Deucalion, was also used for the Babylonian flood in the work of Berossus and for the Biblical flood in the Septuagint, as well as in the other Greek translations of the Bible and in the writings of Josephus Flavius. The Jewish tradition concerning the Flood made a noticeable impression on the Hellenistic world, as we see from local myths like the one associated with the city of Apamea in Phrygia, which was regarded as the place where the ark had rested and was consequently called Κιβωτός, the word used for the ark in the Septuagint and in the other Greek renderings. In the late Midrashim one can observe, as we have already stated earlier, a renewal of the influence, direct or indirect, of the Mesopotamian tradition.

§ 5. The structure of the section in the form before us is perfectly integrated in all its details according to the literary criteria of the ancient East. The section is clearly divisible into twelve paragraphs. Each paragraph deals with a given episode in the sequence of events, and they are all linked together by means of parallelisms of words and expressions.

The first paragraph (vi 9–12) describes the situation in the world before the Flood: the corruption of all flesh and the righteousness of Noah. The second (vi 13–22) relates that God told Noah of His decision to destroy the earth on account of the wickedness of mankind and enjoined him to build the ark. The third (vii 1–5) tells how God spoke again to Noah, informing him that the time had come for him to enter the ark, for in another seven days the Deluge would come upon the world. The fourth (vii 6–9) records the entrance into the ark of all concerned, in accordance with the Divine command. The fifth (vii 10–16) depicts the commencement of the Deluge. The sixth (vii 17–24) narrates how the flood continued and the waters prevailed over the earth. The seventh (viii 1–14) portrays the end of the Flood and the beginning of the return of the world to normality. The eighth (viii 15–17) contains the Divine communication instructing Noah to go forth from the ark. The ninth (viii 18–22) deals with the exit of the occupants from the ark according to the Divine injunction, and with Noah's sacrifice and its favourable acceptance. The tenth (ix 1–7) tells of the blessing God bestowed on Noah and his sons. The eleventh (ix 8–11) announces the covenant that God promised them. The twelfth (ix 12–17) describes the sign that God appointed for the covenant.

The series of paragraphs is composed of two groups, each comprising six paragraphs: the numerical symmetry should be noted. The first group depicts for us, step by step, the acts of Divine justice that bring destruction upon the earth, which had become filled with violence; and the scenes that pass before us grow increasingly gloomier until in the darkness of death portrayed in the sixth paragraph there remains only one tiny, faint point of light, to wit, the ark, which floats on the fearful waters that have covered everything, and which guards between its walls the hope of future life. The second group shows us consecutively the various stages of the act of Divine compassion that renews life upon earth. The light that waned until it became a minute point in the midst of the dark world, begins to grow bigger and brighter till it illumines again the entire scene before us, and shows us a calm and peaceful world, crowned with the rainbow that irradiates the cloud with its colours — a sign and pledge of life and peace for the coming generations.

The first paragraph concludes with the expression *upon the earth,* and the phrase is repeated at the end of the sixth paragraph, which is the last of the first group, and at the end of the twelfth, the conclusion of the entire section. At the end of each of the four intermediate paragraphs of the first group there occur parallel expressions that indicate Noah's obedience to God's instructions: *he did all that God commanded him* (vi 22); *all that the Lord had commanded him* (vii 5); *as God had commanded Noah* (vii 9); *as God had commanded him* (vii 16). In the second group, each of the six paragraphs terminates with the words *the earth,* and two of them — the eighth and the twelfth — actually with the phrase *upon the earth.*

There is a concentric parallelism between the two groups. At the commencement of the first, mention is made of God's decision to bring a flood upon the world and of its announcement to Noah; and at the end of the second, reference is made to the Divine resolve not to bring a flood again upon the world and to the communication thereof to Noah and his sons. In the middle of the first group we are told of the Divine command to enter the ark and its implementation is described; in the middle of the second, we learn of God's injunction to leave the ark and of its fulfilment. At the end of the first group the course of the Deluge is depicted, and at the beginning of the second its termination. Beside parallels of content, there is also discernible a verbal parallelism. The stem שחת *šḥt* ['corrupt'] occurs a number of times in the first two paragraphs and is used again in the last two paragraphs (vi 11, 12 [twice], 13, 17; ix 11, 15). Reference is made to God's *seeing* in the first and last paragraphs (vi 12; ix 16; compare also vii 1, ix 14); similarly, the word *generations* is mentioned in the first paragraph and in the last (vi 9: *in his generations;* ix 12: *for all future generations*). In the second paragraph it is written: *But I will establish My covenant with you* (vi 18), and in the penultimate paragraph it is stated: *I establish My covenant with you* (ix 11; compare also ix 9, 17). The subject of food and the word לְאָכְלָה *le'okhlā* are mentioned in the second and tenth paragraphs (vi 21; ix 3). In the middle of the first and second groups of paragraphs *clean animals* are mentioned (vii 2, 8; viii 20). In the first group, the period of seven days is referred to first, then that of forty days (vii 4, 10, 12, 17), and finally that of one hundred and fifty days (vii 24); in the second, we read first of one hundred and fifty days (viii 3), then of forty days (viii 6) and thereafter of seven days (viii 10, 12). Furthermore, both in the first group in connection with the commencement of the Flood and in the second in relation to its termination, the Bible indicates the date by reference to Noah's age (vii 6, 11; viii 13), and mentions the windows [אֲרֻבֹּת *'ărubbōth*] of heaven and the fountains of the deep (vii 11; viii 2), and the mountains (vii 19, 20; viii 4, 5).

In this section, just as in the preceding, numerical harmony is noticeable. The number *seven,* which, as we have seen, is the number of perfection, is mentioned explicitly in the text many times; periods of seven days (vii 4, 10; viii 10, 12); seven pairs of clean animals, and likewise of the birds of the air (vii 2–3); and if we count the number of times that God spoke to Noah, we shall find that they total exactly seven (vi 13; vii 1; viii 15; ix 1, 8, 12, 17). Similarly in the second paragraph, in connection with the construction of the ark, the stem עָשָׂה *'āśā* ['made'] occurs seven times; in paragraphs 3–5, in regard to the entrance into the ark, the stem בּוֹא *bō* ['come'] is found seven times; the verb שׁחת *šḥt*, which appears, as I have stated, at the beginning and the end of the section, is used in all seven times; in the last two paragraphs, with reference to the covenant, the word *covenant* occurs seven times; the word *water* is employed twenty-one times — seven times three; the word *flesh* appears fourteen times — seven times two; Noah's name, which occurs also in the continuation of the pericope, is found in the whole pericope thirty-five times — seven times five. Apart from seven, the numbers appertaining to the sexagesimal system, which was in general use in the ancient East, also occupy an important place in the section. The age of Noah is expressly given as 600; in keeping with this numerical system are the twelve paragraphs, and the number of times the word *flood* occurs, to wit, twelve times in the whole pericope. So, too, the various categories of living creatures are detailed, in between two general expressions at the beginning and at the end (vi 19; ix 16), twelve times, phrased in twelve different ways, in accordance with the usual stylistic practice of the Bible in repetitions of this nature (vi 20; vii 2–3, 8, 14, 21, 23; viii 1, 17, 19, 20; ix 2, 10).

All these particular features, which are clearly discernible in the architectonic structure of the section and give it perfect harmony, are certainly not a chance phenomenon.

§ 6. *The problem of determining the sources.* In the view of the majority of modern exegetes, the Biblical narrative of the Flood was built up by a complicated process of interwoven excerpts taken over verbatim, or nearly so, from various recensions. These are, according to the generally accepted view, the account of source J (to be exact, the second stratum of J, usually indicated as J²) and that of source P; other conjectures advanced in recent years, to which we shall revert later, increase the number of sources. Several generations of scholars took part in the work of making a detailed and exact analysis of the text according to the sources, and the results are regarded, to quote Gunkel's expression, as a 'masterpiece of modern criticism', or, as Budde wrote earlier, an 'indisputable masterpiece'. This spirit of boastful self-confidence on the part of the professional expositors gave the general public the impression that the existence of the two recensions, one of J and the other of P, was an assured fact. Even in school primers and in popular works intended for the lay reader, the two versions are referred to with the simple certitude with which one may speak of a human being having two eyes; and men of learning in other fields, like the Assyriologists (Heidel, for example), although they are accustomed to scientific caution and to the probe of relentless criticism, accept the prevailing view with closed eyes as though it were an established fact.

Of course, the general public is still unaware of the recent theories, which deviate from the majority opinion, like that of Volz, for example, who holds that we have not actually two different recensions before us but one basic account of J emended and augmented by P; or that of Romanoff, who distinguishes in our section excerpts from three documents, J and P and still another source, which he calls M; or that of Mowinckel, who attributes many fragments to E instead of J²; or that of Gerhard von Rad, who subdivides P into two separate recensions; or that of Kraeling, who conjectures that prior to the versions of J² and P there was an older one of J¹, and who finds vestiges of that recension in several verses of our section and at the beginning of chapter xi.

These conflicting opinions prove that Budde was undoubtedly wrong in regarding the division of the sources accepted in his day as an 'indisputable' mastepiece, and that even the method of literary analysis enables us to come to different conclusions. Anyone who studies the course of this research cannot free himself from the impression that, if the analytical method is capable of producing divergent results, its criteria cannot necessarily be as sound and reliable as many have thought.

In truth, this is but an interesting example of that subjective and mechanical method of exegesis that many European scholars adopted in their study of ancient literatures, without making any attempt to gain a deeper insight into the literary conditions, customs and usages of the environment in which the writings in question were composed — a method that also outside Biblical scholarship (for example, in the field of classical studies) resulted in conclusions that are similar and parallel to those arrived at by Biblical scholars in regard to the Five Books of the Torah.

If we examine the section of the Flood without bias and pay heed to its finished structure, to which we referred previously in § 5, it becomes apparent that the section in its present form cannot possibly be the outcome of the synthesis of fragments culled from various sources; for from such a process there could not have emerged a work so beautiful and harmonious in all its parts and details. If it should be argued that the artistic qualities of the section are the result of the redactor's work, then one can easily reply that in that case he was no ordinary compiler, who joined excerpt to excerpt in mechanical fashion, but a writer in the true sense of the word, the creator of a work of art by his own efforts. Thus the entire hypothesis, which presupposes that the different fragments were already in existence previously in their present form as parts of certain compositions, collapses completely.

But this general observation is not enough. We must examine the arguments on which the division of our section according to the documentary theory relies.

The reasons are: (1) variations in the use of the Divine Names: sometimes אֱלֹהִים *'Elōhīm* occurs and sometimes ה' *YHWH;* (2) linguistic differences: for instances, sometimes we find *male and female* and sometimes *the male* [literally, 'a man'] *and his mate;* (3) repetitions and duplications; (4) conflicting passages. To these criteria, which are based on the section itself, we have to add: (5) features of form or content, regarded [for extraneous reasons] as characteristic of J or P, that are found in certain verses of the section; for example, the expression *established a covenant,* which is considered as distinctive of P in contradistinction to the other sources, which use the term *made* [literally, 'cut'] *a covenant.*

I have discussed these arguments in detail in my Italian work *La Questione della Genesi,* pp. 40–45, 98–101, 112–116, 158–170, 175, 197–198, 205–207, 335–353, and in part also in my book *The Documentary Hypothesis,* English translation, pp. 36, 47 f. There is no need, therefore, to recapitulate that detailed discussion here; it will suffice to refer to the subject briefly.

I shall deal with the general question of the variations in the use of the Divine Names in the Introductory Volume, which I shall publish later. * Here I shall refer only to what I stated above, in Part I, pp. 86–88, concerning the changes in the use of these Names that we encounter in the first two sections of the Book of Genesis, and I shall add a few words relative to the section of the Flood. I have already shown in my aforementioned works that the occurrence of one or other of the two Divine Names depends on general principles, followed both in Israelite and other literatures of the ancient East, that govern the use of the generic and specific designations of the Deity. The Tetragrammaton is the specific name of the God of Israel and signifies the Godhead in His personal aspect according to the Israelite conception, and in His

---

* This volume, owing to the untimely demise of the author, remained unwritten.

direct relationship with His creatures. אֱלֹהִים *'Elōhīm,* on the other hand, was originally a common noun, which became a proper name through the realization that there is but One God and that only *YHWH He is 'Elōhīm;* and therefore it connotes the general concept of Deity that is shared by all peoples. From the rules that I formulated in detail in Part I, pp. 87 f., one would expect the section of the Deluge primarily to use the name *'Elōhīm,* since it speaks of the God of the whole world, not of the specific God of Israel, and the tradition concerning the Flood is found also among non-Israelites. Now it is actually the name *'Elōhīm* that occurs throughout almost the entire section, and the Tetragrammaton appears solely when there is a special reason for it, in accordance with the rules mentioned above. In the third paragraph the Tetragrammaton is used, because the clean animals intended for sacrifice are mentioned there, and wherever oblations are referred to we find the name *YHWH,* which denotes the personal Godhead (compare Sifre Num. § 143, and the parallel passages). So, too, the Tetragrammaton appears in the ninth paragraph, which refers to the offering of sacrifices and their favourable acceptance. The last sentence of the fifth paragraph (*and YHWH shut him in*) reflects the personal and direct — as it were, the palpable — relationship between *YHWH* and Noah, the relationship of a Father full of compassion towards his cherished son. In all the other parts of the section, where there is no special reason for the use of the Tetragrammaton, the name *'Elōhīm* invariably occurs.

Likewise the interchange of certain expressions is not due to the stylistic peculiarity of one source or another. Let us consider, for instance, the most radical example, the fact that sometimes the term *male and female,* which is ascribed to P, is used, and at other times, the expression *the male and his mate,* which is attributed to J. As will be seen from my commentary on vii 2, it was necessary to employ there the phrase *the male and his mate* (which is not identical in meaning with *male and female*) in order to make the meaning clear. Evidence of the weakness of the analytical method of exegesis is to be found immediately in the passage that follows: in verse 3, which is likewise assigned to J, occurs the expression *male and female,* which is regarded as the private property of P. To explain this difficulty, it is asserted that the editor tampered with the text, but this is obviously a desperate solution.

On the face of it, the third argument, which is based on the existence of a number of duplications and repetitions in the section, seems a more serious reason; and the fourth, which points to the conflicting passages, is even more impressive. In *La Questione* pp. 336–337, I give a list of the duplications and repetitions, which include no fewer than thirteen instances; for example, the fact that Noah is told on two occasions to enter the ark (vi 18, vii 1), that the commencement of the Flood is mentioned twice (vii 10, 11), that two separate references are made to the Divine promise not to bring universal destruction again upon mankind (viii 21–22, ix 8–17), and so on and so forth. I have likewise listed there (p. 337) the discrepancies found between various verses. These number five: (1) the creatures that were received into the ark comprised one pair of each species according to vi 19–20 and vii 15–16, but there were seven pairs of each kind of clean animal and bird according to vii 2–3; (2) vii 11 states that the Deluge was formed by the confluence of the upper and lower waters, but vii 12 speaks of ordinary rain; (3) in viii 9 we are told that *the dove found no place to set foot,* but earlier (*v.* 5) we learnt that *the tops of the mountains were seen;* (4) according to viii 6–12 Noah endeavoured to determine by the means at his disposal whether it was possible for him to leave the ark, but according to viii 15–17 he was apprised of this by God; (5) disparities between the various sets of chronological data.

Anyone studying these lists receives the impression that the narrative is in a state of chaos, and that the only way to introduce order into it is to divide it into various accounts. But we must not forget that these lists came to be compiled as a result of the researches of those who were already convinced from the outset, by the fact that different names are used for God, that the section contains elements derived from various documents. But if we approach the text without bias, the impression we gain is totally different.

In so far as the third argument is concerned, we must, first of all, bear in mind the fact that the use of repetition and verbal parallelism is a common feature of the literary style of the ancient

East generally and of the Bible in particular; and any one who wishes to remove from the Scriptural texts all that is in harmony with this practice is simply closing his eyes to a basic and characteristic trait of these passages. Nor is this all. Many matters are referred to more than twice in our section, and if we reject all possibility of repetition in one recension, we shall have to assume that there were more than two versions. For this very reason Romanoff proposed, as we saw, that the verses of the section should be distributed among three sources. But even three are not enough, for some things are mentioned four and five times, and even six. Reference is made to the increase of the water no fewer than six times in chapter vii (*v.* 17: *and the waters increased; v.* 18: *the waters prevailed;* ibid.: *and increased greatly; v.* 19: *and the waters prevailed so mightily; v.* 20: *the waters prevailed; v.* 24: *and the waters prevailed*). If we insist on applying the analytical method consistently, we shall reach a stage of absurdity.

Unquestionably, the repetitions are introduced for the sake of parallelism in accordance with the customary stylistic convention. Moreover, they are not redundant repetitions. Reference to my commentary should easily convince one that whenever the text reverts to a given subject it tells us something new. In God's first communication, Noah is enjoined to build an ark in order that he may enter it when the proper time comes, and in the second communication, when the time has arrived, he is instructed to enter the ark *forthwith.* In verse 10 of ch. vii it is stated generally that the waters of the flood were upon the earth, while *vv.* 11 f. describe in detail the manner in which these waters came. At the end of ch. viii we are told that God decided not to bring another Flood upon the world, and in ch. ix it is narrated, in keeping with the characteristic principles of epic style, that God informed Noah of this decision. In my annotations I shall explain, *ad locum,* all the numerous reiterated references to the waters prevailing upon the earth, and likewise the other duplications and repetitions of the section.

Let us now take a glance at the discrepancies found in the section in accordance with the list we drew up above.

(1) With regard to the first, which is connected with the pairs of living creatures, we must note that wherever the Bible mentions

one pair only, the verb used is בּוֹא bō' ['come', 'go', 'enter'; in *Hiph'îl* 'bring'] (vi 19: YOU SHALL BRING; vi 20: SHALL COME IN *to you;* vii 9: WENT IN *unto Noah;* vii 15: AND WENT IN *unto Noah;* vii 16: AND THEY THAT ENTERED ... WENT IN), but when seven pairs are spoken of the verb is לָקַח *lāqaḥ* ['take'] (vii 2: *Take with you*). In other words, those creatures that felt an inner urge to come to Noah of their own accord in order to be received into the ark, and were permitted by Noah to enter (vi 19: *You shall permit to enter* [literally, 'bring']), comprised two of each kind, a pair. Apart from these, Noah was commanded to *take* additional pairs from his flocks and herds and the birds that he could catch, which he could use, for purposes of which we shall speak later, without endangering the existence of these species. Hence there is no contradiction here at all. On the contrary, it is the analytical method that encounters at this point a grave difficulty. In vii 8–9 one pair is mentioned in regard to both the clean and unclean animals. Since a distinction is drawn between the two categories of animals in the same way as in *v.* 2, which is attributed to J, we ought to conclude that these verses also belong to J; but *v.* 9 contains *'Elōhīm* and not *YHWH*. Furthermore, the number *two* mentioned here with reference also to the clean animals contradicts what is stated elsewhere in source J itself. The difficulty is resolved by attributing *vv.* 8–9 to the redactor, or by regarding them as an excerpt of J radically revised by the compiler. But this is an arbitrary solution, and it is difficult to understand why the editor should have wished to introduce such confusion into the narrative. But according to our interpretation, it is all clear and simple: the passage speaks of going (*they went in unto Noah*) and not of taking; also of these kinds of clean animals, which *went in* of their own accord unto Noah in order to be saved, there were two each, but Noah took others in addition to them.

(2) The second incongruity was discovered between vii 11: *all the fountains of the great deep burst forth, and the windows of the heavens were opened,* and *v.* 12: *and rain fell upon the earth forty days and forty nigths.* Verse 12 is assigned to J on account of the reference to forty days and forty nights, which occurs earlier in a verse ascribed to J (vii 4); thus *v.* 11 is left to P. But this does not solve the problem. On the contrary, this division, which makes

J give us the simpler description and P the more poetic and arresting portrayal, conflicts with the traits that are considered to be typical of the two sources. To avoid this dilemma, it is suggested that when P mentions the fountains of the deep and the windows of the heavens, he is only quoting verbatim a still older source (and undoubtedly according to our theory, too, the words of an ancient epic poem are cited here). But once we have accepted this premise, there is no further need for dissecting the text. The Bible first quotes the words of the ancient poetic source, which tells how from under the earth the waters of the deep burst forth and spread over the face of the earth, and at the same time the windows of heaven were opened wide and no longer held back the upper waters but allowed them to come pouring down. Thus far the narrative describes only how the mighty cataclysm *began*: subsequently, Scripture must relate in what manner and for how many days it continued. This we are told in *v.* 12, which adds that the rain, that terrible rain that came down from the windows of heaven, which were opened wide, continued another forty days and nights without intermission. The text makes no further mention of the water that flowed from the fountains of the deep, since the earth was already covered by a layer of water and the augmentation that came from below was not visible; consequently there was no reason to speak of it.

(3)   Another disparity is pointed out between viii 5: *the tops of the mountains were seen,* and viii 9: *but the dove found no place to set her foot.* But an identical discrepancy exists in the Epic of Gilgameš. There it is first stated (line 139) that mountains were seen on all sides, and then (lines 146–149) it is said: 'I brought out the dove and sent her forth, and the dove went and turned back; there was no resting-place, so she returned.' It is certainly not to be supposed that an astonishing coincidence occurred, to wit, that both in Babylon and in Israel there was written in one recension that the dry land was visible and in another that there was no place for the dove to set foot, and thereafter a redactor came, in Babylon as well as in Israel, and incorporated the two contradictory statements without noticing the discrepancy between them. Such an assumption would assuredly be absurd. Hence another explanation is required. The correct interpretation, with regard to both the

40

Biblical story and the Epic of Gilgameš, is undoubtedly this, that the dove was sent forth to determine whether, apart from the tops of the mountains, which were already visible to the people in the ark or the boat, other areas were free from water, and since the dove found no other sites where to land she had no choice but to return to the place whence she was sent forth.

(4) Any one who sees an incongruity between Noah's attempt to find out, by dispatching the birds, if the waters had subsided from the earth, and the subsequent statement that God commanded him to go forth from the ark, overlooks the fact that the literary criteria of a poetic or semi-poetic narrative are different from the principles of strict exactitude demanded by a mathematical proof. It cannot be gainsaid that logically the information provided by the behaviour of the birds was sufficient for Noah, and he needed no further intimation to realize that he could leave the ark; conversely, if he received a Divine injunction to go forth from the ark, the experiment with the birds was superfluous. Nevertheless, not everything that is unnecessary is impossible; moreover, the requirements of poetic art and the adaptation of traditional material are not the same as those of abstract logic. The tale of the raven and the dove was so integral a part of the tradition, both among Israelites and Gentiles, that it was not possible to ignore it. On the other hand, a story like ours, which shows how Divine Providence constantly guided Noah at every stage, could not refrain from introducing a communication from God to Noah at the decisive moment of the exit from the ark. This apart, the mention of a command to this effect was also required from the artistic point of view, as a parallel to the injunction to enter the ark. Thus the sending of the birds and the Divine command were both necessary, and the Bible linked them together artistically and in a form that avoids any contradiction or redundancy of words. After Noah had learned from the experiment with the birds that the waters had abated from the earth, he waited another month (see below), and then he began to make preparations to leave by removing the covering of the ark. Since, on lifting the cover, he could look in every direction, he saw for himself that the face of the ground had become dry (viii 13), that is, that there was no longer a layer of water on the face of the earth, although the ground was not yet completely dry. After the

41

lapse of another fifty seven days, he saw that the earth was thorough-ly dry (*ibid.* 14), and then he had only to wait for the Divine command to go forth from the ark, and he was ready to obey this injunction forthwith. This is the situation depicted at the close of the seventh paragraph; the eighth paragraph tells of the Divine communication for which Noah was waiting. It should be noted that God's words to Noah contain not the slightest reference to the fact that the earth was dry, a fact of which Noah should have been apprised had he learned only from the Divine instruction that it was possible for him to leave the ark. If so, the seventh and eighth paragraphs not only do not contradict one another, but on the contrary they are complementary and necessary to each other.

(5)   The difficulties connected with the chronological data, I shall discuss specifically in § 7.

There remain still the arguments that I have mentioned in (5) (p. 35). They belong to the general problem of the composition of the Book of Genesis and not to our section as such; I shall not, therefore, deal with them here but in the Introductory Volume that I shall publish later *. In the meantime, the reader can consult on the subject *La Questione* and, in summary form, *The Documentary Hypothesis*, English translation. Here it will suffice to draw atten-tion to the following points:

(a)   In so far as our section is concerned, these considerations are valid only for one who is already convinced to begin with that J and P actually existed; thus the premises still have to be proved.

(b)   The most important contention, which is based on the ex-pressions *established a covenant* and *made* [literally, 'cut'] *a coven-ant*, I shall have the opportunity of discussing in my annotations to vi 18, where it will be seen that the distinction between the two idioms is not a matter of style, which may depend on difference of sources, but one of theme, that is, that the meaning of the two expressions is not the same. The other arguments belonging to this category are not of great consequence and I have already shown their nullity in my Italian book.

It clearly follows from all that we have noted in this subsection and in the one preceding that there is no reason to doubt the unity

---

* This volume remained unwritten.

of our section, and that, on the contrary, the structure of the section in all its parts and details leaves no doubt about its homogeneous character.

§ 7. *The Chronology of the Flood.* Expositors in all ages, from the time of the Talmud to our own day, have dealt with this question at length, and diverse views, in great number, have been advanced thereon. The analysis of the sources does not help us to elucidate the subject, but, on the contrary, complicates it considerably. I shall not enumerate here the various theories that have been put forward, or the difficulties that have been pointed out and the solutions that have been offered; for all this would require an unduly long discussion without corresponding advantage. I shall content myself with stating how I think the matter can be understood in a simple and satisfactory manner.

For the first Divine communication to Noah (vi 13 ff.) the Bible indicates no date, but it may be conjectured, as I shall explain at the end of my commentary on the second paragraph, that the ancient tradition gave it as the first day of the first month, and it related that after God had spoken to him Noah occupied himself with the construction of the ark for forty days. The date of the second communication (vii 1 ff.) is also not expressly stated, but undoubtedly we have to assume that it occurred on the tenth day of the second month, forty days after the beginning of the year, for Noah was told that in another seven days the Flood would commence (vii 4), and the Flood began after seven days (vii 10) on the seventeenth day of the second month (vii 11; on the different reading in the Septuagint see below my annotation to viii 14). The Deluge lasted forty days (vii 4, 12, 17), that is, until the twenty-seventh day of the third month, and the waters prevailed upon the earth one hundred and fifty days (vii 24). The verb וַיִּגְבְּרוּ *wayyighberū* [literally, 'were strong'; E. V. *prevailed*] does not denote an action but a condition, the meaning being that the waters remained in their might upon the ground during one hundred and fifty days. At first glance, it may be doubted if the forty days rain are included in this figure, but a comparison of the dates given in vii 11 (seventeenth day of the second month) and in viii 4 (seventeenth day of the seventh month) shows that they were probably included. The ark came to rest on the mountains — this was the first intimation that

43

the waters were beginning to decrease and no longer prevailed —
exactly five months after the commencement of the Flood, and
five months are, in round numbers, one hundred and fifty days.
Although five lunar months comprise only 147 days, yet the Bible
apparently preferred to use a round figure, just as we also speak
today, for instance, of ninety days to indicate a period of three
months, although the number of days is not precisely ninety. Forty
days after the beginning of the Deluge the rain actually ceased
to come down on the earth, and the fountains of the deep were
closed (viii 2), and consequently no more water was added to that
which already submerged the land; but the layer of water did not
subside for a long time, during which it was impossible to see
aught but sky and water, water and sky. It was not till five months
after the commencement of the Flood that the first sign of the
decline of the layer of water was discernible, to wit, when the
bottom of the ark touched the tops of the mountains and the ark
came to rest. Thereafter, the waters continued to decrease, and
when the first day of the tenth month arrived the tops of the
mountains (viii 5) became visible. In the following lines we shall
see how this date fits in with other dates of the chronology of
the Deluge.

Forty days after the peaks of the mountains were visible, Noah
opened the window of the ark (viii 6) and sent forth the raven
(viii 7). This took place, therefore, on the tenth day of the
eleventh month, exactly nine months after God had spoken the
second time to Noah. Seven days later (see my comments on
viii 8), Noah sent forth the dove. This occurred, therefore, on the
seventeenth of the eleventh month, four months precisely after the
ark stopped, nine months exactly after the beginning of the
Flood — a clear example of harmonious parallelism.

The dove found no place where to set her foot and returned
to the ark, on the same day of course. After another seven days
Noah sent her a second time (viii 10), and in the evening she
returned with a fresh olive leaf in her mouth, indicating that the
lower hills, on which the olive tree grows, were free of water.
At this point we reach the twenty-fourth day of the eleventh month.
When another seven days had passed, Noah sent out the dove a
third time. This time she returned to him no more (viii 12). This

44

brings us to the first day of the twelfth month, and here, too, we discern a parallel to the other dates that fall on the first of the month (viii 5, 13; and, according to my conjecture, also the first Divine communication to Noah). On the first day of the first month of the six hundred and first year, precisely one month after he had sent the dove forth the last time, three months exactly after the summits of the mountains were seen, Noah removed the covering of the ark and saw that the face of the ground was dry (viii 13). And on the twenty-seventh day of the second month, eleven lunar months to the day after the end of the Flood, the land was completely dried out (viii 14). On the same day, an entire solar year — 365 days — had elapsed since the beginning of the Deluge (see below, my annotations to viii 14). The sun had returned to the point at which it was at the commencement of the Flood; the cycle was complete.

Thus the chronological data correspond to, and parallel, each other perfectly. Not only do they not conflict, nor give any evidence of composite sources, but on the contrary they indicate the concordant unity of the section. Those who divide the section among various sources destroy its harmonic structure and create all sorts of difficulties.

§ 8. *The problem of the relationship of the tradition of the Flood to natural phenomena.* Several scholars have endeavoured to determine the nature of the phenomenon upon which, in their view, the Mesopotamian and Israelite tradition of the Deluge is based. It is worth devoting a few lines to this subject.

The section certainly does not imply that the waters of the Flood submerged the whole earth, to wit, all that we denote today by the name globe. The horizon of the narrative includes only the part of the world in which, according to the preceding chapters, the first generations of mankind dwelt, that is, the Mesopotamian region, as is evident particularly from the Mesopotamian parallels to ch. v. To this corresponds the Mesopotamian background of this section and of what follows, especially in the two parts of ch. xi, which mentions, *inter alia*, the land of Shinar and the city of Babylon as the habitation of the human race after the Deluge. So the Sages of the Talmud rightly understood our section, as we see from B. Shabbat 113b (similarly, B. Zebaḥim 113b): 'R. Ammi

said: He who eats earth of Babylon is as though he ate the flesh
of his ancestors (Rashi explains: 'For they died there in exile';
but from the continuation of the passage it appears more probable
that the reference is to the Flood); some say, It is as though he
ate abominations and creeping things, because it is written, *And
he dissolved* [E. .V. *blotted out*] *every living thing*, etc. Resh
Lakish said, Why is it [Babylon] called Shinar? Because all the
dead of the Flood were tossed thither.' The view that the Deluge
did not come upon the Land of Israel we have mentioned earlier
(§ 4, p. 26).

Among the exegetes who attempted to determine the origin of
the Flood tradition as a natural event, there were those who
thought (for example, Koenig), on the strength of the Akkadian
name for the Deluge *abûbu,* that the ancient tradition was founded
on the phenomenon of the annual inundations of the great Mesopotamian rivers. But it is impossible to imagine that a tradition
that narrates a story so far removed from the sphere of the normal
emanated from the observation of an oft-recurring event. A different
view is expressed by the geologist Suess, who based his theory on
certain expressions used in the Babylonian and Biblical narratives.
He conjectures that the origin of the tradition is to be sought in
a colossal earthquake that caused the sea to inundate the region
extending from the Persian Gulf, or south of it, up to the area
north of it. But this hypothesis lacks sufficient foundation; the
collection of a few details from a poetic description is insufficient
material on which to base a reconstruction of actual happenings,
especially if some of the details are not in reality to be found in the
texts themselves but were introduced there hypothetically, for
example, the reading מַבּוּל מִיָּם *mabbūl miyyām* ['flood from the
sea'] in Gen. vi 17, in place of מַבּוּל מַיִם *mabbūl mayim* ['flood
of waters']. Another suggestion was put forward by Sir. L. Woolley.
In his excavations at the site of Ur of the Chaldees, he found
among the strata containing relics of human artifacts a layer of
clay about two and a half metres thick, and he thought that this
layer, which in his opinion belongs to the fourth millenium, was
formed as a result of the Flood of which the Mesopotamian and
Biblical tradition speaks. But similar layers, belonging to various
periods, were subsequently discovered in other places in the same

area, both in the south (in Kiš and in Šuruppak, the city of Utnapištim) and in the north (in Nineveh); whereas other excavations, carried out on sites close to these, showed nothing similar. It is more likely, therefore, that these layers are the result of local occurrences only, which took place at different times.

Generally speaking it may be said that the endeavours to link our section with some given happening is not in keeping with the character and purpose of the section. It is poetic in character, and its aim is to explain how we have to understand and interpret, according to the Israelite conception, the ancient tradition of the Flood, and to point the lessons to be learnt from it. Hence all the attempts at rationalization, such as those we have mentioned in this subsection, are unacceptable.

9. *Bibliography.* In Part I, I arranged the bibliography appertaining to each section at the end of the relevant introduction. But in this Part, notwithstanding my desire to maintain a uniform arrangement, I was compelled, for technical reasons *, to list the bibliographies at the end of the volume, to which the reader is referred (pp. 284 ff.).

RUBRIC OF SECTION

CHAPTER VI

9. *This is the history of Noah.*

This sentence serves as the rubric of the entire section of the Flood, which comes to narrate the *history* of Noah, that is to say, the world events that are particularly connected with the personality of Noah. The history of Noah extends to the point where the narrative gives precedence to his sons (ix 18: *And the sons of Noah ... were,* etc.).

---

* Although these technical reasons no longer obtained in the case of the translation, it was felt desirable to retain the author's original arrangement.

ACT ONE

THE PUNISHMENT

FIRST PARAGRAPH

THE CORRUPTION OF ALL FLESH AND THE RIGHTEOUSNESS OF THE GOOD MAN

[9. Continued] *Noah / was a wholly righteous man / in his generations;*
with God / did Noah walk.

10. *And Noah begot / three sons,*
Shem, / Ham, / and Japhet.

11. *But the earth was corrupt / in God's sight,*
and the earth was filled / with unrighteousness.

12. *And God saw the earth, / and behold, it was corrupt;*
for all flesh had corrupted / their way upon the earth.

9. Just as in the story of Creation, after the opening words, *In the beginning God created the heavens and the earth*, the Bible repeats the last expression *the earth* and places it before the predicate in order to give it prominence and begin therewith the theme that appertains particularly to the earth (see my annotations to i 2), so also here Scripture reiterates the name of Noah with which the rubric ends, and puts it in front of its predicate so as to stress it and commence with it the new narrative that is devoted especially to Noah.

אִישׁ צַדִּיק תָּמִים הָיָה *Iš ṣaddîq tāmîm hāyā* [translated: *was a wholly righteous man*] / The words have been variously explained: (1) Noah was a righteous [צַדִּיק *ṣaddîq*] and perfect [תָּמִים *tāmîm*] man; (2) Noah is a righteous man, and he was perfect; (3) Noah, a righteous man, was perfect; (4) Noah was a completely righteous man, wholly righteous. The first explanation is difficult, since the conjunctive *Wāw* is not normally omitted in such cases; the second is even more difficult, for the Bible certainly did not refer to Noah's righteousness in the present tense and to

48

his perfection in the past tense; the third, which is reflected in the Septuagint and in the Masoretic accents, is connected apparently with homiletical interpretations placed on the word תָּמִים *tāmīm,* and does not accord with the simple sense of the verse. The fourth explanation is the most likely, having regard to Job xii 4: צַדִּיק תָּמִים *ṣaddīq tāmīm is* [or *am*] *a laughing stock,* and Num. xix 2: *a* תְּמִימָה *temīmā* [fem. sing. of תָּמִים *tāmīm*] *red heifer, in which there is no blemish.* The meaning of תְּמִימָה *temīmā* cannot be 'without blemish', for that is distinctly stated in the continuation of the verse; hence the word is not an adjective, but an adverb, and the expression signifies 'perfect in redness' (see Sifre Num. § 123), 'perfectly red', 'wholly red'. Similarly in our verse the meaning is: *wholly righteous.* In Prov. xi 5, צִדְקַת תָּמִים *ṣidhqath tāmīm* [literally, 'righteousness of a perfect one'], apparently connotes, 'the righteousness of one who is wholly righteous'; compare Prov. xx 7: *a righteous man who walks* IN HIS INTEGRITY [בְּתֻמּוֹ *bethummō,* literally, 'in his perfection']. Some dispose of the problem by affixing a *Wāw* copulative ['and'] to the word תָּמִים *tāmīm,* or by deleting the word *righteous.* But the method of Alexander the Great with respect to the Gordian knot is not correct in philology.

In his generations [בְּדֹרֹתָיו *bedhōrōthāw*] / The plural is somewhat difficult; further on (vii 1) we find the singular: *for I have seen that you are righteous before Me in this generation.* The rabbinic glosses (B. Sanhedrin 108a; compare Bereshith Rabba and Tanḥuma) explain the word as though it meant the same as the singular ('R. Joḥanan said: *In his generations,* but not in other generations; and Resh Laḳish said: *In his generations,* how much more so in other generations'). It is on the basis of such interpretations, apparently, that the Septuagint renders: ἐν τῇ γενέσει αὐτοῦ, that is, 'in his generation'. Some modern exegetes are of opinion that we should read בִּדְרָכָיו *bidrākhāw* ['in his ways'] instead of בְּדֹרֹתָיו *bedhōrōthāw,* but this view has nothing to support it. In any case it cannot be correct, since afterwards it is written: *with God did Noah walk,* a figurative expression describing Noah as a man who walked in *God's ways;* it follows that the preceding word cannot refer to Noah's walking *in his own ways.* According to the plain meaning of the text, the purpose of the plural seems to be to glorify Noah: not only was he righteous, but he was wholly

49

righteous; not only was he outstanding in his righteousness among his contemporaries, that is, among those who, like himself, belonged to the tenth generation after Adam, but he was pre-eminent in righteousness relative to all the generations that lived on earth in his days. This is how the Bible expresses itself when it makes an objective statement, but later on when the Lord speaks to Noah, He does not call him 'wholly righteous' but only 'righteous', and He does not say 'in your generations' but in this generation. The sages of the Talmud already noted, in connection with these very verses, that 'a part of a man's praise may be said in his presence, but all of it in his absence' (B. 'Erubin 18b).

With God did Noah walk] In the structure of the verse, this clause is parallel to the first clause, *Noah was a wholly righteous man in his generations;* this clearly shows that the two clauses are equivalent in meaning: walking with God means walking in those ways in which God walks, namely, the ways of righteousness and justice; and whoever walks therein is wholly righteous. Although Enoch is spoken of in similar terms (see Part I, pp. 282 ff.), this does not militate against the explanation we gave above of the expression *his generations,* for Enoch did not belong to the generations that were contemporary with Noah. According to the chronological date in ch. v, Enoch departed from the world in the year 987 of Creation, whereas Noah was born in 1056, sixty-nine years after the death of the righteous man that preceded him.

10. *And Noah begot*] Noah's name occurs three times as the subject of three consecutive clauses: the first time at the beginning of the sentence (*Noah was a wholly righteous man*); the second time at the end (literally, 'with God walked Noah'); and here, the third occurrence, in the middle. The threefold reiteration lends emphasis, as usual, to the name, and the change of its position gives literary grace and symmetry to the recapitulation.

Three sons, Shem, Ham and Japhet] This has already been stated earlier (v 32); but such repetitions are usual at the commencement of the 'histories', as I noted in my commentary on v 1 (Part I, p. 274).

The Bible does not state explicitly whether the three sons were righteous or not; nor whether they were saved by their own merit or the merit of their father. It would seem that the intention of the Bible is to tell us that they were saved because of their own virtue, because (1) the essential purpose of the section is to teach us that the Lord requites every man according to his deeds, the righteous man according to his righteousness and the wicked man according to his wickedness; (2) it has already been stated that Noah was a *wholly* righteous man, and if he had not succeeded in training his sons to walk in the good way, he would not have been *wholly* righteous; (3) the subsequent statement in *v.* 11, *But the earth was corrupt in God's sight,* is antithetic to what precedes and tells us that all the other inhabitants of the earth were corrupt, whereas in this verse, which speaks of the sons of Noah, there is no expression of contrast to what had previously been said about the father's righteousness.

The Bible itself probably reflects this interpretation of the ancient tradition concerning Noah and his sons. In Ezekiel xiv reference is made to the personal responsibility of every human being, and it is stated there that when a land sins against the Lord, even if there be in it righteous men, like Noah, Daniel and Job, they would be delivered by their righteousness (*vv.* 14, 16, 18, 20), but they would deliver *neither sons nor daughters* (*vv.* 16, 18, 20). It is clear that if we do not assume that the prophet had a different tradition from that of the Book of Genesis (see the introduction above, § 4, p. 25), the meaning of our text, according to the prophet's understanding of it, is that Noah did not deliver his sons by his righteousness, but that they, by their own righteousness, saved themselves. On the character of Ham and his sin against his father, see my remarks below, in my annotations to the next section.

11. *But the earth was corrupt* [וַתִּשָּׁחֵת *wattiśśaḥēth;* literally, 'and was corrupt'] / The *Wāw* expresses antithesis, as though to say: But, in contrast to those previously mentioned, all the people of the earth were corrupt, and their corrupt behaviour polluted and corrupted the land that they inhabited. This idea is commonly found in the Bible, and *v.* 12 repeats it in explicit language.

In God's sight [literally, 'before God'] / — that is, before the eyes of God, which rove over the whole earth. Compare x 9: *a mighty hunter before the Lord.*

And the earth was filled with UNRIGHTEOUSNESS [חָמָס *ḥāmās*] / God had bestowed upon them the blessing of fertility: *Be fruitful*

and multiply, and fill the earth (i 28), and this benison was fulfilled for them, but they were ingrates, and instead of thanking
God for *filling* the earth with them, they on their part *filled* the
earth with unrighteousness.

חָמָס *ḥāmās* [rendered: *unrighteousness*] / All the commentators,
both ancient and modern, are accustomed to explain the word to
mean lawlessness perpetrated by force. But this interpretation does
not suit the context, for there is no reason to suppose that the
text speaks of a particular kind of wrongdoing. According to
Talmudic exegesis (B. Sanhedrin 108a), Scripture seeks to show
how great is the evil of חָמָס *ḥāmās*, for the generation of the
deluge committed every transgression, but their fate was not sealed
until they were guilty of robbery. Various other explanations have
been advanced in answer to the question why the Bible stresses
here חָמָס *ḥāmās* in particular. This sin, it is suggested, is notorious
(Naḥmanides); or the reference is to crimes of the kind that
Lamech son of Methuselah committed, mentioned above, iv 23—24
(Dillmann); or the allusion is to the story of the sons of God,
who took them wives of whomsoever they chose, that is, according
to this exposition, to the fact that they violated married women
(Jacob); and the like. But all these interpretations are forced.
The crux of the matter is that the conventional explanation does
not accord with the simple meaning of the text. Although it is true
that in the rabbinic idiom, as in modern Hebrew, the word
חָמָס *ḥāmās* connotes a deed of outrage and violence, yet this was
not its meaning in the Biblical period. In the language of the Bible
it signifies generally anything that is not righteous. A witness of
חָמָס *ḥāmās* is a false witness (Exod. xxiii 1; Deut. xix 16; Psa.
xxxv 11; compare *ibid.* xxvii 12); 'hatred of חָמָס *ḥāmās*' is cause-
less hatred, having no justification (Psa. xxv 19). Of one who
is innocent of all transgression it is said that 'he did no חָמָס *ḥāmās*'
(Isa. liii 9) or that 'he has no חָמָס *ḥāmās* in his hands' (Job xvi
17; i Chron. xii 17). As parallels to חָמָס *ḥāmās* we find words
with a general signification, like רַע *raʿ* ['evil'], רֶשַׁע (רָשָׁע) *rešaʿ*
(*rāšāʿ*) ['wickedness' ('wicked')], עַוְלָה *ʿawlā* ['wrong'], אָוֶן
ʾāwen ['iniquity'] (Isa. lix 6; Jonah iii 8; Psa. lviii 3; cxl 2, 5;
Prov. iv 17); and in antithesis to חָמָס *ḥāmās* there occur expressions
like יְשָׁרִים *yešārīm* ['upright'], צַדִּיקִים *ṣaddīqīm* ['righteous'] (Prov.

iii 31–32; iv 17–18). The term חָמָס *ḥāmās* is applied to various sins, for example to idolatry (Ezek. viii 17, in an expression that is actually an imitation of the language of our verse: *that they should fill the land with* חָמָס *ḥāmās*), to the business methods of Tyre (Ezek. xxviii 16), to divorcing the wife of one's youth (Mal. ii 15 f.), or to words of guile and slander (Psa. cxl 2–4, 12; Prov. iii 31–32 [*perverse*]; xvi 29); and so on and so forth. This is also true of our verse: the reference is to wickedness generally, to unrighteousness as a whole. In contrast to Noah, who was wholly righteous, the entire earth was filled with deeds of unrighteousness.

12. *And God saw the earth and behold it was corrupt*] In the previous verse it was stated objectively that the earth was corrupt, and now Scripture tells us of God's subjective attitude to the world situation. The Judge of the universe did not remain indifferent to the position, but He saw and knew and made the requisite decisions.

The expression *And God saw* recalls to the reader's mind the story of Creation (i 31): *And God saw everything that He had made, and behold, it was very good.* The world as it emerged from the hands of the Creator was exceedingly good, but now, because of man's conduct, it was corrupt. In order to grasp the full significance of the verb שָׁחַת *šāḥath* here, we must bear in mind the words of Jer. xviii 3–4 concerning the potter: *So I went down to the* POTTER'S [יוֹצֵר *yōṣēr*] *house, and there he was working at his wheel. And the vessel he was making of clay* WAS SPOILED [נִשְׁחַת *nišḥath*]. The material did not receive the form that the potter wished to give it; it assumed another shape and the vessel was spoiled in his hand. Then the potter changed the material back into a shapeless mass, and made of it another vessel in accordance with his desire (*ibid. v.* 4: *and he reworked it into another vessel, as it seemed good to the potter to do*). In similar vein, our section speaks about the Creator [יוֹצֵר *yōṣēr;* the same word as for potter] of the world: He saw that the man whom He had formed of the dust from the ground did not conform to His will, and that His creature was malformed; He thereupon resolved to annihilate mankind, who had become corrupt, and to fashion in their stead another human race. Actually the moral that the prophet wishes to inculcate by means of the parable of the potter is different

53

from the basic teaching of our section, but it is manifest that the two sections have the same allegory in mind, although they apply it to different purposes.

The expression *the earth* occurs in this sentence, as in the two preceding clauses, at the end of the first hemistich; we thus have a graceful reiteration of one of the key words of the paragraph three times consecutively, at corresponding points in the structure of the sentences, as is clear from the division of the verses that I have indicated above, p. 48 [this is seen in the Hebrew; the translation cannot reproduce the terminal position of the *earth* in each clause]. After this threefold mention of *the earth* we hear an echo of it at the end of the paragraph (*upon the earth*), to give, as it were, a harmonious touch to the conclusion.

The name אֱלֹהִים *'Elōhim* also appears three times in the paragraph; but since it occurs twice as the complement in its clause, it is not particularly emphasized.

For all flesh had corrupted their way upon the earth] This sentence comes, as it were, to explain explicitly the nature of the earth's corruption that was mentioned twice earlier; the corruption of the earth means the moral corruption of all flesh. The verb שָׁחַת *šāḥath* also occurs thrice, and is clearly emphatic; in the first and third instances it is placed at the commencement of the clause, and in the second case at the end.

All flesh] This phrase which sometimes denotes human beings only (for example, Isa. xl 6; Jer. xxv 31), includes in our section all living things, as we learn expressly from the subsequent verses (vi 17, 19; vii 15, 16, 21; viii 17; etc.). Possibly the ancient poetic tradition, like the later rabbinic legends, spoke also of the corruption of the creatures. The Torah did not wish to dwell on this detail, since it was not of importance to its purpose. It could be of literary interest, but for the moral education of humanity, which is the Torah's aim, it had no significance; hence the Torah passed it over in silence. But possibly not in complete silence; Scripture may have wished to hint at it here, in order to forestall the question: But why were the animals destroyed, if they were free from transgression?

Their way] The mention of *way* at the conclusion of the paragraph corresponds to the reference to *walking* at the beginning.

54

Noah walked with God, that is, his way was the way of God; but all the other inhabitants of the earth, save his family, corrupted their way.

Upon the earth] These words are related to the preceding expression *their way;* all flesh corrupted the way that they walked on the earth. Hence it was possible to say that *the earth* was corrupt.

SECOND PARAGRAPH

NOAH IS TOLD OF THE COMING DOOM AND
IS ENJOINED TO MAKE THE ARK

13. *And God said to Noah,*
    'An end of all flesh / I have determined to make;
    for the earth is filled / with unrighteousness through them;
    and behold, I am about to destroy them / with the earth.

14. *Make yourself / an ark of gopher wood;*
    rooms / make in the ark,
    and cover it / inside and out / with pitch.

15. *This / is how you are to make it;*
    three hundred cubits / the length of the ark,
    fifty cubits its breadth, / and thirty cubits its height.

16. *A window / make for the ark,*
    and to a cubit / finish it above;
    and the door of the ark / set in its side;
    with lower, second, and third decks / make it.

17. *And I —*
    behold, I am about to bring a flood, / water upon the earth,
    to destroy all flesh / in which is the breath of life, / existing
        under heaven;
    everything that is on the earth / shall expire.

18. *But I will establish My covenant / through you;*
    and you shall come into the ark, / you,
    your sons, your wife, and your sons' wives / with you.

19. *And every living thing / of all flesh,*
    two of every sort / you shall bring into the ark,
    to keep them alive with you; / they shall be male and female.

20. *Of the flying creatures according to their kinds, / and of the*
    animals according to their kinds,
    of every / creeping [i.e. moving] *thing of the ground accord-*
    ing to its kind,
    two of every sort / shall come in to you, to keep them alive.

21. *And you —*
    take with you / of every sort of food that is eaten,
    and store it up for yourself; / and it shall serve for you and
    for them / as food.

22. *And Noah did this; / according to all that God commanded*
    him,
    so did he.

13. *And God said to Noah*] God informs Noah that He has decided to destroy all flesh in the waters of the Flood, and to fulfil through him and his descendants after him the promises that He made to Adam. Hence, He commands him to build an ark that can serve as a refuge for him and his family and for a pair of each kind of living creature during the Deluge. This is not an unnecessary repetition of vi 7; there the Bible tells us of God's decision, and here of its announcement to Noah.

An end of all flesh, etc.] The beginning of this paragraph is linked to the end of the preceding paragraph. Various expressions that appeared in the latter are repeated here: כָּל בָּשָׂר *kol bāśār* ['all flesh']; לְפָנַי *lephānay* ['before Me'] (in the first paragraph, לִפְנֵי הָאֱלֹהִים *liphnē hā'Elōhīm* [literally, 'before God'; rendered: 'in God's sight']); מָלְאָה הָאָרֶץ חָמָס *māle'ā hā'āres ḥāmās* ['the earth is filled with unrighteousness'] (in the preceding paragraph וַתִּמָּלֵא הָאָרֶץ חָמָס *wattimmālē' hā'āres ḥāmās* ['and the earth was filled with unrighteousness']); and the verb הִשְׁחִית *hišḥīth* ['destroyed'].

בָּא לְפָנַי *bā' lephānay* [literally, 'has come before Me'; translated: 'I have determined'] / According to Abraham ibn Ezra the meaning is: the end of man 'has come', as in Amos viii 2: *the end has come upon My people Israel*. This, however, explains only the word בָּא *bāʿ* ['has come'], but not לְפָנַי *lephānay* ['before Me']. Dillmann interprets it to mean: according to my intention and desire; but this is a forced interpretation. More probably the meaning is the same as in Esther ix 11: *That very day the number of those slain . . .* WAS BROUGHT [בָּא *bā'*; literally, 'came'] BEFORE *the king*. When a matter is brought for the consideration and decision of the king, it is said to come before the king. This is also the case here: [God, as it were, says:] sentence of destruction upon all flesh has been presented before My Court of Justice, and I have already come to a decision concerning it, and I am about to execute it.

For the earth is filled with unrighteousness through them] This is the reason for the decree of destruction. The earth is filled with unrighteousness; therefore it follows that the unrighteousness must be removed from its midst and the world must be remoulded. Since the unrighteousness comes *through*, that is, *on account of*, mankind, justice demands that they who brought about this situation should receive their punishment. The word מִפְּנֵיהֶם *mippenēhem* ['through them'; literally, 'from before them'], in which the noun פָּנִים *pānīm* [literally, 'face'; rendered: 'before', 'through'] appears for the third time, comes to emphasize, as it were, the source of the evil: *through them* [מִפְּנֵיהֶם *mippenēhem*] the matter has come *before Me* [לְפָנַי *lephānay*].

וְהִנְנִי מַשְׁחִיתָם *wehinenī mashḥīthām* [literally, 'and behold, I destroy them'; rendered: 'and behold, I am about to destroy them'] / the word הִנֵּה *hinnē* ['behold'], followed by the participle, indicates an act that is about to be performed immediately; here the meaning is: I am about to destroy. The retribution will be measure for measure; they *destroyed* [i. e. corrupted] their way, therefore I am about to *destroy them*.

אֶת הָאָרֶץ *'eth hā'āreṣ* [rendered: 'with the earth'] / Various suggestions have been put forward to explain or amend these words:

(1) From the earth (Rashi, first explanation; Ibn Ezra, first explanation; and so Graetz, who doubles the preceding final *Mēm* [of מַשְׁחִיתָם *mashḥīthām*] and reads מֵאֵת הָאָרֶץ *mē'ēth hā'āreṣ*; similarly others, who read מִן הָאָרֶץ *min hā'āreṣ* ['from the earth'] or מֵעַל הָאָרֶץ *mē'al hā'āreṣ* ['from upon the earth']).

(2) Behold, I am about to destroy them and the earth (Ibn Ezra, second explanation, and so several moderns, who actually read on the basis of the Septuagint: 'And behold, I am about to *destroy them* [מַשְׁחִיתָם *mašḥīthām*, or מַשְׁחִית אוֹתָם *mašḥīth 'ōthām*] *and* [וְאֶת *we'eth*] the earth').

(3) And behold, I am about to destroy them, that is to say, destroy the earth (Jacob).

(4) Other emendations, like: 'And behold, I am about to destroy them, *for they destroy the earth* [כִּי (הֵם) מַשְׁחִיתִים אֶת הָאָרֶץ *kī* (*hēm*) *mašḥīthīm 'eth hā'āreṣ*]' (Budde); 'And behold, *they are about to destroy* [וְהִנָּם מַשְׁחִיתִים *wehinnām mašḥīthīm*] the earth' (Gunkel); 'And behold, we [the gods] intend to destroy [וְהִנְנוּ מַשְׁחִיתִים *wehinenū mašḥīthīm*] the earth' (Eerdmans, who finds in this emendation, which he himself introduced into the text, a proof of his view that the Torah contains polytheistic tales).

(5) Together with the earth (Onkelos; Peshiṭta; Vulgate; Rashi, second explanation; and other medieval and modern exegetes).

The first explanation is ruled out for the reason that the concept of destruction is absolute and not relative like that of wiping out' (see my note on the verb מָחָה *māḥā* in Part I, vi 7, pp. 304–305), and therefore it is not possible to add a complement to it to indicate the place from which one destroys; he who is destroyed is completely destroyed, without qualification. Verse 17, in which we find מִתַּחַת הַשָּׁמַיִם *mittaḥath haššāmayim* [literally, 'from under heaven'] after *leśaḥēth* ['to destroy'], presents no difficulty, because the *Mēm* there does not signify 'motion away from', the meaning being: all flesh that exists under the heaven (see below, on the verse). The second interpretation is difficult from the grammatical point of view, and the third encounters both grammatical and thematic difficulties. The emendations do not solve the problem but nullify it by force, and introduce into the text the expositor's own ideas. The fifth explanation appears to be correct. There is no objection to it grammatically, and so far as the thought is concerned it fits in with the central idea of the text: they destroyed [i. e. corrupted] their way, therefore, I shall destroy them; the earth was destroyed [i. e. corrupted] on account of them, therefore I shall destroy also it with them.

14. *Make yourself*, etc.] God commands Noah to make himself

an ark, although it is only later, in *vv.* 17–21, that He tells him
that it is by water that He will destroy all flesh, and that it is His
will to save him and his family. In this way it is possible to speak
to a wholly righteous man, who accepts his Master's bidding even
when he does not know its reason or purpose. The command to
build the ark, which is one of the key themes in this paragraph,
is stressed by the reiteration of the verb עָשָׂה *ásá* seven times in the
paragraph, as I noted in the introduction to the section.

An ark] The word תֵּבָה *tēbhā* ['ark'] occurs in only two sections
of Scripture: here and in the section that describes the birth and
rescue of Moses (Exod. ii 3–5). This is certainly no coincidence.
By the verbal parallel, the Torah wished, apparently, to draw
attention to the parallelism of theme. In both cases there is to be
saved from drowning one who is worthy of salvation and is destined
to bring deliverance to others; here it is humanity that is to be
saved, there it is the chosen people; here it is the macrocosm that
has to be preserved, there it is the microcosm. The experiences of
the fathers foreshadow the history of their descendants. Hence,
similar expressions occur in both sections: here it is stated, *Make
yourself an ark of gopher wood ... and cover it, inside and out,
with pitch;* there it is written, *she took for him a basket* [the same
word as for *ark*] *made of bulrushes, and daubed it with bitumen and
pitch.* The difference in the materials used is due to the difference
of locality, custom and the beings to be saved: there it is a child,
and here it is a complete family of people together with a great
number of creatures. Here it is written, *Make yourself,* because
a huge ark of the requisite dimensions was certainly not ready to
hand; there it says, *she took for him,* because small baskets of
bulrushes could be obtained ready-made in Egypt. But the essential
point is identical: each passage speaks of a תֵּבָה *tēbhā;* the parallelism is therefore clear.

The word תֵּבָה *tēbhā* is apparently a loan-word. Although the
Akkadian derivation is no longer tenable, yet the view that it is of
Egyptian origin is still accepted. The Egyptian word *ḏbȝ.t* denotes
a coffin or a chest in general, and also a big building such as a
palace and the like. There is also a form of the word that is nearer
to the Hebrew, namely, *tb.t,* which signifies a chest or box. The
substantive *ḏbȝ,* without the feminine ending, means a bird's cage.

The original signification common to them all seems to have been: an object made in the shape of a parallelepiped, and this is precisely the primary meaning of the Hebrew word תֵּבָה *tēbhā,* which is used also today as a term for this geometrical form. Undoubtedly the Biblical narrative refers to such a structural shape and not to that of a ship. The sentence, *and the ark went on the face of the waters* (vii 18) is not suited to a boat, which is navigated by its mariners, but to something that floats on the surface of the waters and moves in accordance with the thrust of the water and wind. Similarly the subsequent statement (viii 4): *the ark came to* REST ... *upon the mountains of Ararat,* implies an object that can *rest* upon the ground; this is easy for an ark to do, since its bottom is straight and horizontal, but not for a ship.

This is not the case in the Mesopotamian documents. They all relate, without exception, that the hero of the Deluge was saved in a ship. Although the details in the Epic of Gilgameš regarding the construction of the vessel are capable of different explanations, and the commentators are not agreed on their interpretation, yet it seems probable that the observation there that the measurements of its length breadth and height were equal (lines 30, 57–58) does not refer to the boat itself, but to a cubic structure within it, which is called *êkallu,* 'palace', in line 95. Unquestionably this poem, like all the other Mesopotamian texts, refers to a proper ship; not only is it invariably called *elippu,* which means *ship,* but the epic indicates that Utnapištim entrusted the navigation of the vessel to the boatman, and that he brought into it the craftsmen, that is, the sailors; and when it speaks of the end of the Flood, it does not use a word like *rested,* which is found in the Torah, but terms more suited to a boat that is held up among the mountain crags (particularly noteworthy is the statement that the mountain held the ship fast (*iṣbat*)). Berossus, too, in agreement with the ancient sources, always speaks of a boat, and even mentions its pilot (κυβερνήτης).

In the Torah there is no reference to a ship or to a pilot or to navigation. The ancient exegetical tradition likewise understood the Biblical word תֵּבָה *tēbhā* specifically as a box: in the Septuagint, κιβωτός; in Josephus, λάρναξ; in the Vulgate, *arca.* We also find the תֵּבָה *tēbhā* depicted as a box (apparently, under the influence of Jewish tradition) on the coins of Apamea in Phrygia, and on some of the monuments of early Christian art. In other Christian represent-ations, however, a boat or ship appears, and in it there is a house-like structure; but this may be due, directly or indirectly, to the influence of the Babylonian tradition, which is known to us from the account of Berossus. This is mostly the case, too, in medieval and modern art. It was to such a conception, apparently, that Ibn Ezra alluded, when he wrote: its name is תֵּבָה *tēhbā* and not boat, for it did not have the shape of a ship, nor did it have oars.

Perhaps the difference between the Torah and the Mesopotamian tradition is not accidental, and the Torah wished of set purpose to oppose the Gentile tradition and to declare that Noah's deliver-ance was not due to his seafaring skill but only to the will of His Heavenly Father. He had only to make an ark that would not sink in the water; that was all that was required of him; in all that concerned the unfoldment of events, he had to put his trust in the Lord, and He would do what was necessary.

The parallel drawn between a broken box and a ship's keel [literally, 'a rocking ship'] in the dispute about the shape of the shewbread (B. Menaḥot 94b) is a pure coincidence.

Gopher] This tree is mentioned nowhere else in the Bible, and it is difficult to identify it exactly (see the various attempts in B. Sanhedrin 108 b, and compare B. Rosh Hashana 23 a). Appar-ently it is a kind of pine, belonging to the species of cedar. In Targum Onkelos: קַדְרוֹס *qadhrōs*, that is, κέδρος, 'cedar' (the reading קַדְרוֹם *qadhrōm* is a scribal error); In Targum Pseudo-Jonathan [Palestine Targum] A and B: קַדְרִינוֹן *qadhrīnōn* (the *reading* קַדְרוֹנִין *qadhrōnīn* is also incorrect); and in one of the Greek versions ἐκ ξύλων κεδρίνων. The signification of the botanical name *giparu* in Akkadian, and whether there is any connection between it and *gopher*, is uncertain. The Septuagint and Vulgate used general terms in their translation, possibly because they did not know the identity of the tree; the Septuagint, ἐκ ξύλων τετραγώοων, i.e. of quadrangular timber; the Vulgate, *de lignis levigatis*, i. e. of smoothed wood. Possibly the word *gopher*, like the word כֹּפֶר *kōpher* ['pitch'] at the end of the sentence, belonged to the ancient poetic tradition concerning the Flood.

Rooms [קִנִּים *qinnīm*; literally, 'nests'] *make in the ark*] The

Rabbis in Bereshith Rabba xxxi 9, rightly translated, קִילִין וּמְדוֹרִין *qīlīn ūmᵉdhōrīn* (Onkelos: מְדוֹרִין *mᵉdhōrīn;* Targum Pseudo-Jonathan [Palestine Targum], קִילִין *qīlīn*), that is, 'compartments and dwellings.' This is the usual interpretation placed on the word today. Several scholars, following Lagarde, have suggested the reading קִנִּים קִנִּים *qinnīm qinnīm,* repeating the word in accordance with the usual form of distributive expressions; but the sentence has no distributive sense, and if the text had read, קִנִּים קִנִּים *qinnīm qinnīm* make the ark', the meaning would have been: break the ark to pieces and make thereof many compartments. Recently A. S. Yahuda has suggested that קִנִּים *qinnīm,* on the basis of the Egyptian *ḳn,* means papyrus fibre, which the Egyptians used for caulking their boats. But this interpretation is also not possible, since the extension of the accusative relating to *make (in) the ark* doubtless indicates the way in which the ark was built as a whole, not how a particular detail of the work was carried out.

And cover it, inside and out, with PITCH [כֹּפֶר *kōpher*] / The word כֹּפֶר *kōpher* in this signification is not found elsewhere in the Bible. It corresponds exactly to the Akkadian word *kupru,* which occurs in the Epic of Gilgameš, and appears to have been commonly used in the literary tradition of the Deluge.

The purpose of the instructions given in this verse is not yet stated; it will become clear later. The ark was to provide a refuge from the waters of the Flood; the rooms were to accommodate therein all sorts of creatures; the ark was to be covered with pitch so that the water should not seep into it.

15. *This is how you are to make it*] The general and principal instructions are followed by detailed directions, which commence with a formula of the kind that is normally used in such cases (Num. viii 4: *And this was the workmanship of the lampstand;* Deut. xv 2: *And this is the manner of the release;* i Kings vii 28: *This was the construction of the stands;* the Siloam inscription, line 1: 'And this is the story of the conduit'.

Three hundred cubits the length of the ark] The number 300 is one of the round figures in the sexagesimal system (see my remarks on this system above, Part I, in the introduction to *The Book of the History of Adam,* pp. 258 ff.), being half 600, which is 10×60. Although a length of 300 cubits is no small measurement, yet it is not so very big when compared to the extravagant measurements of the ship given in the Babylonian tradition of the Flood. According to Berossus the length of the boat was five stadia, that is, almost a kilometre. The Torah as usual reduces the figure (one hundred and fifty metres approximately), in keeping with the tendency that we observed in ch. v. The same applies to the width (see the introduction, p. 17).

Fifty cubits its breadth] Half of one hundred, one of the basic numbers of the decimal system.

And thirty cubits its height] Half of sixty, the fundamental number of the sexagesimal system.

To ask how so many living beings could enter into an ark of such dimensions, or other 'practical' questions of this nature, is to ignore the poetic and exalted character of so noble a narrative as the one before us.

16. *A* צֹהַר *ṣōhar* [rendered: 'window'] *make for the ark*] Also the word צֹהַר *ṣōhar* is found only here. Possibly this word, too, like the nouns גֹּפֶר *gōpher* and כֹּפֶר *kōpher,* which are of the same grammatical structure, belong to the ancient literary tradition of the Flood. Its meaning is in dispute. The Septuagint translates: ἐπισυνάγων, that is, 'gathering', 'collecting' (perhaps on the basis of Job xxiv 11, which means apparently: among the rows of the harvesters they glean); but this translation is improbable. Another explanation is: something with which to illumine the ark, the word being related to צָהֳרַיִם *ṣohŏrayim* ['noon']. This is how Onkelos translates it: נְהוֹר *nehōr* ['light']; similarly Aquila: μεσημβρινόν a derivative of μεσημβρία, 'noon-day'; and so, too, Symmachus: διαφανές that is, 'something transparent'. According to rabbinic interpretation צֹהַר *ṣōhar* was a precious stone that shone in the ark. The Vulgate renders: *fenestra,* 'window', and this is how most of the medieval expositors and many moderns have understood the term, on the strength of what is subsequently related (viii 6): *Noah opened the window of the ark which he had made.* Likewise in the Epic of Gilgameš, mention is made of the window of the ship (Tablet xi, line 135). A third explanation is 'covering', on the basis of ظَهْر *ẓahrun* in Arabic, *ṣēru* in Akkadian, *zukhru* in the El Amarna writings, and *ẓr* in Ugaritic, which mean *back.* The covering is also mentioned later on (viii 13): *and Noah removed*

the covering of the ark. In the Babylonian fragment discovered in Nippur it is stated in connection with the making of the boat: 'with a strong covering you shall cover it.' The most probable interpretation is *window*, for the following reasons: (1) when we read later on, *the window of the ark which he had made*, we find in the words *which he had made* an allusion to an earlier statement in which the term 'making' was actually used (here תַּעֲשֶׂה *ta'ăśe* ['make'], and in *v.* 22, in a general statement, וַיַּעַשׂ ... עָשָׂה *wayya'aś* ... *'āśā* ['did ... he did']); (2) an instruction to make a covering would have been superfluous, since you cannot have an ark without a covering; whereas a window is not a common feature in an ark, and therefore a special instruction to make it was necessary.

And to a cubit FINISH IT [תְּכַלֶּנָּה *tekhallennā*] *above*] Many interpretations of the verse have been suggested. The pronominal suffix of the word תְּכַלֶּנָּה *tekhallennā* refers, according to some commentators, to the ark, and, according to others, to צֹהַר *ṣōhar* (which they regard as a feminine noun, or else they point it תְּכַלֶּנֻה *tekhallenhū*). The latter exegetes are again divided into two groups on the question of the meaning of the word צֹהַר *ṣōhar* — whether it is a window or a cover; and they all disagree further as to the interpretation of the words *to a cubit*, which lends itself to various explanations.

In order to arrive at the correct interpretation, we must pay attention, as I indicated on p. 55, to the structure of the verse. We have here two pairs of clauses, and in each pair the first clause contains the word תֵּבָה *tēbhā*, and the second a pronominal suffix in the third person feminine singular. According to the rules of parallelism, we must conclude that since this suffix in the second couplet undoubtedly refers to the ark, it must likewise allude to it in the first couplet; and just as in the second pair the two clauses denote two different acts (the fixing of the door and the division of the ark into three storeys), so the two clauses of the first pair contain directions concerning two different tasks (the making of the צֹהַר *ṣōhar* in the first line and a totally different work in the second). Hence we must conclude that all the varied and extra-ordinary explanations that consider the suffix of תְּכַלֶּנָּה *tekhallennā* to relate to צֹהַר *ṣōhar* cannot be regarded as correct. The true

64

interpretation is as follows: Finish the construction of the ark on top in such a way that there should remain a cubit's breadth only, that is (see Rashi, S. D. Luzzatto), that the roof should slope down on both sides along the length of the ark, leaving above, between the two sloping sides, a horizontal area one cubit wide, likewise along the whole length of the ark. No specific instructions were necessary, as I have already stated, to inform Noah that an ark *must have* a covering; but with regard to its *form,* he needed a directive. This is appropriately given in this sentence.

And the door of the ark set in its side] In this huge ark there shall be a door, which shall permit entry and exit. This door was not to be a big one in proportion to the size of the ark, but a side entrance, small and unimposing, in order that it should be easily closed and firmly secured. Also in the Mesopotamian tradition the door of the boat is mentioned.

With lower, second and third decks make it] This is the fourth directive in the verse: divide the ark into three storeys. The plural of the words תַּחְתִּים שְׁנִיִּם וּשְׁלִשִׁים *taḥtiyyīm šeniyyīm ūšelīšīm* ['lower, second and third decks'], indicates that there were many rooms on each deck. In the Epic of Gilgameš (ll. 60–62) reference is also made to the division of the boat; but there the meaning is not quite clear, and it is difficult to decide whether rooms or places or both together are intended.

17. *And I — behold, I will bring a flood, water upon the earth*] Now the Divine announcement clarifies what was previously left obscure. At first God had said: *and behold, I will destroy them with the earth* — a general statement that did not specify how He would carry out the destruction. In similar terms He commanded Noah to build the ark — a general instruction that did not explain the purpose of the ark. Now the matter is elucidated: the destruction would be accomplished by means of a deluge of water, and the ark would serve as a refuge for Noah and his household and the pairs of creatures from the waters of the Flood.

And I] In antithesis to 'you', which is contained in all the verbs in the second person that occur in verses 14–16: you, on your part, do all that I bid you, and I, on my side, shall implement my decision.

Behold, I am about to bring] The syntactic construction is the

65

same as that of *v.* 13, *and behold I am about to destroy;* see my note there.

The flood [מַבּוּל *mabbūl*] / *The word* מַבּוּל *mabbūl* is found only in our section and in Psa. xxix 10: *The Lord sits enthroned over the* מַבּוּל *mabbūl,* etc. In the latter verse, too, if the meaning of מַבּוּל *mabbūl* is not altogether different ('throne', according to Epstein, *Tarbiz,* xii, p. 82), and if we are not to read in its stead לִמְלֹךְ *limlōkh,* as many have proposed (Lambert, Torczyner [Tur-Sinai], Ginzberg), the reference is to the waters of Noah. This word, too, which is specifically applied in the Bible to the waters of Noah, belonged, it seems, to the vocabulary of the ancient poetic tradition on this subject. Its etymology is disputed. It has been suggested that it is derived from (1) the Hebrew stem נָבַל *nābhal,* in the sense of destruction (Ibn Ezra, Jacob), or the Akkadian root *nabālu,* which has the same meaning (Delitzsch, Koenig and others); (2) the stem בָּלַל *bālal,* a contraction of מַבְלוּל *mabhlūl,* formed like the noun מַסְלוּל *maslūl* (an alternative explanation by Ibn Ezra); (3) the stem יָבַל *yābhal,* which appears in the expression יִבְלֵי־מַיִם *yibhlē mayim* ['watercourses', 'flowing streams'] (Isa. xxx 25; xliv 4), the *Yōd* being assimilated as in the word מַדּוּעַ *maddūaʿ* (Gesenius, Dillmann and others); (4) the Akkadian *abûbu,* the usual term for the Deluge in the Babylonian tradition; (5) the Akkadian *bubbulu,* which is taken to mean 'a flood'. In order to decide between the various theories, we may be guided by the Ugaritic writings. In one of the Ugaritic inscriptions (I D, ll. 44–45) it is written: *bl ṭl bl rd bl šrʿ thmtm.* According to my interpretation (*Orientalia,* New Series, viii [1939], p. 239), these are the words of Daniel who prays to Baal and entreats him to water his fields with dew and rain and the fountains of the deep. The word *bl* is, to my mind, the imperative of the verb *ybl* in the sense of *cause to come, bring* (in Arabic وبل *wabala,* especially, *to bring down rain*). Now in the same Ugaritic verse mention is made both of the waters coming down from heaven and the waters that ascend from the deep, exactly as it is worded in our section (vii 11): *all the fountains of the great* DEEP *burst and the windows of the heavens were opened.* It seems clear, therefore, that the word מַבּוּל *mabbūl* is formed from the Hebrew and Canaanite stem יבל *ybl;* it is not a loan-word but a pure Hebrew substantive, and is well-suited to the theme. Nevertheless, it is possible that the early Hebrew poets who began to compose poems on the Deluge chose particularly this word, because it sounded like the word normally used in Akkadian, *abûbu,* and the Torah continued this linguistic tradition.

Water upon the earth] The word הָיָה *hāyā,* which occurs later (vii 6) between *flood* and *water,* shows that they have to be separated here, too, contrary to the Masoretic accents. Many exegetes regard the words *water upon the earth* as a later addition, but this view has nothing to support it. On the contrary these words are necessary; since the term מַבּוּל *mabbūl* described something that had not yet come into existence, it was impossible for Noah to understand it without an explanation of its nature. Below (vii 6), in the story of the implementation of this announcement to Noah, the Bible repeats, as usual, the expressions of the original communication.

In which is the breath of life] Here, too, we have an explanatory note, which is needed to make it clear that the phrase *all flesh* is not to be understood in its restricted connotation, 'all human beings', but in its wider signification, 'all living creatures' (see above, the end of the commentary on the first paragraph, p. 54).

מִתַּחַת הַשָּׁמַיִם *mittaḥath haśśāmayim* [rendered: 'existing under heaven'; literally, 'from under'] / The *Mēm* ['from'] of מִתַּחַת *mittaḥath* is not connected with the verb *destroy* but with the expression *all flesh,* etc. The sense is: all flesh in which is the breath of life and whose life is lived beneath the heavens. This excludes those who exist in the water under the earth (Exod. xx 4; Deut. v 8).

Everything that is on the earth shall perish] I bring the flood with this intention, and according to my intention it shall be.

18. *But I will establish My covenant through* [literally, 'with'] *you*] The meaning, according to some commentators (Naḥmanides, Gunkel) is: but I make a covenant with you now to deliver you from the water of the flood; according to others (for instance, Skinner): after the flood I shall make a covenant with you (ix 9f.). But as I have already noted in the introduction to this section (§ 6. p. 35), a distinction has to be drawn between 'making [literally, 'cutting'] a covenant' and 'establishing a covenant':

67

making a covenant means the giving of an undertaking by the parties to the covenant; whilst establishing a covenant signifies to fulfil and implement this undertaking. Hence the aforementioned explanations are unacceptable. For the same reason, it is difficult to agree with the view of Gersonides and Abravanel that the reference is to the preservation of the established order of creation, to which there is an allusion, according to their view, in the word 'covenant' in Jer. xxxiii 20, 25; but for Noah, too, the normal order of nature was changed during the period of the flood, and the difference between him and other people lay only in this, that he did not suffer from these changes to the same extent as they did. The key to the understanding of the text is provided by the wording of a similar verse further on (xvii 21): *But I will establish my covenant with Isaac.* There God tells Jacob that in truth Ishmael, too, shall be fruitful and multiply and become a great nation, but the covenant that God made with Abraham would not be fulfilled through Ishmael, his son by Hagar, but through Isaac, his son by Sarah. A similar situation obtains here. Noah is informed that all mankind would perish in the waters of the Deluge; and if this came to pass, what would become of the promises that God had made to Adam? It is written in Gen. i 28: *And God blessed them and God said to them, 'Be fruitful and multiply and fill the earth.'* Thus a covenant was made with the human race that they would be fruitful and multiply and fill the earth — a *covenant* not in the sense of a bilateral undertaking, but of a unilateral promise in favour of man, like that which was given to Phineas when God declared (Num. xxv 12): *Behold, I give to him My covenant of peace.* Since it is not possible for God not to fulfil His word, therefore the statement, *everything that is on the earth shall die,* is immediately followed here by, *But I will establish My covenant through you,* as though to say: and as for My covenant with the first man, I shall fulfil it through you and your seed after you; through you shall the existence of mankind be continued, and through you shall the blessing that I bestowed upon Adam be realized. It is not without reason that later in the story (ix 1) Noah and his sons are blessed in the very words used in Adam's benison: and God blessed Noah and his sons, and said to them: *Be fruitful and multiply, and fill the earth.*

And you shall come into the ark, etc.] The thought of the previous sentence is continued: in order that the establishment of the covenant and the fulfilment of God's promise to Adam may be attained, let Noah and his sons, and their wives with them, pair by pair, enter the ark, and they would all be delivered thereby from the waters of the Flood. The emphasis placed on the women (*and your wife and the wives of your sons with you*) points to the primary motive, the preservation of the species.

The parallelism of the words *through* [literally, 'with'] *you — you — with you* at the end, respectively, of each of the three parts of the verse is clearly seen in the way I have marked the verse-division on p. 55.

19. *And of every living thing,* etc.] Even as the human species would continue to exist, so all the various kinds of creatures that had been created would be preserved; and to this end, just as the human beings would enter the ark in pairs, so would also a pair of every species of creature enter.

You shall bring into the ark] See below, the annotations to *v.* 20 (*two of every sort shall come in,* etc.).

To keep them alive with you] The immediate object of their entering the ark would be *to keep them alive with you,* that is to say, that you, Noah, would give them the opportunity to continue their own life in your proximity; the ultimate goal would be to keep their species alive. For this reason emphasis is given at the end of the sentence to the words *they shall be male and female.*

20. *Of the birds according to their kind,* etc.] In this verse expressions occurring in the story of Creation are repeated, in order to indicate that every kind of creature deserves to be, and will be, saved. The Bible changes slightly the form of the expressions and their order, in accordance with the usual practice in repetitions. On this feature of reiteration with variations of form and nuance, see my observations in Part I, in my annotations on i 26, p. 57. Here the beasts are not expressly mentioned, and are included in the phrase *every creeping thing of the ground according to its kind,* which denotes every creature that creeps, that is, that moves, on the face of the ground.

Two of every sort shall come in to you, to keep them alive] On the face of it, it appears as though this is an unnecessary

69

repetition of what has already been stated in the previous verse. But actually there is no repetition here but an additional explanation. Above it is stated: *you shall bring into the ark;* now Noah might have queried this instruction and said: How is it possible for me to search out all the different kinds of creatures upon earth and bring them with me into the ark? (see Bereshith Rabba, xxxii 8: 'he [Noah] said unto him: "Am I a hunter?"'). To this potential question the following answer is given: *two of every sort shall* COME IN *to you* — of their own accord, as a result of an inner urge that God would arouse within them for their own preservation and the preservation of their species. There will be no need for you to take the trouble to search for them; they will come in of their own accord to you, so that you may keep them alive (already in B. Zebaḥim 116a we find the comment: *by themselves*). In the light of this interpretation, the meaning of the word *bring* in the preceding verse is: you shall permit them to come into the ark. Proof of this is to be found in what we are told later on about the dove (viii 9): *and* BROUGHT *her into the ark with him;* and it is certain that the dove came by herself.

To keep them alive [לְהַחֲיוֹת *lehaḥăyōth*] / The fondness for variation, which is discernable, as we have noted, in Biblical style, is also noticeable in the work of the Masoretes, who fixed at a later period the spelling of the text. The word לְהַחֲי(וֹ)ת *lehaḥăyōth,* which occurs in two consecutive verses, is spelt the first time defectively לְהַחֲיִת *lehaḥăyōth* [without a *Wāw* after the *Yōdh*], and the second time *plene* לְהַחֲיוֹת *lehaḥăyō(w)th* [with *Wāw*]. Similarly, the word טְהֹ(וֹ)רָה *ṭehōrā* ['clean'], which is found twice in vii 2, is written the first time *plene,* טְהוֹרָה *ṭehō(w)rā* [with *Wāw*] and afterwards defectively טְהֹרָה *ṭehōrā* [without *Wāw*]; and when it reappears twice in *v.* 8, it is again spelt once in full and once defectively. Conversely, in viii 20, it is first written defectively טְהֹרָה *ṭehōrā* and then *plene,* טָהוֹר *ṭāhō(w)r.*

21.   *And you*] — in antithesis to the third person (יָבֹאוּ *yābhō'ū*) in the preceding verse, as though to say: they shall do their part and come in to you, and you do your duty and prepare food for yourself and for them.

Of every sort of food that is eaten] — vegetarian food, in accordance with i 29–30; see my comments there pp. 58–59. The word

לְאָכְלָה *leʾokhlā* ['as food'], which is found there and recurs here.
serves to recall those verses.

22. *And Noah did this,* etc.] The words form a solemn conclusion
to the second paragraph, and also indicate a pause in the course of
events, leaving Noah at work in fulfilment of God's command. This
verse, which states, and reiterates, that Noah did all that he was
commanded, provides us with a graphic picture of Noah working
devotedly, with complete faith in all that the Almighty had told
him, and in absolute obedience to the word of his Creator.

The Bible undoubtedly intends to convey that Noah's work in
making the ark required considerable time. Possibly the ancient
poetic tradition related that the first Divine communication came to
Noah on the first day of the first month, and that his work on
the construction and equipment of the ark lasted forty days, corresponding to the periods mentioned later in our section (vii 4, 12,
17; viii 6). This would be in keeping with what becomes evident
a little later, namely, that also according to the Bible the date
of the second communication, which came to Noah at the end of
his work, was the tenth day of the second month, that is, forty
days after the commencement of the year. But this emerges from the
text indirectly; it is not expressly stated. The Torah was concerned
to mention only the dates of the phases of the Deluge, and did
not record the dates of the Divine revelations to Noah; God's word
is not related to time as are the happenings of nature.

THIRD PARAGRAPH
THE COMMAND TO ENTER THE ARK
CHAPTER VII

1. *Then the Lord said to Noah,*
   'Go, you and all your household / into the ark,
   for I have seen that you / are righteous before Me /in this
      generation.

2. *Of all / the clean animals*
   take with you / seven pairs, / the male and his mate;

1THE FLOOD

and of the animals / that are not clean,
a pair / the male and his mate;

3.   *also of the flying creatures of the air / seven pairs, / male and*
     female,
    to keep their kind alive / upon the face of all the earth.

4.   *For in seven days / I will send rain upon the earth*
    forty days / and forty nights;
    and I will blot out / every living thing that I have made
  from the face of the ground.'

5.   *And Noah did / all that the Lord had commanded.*

The ark was completed; in verse 1 it is referred to as something existing. Noah had already finished all that he had been enjoined to do, and he was waiting for new instructions to apprise him when to enter the ark that he had prepared. Meanwhile the second month had arrived, that is, the month of Marḥeshvan (counting the months of the year from Tishri), and the rainy season was drawing near. The day appointed by the Divine plan for the commencement of the Deluge was fast approaching. And lo! Noah again hears the Lord addressing him and commanding him to go into the ark together with all those destined to be rescued with him, for in another seven days the waters of the Flood would be upon the earth. Since it is subsequently stated (*v.* 11) that the Deluge began on the seventeenth day of the second month, it follows that according to the Bible the second communication from God came to Noah on the tenth day of the second month.

1. *Then the Lord said to Noah*] On the reason for the change of the Divine Name (in the previous paragraphs we find אֱלֹהִים *'Elōhīm,* but in this paragraph the Tetragrammaton) see the introduction to the section of the Flood, § 6, pp. 35 f.

Go, you and all your household, into the ark] Now the time has arrived for your entrance into the ark — *the* ark, with the definite article, the ark that was well-known and already prepared.

For I have seen that you, etc.] In contradistinction to what was stated earlier (vi 12): *And God saw the earth, and behold, it was corrupt.* I have seen [God declares] all the other inhabitants of the world, and behold, they are corrupt; I have seen you, and behold,

72

you are righteous before Me. The fact, also, that Noah believed in all that was told him in the first Divine communication and did everything that he was enjoined was an additional indication of his righteousness, as the Bible states in the case of Abraham (xv 6): *And he believed in the Lord; and He reckoned it to him as a righteousness.*

Righteous before Me in this generation] See above, on vi 9 (*in his generations*).

2. *Of all the clean* [טְהוֹרָה *ṭehō(w)rā*, with *Wāw*] *animals*, etc.] At this point, Noah was given a new precept. Apart from the two creatures of every species that would *come* of their own accord, he was to *take* from his flocks and herds seven pairs of every kind of clean animal. For the time being the purpose was not revealed to him; again we have an injunction for which no reason is given, and once more the righteous man, who obeys God's commandment unquestioningly, is put to the test. The reason for the precept, as many expositors have perceived, becomes apparent later, when we are informed (viii 20): *Then Noah built an altar to the Lord, and took of every clean animal and of every clean bird, and offered burnt offerings on the altar.* Had not Noah taken extra pairs of clean animals and birds into the ark, he would not have been able to offer sacrifices without completely exterminating the species involved.

Take with you] — for every purpose that you may require. The sacrifices are not mentioned to him at this stage; for had he been told about them at the beginning, his offerings would not have been so meritorious as when he brought them in response to an inner urge to forgo a part of the little that remained to him in order to give thanks to the Lord for his deliverance. The intention is not to *command* Noah to bring sacrifices, but to make it *possible* for him to do so. In any case, there may be an allusion to the subject in the verb לָקַח *lāqaḥ* ['take'], which is commonly used when the preparation of animals for sacrifices is spoken of (for example, Gen. xv, 9–10; Exod. x 26, etc. etc.).

The male and his mate [אִישׁ וְאִשְׁתּוֹ *'iš we'ištō*, literally, 'a man and his wife'] / This expression, which replaces the usual formula *male and female*, is not an indication of another source, as most modern scholars think. It was essential to employ here a different ex-

73

pression. The meaning of the words *male and female*, coming after the number *two*, is unmistakable; but here, following the number *seven* [literally, 'seven, seven'; rendered: 'seven pairs'], there would have been need for further clarification. Had the text read, *seven seven, male and female*, we should have been in doubt as to the respective number of males and females, and we might have taken the sense to be seven animals of every kind of clean animal, some of them males and some females. To make the position clear, it was necessary to state here אִישׁ וְאִשְׁתּוֹ *'îš we'ištō*, the word אִישׁ *'îš* ['man'] having a distributive connotation: each one of the males together with his female. Hence the phrase signifies: *seven pairs* of each kind of clean animal. And since the text has here *the male and his mate*, the expression is repeated in the second half of the verse, in order to preserve the parallelism, and to make it clear that the clean and unclean animals differed only in regard to the *number* — not the principle — of (mated) pairs. In verse 3, after the signification of the numerical idiom *seven seven* had been established, it was possible to revert to the use of the normal formula *male and female*.

And of the animals that are not clean [טְהֹרָה *tehōrā*, without *Wāw*] / At first sight, it seems strange that the Bible did not say simply: *and of the unclean animals*. The rabbinic explanation (B. Pesaḥim 3a, and parallels) that the Torah prefers to use chaste language is well-known, but this is only a homiletical interpretation that seeks Scriptural support for instruction in good manners, and does not represent the true sense of the verse, for numerous Pentateuchal passages contain expressions of impurity. The simple meaning of the words requires us to explain the matter differently. When the Torah speaks of unclean animals and refers to them by this term, it wishes to emphasize positively the quality of uncleanness and its laws; but here the only positive quality of interest is that of the clean animals, which excludes them from the rule of *two of every sort;* all the other animals (including, of course, the wild beasts), since *they do not possess* this attribute, are not excepted from the general rule.

On the change from the full spelling of טְהוֹרָה *tehō(w)rā* [with *Wāw*] to the *defective spelling* טְהֹרָה *tehōrā* [without *Wāw*], see the end of the commentary on vi 20.

74

The verse raises a question: how is it possible to speak of animals that are clean and not clean at a time when the Torah laws distinguishing between these categories had not yet been formulated? The explanation may be that the concepts of clean and unclean animals were already in existence prior to the Torah, even among the Gentiles, particularly in relation to sacrifices (our verse does not refer to a distinction in human food, for according to the Bible, as we have noted, the diet at the time was purely vegetarian). The Babylonians and Assyrians, as a rule, brought oblations only of herds and flocks, and in rare instances of mountain goats. When they sacrificed dogs or swine, these were not offerings to the gods but gifts to the demons (for example, the female demon *lamaštu*), or served as a substitute for a sick person, so that his ailment would be transferred to the animal. If by chance a dog entered one of the temples of the gods, the sanctuary required a ceremony of purification (the inclusion of wild boars among offerings of sheep and oxen in the list of sacrifices that were customary in Ur of the Chaldees at a later period, in the time of the Seleucids, is quite exceptional). Already in the Sumerian story of the Flood, the oldest recension we have of this tradition, it is expressly stated that the hero of the Deluge offered up, after his deliverance, an ox and sheep.

3. *Also of the flying creatures of the air, seven pairs, male and female*] The fact that the Bible does not differentiate here between clean and unclean flying creatures, as it did above in the case of the animals, constitutes at first sight a difficulty. According to the exegetical traditions of the Talmudic sages and of the medieval commentators, this verse is to be understood, on the strength of the distinction drawn in the preceding sentence, to refer to the clean birds only. But such an interpretation is very forced. Today the prevailing view calls for the emendation of the text. Several expositors hold that the whole of the first part of the verse, up to the word *female,* does not belong to the original text. Others, in accordance with the Samaritan Pentateuch and the Septuagint, add the adjective *clean* to the term *flying creatures.* There are even some exegetes who not only supply the word *clean,* but, following the Greek text, also insert the words: *and of all the flying creatures that are not clean, a pair, male and female.* But even if we suppose

that it was possible for a scribe to omit this line in error by skipping from the first mention of *male and female* to the second, it is hard to imagine that yet another mistake was made in the verse and that, without adequate reason, the word *clean* was likewise left out. The Septuagint and Samaritan Version simply conformed to their usual tendency of giving uniformity to the text and harmonized the verses. There is no need, however, for forced interpretation or for textual emendations. The Torah has also in mind the unclean species of flying creatures, or at least some of them — to the extent that Noah was able to catch them (in regard to the flying creatures the word *all* is not used, as it is in connection with the clean beasts). Of these, too, Noah had to take seven pairs, since he would have need, in the future, to make use of both categories — not only of the clean birds for sacrifices, but of the two kinds together for the purpose of sending some of them forth to ascertain the state of the water upon the earth. Thus we are told later that Noah employed to this end both a raven (an unclean bird) and a dove (a clean bird). He could not tell at the outset how many birds would be necessary for this task; nor could he be sure that an accident would not befall one of them. If there were only two and a mishap occurred to one, that entire species would be destroyed.

To KEEP *their kind* ALIVE [לְחַיּוֹת *leḥayyōth*] / Above (vi 19, 20) the verb לְהַחֲיוֹת *lehaḥăyōth* ['to keep alive' — *Hiphʻil*] is used, and here לְחַיּוֹת *leḥayyōth* [*Piʻel*]. The change of conjugation corresponds to the change of context. In the earlier passage the sense is: in order, that you, Noah, should keep the creatures alive by the care that you would give them (compare Gen. xlv 7; l 20); here the meaning is that seven pairs would be needed to save the *kind* alive, that is, to assure the perpetuation of the species.

4. *For in another seven days*] See my observations in Part I, pp. 12f., on the fact that in the ancient Eastern literature a series of seven consecutive days was considered a perfect unit of time, in which an important enterprise could develop; the work continued for six days and reached, on the seventh, its conclusion and results. Here this unit of time is devoted to the task of bringing the creatures and the various types of food into the ark. This would occupy Noah for six days, and on the seventh everything would be ready.

Forty days and forty nights] — day and night without cessation. The Mesopotamian tradition relates that the Flood lasted seven days, which, as I have explained, was the customary period of time. The Torah, as usual, presents the matter in a more reasonable form. It is hard to conceive that seven days of rain would suffice to flood the whole earth. In the Pentateuchal narrative, the extremely long period of rain explains the terrific consequences. For the fact that a series of forty days was also a traditional unit of time, see the introduction to this section, § 7, pp. 43–45.

And I will blot out ... from the face of the ground] The expressions that were used earlier (vi 7), and which will also recur later (*v.* 23), are repeated here. On the first occasion the Lord made a decision; here He announces His resolve to Noah; further on we shall be told that it was fulfilled.

[*Every*] *living thing* [הַיְקוּם *hayᵉqūm*] / The word is found only in this section and again in Deut. xi 6, where, also, the term is used in the context of general destruction. Perhaps it, too, belonged to the vocabulary of the ancient poetic tradition relating to the Flood.

5. *And Noah did,* etc.] — the conclusion of the paragraph, corresponding to the ending of the preceding paragraph and also of the following paragraphs.

FOURTH PARAGRAPH

THE FULFILMENT OF THE INJUNCTION
TO ENTER THE ARK

6. *Noah / was six hundred years old*
   when the flood came, / water upon the earth.

7. *And Noah went in, / and his sons*
   and his wife and his sons' wives / with him,
   into the ark, / because of the waters of the flood.

8. *Of the clean animals, / and of animals / that are not clean,*
   and of the flying creatures, / and of everything that moves on
      the ground,

9. *two and two went in unto Noah / into the ark,*
   male and female, / as God had commanded Noah.

Although at the end of the two previous paragraphs it was stated
generally that Noah did all that he had been enjoined by his
Creator, this paragraph now comes to describe in detail the fulfilment of the command to enter the ark. We thus find here another
interesting example of the literary expedient of first making a
general statement and thereafter setting out the details, a feature
on which we have already dwelt in Part I (p. 91). Of even
greater interest in this paragraph is the manner in which the
detailed description is presented and its similarity to the method
employed in epic poetry.

In the history of world literature, heroic poetry — or the epos, to
call it by its Greek name—preceded narrative prose; and apparently
there is reason to believe that the latter (in which, for instance,
the vast majority of the sections of Genesis and many other sections
of the Torah are written) first came into being as a sequel to, and
development of, epic poetry, which, both in its Eastern and Western
forms, evinces a great love of repetition, due to the very nature of
the epos, which was originally intended to be heard and not read.
People who are gathered to listen to epic songs by a minstrel are
particularly pleased when he begins a familiar and popular stanza;
they find it easier then to follow the singer and, as it were, to participate in his song. Many and varied are the circumstances that con-
duce to reiteration in heroic poetry, and all of them are represented
in the books of the Bible. I dealt with these factors in my Hebrew
essay 'The Epic Poetry of Israel', published in *Keneseth,* dedicated
to the memory of H. N. Bialik, viii, pp. 121–142, where the reader
will find, on pp. 126–127, a detailed discussion of the material.
Here it will suffice to indicate that one of the most common
instances is that in which a poem tells of the giving of an order
and afterwards of its execution. The poet then begins by stating:
So-and-so commanded so-and-so and said to him, Do this and this
and this. After citing the words of the one who gives the command,
he continues: And so-and-so did that and that and that. All the
details of the action are reiterated in the very words used by the
poet when quoting the injunction.

On the other hand, narrative prose is not so fond of verbal repetitions, for it was meant to be read rather than heard, and the reader, unlike the listener, has no predilection for what he already knows by heart. On the contrary, reiteration, in the *ipsissima verba*, may at times be burdensome to him. Consequently, prose is inclined, when reverting to a given subject, to modify the expressions, or to shorten them, or to change their order. This is what happens in the narrative prose of the Pentateuch. However, abridgement and variation are not possible in every instance. For example, when the topic is essentially technical, as in the sections dealing with the work of the Tabernacle (Exod. xxv–xxxi; xxxv–xl), it is impossible to abbreviate or to vary the text. Then verbal repetitions occur as in epic poetry. First it is related that the Lord commanded Moses to make the Tabernacle and all its appurtenances and explained to him all the details of the work, and then we are told that Moses carried out the task, and the particulars are restated in full. Complete sections recur in identical form, with one change: in place of verbs in the imperative, like *make* etc., we find verbs of implementation, *made* etc. But when the subject is not primarily technical as in the case of the construction of the Tabernacle, and hence does not require meticulous exactitude of detail, the repetitions in prose are not word-for-word restatements.

In the section of the Flood, which is mainly concerned with the narration of events, and in which technical matters, like the particulars of the building of the ark, do not predominate, the Torah uses chiefly the method of abridgement. After stating that God commanded Noah: *Make yourself an ark of gopher wood; rooms make in the ark, and cover it inside and out with pitch*, etc., the execution of the command is not narrated in the same words. If it were an epic poem that we had before us here, or if the details of the construction of the ark were the main theme of our section, it would subsequently have been written: So Noah made for himself an ark of gopher wood; he made rooms in the ark, and covered it inside and out with pitch, etc. But since this is not consonant with prose style and there was no specific need for it, the Torah did not reiterate the words of the Divine command, and was content to state with extreme brevity (vi 22): *And Noah did this; according to all that God commanded him, so did he.*

79

The position is different, however, in this, the fourth paragraph. Here we have a mighty and amazing spectacle: the tremendous, endless procession of all the creatures streaming from all parts of the earth to Noah's abode in order to find shelter with him in the ark. This time a brief and anaemic expression, such as *And Noah did this; according to all that God commanded him,* or the like, would have been inadequate; a detailed description was necessary. Hence the matters on which Noah was previously instructed are repeated here, and this reiteration presents us, as it were, with a magnificent and graphic picture of that wondrous scene, the mass pilgrimage from all parts of the world to the one place that promised salvation to every species of creature. But it is not an exact verbal and mechanical repetition as it might have been in epic poetry; there are variations that give greater vividness to the entire account and heighten its effect, but in general the phrases of the Divine commands are reiterated and this conforms basically to the age-old literary tradition.

We shall now tabulate all the verses of our paragraph with their corresponding parallels, in order to demonstrate clearly how each expression of our passage echoes the statements made earlier in the two preceding paragraphs:

ch. vii	ch. vi
6. *Noah was six hundred years old when the flood came, water upon the earth.*	17. *...a flood, water upon the earth...*
7. *And Noah went in, and his sons and his wife and his sons' wives with him into the ark, because of the waters of the flood.*	18. *...and you shall come into the ark, you, your sons, your wife, and your sons' wives with you.*
8. *Of clean animals and of animals that are not clean, and of flying creatures, and of everything that moves on the ground,*	vii.2. *Of all the clean animals ... and of the animals that are not clean, ...* vi. 20. *Of the flying creatures according to their kinds, ... of every moving thing of the ground according to its kind, ...*

9. *two and two went in unto Noah into the ark, male and female, as God had commanded Noah.*

vi. 19. *...two of every sort you shall bring into the ark, ... they shall be male and female.*

Having considered the general character of the paragraph, let us proceed to examine the details. A few observations will suffice, since most of the points were explained earlier, when they first occurred in the preceding paragraphs.

6. *Noah was six hundred years old*] As I have already indicated in the introduction to this section (pp. 17, 22.), Noah's age affords a parallel to the Mesopotamian tradition, which gives Ziusudra's age before the Deluge as ten *šar*, that is, 36,000 years, or 600 units of sixty years; only the Torah, in accordance with its trend, has reduced the figure. Noah's age was, in truth, 600 units of time when the Flood occurred, but the unit was one year not sixty years. Although the figure seems at first unduly high, it is modest by comparison with the notions current at the time when the Torah was written.

When [literally, 'and'] *the flood* CAME [הָיָה *hāyā;* literally, 'was'] / The word הָיָה *hāyā* connotes here, *came into being, happened.* The verse corresponds, in Biblical usage, to a complex sentence. The English idiom would require us to say: Noah was six hundred years old when the flood came.

7. *Because of the waters of the flood*] — on the seventh day, when the first rains were about to come down. The meaning is that Noah and his household entered at the last moment (compare *v.* 13), but the creatures mentioned in *vv.* 8–9 had arrived and were settled in during the previous six days, although this is not expressly stated and one might have supposed that they all came together.

8–9. *Of clean animals,* etc.] Scripture does not again mention here the taking of the additional seven pairs, since there was nothing extraordinary about it. It was quite a simple matter for Noah to take a few animals of his flocks and herds, and the point is implied in *v.* 5: *And Noah did all that the Lord had commanded him.* What needed special stressing was the fact that two of every species, both of the clean and unclean kinds, male and female, came of their own accord.

81

On the difference in spelling between טְהוֹרָה *ṭᵉhō(w)rā* [with *Wāw*] and טְהֹרָה *ṭᵉhōrā* [without *Wāw*], see above.

As God had commanded Noah] — to take two of every sort into the ark, when they would come to him (vi 19–20).

FIFTH PARAGRAPH

THE BEGINNING OF THE FLOOD

10. *And it came to pass / at the end of the seven days,*
that the waters of the flood / were upon the earth.

11. *In the six hundredth year / of Noah's life,*
in the second month, / on the seventh day of the month,
on that day —
there burst forth all the fountains / of the great deep,
and the windows of the heavens / were opened.

12. *And rain fell / upon the earth*
forty days / and forty nights.

13. *On the very same day / entered Noah*
and Shem and Ham and Japheth, the sons of Noah, / and Noah's wife
and the three wives of his sons / with them, / into the ark;

14. *they —*
and every beast / according to its kind,
and all the cattle / according to their kinds,
and every moving thing that moves on the earth / according to its kind,
and every flying creature / according to its kind,
every bird / of every sort.

15. *They went in unto Noah / into the ark,*
two and two / of all flesh
in which there was / the breath of life.

16. *And they that entered, / male and female of all flesh,*
went in / as God had commanded him;
and the Lord shut him in.

In this paragraph, too, we find a comprehensive statement followed by particulars. Above it was stated generally, *when the flood came*; now the event is described in detail.

10. *And it came to pass at the end of the seven days*] — a formal opening: and it came to pass when the seventh day that God had appointed when He spoke to Noah (*v.* 4: *in seven days*) arrived, that it happened as He had announced at the beginning.

11. *In the six hundredth year of Noah's life*] This would appear, at first sight, to be a redundant duplication of what we were told in *v.* 6; but a brief examination of the passages will suffice to show us that the context is different. Verse 6 comes to tell us Noah's age at the time of the Deluge; but here the intention is to give the exact date of the commencement of the Flood. The Bible indicates the day, as usual, by the date of the month; the month is specified, as is customary, by its position among the months of the year; the year is determined in accordance with the system, which was likewise in common use, of counting by the ages of kings. At this period all the kings of the earth passed away. Noah is thus the head of the new humanity; hence the date can be established only by reference to Noah's age. Nor should it be forgotten that in the Mesopotamian legends the hero of the Flood was a king.

In the second month] This is the month of 'Iyyār according to R. Joshua, or Marḥeŝwān according to R. Eliezer (B. Rosh Hashana 11b); and each of the two Tannaim * had his reason for his particular view. The simple interpretation of the text favours the month of Marḥeŝwān, when the rainy season usually begins; for there is no indication in the Bible that the established order of nature had undergone seasonal changes, too. However, the Babylonian tradition, which is reflected in the account of Berossus, states that the Deluge took place in the month of Daisios, that is, in Nīsān.

On the seventeenth day of the month] On the significance of this date see above, the end of my commentary to the second paragraph. The Septuagint reads: *in the twenty-seventh day of the month;* see on this my annotation to viii 14.

On that day] Compare Exod. xix 1: *On the third new moon after*

---

* Teachers of the Oral Law in the period of the Mishnah.

the children of Israel had gone forth out of the land of Egypt,
ON THAT DAY *they came into the wilderness of Sinai.* There, too,
as in our verse, the words *on that day* come after the mention of
the exact date, the purpose being to emphasize the date and to
focus on it the reader's attention. In the former passage, also, as
in our own, the date of the Divine communication is given only
indirectly. Only by inference, on the basis of the date of the arrival
of the children of Israel in the Wilderness of Sinai, is it possible
to deduce that the day on which the Decalogue was given was,
according to the Bible, the sixth day of the third month, as the
Talmudic sages rightly concluded (if we assume that each ascent
of Moses on the Mountain [*ibid. vv.* 3, 8, 9] took place in the
early morning, it follows that *vv.* 10–11: *consecrate them today
and tomorrow ... for on the third day the Lord will come down
upon Mount Sinai,* were uttered on the fourth day of the month).
A precise date is not assigned to a Divine communication except
when there is a special reason for it, for example, Num. i 1; ix 1,
and so on.

On the expression *on the very same day,* see below, on *v.* 13.

There BURST FORTH [נִבְקְעוּ *nibhqeʿū*] *all the fountains of the*
GREAT [רַבָּה *rabbā*] DEEP [תְּהוֹם *tehōm*] *and the windows of the
heavens were opened*] — an actual verse of poetry, as one can
see from its structure, rhythm, parallelism and the poetic words
that it contains. Possibly the Torah quoted it in the exact form
in which it was found in the ancient Israelite poetry on the Deluge.

On the use of the term תְּהוֹם *tehōm* by Israelites and Gentiles,
and on the various concepts expressed by it, see my remarks in
Part I, pp. 23–24. Here the reference is undoubtedly to the sub-
terranean waters, which are the source of the springs that flow
upon the ground. The word רַבָּה *rabbā* is the regular adjective
applied to תְּהוֹם *tehōm* in the literary tradition. Examples are: Isa.
li 10: *Was it not thou (O arm of the Lord) that didst dry up the
sea, the waters of the* GREAT DEEP [תְּהוֹם רַבָּה *tehōm rabbā*]; Amos.
vii 4: *and it devoured the* GREAT DEEP [תְּהוֹם רַבָּה *tehōm rabbā*]
and was eating up the land; Psa. xxxvi 6 [Hebrew, *v.* 7]: *Thy
judgments are like the* GREAT DEEP [תְּהוֹם רַבָּה *tehōm rabbā*]; ibid.,
lxxviii 15: *He cleft rocks in the wilderness, and gave them drink
as the* GREAT DEEP [כִּתְהֹמוֹת רַבָּה *kithehōmōth rabbā*] (that it, as

though from the great deep; the form תְּהֹמוֹת tehōmōth is apparently singular, like the form חָכְמוֹת ḥokhmōth ['wisdom'], which is used as a singular in Prov. ix 1: *Wisdom has built her house, she has hewn her seven pillars;* compare *ibid.* i 20; xiv 1). Evidence of the antiquity of this attributive is to be seen in the fact that in the classic period of the Hebrew language the word גְּדוֹלָה gedhōlā ['great', fem. sing.] was used both in speech and in writing, and not רַבָּה rabbā, as in the ancient Canaanite tongue. The phrase תְּהוֹם רַבָּה tehōm rabbā became, as it were, a compound noun, and its form was stereotyped, the definite article being omitted not only before the word תְּהוֹם tehōm but also before רַבָּה rabbā; and so it is written here, although in the continuation of the verse the definite article is prefixed to שָׁמַיִם šāmayim ['heav‚ens'].

The verb בָּקַע bāqaʿ ['burst forth', 'cleave', 'divide'] is also traditionally connected with תְּהוֹם tehōm. The origin of this tradition is discernible in the Babylonian Account of Creation, which relates (Tablet iv, line 137) that the god Marduk cleft with his sword the body of Tiamat (= תְּהוֹם tehōm), the goddess of the primitive ocean, after slaying her. The use of this verb seems to have continued also in the epic poetry of Israel describing the revolt of the sea against its Creator (see above, Part I, pp. 37 ff.). It is likewise frequently found in Biblical literature, not only when the text refers to the crushing of the rebellious sea and its confederates, the rivers (for instance, Hab. iii 9: נְהָרוֹת תְּבַקַּע־אָרֶץ *nehārōth tebhaqqaʿ ʾāreṣ* [E. V. *Thou didst* CLEAVE *the earth with rivers*], which according to the context is to be interpreted: Thou didst cleave upon the earth the rebellious rivers; so, too, in Psa. lxxiv 15: *Thou didst* CLEAVE OPEN *springs and brooks*), but even in passages that allude to any example of God's unlimited dominion over the waters of the world, such as the dividing of the Red Sea or the bringing forth of the water from the rock (Exod. xiv 16: *and stretch out your hand over the sea and* DIVIDE IT; *ibid. v.* 21: *and the waters* WERE DIVIDED; Jud. xv 19: *And God* SPLIT OPEN *the hollow place that is at Lehi, and there came water from it;* Isa. xxxv 6: *For waters* SHALL BREAK FORTH *in the wilderness; ibid.* xlviii 21: *He* CLEFT *the rock and the waters gushed out; ibid.* lxiii 12: *Who* DIVIDED *the waters before them;* Psa. lxxviii 13: *He* DIVIDED *the sea and let them pass through it; ibid. v.* 15:

85

He CLEFT *rocks in the wilderness and gave them drink as from the great deep;* Prov. iii 20: *by His knowledge the deeps* BROKE FORTH; Job xxviii 10: *He* CUTS OUT *channels in the rocks;* Neh. ix 11: *And Thou* DIDST DIVIDE *the sea before them* [in all these verses some form of the verb *bāqaʿ* occurs]). In our verse the meaning is that the fountains, which in normal times furnish sufficient water for the needs of man, the animal world and the irrigation of the fields, on that day burst open and poured out terrific quantities of water that augmented the water raining down from the heavens and together with them, created the mighty Flood.

And the WINDOWS [אֲרֻבֹּת *ʾărubbōth*] *of the heavens* WERE OPENED [נִפְתָּחוּ *niphtāḥū*] / Also in this sentence a literary tradition is continued that has its origin in the early poetry of the ancient Orient. From the Ugaritic writings we know that the Canaanites used to tell of the god Baal that he built for himself a palace in the sky and opened therein windows or lattices (the very verb *pth* ['opened'] and the nouns *hln* [= Hebrew חַלּוֹן *ḥallōn,* 'window'] and *ʾurbt* [= *Hebrew* אֲרֻבָּה *ʾarubbā,* 'lattice'] are found in Tablet II AB, col. vii, lines 17f.), and through these windows Baal caused his thunders to be heard. And since the Canaanites attributed to Baal also the sending down of rain from heaven, it is probable, although there is no definite reference to it in the texts known to us at present, that they also conceived this action to take place through the windows, and the term *the windows of heaven* was used in their language to denote the source of rain. One should not be surprised at the fact that this expression was inherited by the Hebrew tongue. The different forces and phenomena of nature and the fundamental principles of life, which the pagan peoples embodied in the form of entirely separate deities, were integrated and united, in the monotheistic consciousness of the Israelites, as the various acts of the One and Only God; and when the ancestors of Israel accepted the tongue and phraseology of the Canaanites, it was but natural that they should also take over, as part of the vocabulary and idioms of the Canaanite language, the Divine designations and other terms that signify these acts or are connected with them. In this way the Israelites appropriated two titles of the God of Melchizedek, *God Most High* and *Maker of heaven and earth* (see Part I, pp. 200 f.); similarly the Israelites employed the Divine appellation רֹכֵב בָּעֲרָבוֹת *rōkhēbh bā'ărābhōth* ['who rides upon the clouds'], which the Canaanites applied to Baal (*rkb 'rpt*); and so, too, the Israelites accepted the use, if only as metaphorical expressions, of such idioms as 'the opening of the windows of heaven'. We find the phrase, in the undoubted sense of sending down rain, in Mal. iii 10: *if I will not open the windows of heaven for you and pour down for you an overflowing blessing.* In ii Kings vii it is recorded that one of the king's captains did not believe in the words of the prophet who announced in the Lord's name: *Tomorrow about this time a measure of fine meal shall be sold for a shekel, and two measures of barley for a shekel, at the gate of Samaria,* and in mockery of these good tidings he said (*v.* 2; compare *v.* 19): *If the Lord Himself shall make windows in heaven, could this thing be?* as though to say: Is it possible to believe that the Lord would open windows in heaven and send down therefrom not rain, as usual, but fine flour and barley? On Isa. xxiv 18: *For the windows on high are opened,* see below. The substantive חַלּוֹן *ḥallōn* ['window'], which is used in Ugaritic as the equivalent of *'urbt* ['lattice'], is likewise found in the Hebrew linguistic tradition as a synonym for אֲרֻבֹּת הַשָּׁמַיִם *'ărubbōth haššāmayim* ['the windows of the heavens], from which the waters of the Deluge came down. Although it does not occur in the Bible — possibly, this is accidental — it is found in rabbinic literature. In Bereshith Rabba xxxi 12 we are told of the giants (see the variant readings in Theodor's edition, p. 285): 'They set down their feet and closed up the deep, and they placed their hands on the *windows* [חַלּוֹנוֹת *ḥallōnōth*] and closed them up', etc. Apparently, this word preserves traces of the ancient tradition, which survived among the Israelites through the generations.

Here in our verse, in keeping with the previous sentence, which speaks of the fountains of the great deep, the expression connotes that during the Flood it did not rain in normal measure, but the windows of heaven were opened wide and the water poured from them in large quantities without any restraint.

It is thus manifest that according to this verse two different constituents intermingled in the waters of the Deluge — the waters of the deep from below and the rain-water from above. The Mesopotamian texts mention only a terrific storm that brought down water from the heavens. The Torah does not refer actually to a storm but to rain, adding thereto the waters of the deep. Scripture's intention apparently is to teach us that the Judge of the whole earth, who directs His world with righteousness and rules over the whole of nature according to His will, is able to turn the waters of the springs and of the rain, which He utilizes as sources of blessing to humanity when they are guiltless, into an instrument of blight to mankind when they are guilty. In a similar sense, which was possibly not uninfluenced by our verse, it is written in Isa. xxiv 18: *For the windows on high are opened, and the foundations of the earth tremble.*

12. *And rain* FELL [literally, 'And the rain *was*'] *upon the earth forty days and forty nights*] — that is to say, rain came *down* upon the earth for forty days and forty nights, as the Lord had previously told Noah (*v.* 4).

13–16. In these verses the Bible musters, as it were, all the living beings that were in the ark on that fateful day (*on the very same day* — an expression that also occurs in other passages of Scripture, for example, Gen. xvii 26, in connection with the circumcision; Exod. xii 41, 51, in regard to the exodus from Egypt — serves to indicate the day that the will of God had appointed from the beginning). Before the door of the ark is closed (*v.* 16) and all that it contains disappears from our sight, the Bible passes before us, one by one, all the human beings and the various types of animal life that found refuge within it, in order that we should realize the importance and value of the living treasures entrusted to the ark's protection. We are not presented here with a general review, such as we found in the preceding paragraphs (where the main items only are mentioned and one species is included in another), but with a properly detailed and complete muster-roll. The sons of Noah are not just mentioned in general terms — anonymously — but each one is listed by name (*and Shem and Ham and Japheth, the sons of Noah*); likewise his wife is referred to, if not actually by her personal name, at least by her designation, *the wife of Noah,* which is part of her full name in the description *so-and-so the wife of so-and-so* (for example, *Jael the wife of Heber the Kenite*; the formula is also customary on Hebrew seals). In regard to the wives of Shem, Ham and Japheth, the Torah is not content with the general expression, *the wives of his sons*, but also adds the number—*three*—as though to introduce the three of them as a group (see below). Also the living creatures are presented to us this time in great detail: the beasts are expressly mentioned and not implied in another species of animal as above, and the name [i. e. the word 'beast'] is preceded by the word *every* and followed by *according to its kind*. The same applies to the cattle and moving things and all the winged creatures.

And the THREE [שְׁלֹשֶׁת *šelōšeth*] *wives of his sons*] The numeral occurs here exceptionally with the feminine ending in relation to a feminine noun; so, too, in Job i 4: *and they would send and invite their* THREE [שְׁלֹשֶׁת *šelōšeth*] *sisters* (the similar instances in i Sam. x 3, and in Ezek. vii 2, are in doubt; the first because the gender of the noun כִּכָּר *kikkār* ['loaf'] there is uncertain, and the second on account of the difference between the *Qerē* [the *pronunciation* of the word according to the Masorah] and the *Kethībh* [the Masoretic *spelling* of the word]). There may be a reason for this. If we take note of the fact that in the Book of Job it is first stated that there were born to Job שָׁלֹשׁ בָּנוֹת *šālōš bānōth* (i 2), and subsequently that his sons were accustomed to send and invite *their* THREE [שְׁלֹשֶׁת *šelōšeth*] *sisters to eat and drink with them* (i 4), we shall see that there is a difference between the two verses. When the purpose of the text is to fix a number, as in *v.* 2, which apprises us that Job's daughters numbered three—not two or four or more—the regular numeral is used, without a suffixed *Tāw* before a feminine substantive; but when a certain group of women (or of things in the feminine gender), comprising a number already known to us, is spoken of, and it is desired to emphasize that the reference is to *all of them together,* then the numeral with the feminine termination is employed. The phrase שָׁלֹשׁ נָשִׁים *šālōš nāšīm.* without definition, means in general: a woman and another woman and another woman; the expression שְׁלֹשֶׁת הַנָּשִׁים *šelōšeth hannāšīm* denotes the *entire* group, known to us already and consisting of three women. So we must explain the words in Job i 4: לִשְׁלֹשֶׁת אַחְיֹתֵיהֶם *lišelōšeth 'aḥyōthēhem* ['their three sisters'], and so also the text before us, וּשְׁלֹשֶׁת נְשֵׁי בָנָיו *ūšelōšeth nešē bhānāw* ['and the three wives of his sons'] (the definition is expressed here in the pronominal suffixes of the words אַחְיוֹתֵיהֶם *aḥyōthēhem* and בָנָיו *bhānāw*). This premise enables us also to explain why, when the pronominal suffix is added to a numeral, it takes the ending *Tāw* even if the thing counted is feminine, for example, אַרְבַּעְתָּן *'arbaʿtān* ['they four'] (Ezek. i 10), and in Mishnaic language חֲמִשְׁתָּן *ḥămištān* ['the five of them'; M. H. Segal, *A Grammar of Mishnaic Hebrew*, p. 195, vocalizes: חֲמִשְׁתָּן *ḥămiššāthān*] (Mena-ḥoth xiii 2), and so forth. The reference is to all those comprised by the number, and the pronominal suffix serves to define them.

14. *They and every beast, etc.*] — that is to say: not only they — Noah and his household—were there, but the representatives of all the creatures. As I have explained earlier, it does not imply that the latter also came into the ark on the selfsame day; they entered in the course of the week, and on the last day of the week they were all to be found there.

EVERY BIRD [כֹּל צִפּוֹר *kōl ṣippōr*] *of* EVERY SORT [כָּל־כָּנָף] *kol kānāph*; literally, 'every wing'] / This is in apposition to *every flying creature, according to its kind.* The significance of this apposition is not at first glance quite clear. Many have explained it to mean: every bird and every winged creature, including שֶׁרֶץ הָעוֹף *šereṣ hāʿōph* (Lev. xi 20), that is, *flying insects* of every sort (compare B. Ḥullin 139b.) But this interpretation is impossible, because the term צִפּוֹר כָּנָף *ṣippōr kānāph* ['winged bird'] (Deut. iv 17; Psa. cxlviii 10) signifies only birds proper. Furthermore, had this been the meaning, a copulative *Wāw* would have been required before כָּל־כָּנָף *kol kānāph*. Actually there is no specific need for the insects to be expressly mentioned; even when Scripture wishes to go into detail, as in the present case, it is certainly not bound to concern itself with minutiae of such little importance. Clearly, the Masoretes did not understand the verse in this way, for they separated כֹּל *kōl* from צִפּוֹר *ṣippōr* by means of a disjunctive accent (although some printed editions hyphen the two words, this is an error, as reliable MSS from the School of Ben Asher prove). It should be noted that in Ezek. xxxix 4, 17, the text reads צִפּוֹר כָּל־כָּנָף *ṣippōr kol kānāph* ['birds of every sort'], and *ibid.* xvii 23, exactly as here, כֹּל צִפּוֹר כָּל־כָּנָף *kōl ṣippōr kol kānāph* (there, too, as in our passage, the first כֹּל *kōl* has a disjunctive accent, יְתִיב *yethībh*, and not מַהְפָּךְ *mahpākh*, as we find in inaccurate editions), and unquestionably the prophet had birds in mind. Others (like Dillmann) take the view that since the Bible has mentioned *and every flying creature, according to its kind,* which includes also insects, the apposition comes to emphasize the birds in particular. But this, too, is not feasible, because it is illogical to suppose that the apposition serves here to restrict the signification of the preceding term, which is more comprehensive. The clue to the correct interpretation is to be found in Ezekiel xliv 30: *And the first of* ALL THE FIRST FRUIT OF ALL KINDS [כָּל־בִּכּוּרֵי כֹל *kol bikkūrē khōl*], AND EVERY OFFERING OF ALL KINDS [וְכָל־תְּרוּמַת כֹּל *wekhol terūmath kōl*] *from all your offerings,* and in ii Chron. xxxii 15: NO GOD OF ANY [כָּל־אֱלוֹהַּ כָּל־ *kol ʾElōah kol*] *nation or kingdom.* Accordingly the meaning here is: every bird of every sort of winged creature. It is an elaboration of the preceding expression in keeping with all that follows in these verses.

15. *They went in* [וַיָּבֹאוּ *wayyābhōʾū*] / Those who explain this word (and the other forms of the stem בּוֹא *bōʾ* that appear in this paragraph) as a pluperfect, namely, that they had already come before, are motivated by harmonistic reasons, and their exegesis is valueless. We must not forget that the concept of the *tenses* of verbs, to which we are accustomed today, was unknown in the classic period of the Hebrew language. The Bible merely states that *they came* — and no more. It reverts to the important subject of the coming of the creatures of their own accord in order to stress once again, at the time of the final muster, that precisely two came, that they came of their free will, that literally representatives of all flesh came. For added emphasis it is stated here, *of all flesh in which there was the breath of life,* and not merely *of all flesh* as above.

16. *And they that entered, male and female of all flesh, went in*] Once more an important detail is emphasized as in the preceding verse. Those who came were not just two, but exactly one male and one female of every kind of living creature, as God had previously commanded Noah (vi 19; vii 2–3; compare vii 9).

And the Lord shut him in] Many propose to read: ʾAnd *Noah* shut himself in' for in their view it is incomprehensible that the door should not have been closed from within; in the Epic of Gilgameš, too, it is stated that Gilgameš closed the door of the ship. But it seems that this very divergence represents one of the innovations introduced by the Torah. The closing of the door by Noah from inside is self-understood, even though it is not expressly mentioned. What Scripture wished to tell us and to emphasize at the close of the paragraph is this, that the All-merciful Father took care of those things that Noah could not see from within, and ensured that outside, too, the ark should be perfectly closed, that every crevice should be properly sealed, so that not a drop of water should be able to seep into the ark. It is for this reason that the Tetragrammaton and not אֱלֹהִים *'Elōhīm* is used here, in conformity with the customary usage of the Hebrew tongue, which prefers the name *YHWH* when a direct relationship between God and His creatures is referred to (see Part I, pp. 87 f.).

SIXTH PARAGRAPH
WATER UPON THE EARTH

17. *And the flood continued / forty days / upon the earth,*
    and the waters increased, / and bore up the ark, / and it was
        lifted up above the earth.

18. *The waters prevailed / and increased greatly / upon the earth;*
    and the ark floated / on the face of the waters.

19. *And the waters / prevailed so mightily / upon the earth*
    that all the high mountains / under the whole heaven / were
        covered.

20. *Fifteen cubits / upward*
    did the waters prevail, / and the mountains were covered.

21. *And there expired / all flesh / that moved upon the earth,*
    flying creatures and cattle and beasts / and all swarming
        creatures / that swarm upon the earth,
    and every man;

92

22. *all that had the breath of the spirit of life / in its nostrils,
— whatsoever was on the dry land — / died.*

23. *He blotted out / every living thing / that was on the face
of the ground,
man and animals and creeping things / and flying creatures
of the air;
they were blotted out / from the earth.
Only Noah was left, / and those that were with him / in
the ark.*

24. *And the waters prevailed / upon the earth
a hundred and fifty days.*

The symmetrical structure that is discernible through the entire
section is particularly apparent in this paragraph. Each of the first
three sentences concludes with the phrase *upon the earth,* and in each
of them the word *flood* — or its synonym, *waters* — occurs as the
subject, coming immediately after the initial word [in the Hebrew].
These words — *flood, waters, upon the earth* — are the key words
of the paragraph, which depicts the dominion of the *waters of the
flood upon the earth* during a hundred and fifty days; and they
recur a number of times in the paragraph until the last verse, in
which, too, the subject *waters* appears as the second word, followed
by the phrase *upon the earth.* This phrase is found in all seven
times in our paragraph, and on each occasion forms the end of
the sentence, like an oft-repeated echo heard when one pauses in
speaking. Similarly the word *waters* occurs six times, echoing its
synonym, *flood,* which appears [in the Hebrew] as the second
word in the first sentence; thus they are used jointly seven times in
the paragraph.

17. *And the flood continued forty days upon the earth, and the
waters increased,* etc.] Only one who does not understand the
structure of the verse, or its meaning, can regard it as a redundant
repetition of what was stated in *v.* 12. The sense is: since the flood
lasted forty days upon the earth, the waters increased and carried
the ark; thus the ark was not left resting on the ground, but was
lifted up on the waters. In the following verses, too, there are no
superfluous duplications, if they are rightly understood.

93

18. *The waters prevailed,* etc.] The narrative unfolds by grada-
tions. Not only did the waters increase, as the previous verse states,
but the waters prevailed and increased *greatly;* not only was the
ark lifted off the ground, but it floated on the face of the waters,
moving away from its original position.

19. *And the waters*] The meaning is: As for the waters (on the
subject preceding the verb see above Pt. I, p. 21). The preceding
verse relates what happened to the ark; now we are given, as it
were, this additional information: the ark was, indeed, floating on
the face of the waters, but these waters prevailed mightily beneath
it. Compare viii 5.

Prevailed so mightily, etc.] Another step forward: not only did
the waters prevail and increase *greatly* [מְאֹד *me'ōdh*], but they
prevailed *so mightily* [מְאֹד מְאֹד *me'ōdh me'ōdh,* literally, 'greatly
greatly'].

That [literally, 'and'] *all the high mountains . . . were covered*]
The waters prevailed to such an extent that even the highest
mountains were covered with water. The Septuagint read the verb
ויכסו *wyksw* as the active form (וַיְכַסּוּ *wayekhassū* [*Pi'ēl,* 'and they
covered', instead of וַיְכֻסּוּ *wayekhussū, Pu'al,* 'and they were
covered']); the subject of the sentence is accordingly *the waters.*
But if this were the meaning of the text, the particle אֶת־ *'eth*
would be required before כָּל־הֶהָרִים *kol hehārīm* ['all the
mountains'].

20. *Fifteen cubits,* etc.] Further progression: not only were the
mountains covered with water, but there was a tremendous layer
of water over them. At the same time the verse indicates that the
depth of this layer reached fifteen cubits, in order to explain why
the mountains did not halt the ark. The height of the ark was
thirty cubits (vi 15); hence, even if we assume that only half
its height floated above the water, it was able to clear the highest
mountain peaks.

And the mountains were covered] At first sight it would appear
that there is an unnecessary repetition here of what had already
been stated in *v.* 19: *all the high mountains . . . were covered,* etc.
But this is not so. The verb *covered* here is still connected with the
adverbial phrase *fifteen cubits upward.* In *v.* 19 we are informed
in general terms that the mountains were covered; but here we are

94

told to what extent they were covered (see Ibn Ezra). The Septuagint has translated the verb in this sentence, too, as an active form
(וַיְכַסּוּ *wayᵉkhassū:* 'and they covered'); but this rendering is open
to the same objection as that of *v.* 19.

21. *And there expired, etc.*] God had already told Noah of his
intention *to destroy all flesh in which is the breath of life, existing
under heaven; everything that is on the earth shall expire* (vi 17).
Here and in the following verse, in conformity with epic style, it is
related in similar, and partly in identical, language that this
announcement was fulfilled.

All flesh that moved upon the earth] — a general statement
followed by a detailed enumeration: flying creatures, cattle, beasts,
swarming creatures, and finally — the last being most cherished —
man. The function of the prepositional *Bēth* (בָּעוֹף וּבַבְּהֵמָה *bāʿōph
ūbhabbᵉhēmā;* literally, 'in [among] the birds and the cattle') is
to elucidate and detail.

And every man] Thus the verse ends on a note, as it were, of
bitter sorrow: there perished not only the flying creatures, accustomed to fly in the heights of the heavens, and the cattle, cherished
by man, and the wild beasts, further removed from man, and the
swarming creatures, which are mostly despised by man, but also the
most important of the created beings — man; not just a part of
the human race, but the whole of it! Even the swarming creatures,
which the Torah was not concerned to mention expressly in the
previous paragraphs, are mentioned here, in order to reach down
to the lowest level in the scale of life and then, with a sudden
leap, to ascend to the highest: *and every man.*

22. *All that had the breath of the spirit of life in its nostrils*]
The detailed description is now followed by a comprehensive statement, as though to sum up, in a single, broad portrayal, all the
terrible consequences of the Deluge. Every species of creature into
whose nostrils, at the time of the creation of the world, the Lord
had breathed the breath of life — to use the expression employed
in Gen. ii 7 with reference to man — was swept from the world.

Whatsoever [מִכֹּל *mikkōl;* literally, 'from all'] *was on the dry
land*] The *Mēm* (מִן *min,* 'from') of the word מִכֹּל *mikkōl* is
من البيان *mina 'lbayâni,* the explicative מִן *min,* which has the
force of: 'that is to say'. When the Torah states, *all that had the*

breath of the spirit of life in its nostrils, the reference is to all those who lived upon the land, not to those who existed in the water. This use of *Mēm* will be found again later (viii 17; ix 10).

Died [מֵתוּ *mēthū*] / The verb וַיִּגְוַע *wayyighwa'* ['expired'] at the beginning of the verse signifies the moment of transition from life to death; this verb — מֵתוּ *mēthū* — indicates the condition obtaining after that moment.

23. *He blotted out every living thing,* etc.] Then the Lord executed what He had resolved (vi 7) and had announced to Noah beforehand (vii 4). The earlier expressions are here repeated, in accordance with epic stylistic requirements in such circumstances. A comparison of the three verses is instructive:

vi 7:	vii 4:	vii 23:
I will blot out man whom I have created	and I will blot out every living thing that I have made	He blotted out every living thing
from the face of the ground,	from the face of the ground	that was on the face of the ground,
man and beast and creeping things		men and animals and creeping things
and flying creatures of the air		and flying creatures of the air.

The correct vocalization of the word וימח *wymḥ* is וַיִּמַח *wayyimaḥ,* the shortened form of the *imperfect Qal* ['and He blotted out'], and not וַיִּמָּח *wayyimmāḥ,* the apocopated *imperfect Niph'al* ['and was blotted out'], which is found in inaccurate editions. The particle אֶת־ *'eth* proves this.

They were blotted out from the earth] Here we have the *Niph'al,* the active form being followed by the passive of the same root. This is a traditional stylistic usage that was inherited by Hebrew literature from Canaanite writings, as we learn from Ugaritic texts. Compare, for example, Jer. xvii 14: *Heal me, O Lord, and I shall be healed; save me, and I shall be saved;* ibid. xxxi 4 [Hebrew, v. 3]: *Again I will build you, and you shall be built, O virgin Israel!;* Psa. xix 12–13 [Hebrew, vv. 13–14]: CLEAR THOU ME [נַקֵּנִי *naqqēnī*] *from hidden faults . . .* AND I SHALL BE CLEAR [וְנִקֵּיתִי *weniqqēthī*] *from great transgression;* ibid. lxix 14 [Hebrew, v. 15]: *Deliver me out of the mire, and let me not sink;*

96

let me be delivered from them that hate me, and out of the deep waters. In Ugaritic texts we find: 'Quickly build houses, quickly raise up palaces; quickly shall houses be built, quickly shall palaces be raised up (Tablet II AB, v, 113–116).

Only Noah was left, and those that were with him in the ark] These alone were left after the universal destruction. The survivors do indeed represent a ray of hope for the future, but for the moment they are but a meagre and woeful remnant.

24. *And the waters prevailed upon the earth a hundred and fifty days*] The verb *prevailed* connotes here a continuing state: the power of the water upon the earth continued a hundred and fifty days, and did not decline in appreciable measure till after this period, which comprised, as we shall see later (viii 4; see also the introduction, § 7), the tremendous downpour of rain for forty days followed by another hundred and ten days. The word מְאֹד *meʾōdh* ['greatly', 'mightily'] is not used here as in *vv.* 18–19; hence the reference is not to the peak of the waters' strength but to their power in general.

So the paragraph closes, with an awe-inspiring picture of the mighty waters covering the entire earth. We see water everywhere, as though the world had reverted to its primeval state at the dawn of Creation, when the waters of the deep submerged everything (see Part I, pp. 23 ff.). Nothing remained of the teeming life that had burst forth upon the earth. Only a tiny point appears on the face of the terrible waters: the ark that preserves between its planks the seeds of life for the future. But it is a mere atom and is almost lost in the endless expanse of water that was spread over the face of the whole earth. A melancholy scene that is liable to fill the reader with despair. What will happen to this atom of life?

97

ACT TWO

THE DELIVERANCE

SEVENTH PARAGRAPH

THE FIRST RAYS OF LIGHT

CHAPTER VIII

1. *But God remembered / Noah*
   and all the beasts / and all the cattle
   that were with him in the ark.
   And God caused a wind to pass / over the earth,
   and the waters subsided;

2. *the fountains of the deep were closed, / and the windows*
   of the heavens;
   and the rain was restrained / from the heavens.

3. *And the waters receded / from the earth / gradually;*
   and the waters abated / at the end of a hundred and fifty days.

4. *And the ark came to rest / in the seventh month,*
   on the seventeenth day of the month, / on the mountain of
   Ararat.

5. *And the waters, / continued to abate / until the tenth month;*
   in the tenth month, on the first day of the month, / the tops
   of the mountains were seen.

6. *And it came to pass / at the end of forty days,*
   that Noah opened / the window of the ark which he had
   made.

7. *And he sent forth a raven, / and it went to and fro*
   until the waters were dried up / from the earth.

8. *Then he sent forth a dove / from him,*
   to see if the waters had subsided / from the face of the
   ground.

9. *But the dove did not find / a place to set her foot,*
   and she returned to him / to the ark,

for the waters were / on the face of the whole earth;
so he put forth his hand / and took her
and brought her in unto him / into the ark.

10. *He waited again / another seven days,*
and once more he sent forth the dove / out of the ark.

11. *And the dove came back to him / in the evening,*
and lo, there were olive leaves, / fresh ones, in her mouth;
so Noah knew / that the waters had subsided / from the earth.

12. *Then he waited again / another seven days,*
and sent forth the dove; / and she returned not again unto
him / any more.

13. *And it came to pass / in the six hundred and first year,*
in the first month, the first day of the month, / the waters
were dried / from off the earth;
and Noah removed / the covering of the ark,
and looked, / and behold the face of the ground was dry.

14. *In the second month, / on the twenty-seventh day of the*
month,
the earth was dried out.

The question with which the end of the commentary on the
preceding paragraph closes is immediately answered at the beginning of this paragraph: *But God remembered Noah*, etc. The
Creator of the world did not forget his creatures.

1. *But [God] remembered]* The meaning is not that He
remembered at the termination of the hundred and fifty days
mentioned in the previous verse, for we are subsequently told
(*v.* 2): *the fountains of the deep were closed, and the windows
of the heavens, and the rain was restrained from the heavens,* and
this took place, of course, at the end of the forty days of rain.
To understand these verbs (remembered, were closed, etc.) as
pluperfects (He had already previously remembered, [the foun-
tains] had already previously been closed, etc.) is certainly incorrect
and not in keeping with Hebrew idiomatic usage, as we saw above
in similar cases. The interpretation here must follow the same lines
as the explanation we advanced regarding the relationship between

the story of Creation and the story of the Garden of Eden. The preceding paragraph tells how the waters prevailed upon the earth, and this episode forms the theme of that paragraph up to the end; whereas this new paragraph deals with a different topic — the first stage of the deliverance of the survivors — and commences the narration of this story from the beginning, although the commencement antedates the conclusion of the episode described above.

It is not the covenant (vi 18) that God remembers, as many have explained, for the covenant mentioned there was not made with Noah, as we have seen; furthermore, it is distinctly stated here that *God remembered Noah* etc., and not that He recalled the covenant. This act of remembrance is similar to that recorded later with reference to Sarah (xxi 1): *The Lord* VISITED [פָּקַד *pāqadh*] *Sarah as He had said, and the Lord did to Sarah as He had promised ... at the time of which God had spoken to him.* 'Visiting' in this passage means 'doing', as is clearly shown by the parallelism פָּקַד *pāqadh* — וַיַּעַשׂ *wayya‘aś*, and especially doing a thing at a predetermined time. The same applies to God's remembrance of Noah, for 'visiting' and 'remembering' are synonymous concepts. Even as the Lord had announced to Noah beforehand (and on the day that He had previously appointed), so He did — on that very day. God had told him that the rain would last forty days (vii 4), and at the termination of this period He put an end to the downpour of the waters of the Flood.

Noah] Only Noah's name is mentioned, for he is the father of the family and the head of the house (Ibn Ezra); but his wife and sons and sons' wives are implied. Similarly it is written further on (xii 10): *So Abram went down to Egypt,* but from the continuation of the story it is clear that both Sarai (*v.* 11) and Lot (xiii 1) went down to Egypt with Abram.

And all the beasts and all the cattle) We are already fully cognizant, from what was stated earlier, of the various kinds of creatures that were with Noah in the ark, and there is no need to detail them again. The term *beast* [חַיָּה *ḥayyā*] includes all creatures that are not domestic or tame *cattle*. The Septuagint adds *all the birds and all creeping things,* in order to harmonize this verse with the parallel passages, in accordance with its usual practice.

100

Regarding God's compassion on the dumb creatures, compare the end of the Book of Jonah.

And God caused a WIND [רוּחַ *rūaḥ*] *to pass over the earth*] Just as God's רוּחַ *rūaḥ* was hovering over the face of the waters at the beginning of the world's creation, when the waters of the deep covered the earth, so now that the waters again submerged the earth, God made a רוּחַ *rūaḥ* pass over them. However, it appears that in the story of Creation not an actual wind is meant — that is, a movement of air — but the Divine spirit, God's presence; but the difference is felt only when we render the Bible into another language and cast the notions of antiquity into a modern mould. The ancient Hebrew tongue denotes both concepts by the same word, because in ancient Hebrew thought the two ideas were closely related. Hence the parallelism between the two verses is clear; and in the same way as in the earlier passage God's רוּחַ *rūaḥ* represents the principle and source of life, so here the רוּחַ *rūaḥ* that God causes to blow over the earth indicates the beginning of new life.

The blowing of the wind must be regarded as taking place immediately after the forty days of rain (see the beginning of the commentary on this verse).

And the waters subsided] The waters still prevail over the earth, but their power begins to wane and subside; due to the action of the wind, the waters begin to evaporate.

2. *The fountains of the deep were closed, etc.*] An end was put to the situation described above, in the second part of vii 11. The fountains of the deep, which had then burst forth, were now closed, that is, were shut tight and the waters ceased to flow from them. Similarly the windows of heaven, which were then opened, were now closed, and consequently the rains were held back and could no longer come down from the heavens. Thus, on the one hand, there was the positive action of the wind, which caused the waters to evaporate from above, and on the other, there was the effect of these two negative factors — the closing of the fountains and the heavenly windows — which prevented new waters accumulating either from below or from above.

The Torah does not refer to the heat of the sun as one of the factors contributing to the evaporation of the waters, although it would have been but logical to mention this detail. It may be that Scripture's omission of this point was not unintentional. In the pagan myths stress is laid on the action of the God Šamaš at the end of the Flood, when he shed his light in the heavens and on the earth; and Ziusudra or Utnapištim opened the window of the ship and let his light in and prostrated himself before him. In order to oppose this heathen ideology, which represents the sun as the deity that terminated the Deluge, the Bible ignored the incident and even avoided any specific mention of the dispersion of the clouds by the power of the sun and the wind.

3. *And the waters receded* [וַיָּשֻׁבוּ *wayyāšūbhū*, literally, 'returned'] *from the earth gradually* [הָלוֹךְ וָשׁוֹב *hālōkh wāšōbh*, literally, 'going and returning'] / As a rule, the commentators pay no special attention to the verb שׁוּב *šūbh*, which occurs twice here, and merely explain generally that the waters were reduced. But since the text emphasizes this verb, it is clear that it refers to the waters returning to the places whence they issued (not to the heavens only, as Jacob says in his commentary). The waters came from both the heavens and the great deep and returned to each of them. Since God now wishes to restore the world to its normal state, it is essential that the waters should return to their sources, and that the reservoirs of upper and lower waters should be replenished. Hence, וַיָּשֻׁבוּ *wayyāšūbhū*: the evaporation upwards restores the water to the heavens; and the earth, which absorbs the water downwards, returns it to the deep. The process is, of course, protracted: the waters return, *going and returning* — little by little. When the fountains burst forth, the waters gushed out from there with force and speed, and when the windows of the heavens were opened, the water poured down from them fast and furious; but now that these openings, below and above, have been closed, the waters recede slowly, by a gradual and continuous movement, according to the normal way of nature. Consequently, the layer of water that was formed in the course of the short period of forty days did not disappear till after a much longer time.

And the waters abated at the end of a hundred and fifty days] Only 150 days after the commencement of the Flood was the abatement of the waters noticed; till then their might alone was felt, as was stated earlier (vii 24). Their decrease became apparent

through the fact that the ark came to rest on the mountains (*v.*
4). Until the ark came to a halt, Noah saw only water and sky, and
it was not possible for him to sense that the level of the waters was
steadily falling. But the stopping of the ark made him aware that
the waters had decreased to an appreciable extent.

4. *And the ark came to rest*] There were no longer fifteen cubits
of water above the tops of the mountains, and consequently, even
if less than half the height of the ark was immersed in the water,
its bottom was able to touch them, and the ark could rest on them
(see above, vii 20). There is a word-play between the verb וַתָּנַח
wattānaḥ ['come to rest'] and the name נֹחַ *Nōaḥ*.

In the seventh month, on the seventeenth day of the month]
This was exactly five months after the commencement of the
Flood; and five months are actually the period indicated earlier in
the round number 150 days (see the introduction, § 7). The
Septuagint reads: *on the twenty-seventh day of the month,* as above,
vii 11. For the reason of this difference, see below, my annotation
to *v.* 14.

On the mountains of Ararat] — that is, on one of the mountains
of the land of Ararat. The name Ararat, in Assyrian *Uraṛṭu,* was
the designation of a region north of Assyria; and after the Armenians had invaded that area and settled there (apparently in the
sixth century B.C.E.), their country was called Armenia after
them. In ii Kings xix 37 and Isa. xxxvii 38 (and thence in the Book
of Tobit i 21) it is recorded that the sons of Sennacherib, king of
Assyria, who had murdered their father, escaped to the land of
Ararat; the political conflicts between Assyria and Uraṛṭu explain
why the murderers of the Assyrian king sought refuge in this
particular land. The name Ararat is further mentioned in the
prophecy against Babylon at the end of the Book of Jeremiah
(li 27): *Set up a standard on the earth, blow the trumpet among
the nations; prepare the nations for war against her, summon
against her the kingdoms, Ararat, Minni, and Ashkenaz.* The
prophet comes, as it were, to invite the peoples of the north, and
amongst them the children of Ararat, to fight a war of annihilation
against Babylon.

The Book of Jubilees, which is accustomed to give names to
people and places that are mentioned or alluded to anonymously

103

in the Torah, also assigns a specific name to the mountain on which the ark came to rest. It states (v 28; vii 1) that the ark halted on the summit of Mount Lubar, one of the mountains of Ararat (compare also *ibid.* vii 17, x 15). This name passed from the Book of Jubilees to Epiphanius, to other Christian writers, and also to the Midrashic literature (The Book of Noah).

In the Flood story of the Epic of Gilgameš it is related, as we have already observed, that the ship of Utnapištim stopped on Mount Niṣir. This mountain is apparently to be identified with the modern Pir Omar Gudrun, and is more to the south than the land of Ararat — south of the Lower Zab. What the other ancient texts on the Flood, which are written in the Sumerian or Akkadian tongues, recorded on this point we do not know, since in none of them is the part dealing with the Deluge preserved; even of Tablet XI of the Gilgameš Epic, which contains the story of the Flood, only the Assyrian, not the Babylonian, recension has reached us. But there is another Babylonian tradition corresponding to that of the Torah, which is found in the Greek summary of Berossus, where it is related that the ship came to a halt in the land of Armenia. This name, as we have noted earlier, designated in the time of Berossus approximately the region that was called in the ancient period Ararat; and in the Septuagint version of Isa. xxxvii 38 the name Armenia is specifically used in place of Ararat of the original Hebrew. It is difficult, however, to determine if Berossus derived this geographical detail from an ancient Babylonian tradition or whether he reflects here a later theory. Be that as it may, there is another point of agreement between Berossus and the Jewish tradition in the identification of the particular area in the land of Armenia in which the ship or the ark grounded: Berossus relates that in his days the remains of the ship were still to be seen on the mountains of the Kurds in Armenia (or, according to the quotation in Josephus, *Antiquities,* I, iii, 6: 'on the mountain of the Kordyaeans [Kurds]' — in the singular). Likewise Jewish tradition, followed by that of the Christians and Moslems, locates the landing-place of the ark on those mountains (see, for example, the Aramaic translations, both Jewish and Christian, of our verse: Targum Onkelos: 'on the mountains of Qardu [Cordyene]'; Targum Pseudo-Jonathan [Palestine Targum] A: 'on the mountains of Qardun';

the Peshiṭta: 'on the mountains of Qardu'; similarly, in Bereshith Rabba, xxxiii 4: 'on the mountains of Qardunia [Cordyene]'). The reference is probably to Jebel Jûdî, south of Lake Van, which is still looked upon by the local inhabitants as the mountain on which Noah's ark stranded. Possibly this agreement may be regarded as indicative of the fusing of the traditions of different peoples that took place in the Hellenistic world. Such a synthesis is apparent in the statement of Nicolaus of Damascus cited in *Antiquities, loc. cit.*; he writes that, as the story goes, people fled from the waters of the Deluge to Mount Βάρις in Armenia, where they were saved, and that one man reached the top of that mountain in an ark, and that part of the timber of the ark was preserved a long time. He adds that this may have been the man of whom Moses, the Jewish lawgiver, speaks. The possibility should also be considered that Mount Baris is identical with Mount Lubar of the Book of Jubilees.

Another tradition, which is based on a wrong interpretation of the expression 'the mountains of Ararat' as meaning *the mountains called Ararat* (so several exegetes and translators understood it), and which locates the resting-place of the ark on the highest mountain of the land of Armenia, south of the city of Erivan, has resulted in this mountain and the one adjacent to it being called by the Biblical name Ararat to this day; these are the great Ararat — called by the Turks *Aghri-dagh,* and by the Persians *Kūh-i-Nūḥ,* that is, 'the mountain of Noah' (5156 metres high) — and the Little Ararat (3914 metres high). There were also other local traditions that sited the mountains of Ararat mentioned here in regions other than the land of Ararat. Particularly worthy of mention is the tradition that the ark came to a halt on a mountain near to the city of Celaenae, otherwise known as Apamea of Phrygia, which was consequently designated Κιβωτός, that is, 'ark', and its coins were stamped, as we have mentioned earlier, with the representation of the ark and the name of Noah. The kinship between the Phrygians and Armenians may have influenced this tradition.

However, none of the identifications of the Biblical Ararat with a specific mountain has any basis in the Scriptural text, for the expression *on the mountains of Ararat,* correctly interpreted, only connotes a mountain — unspecified — in the land of Ararat.

5. *And the waters*] The sense is: As for the waters (see above, vii 19). Although the ark came to rest and was stationary, the waters did not stand still; they continued to sink.

Continued to abate [literally, 'they were going and diminishing'] / They were still in the process of gradually diminishing; they became less and less day by day.

Until [עַד *'adh*] *the tenth month*] The meaning is not that until this month they diminished and no more. The word עַד *'adh* often indicates not the end of a process but the completion of an important part of it. Thus, for example, in Gen. xxviii 15, the Lord declares to Jacob: *for I will not leave you until I have done that of which I have spoken to you*. It is obvious that the meaning is not that after doing what He had promised him, God would forsake Jacob, but that the Patriarch is given an assurance till the end of a vital period of his life, the period of his exile. In our case, a significant phase in the course of the Flood is referred to, until *the tops of mountains were seen*.

In the tenth month, on the first day of the month] — that is, counting lunar months, seventy-two days after the ark had landed on the mountains of Ararat. This number is not fortuitous; it is based on the sexagesimal system (12×6), and its importance in the Israelite and Jewish tradition is well known (72 elders, the Divine Name composed of seventy-two letters, and the like).

The tops of the mountains were seen] Again we have a parallel to the process of Creation (Gen. i 9: *and let the dry land* APPEAR).

6. *And it came to pass at the end of forty days*] This is equal to the duration of the Flood; thus the numerical harmony continues. Forty days after the date mentioned in the previous verse was the *tenth* day of the eleventh month, which corresponds to the *tenth* day of the second month, when God spoke for the first time to Noah (see above, at the beginning of my commentary on the third paragraph).

That Noah opened the window of the ark which he had made] The episode of the opening of the window in the Sumerian and Babylonian accounts partly parallels, and partly differs from, our narrative; see my remarks above, on *v*. 2. On the window in general, see on vi 16.

7. *And he sent forth*, etc.] The story of the sending forth of the

birds, which is recounted in a very similar form also in the Mesopotamian tradition (on the details see below), is easily understood,
if we bear in mind the custom of the ancient seamen who, when
they were on the high seas, used to send forth birds from their ships
in order to learn from their flight if there was dry land near, and
in which direction it lay. Thus Pliny relates of the Indians (*Naturalis
historia,* vi 83), that when they travel on the sea they do not gaze
at the stars but they bring with them birds, which they send forth
at frequent intervals, and they follow them as they turn towards
the land. It is self-understood that only such birds can be considered
for the purpose as are accustomed to fly long distances, like the
raven and the dove, and also the swallow, which is added to the
raven and the dove in the Epic of Gilgameš. The use of the verb
שׁלח *šālaḥ* in the *Piʿel,* which means to *send away,* and not in the
Qal, which signifies *sending on a mission,* is suited to the context,
for the intention was to *let* the birds *go free,* in order to see how
they would act and to learn from their actions.

The raven and the dove, which are mentioned successively in the
Biblical narrative, represent two different types of birds capable of
serving this purpose. They are similar to each other in size, but
dissimilar in their attributes: the raven is black and the dove white;
the raven is unclean and the dove clean; the raven is wild and the
dove can be domesticated and become a pet; and each one is
characteristic of its class. Among the unclean birds express mention
is made of *every raven according to its kind* (Lev. xi 15; Deut. xiv
14). In order to show that the Creator of the world provides food
for all His creatures, even for the wild birds, the raven is particularly
specified. Thus we find in Psa. cxlvii 9: *He gives to the beasts their
food, and to the young ravens which cry;* in Job xxxviii 41: *Who
provides for the raven its prey, when its young ones cry to God, and
wander about for lack of food?;* similarly in the New Testament,
Luke xii 24: *Consider the ravens: they neither sow nor reap, they
have neither storehouse nor barn, and yet God feeds them.* Also in
the Book of Proverbs, the ravens of the valley are cited as a typical
example of wild birds (xxx 17): *will be picked out by the ravens
of the valley and eaten by the vultures.* The raven lives in isolation
and has no direct relationship with human beings; only as a marvel
is it recounted that ravens brought bread and meat to Elijah (1

107

Kings xvii 6). The dove is the polaric opposite of all this. It is the symbol of beauty and gentleness, integrity and friendship. Time and again the maiden in the Song of Songs is called *my dove* or *my dove, my perfect one* (ii 14; v 2; vi 9); and her eyes and the eyes of the youth are compared to doves (i 15; iv 1; v 12). In rabbinic literature, the comparison of Israel to a dove, is as we know, a common figure. Also as an example of birds that travel long distances, the dove is mentioned several times in the Bible (Isa. lx 8: *Who are these that fly like a cloud, and like doves to their windows?* Hos. xi 11: *they shall come eagerly like birds from Egypt, and like doves from the land of Assyria;* Psa. lv 6 [Hebrew, v. 7]: *O that I had wings like a dove! I would fly away and be at rest;* possibly also Psa. lvi 1: *The Dove on Far-off Terebinths*). The contrast between the dove and the raven is likewise found in rabbinic literature; it will suffice to quote, for instance, B. Qiddushin 70b: 'There are two families in Nehardea, one called The House of Jonah ["dove"] and the other, The House of 'Urbathi ["raven-like"]'; and B. Sanhedrin 99b–100a: 'Of what use are the Rabbis to us? They have never permitted us the raven, nor forbidden us the dove.'

The same obtains in medieval Jewish literature. Thus in an elegy for the Ninth of Ab, called *Wolves of the Evening,* Zeraḥiah Hallevi Gerondi (twelfth century) writes: 'Lo, I the dove am black as a raven because of my sanctuary that lies in ruins.' In classical literature, too, this antithesis is noted (see, for example, Juvenal, ii 63: *dat veniam corvis, vexat censura columbas* ['Our Censor absolves the ravens and passes judgement on the doves']).

In the Epic of *Gilgameš,* as we have already observed (p. 9), the story of the sending forth of the birds is told as follows: On the seventh day after the ship had grounded on Mount Niṣir, Utnapištim put forth a dove, but she found no resting-place, so she returned to him. Then he put forth a swallow, but she also found no resting-place and returned to him. Thereafter he sent forth a raven, and the raven saw that the waters had abated and it found something to eat, and so it did not return. The similarity to the Biblical narrative is manifest. Both in the Babylonian epic and in the Biblical account (*vv.* 10, 12) seven days are mentioned; the raven and the dove are sent forth; the birds that are sent out on the first two occasions return, but the last bird to be sent does not come back; the reason for the birds' returning is the lack of a resting place.

But there are also differences. The Gilgameš Epic speaks also of the putting forth of a swallow, but in the Scriptural story there is no mention of this bird. Whether the sending of the swallow was part of the ancient tradition and the Torah omitted it for some reason, or on the contrary it is an addition of the Babylonian poet, it is not possible to decide. Furthermore, according to the Babylonian Epic the dove was sent forth only once, but in the Torah account three times. And again, the order in which the two birds are mentioned is different in the Bible from that of the Gilgameš Epic, which speaks of the dove first and of the raven last. The Pentateuchal order is more in keeping with the general character of the Scriptural narrative, which is wholly based on an ethical interpretation of the story. It was fitting that the good tidings of salvation should reach Noah through the medium of the gentle and pure-hearted bird, and that the olive-leaf, the symbol of the Creator's compassion, should be brought to the perfectly righteous man in the mouth of his perfect dove.

A raven [literally, 'the raven'] / — one of the ravens that were with him in the ark. The definite article indicates here only what is termed a general definition: he sent forth the raven that he sent; similarly in *v.* 8: one of the doves that were with him in the ark, the dove that he put forth; and so, too (below, xiv 13): *and the survivor came,* that is, one of the survivors, the survivor that came.

The purpose for which Noah sent the raven is not expressly stated as in the case of the dove in *v.* 8, *to see if the waters had subsided from the face of the ground.* One may suppose, as most commentators do, that the object was the same; but this is difficult, for if the two birds had been put forth for the identical reason, it should have been indicated in connection with the first bird rather than the second. More probably Noah sent forth the raven without any specific intention; he let it go to see how it would act so that he might learn something from its behaviour — whatever there was to learn from it. Actually, however, it taught him nothing. The Septuagint adds also here the words, *to see if the waters had subsided* (with slight variations in the MSS) in order to harmonize, in accordance with its usual practice, this verse with *v.* 8. The Biblical text should not, therefore, be emended on the basis of the Septuagint as many contemporary expositors have suggested.

And it went to and fro] True to its nature, the raven is concerned only with itself and pays no heed to man's needs. It goes forth and comes back, goes and returns, and Noah can draw no inference from its going and coming. Instead of *to and fro* [literally, 'going and returning'] the Septuagint reads: *and did not return.* Actually this clause does not fit in well with the rest of the verse. But it is interesting to note that it corresponds to what is related in the Epic of Gilgameš.

Until the waters were dried from the earth] — that is, until the twenty-seventh day of the second month of the second year (*v.* 14). 8. *Then he sent forth a dove*] In our text we are not told when she was sent forth. Undoubtedly the meaning is not that Noah let her go immediately after sending the raven, since it is said of the raven that *it went to and fro,* and Noah could not have known this till several days had passed. Further, it is stated in *v.* 10: *He waited again another seven days,* implying that he had already waited and that seven days had elapsed prior to this (compare *v.* 12: *Then he waited again another seven days* — after the week mentioned in *v.* 10). The view has been expressed that in the original text *v.* 8 commenced with the words *and he waited seven days* and that these words were omitted in error. But it is hard to imagine how such a mistake could occur. In any case, even without this clause, it is clear from *v.* 10 that according to the Biblical narrative seven days passed between the sending forth of the raven and the first time he sent the dove.

On the dates see the introduction, § 7.

From him] In connection with the putting forth of the raven Scripture does not say *from him,* but the expression is used in regard to the dove, thus indicating the friendly relations between Noah and her.

To see if the waters had subsided, etc.] This time Noah has a specific purpose: he lets the dove go free, and he relies on her understanding and friendship, so that the sending forth becomes a mission. He hopes to be informed (that is the sense of *to see*) by the dove's behaviour on a definite point, namely, *if the waters had subsided from the face of the ground,* that is to say, if the waters had further abated since the ark had landed.

9. *But* [literally, 'And'] *the dove did not find a place where to set her foot,* etc.] The *Wāw* of *weʾlōʾ* ['and . . . not'] is antithetic: It is true that Noah was hoping to receive some tidings, but the dove found no place where to rest her feet, *for the waters were on the face of the whole earth;* therefore she could not bring Noah any news. Or, more exactly, since she returned as she had left, Noah came to a negative conclusion, to wit, that there was still *water on the face of the whole earth.*

Also the word מָנוֹחַ *mānōaḥ* [literally, 'resting-place'; rendered: 'place where to set'] forms a word-play with the name נֹחַ *Nōaḥ* (see above, on *v.* 4).

So he put forth his hand and took her and brought her in unto him, into the ark] — expressions of affection. Noah sympathizes with the dove, which sought *a place to set her foot* but did not find it, and he helps her with his hand to return to him and find refuge in the ark. Again we have a word-play: וַיְשַׁלַּח *wayeˊšallaḥ* ['and he sent forth'] — וַיִּשְׁלַח *wayyišlaḥ* ['and he put forth'].

10. *He waited again another seven days*] — that is, apart from the days that elapsed between the sending forth of the raven and the first time the dove was sent, which were apparently also seven (see above, on *v.* 8).

11. *And the dove came back to him in the evening*] At the time when birds are accustomed to return to their nest in order to spend the night there, the dove returned to her cote in the ark — to the man who loved her and whom she loved in turn — and brought him good tidings, in the form possible to a creature that cannot speak.

And lo] What an encouraging novelty! It was a small thing that the dove brought in her mouth, but this small thing was a harbinger of peace and announced salvation.

Olive LEAVES [עֲלֵה *ʿălē,* singular construct] / עָלֶה *ʿălē* has a collective sense, as above (iii 7): *and they sewed fig* LEAVES [עָלֶה *ʿălē*] together. The reference is to a twig containing several leaves.

Fresh ones [טָרָף *ṭārāph*] *in her mouth*] According to Rashi: which the dove had plucked with its mouth; the verb has the masculine form because the bird was a male dove, and the *Rēš* of

111

טָרָף *ṭārāph* is pointed, exceptionally, with a *Qāmeṣ*, although the verb is not at a pause. This is altogether difficult. It seems more probable, in accordance with the view of most exegetes, that טָרָף *ṭārāph* is an adjective qualifying עָלֶה *ʿālē*, formed like רָחָב *rāḥābh* ['wide'], and its signification is 'fresh', 'green' (in Arabic طرف *ṭarufa* and طريف *ṭarîfun*, 'plucked whilst it is still fresh'). It has been suggested that the word טָרָף *ṭārāph*, signifying 'a leaf', as in Aramaic, was added as an explanation of the word עָלֶה *ʿālē;* but this conjecture does not appear to be correct, because the crux of the good tidings was that the leaves were fresh and green. This fact proved that the lower hills, which are suited to the cultivation of the olive, were already free of water, and that the trees growing on them had begun to put forth new branches and leaves.

So Noah knew] He inferred from what he saw.

That the waters had subsided, etc.] — precisely what he wanted to know when he sent the dove forth the first time (*v.* 8).

12. *Then he waited* [וַיִּיָּחֶל *wayyiyyāḥel*] / It means the same as וַיָּחֶל *wayyāḥel* ['he waited'] in *v.* 10. Biblical style is normally fond of variation and changes of form, as we have already noted several times. Grammarians regard וַיִּיָּחֶל *wayyiyyāḥel* as the *Niphʿal* of the stem יָחַל *yāḥal*, and וַיָּחֶל *wayyāḥel* as the *Hiphʿîl* of the stem חִיל *ḥîl;* but to the ancients who spoke Hebrew they were just parallel forms, deriving from the same root and having the same meaning, and hence they could be interchanged for the sake of variety.

And she returned not again unto him any more] Although he had sent her forth *once more*, she did not return to him *again* (another example of variation and change from what we call *Hiphʿîl* [*v.* 10: וַיּוֹסֶף *wayyōseph*, literally, 'and he continued'; rendered: 'and once more'] to what we call *Qal* [our verse: יָסְפָה *yāsephā*, literally, 'she continued'; rendered: 'again']); this showed that the dove had found a place where to rest and to place her nest and to sustain herself. Life begins to renew itself upon the earth.

13–14. These two verses provide a formal conclusion to the paragraph, corresponding to the opening of the fifth paragraph, which deals with the commencement of the Flood (vii 11). The beginning and the end constitute a kind of framework for the description of the wonderful yet terrible happening.

And it came to pass in the six hundred and first year] The reference, of course, is to Noah's life. At the beginning of the story (vii 11), the words *of Noah's life* are explicitly used in giving the date. Now there is no need for this. For now there is no other era in existence; there are no kings or governments, and it is impossible to number the years except by reference to the father and head of renascent humanity.

In the first month, the first day of the month] Precisely at the commencement of the year, on the anniversary of Creation, the world resumed again the form that God had given it when first it came into being.

The waters were dried from off the earth] Here Scripture narrates the story objectively. Noah was not yet able to perceive the position clearly, for through the narrow window, which opened on to one side only, he could not see much.

And Noah removed the covering of the ark] The rain having stopped, the covering was no longer required; and once the covering was removed, it was possible to view the landscape from all sides.

Regarding the covering, see above, on vi 16.

And looked, and behold the face of the ground was dry] Here the Bible tells of Noah's subjective observation of what had been objectively stated previously in the first part of the verse.

14.   *In the second month, on the twenty-seventh day of the month, the land was dried out*] Above we were told that already on the first day of the first month *the face of the ground* WAS DRY [חָרְבוּ *ḥārebbū*], that is, that there was no longer a layer of water over it, but the ground was still wet (Bereshith Rabba xxxiii 7: 'it had been turned into muddy soil'; in Seder Olam ch. iv: 'became like pulp'), and completely covered by mud. Hence, the proper time had not yet arrived to leave the ark, and it was necessary to wait until the earth was *dried out* [יָבְשָׁה *yābbeša*] and returned to the state befitting the name it had received at the time of Creation, when it was said (Gen. i 9): *let the* DRY LAND [יַבָּשָׁה *yabbāša*] *appear*. It attained this state again on the twenty-seventh day of the second month of the six hundred and first year, that is, if we count both the first and the last day, a year and eleven days after the commencement of the Deluge: a complete solar year of 365 days in all. The Septuagint, which was composed in Egypt for

113

the use of the Jews living there, who were accustomed to the Egyptian year of 365 days, also had in mind a complete year, and with this in view wrote twenty-seven instead of seventeen in vii 11 and in viii 4 (for the chronological details of the Flood, see the introduction to this section, § 7).

The cycle was complete: the sun returned to the point at which it was on the day the Deluge began, and the earth returned to the state in which it then found itself. The time for leaving the ark had at last arrived, and Noah stood ready, awaiting the Divine command to go forth.

EIGHTH PARAGRAPH

THE COMMAND TO LEAVE THE ARK

15. *Then God spoke / to Noah, saying*:

16. *'Go forth from the ark, / you*
    and your wife, / and your sons and your sons' wives / with
        you.

17. *Every living thing / that is with you*
    of all flesh / — flying creatures and animals
    and every creeping thing / that creeps on the earth — / bring
        forth with you,
    that they may breed abundantly on the earth, / and be fruitful
        and multiply / upon the earth.'

15. *Then God spoke to Noah, saying*] — a more formal expression than that used for the first communications to Noah, and identical with the formula that introduces the Lord's words to Moses. The intimation of a bitter experience is not comparable to the announcement of liberation from it.

16. *Go forth from the ark*] — a parallel injunction to that of vii 1: *Go into . . . the ark.*

You, etc.] Again we have a variation in the listing of the members of Noah's family. The change is introduced for its own sake without any hidden intention, as several commentators have supposed.

17. *Every living thing* [חַיָּה *ḥayyā*], etc.] Here, too, there is a modification in the enumeration of the various types of living creature. חַיָּה *ḥayyā* [usually translated: 'beast', 'animal'] has also in this instance a general signification. מִכָּל בָּשָׂר *mikkol bāśār* ['of all flesh'] is another example of من البيان *mina 'lbayâni*, as above (vii 22). The general statement is followed by details: *flying creatures and animals*, etc. The *Bēth* [prefixed to each of these Hebrew nouns] is that of explanation and specification, as in vii 21.

Bring forth] (The *Kethîbh* [the text as it is *written*] is הוֹצֵא *hôṣē'*, the regular form of the imperative *Hiph'il;* the *Qerē* [the marginal recommendation that is *to be read*] is הַיְצֵא *hayṣē'*, a variant grammatical form based on the conjugation of the verbal stem יָצָא *yāṣā'*, which is a *Pē'-Wāw* verb, as though it were a *Pē'-Yōdh* verb of the type of יָשַׁר *yāśar,* יָטַב *yāṭabh,* and the like). Just as in the second paragraph, after the instruction *and you shall come,* referring to Noah and his household (vi 18), we have the command *you shall bring* with regard to the creatures (*ibid. v.* 19), so here, after the injunction *Go forth* directed to Noah and his family, comes the order *bring forth* relative to the creatures. And in the same way as the clause *you shall bring* in the earlier passage signifies, 'you shall permit to enter', so in this verse *bring forth* means, 'permit them to go forth'.

That they may [literally, 'and they will'] *breed abundantly on the earth, and be fruitful and multiply upon the earth*] The sense is: Permit them to go forth in order that they may be able to breed abundantly and be fruitful and multiply. At present there are only two of each kind, but in the course of a short time they will breed abundantly and be fruitful and multiply. What was said in the story of Creation specifically with regard to the creatures of the water (i 20, 22), and to a more limited extent also of the flying creatures of the air (*ibid. v.* 22), is said here of all the living creatures of the earth.

You — with you — with you — with you] These oft-repeated expressions of our paragraph, with which members of the verses conclude, form a harmonious reiteration as in vi 18.

18. *So Noah went forth, / and his sons*
and his wife and his sons' wives / with him;

19. *every beast, every creeping thing,*
and every flying creature, / everything that moves upon the
earth,
by their families / they went forth out of the ark.

20. *Then Noah built / an altar to the Lord,*
and took —
of every clean animal / and of every clean bird,
and offered burnt offerings / on the altar.

21. *And when the Lord smelled / the pleasing odour,*
the Lord said / in His heart,
'I will not again / curse any more
the ground / because of man,
for the imagination of man's heart / is evil from his youth;
neither will I ever again / destroy every living creature
as I have done.

22. *While the earth remains, / seedtime and harvest,*
cold and heat, / summer and winter,
day and night, / shall not cease.'

18. *So Noah went forth*] He was told, *Go forth,* and *he went*
forth. This parallels the fourth paragraph, which relates that
Noah went in (vii 7) immediately after he was commanded, *Go*
'[into the ark] (vii 1).

And his sons, etc.] Once again the order of the words is changed,
and here, too, as in *v.* 16, there is no cryptic reason such as
Jacob has suggested in his commentary. It is but another example
of variation for its own sake, with a view to stylistic elegance and
nothing more.

19. *Every* BEAST [חַיָּה *ḥayyā*], etc.] This verse begins with the
same words as *v.* 17 in order to create a parallelism between the
command and its execution. Similarly, we have here, too, a general
statement followed by details, and also the usual variation of style.

116

They went forth out of the ark] Another instance of stylistic symmetry: the story of the exit begins with the words, *Go forth from the ark* (*v.* 16), uses, in the continuation, the verb יָצָא *yāṣā'* by itself twice (*vv.* 17, 18 ['bring forth' — 'went forth']), and ends with the complete expression, *they went forth out of the ark.* Thus the conclusion corresponds to the opening words.

20. *Then Noah built an altar unto the Lord* [*YHWH*] / The reason for the occurrence of the Tetragrammaton here, as in the third paragraph, and not *'Elōhīm,* we have noted in the introduction to this section, pp. 35–36.

And took] This expression reminds us of the word *take* in the third paragraph (vii 2), and points, as it were, to the connection between that paragraph and the sacrifices mentioned in this passage.

Of every clean animal and of every clean bird] — that is to say, some of every kind of clean animal and every kind of clean bird.

טְהֹרָה *ṭehōrā* ['clean' fem. sing.; spelt without *Wāw*] — טָהוֹר *ṭāhō(w)r* ['clean' mas. sing.; spelt with *Wāw*] / In the Leningrad MS the reverse obtains: טְהוֹרָה *ṭehō(w)rā* [with *Wāw*] — טָהֹר *ṭāhōr* [without *Wāw*]. We have already observed above the tendency of the Masoretes to use full and defective spelling alternately.

And offered burnt offerings on the altar] These were not sacrifices of atonement, as several expositors have surmised; for there was no need for atonement, since suffering and death purge away human iniquities. Nor was their purpose to beseech protection and blessing for the future, as others have supposed, for there is no reason to suppose that the Bible attributed to Noah a desire to make further requests after the wondrous salvation that had been vouchsafed to him. In the Mesopotamian texts likewise we are told that the hero of the Flood offered sacrifices to the gods after his deliverance. In both cases the explanation is very simple. When a person has been saved from a terrible danger, or has escaped from a general catastrophe, his first reaction is to give thanks to him who saved him or helped him to escape. And there could be no greater thanksgiving than these sacrifices. Of the few domestic animals and birds that constituted his sole, meagre possessions for the new period of his life in a world that was completely waste, Noah gave up several animals and birds in honour of his Divine Saviour for the purpose of a burnt offering (which is entirely burnt, the owners having no share in it), so as to express thereby, after the manner of first-fruits and the like, his acknowledgement that everything was from God's hand, and the trust that He would provide everything in the future. As though to say: 'Ere I come to enjoy Thy gifts, let a portion of them first be sanctified unto Thee, so that I on my part may show Thee honour.'

21. *And when the Lord smelled the pleasing odour*] We have noted in the introduction both the points of agreement and difference between the Biblical account and that of the Gilgameš Epic. In contrast to the corporeal and unedifying picture of the Babylonian poem, which depicts the gods swarming from all sides 'like flies' to enjoy the sacrifices, and squabbling among themselves as to who should and who should not enjoy Utnapištim's offerings, we have here the smelling of the odour only. We can appreciate the Biblical expression only when we set it against the terms used in the pagan saga, which it seeks, as it were, to oppose. The God of Israel has no need of sacrifices. *Do I eat* — the Biblical poet asks in His name — *the flesh of bulls, or drink the blood of goats?* (Psa. 1 13). Noah's sacrifices are burnt offerings, whose flesh is wholly burnt and not eaten. Only the odour reaches the throne of the Lord — a thing without substance. Undoubtedly, the reference is not to the smell of burnt meat, which is certainly not pleasant, but to something more important. To understand the Scriptural concept of smelling the pleasing odour, we have to consider such passages as Amos v 21 [the literal rendering of which is]: *I will not smell* [scil. a pleasing odour] *on your solemn assemblies.* If the prophet, who comes to declare that the Lord has no desire for the oblations of the people who transgress against Him, says, *I will not smell,* it means that it was possible for Him to smell, but He does not wish to do so. Had the prophet intended to negate this possibility, he would have put it in the form of a question: *Shall I smell?* just as the Psalmist asks: *Do I eat?* in the verse quoted above. If now a prophet like Amos thinks that the smelling of the sacrificial odour is possible, it certainly has no material import. The expression *He smelt an odour* had already lost in Hebrew its original and literal signification and acquired a figurative connotation, such as: 'He received favourably', 'He esteemed the inner intent of the

118

sacrifice.' In Psalm 1, immediately after the verse cited, we read: *Offer to God a sacrifice of thanksgiving,* the meaning being: Do not think, as do the Gentiles, that God derives material enjoyment from what you offer to Him, and that He eats the flesh of bulls and drinks the blood of he-goats; instead offer to God a sacrifice that is pleasing in His sight, namely, an oblation that expresses your thanksgiving and is indicative of the feeling of gratitude in your heart. Such was Noah's offering; hence it was pleasing to the Lord.

In the expression רֵיחַ נִיחוֹחַ *rēaḥ nīḥōaḥ* ['pleasing odour'], a common sacrificial term, there is apparently a play on the name נֹחַ *Nōaḥ,* similar to the word-play we noted in connection with the words וַתָּנַח *wattānaḥ* ['came to rest'] (viii 4), and מָנוֹחַ *mānōaḥ* ['place where he set'] (viii 9). The combination of the two words רֵיחַ *rēaḥ* and נִיחוֹחַ *nīḥōaḥ* may have become popular also on account of the assonance of their endings. The word נִיחוֹחַ is derived from the stem נוּחַ *nūaḥ* ['to rest'], and signifies something that inspires, and is received with, gratification [literally, 'resting of the spirit']— a meaning well suited to our subject.

The Lord in His heart] — a decision reached with Himself. Compare the expression *to His heart* in the account of God's decision to bring the Flood (vi 6); the two verses parallel each other.

I will not, etc.] When the Lord observed the good intention of Noah, He recognized that this righteous man was truly worthy of being saved; for after his deliverance he did not forget his Deliverer, and did all in his power to show Him his gratitude. Since Noah, the head of the one family left after the Deluge, showed these good qualities of heart, it was possible to hope that the offspring of this family would be of fine character and worthy of blessing. In this way we can understand the connection between God's smelling the pleasing odour and His resolve not to bring universal disaster again upon mankind, and likewise the Divine benison mentioned in the following paragraphs.

The expression לֹא אֹסִף *lō 'ōsīph* [literally, 'I shall not continue'; rendered: 'I will not', 'neither will I ever'] occurs twice in this verse, but the reference in each case is to a different matter: the first time, the words refer to the cursing of the ground because of

Adam (iii 17: *because of you;* similarly here: *because of man*);
the second time, to a world-cataclysm like the Deluge. The position
of the word עוֹד *'ōdh* ['again'] differs in the two clauses: in the
first, it comes after the verb *curse;* and in the second, before the
verb *destroy.* There is a reason for this. As is usual with repetitions
in the Bible, change of form is not without relevance to the subject matter. The curse on the ground — that is to say, the decree
that the ground would not again produce of its own accord,
without human labour, what was needed for man's sustenance, and
that he would eat his bread only with toil and the sweat of his
face — remained valid, except that the Lord promised not to add
thereto, that is, not to aggravate further man's position on earth.
I will not curse any more — more than it is already cursed. In the
second instance, the meaning is that the Lord would not bring
universal retribution upon humanity as He did in the days of Noah:
I will never again destroy, that is, I shall not destroy a second
time. On this subject compare further below, ix 11, and the
commentary there.

For the imagination of man's heart is evil from his youth] Two
interpretations of this sentence have been suggested. According to
the first, it gives the reason for the preceding assurance, *I will not
again:* since the imagination of man's heart is evil from his youth,
he is a fit subject for forgiveness, and therefore I shall not judge
him severely. The second explanation interprets the clause as giving
the reason for the curse upon the ground: I shall not curse the
ground any more on account of man's evil imagination. The first
explanation appears more in accord with the sense of the words,
but it is difficult thematically, for before the Flood, too, human,
nature was no different (vi 5: *and that every device of the thoughts
of his heart was only evil continually*), and it was this very attribute
of character that brought upon him world-wide punishment by the
waters of the Flood. Consequently, the second exposition is to be
preferred. The divergences between vi 5 and our verse are only
differences of wording, as is usual in repetitions, and in this
instance, too, the variations are in keeping with the change of
circumstances. In the earlier passage we find כָּל־יֵצֶר *kol yēṣer*
['every device'], in our verse, יֵצֶר *yēṣer* ['imagination']; there it is
written רַק רַע *raq ra'* ['only evil'], here רַע *ra'* ['evil']; there we

have כָּל הַיּוֹם *kol hayyōm* ['continually'] here מִנְּעֻרָיו *minne'ūrāw* ['from his youth']. In ch. vi, since the evil nature of man was cited as the cause of the terrible punishment, it was proper to indicate it fully (כָּל *kol* ['all', 'every'] twice; רַק *raq* ['only']); in our passage, since it is mentioned only incidentally, in connection with the resolve to apply the attribute of mercy, it is inappropriate to emphasize it unduly.

22. עֹד *'ōdh* [rendered here, 'while'; above, 'again'] / This is the third occurrence of the word in our paragraph, and, as usual, the threefold reiteration indicates emphasis; what has happened now will not happen *again*.

[*While*] *the earth remains*] According to the view reflected in this verse, the earth is not eternal; only the Creator is eternal. Since the earth had a *beginning* (i 1), it stands to reason that it will also have an *end*.

Seedtime and harvest, cold and heat, summer and winter] Six periods of the year, according to rabbinic interpretation, are referred to here (Tosefta Ta'anith i 7; B. Baba Meṣi'a 106b; Bereshith Rabba xxxiv 11, and parallel passages). But it is difficult to accept this as the simple sense of the verse, because there is no proper time-sequence here; furthermore, *summer* and *winter* are essentially the same as *heat* and *cold*. Nor have the attempts to connect this interpretation with the agricultural calendar of Gezer been successful. Dillmann was of opinion that the year is divided here into two seasons: *seedtime, cold, winter* represent one season — the rainy period; while *harvest, heat, summer* constitute another season — the hot period. But this explanation is also difficult, because harvest and summer are two separate times of the year (Jer. viii 20: *The harvest is past, the summer is ended, and we are not saved*). The key to the problem is to be sought in the word-pair that follows in our verse: *day and night*. These two words certainly stand by themselves and are not part of a series with the three preceding pairs. Now just as the last pair of words is unrelated to the rest, so it seems are the other word-pairs. The sense of the verse is that all the mutations that occur in normal times, even though they became blurred or were altogether obliterated during the year of the Deluge, would not be wanting in future — be they the agricultural seasons, like seedtime and harvest, which in the

Flood year were completely non-existent; or the primary distinction between cold and heat, which during this year was not clearly felt on account of the vast quantity of water on the earth; or the change from summer to winter, which is the regular consequence of heat and cold and other factors, and likewise did not take place during this exceptional year.

J. Martin conjectures (*JBL,* xlv [1926], pp. 129–133) that this verse contains an allusion to a tradition concerning years of hunger that preceded the Flood as in the Epic of Atraḥasis, because according to source J, to which this paragraph is attributed, the Deluge lasted forty days, and rain in the course of forty days cannot produce a radical change in agricultural activity. But in view of the fact that according to the complete narrative in its present form the earth did not return to its normal state till after a complete year, there is no basis for this theory.

Day and night] This is difficult, for the difference between the two had not been abolished during the Flood, which lasted, it is expressly stated, forty days and forty nights (vii 4, 12), implying that also then there was day and night. Possibly it means that it was hard to distinguish between day and night on account of the clouds that obscured the sun continuously. We may perhaps conjecture that the ancient saga on the Flood related that during this period the light of the sun was completely quenched, and that a fragment of the epic survives here. The Midrashic literature also speaks of the extinction of the light of the heavenly host at the time of the Flood (Bereshith Rabba xxv 2, xxxiii 3, xxxiv 11, and parallel passages; compare Theodor's commentary on Bereshith Rabba, *loc. cit.,* and Rashi's annotation to our verse). Although it is possbile to regard this as a homiletical interpretation based on the wording of the verse, it is also possible that we have here a vestige of an ancient tradition that was preserved in the memory of the people. In the Midrashic interpretation quoted in Yalkut i 57, the idea of the sun's obscuration is derived from other verses: *and the Lord shut him in* (vii 16) — the Holy One blessed be He shut up the sun and the moon so that they did not shine throughout twelve months, for it is said: *Who commands the sun, and it does not rise* (Job ix 7).'

It appears that the prophet Jeremiah alluded to a promise of this kind, concerning the continued existence of day and night in the future, when he declared in the name of the Lord that the covenant made with David and the seed of Jacob would not be broken just as the covenant with day and night would not be abrogated (Jer. xxxiii 17–26). In this same passage there occurs twice (*vv.* 17–18) the expression *shall not be cut off*, which is found in the continuation of our section with reference to the Flood (ix 11). There is also a similar section in another part of Jeremiah (xxxi 35–37), and there, too, we find an expression resembling one that is used here: וְיִשְׁבְּתוּ *weyišbethū* ['then . . . shall cease'] *ibid. v.* 36, and יִשְׁבֹּתוּ *yišbōthū* ['shall (not) cease'] at the end of our verse. However, in our section the assurance with regard to the continuation of day and night is not called a covenant as in the words of the prophet; only in the promise given to Noah and his sons is the term *covenant* employed. Apparently, the covenant with day and night was one of the details mentioned in the ancient saga of which only an echo is heard in the Torah. See above, the introduction p. 26.

Shall not cease [לֹא יִשְׁבֹּתוּ *lō' yišbōthū*] / Another parallel to the story of Creation. The verb שָׁבַת *šābhath* ['cease'] comes near the end of both sections, and here specifically as an assurance that the order of Creation would not be changed. Although God ceased (from His work) after He had completed the task of creation, yet the world He created and its natural order would not cease while the earth remained. The reference, of course, is to total and universal cessation, for it is obvious that a partial interruption of the normal order may occur in many instances. In years of drought, sowing and harvesting come to a stop (Gen. xlv 6: *and there are yet five years in which there will be neither ploughing nor harvest*); so, too, the children of Israel are commanded to refrain from any agricultural work during the seventh year; and in the plague of darkness that came upon Egypt (Exod. x 21–23) there was no difference between day and night. But in all these cases there is only a temporary, localized intermission.

On the use of a synonym for the verb שָׁבַת *šābhath* in the Sumerian tradition of the Deluge, see above, p. 18, in the list of correspondences of detail, No. 19.

GOD'S BLESSING TO NOAH AND HIS SONS

CHAPTER IX

1. *And God blessed / Noah and his sons,*
    and said to them,
    'Be fruitful and multiply, / and fill the earth.

2. *The fear of you and the dread of you / shall be*
    upon every beast of the earth, / and upon every flying creature
    of the air,
    together with everything that creeps on the ground / and all
    the fish of the sea;
    into your hand they are delivered.

3. *Every moving thing that lives / shall be food for you;*
    as the green plants, / I give you everything.

4. *Only flesh / with its life, that is, its blood, / you shall not eat.*

5. *And surely for your own blood / I will require a reckoning;*
    of every beast / I will require it;
    and of man, / of every man's brother,
    I will require / the life of man.

6. *Whoever sheds the blood of man, / by man shall his blood*
    be shed;
    for in the image of God / was man made.

7. *And you, / be fruitful and multiply,*
    bring forth abundantly on the earth / and multiply in it.

1. *And God blessed Noah and his sons*] In this communication
and in the two announcements following, God apprises Noah and
his sons of what He resolved in His heart (viii 21–22). First of
all, He promises them the blessing of life.

And said to them, 'Be fruitful and multiply, and fill the earth']
The benison vouchsafed to the first man (i 28) is confirmed and
renewed in identical terms. This was the wording of the earlier
blessing: *Be fruitful and multiply, and fill the earth,* and it will
be realized through its bestowal upon Noah and his sons, who are
descendants of Adam.

2. *The fear of you* [מוֹרַאֲכֶם *mōraʾăkhem*] *and the dread of you*
[חִתְּכֶם *ḥittekhem*] / A single idea is expressed by two synonymous
terms; this is demonstrated by the frequent use of the two stems
יָרֵא *yārēʾ* ['fear'] and חָתַת *ḥāthath* ['dread', 'be dismayed'] as verbs
in juxtaposition or parallelism to each other, in such expressions as
אַל (לֹא) תִּירָא וְאַל (לֹא) תֵּחָת *ʾal (lōʾ) tīrāʾ weʾal (lōʾ) tēḥāth* ['do
not fear or be dismayed'] and the like (Deut. i 21; xxxi 8, and
in many other passages, seventeen times in all). Compare also
פַּחְדְּכֶם וּמוֹרַאֲכֶם *paḥdekhem ūmōraʾăkhem* ['the fear of you and the
dread of you'] in Deut. xi 25.

Also this sentence, *The fear of you and the dread of you shall be
upon every beast*, etc., is in keeping with what God said to the first
human being: *and have dominion over the fish of the sea and
over the flying creatures of the air*, etc. (i 28). But a new point
emerges in our verse, to wit, the reference to the subjective attitude
of the creatures towards man. This attitude of fear and dread may
be due to the fact that the creatures were saved from the Flood on
account of man and through his action; from now on they would
realize more clearly the superiority of the human species. On the
change in the relationship between man and the animate world, see
further my annotation to the next verse.

*Upon every beast of the earth and upon every flying creature
of the air*, etc.] Again we find variation of form in listing the
categories of creatures, in accordance with the principles that we
have already discussed. Since the fear of mankind is spoken of here,
there are first mentioned, in order to show how far it reached, those
kinds of creatures that naturally have less reason to be afraid than
other kinds, namely, the beasts of the earth, which are strong and
fierce, and the flying creatures of the air, which can wing their
way on high above the sphere of human life. It seems as though
Scripture meant to say: Even the savage animals and the birds that
soar aloft in the sky will fear you. The Septuagint, in conformity
with its usual tendency to harmonize the verses, adds *and all the
cattle* after *every beast of the earth*. But the addition only detracts
from the significance of the verse.

Together with [בְּ- *be-*] *everything that creeps on the ground*,
etc.] The preposition *Bēth* signifies here '(together) with', as in
Exod. x 9: *We will go with our young and our old*, etc.

125

(Dillmann): even the beasts and the birds, together with all the creeping things of the ground and the fish of the sea, are all delivered into your hand.

3. *Every moving thing* [רֶמֶשׂ *remeś*, literally, 'creeping thing'] *that lives shall be food for you*] This verse marks an innovation compared with what was permitted to Adam. God allowed the latter only vegetarian food (i 29); now He grants Noah and his sons permission to eat the flesh of all living creatures (*every creeping thing that lives*, that means, every moving creature in which there is the breath of life), since they rescued the living creatures in their ark and made the continued life of their kinds possible in the future, and thus became, as it were, partners of the Creator in the creation of the life of these species. Why the Torah first forbade the eating of flesh and afterwards permitted it, I endeavoured to explain in Part I, in my commentary on i 29–30 (pp. 58 f.).

Shall be food for you] The very words spoken to the primo-genitor of the human race (i 29–30; compare also vi 21).

As the green plants, I give you everything] A still clearer reference to what God said at the beginning in similar language (i 30). Now it will be permissible for the sons of Noah to eat flesh as it was then permitted to the first man and the creatures to eat the green plants.

4. *Only* [אַךְ *'akh*] *flesh with its life, that is, its blood you shall not eat*] Since the permission to eat meat is only a concession, as I noted in my commentary to i 29–30, it is made conditional on not eating blood, so as to do honour to the principle of life (*for the blood is the life*), and to serve, at the same time, as a reminder that in truth all flesh should have been forbidden, and hence it behoves us to avoid eating one part of it in order to remember the former prohibition.

With [בְּ *be-*] *its life* [literally, 'its soul'], *that is, its blood*] The preposition *Bēth* signifies here *with*, as above in *v.* 2, the meaning being: together *with its soul*, with the element of life therein, which is its *blood*.

5. *And* SURELY [אַךְ *'akh*] *for your own blood, etc.*] — one restriction followed by another [expressed in each case by אַךְ *'akh*, rendered above, 'only', here, 'surely']. The injunction to respect

the blood as the basis of life is not just an obligation imposed upon
you and a limitation of your right to enjoyment; it operates also
for your benefit.

Your own blood [literally, 'your blood unto your souls'] / Many
explanations have been offered regarding the expression 'unto
your souls'; the correct one appears to be that of Ibn Ezra: 'of your
souls', that is, your own blood.

I will require a reckoning] The expression 'require' occurs three
times in the verse for emphasis. God insists on requiring this
reckoning with the utmost rigour.

Of every beast I will require it] At first sight this seems bizarre.
But one should bear in mind the Pentateuchal law relating to the
ox that had to be put to death by stoning (Exod. xxi 28–32).

And of man, of every man's brother] How much more so shall
I require a reckoning for the blood of man in this instance, seeing
that the slain person is the *brother* of the slayer. Whoever takes
human life is like Cain.

I will require the LIFE [נֶפֶשׁ *nepheš*] *of man*] These verses
(4–5) contain a word-play. The word נֶפֶשׁ nepheš [literally, 'soul']
is used here in three different senses: בְּנַפְשׁוֹ *benaphšō* ['with the
soul'] means: together with the element of life therein; לְנַפְשֹׁתֵיכֶם
lenaphšōthēkhem ['unto your souls'] signifies: which is in you, of
yourselves [rendered: 'your own']; אֶת נֶפֶשׁ הָאָדָם *'eth nepheš
hā'ādhām* ['the soul of man'] connotes his actual life.

6. *Whoever sheds the blood of man, by man shall his blood be
shed*] — a judicial statute formulated in lapidary style. Note the
chiastic parallelism, which repeats in the second member of the
sentence every word of the first in reverse order, as though reflecting
the principle of measure for measure.

By man] — by the hand of man. The other suggested explanations of the verse do not accord with the simple sense of the text.

For in the image of God, etc.] — the reason for the penalty of
death. Whoever slays a human being expunges God's image from
the world. At the first blush one might indeed suppose that on the
basis of this reason it would be wrong to put a murderer to death,
for he, too, was created in the Divine image. But the Bible apparently implies that the murderer has, as it were, erased the Divine
likeness from himself by his act of murder.

127

Was man made [literally, 'made (masc. sing.) man'] / It does not mean: God made man, for in that case the text should have read: *I made* (and so the Septuagint translated, wishing, apparently, to interpret the verse as simply as possible). The verb in the third person is to be construed as having an indefinite or impersonal subject, connoting: *man was made.*

7. *And you,* etc.] In order to end on a happy note, the conclusion of the address reiterates the blessing with which it began and corroborates it. The word *you* stands, as it were, in antithesis to the *I* of the Speaker: *I,* on my side [God declares], have set forth in My present utterance your primary rights and duties, which serve as the foundation of human social life; and *you,* on your side, will be able to live securely in the shadow of My paternal care, be fruitful and multiply on the earth, and bring forth abundantly therein in order to renew the life of mankind. *You* fulfil your part, and *I* (*v.* 9) shall fulfil Mine.

And multiply [וּרְבוּ *ūrebhū*] in it] The Septuagint reads: *and have dominion* [וּרְדוּ *ūredhū*] *over it.* Many modern exegetes consider this reading correct, for in their view it is not possible that one word should occur twice in parallelism. Similarly, most expositors emend the text of such verses as Psa. xxxviii 11 [Hebrew, *v.* 12]: *My friends and companions* STAND [יַעֲמֹדוּ *yaʿămōdhū*] *aloof from my plague, and my kinsmen* STAND [עָמָדוּ *ʿāmādhū*] *afar off,* because they consider it inconceivable that the Psalmist should twice use the same verb in two hemistichs of a verse. But Biblical style evinces a fondness for verbal repetitions of this kind, with some change in the form or connotation of the word repeated. I have shown in an article in *Tarbiz* (xiv, pp. 9–10) that parallelism between the perfect and imperfect of the same stem, as in the verse from Psalms quoted above, was common already in Ugaritic poetry, and the practice continued in Biblical poetry; the change in the form of the verb was sufficient. With regard to change of signification, it will suffice to mention a passage like Gen. xlix 2: *Assemble and* HEARKEN [שִׁמְעוּ *šimeʿū*], *O sons of Jacob, and* HEARKEN [שִׁמְעוּ *šimeʿū*] *to Israel your father.* In this sentence, too, emendations have been proposed (to substitute הַאֲזִינוּ *haʾăzīnū* ['give ear'] or הַקְשִׁיבוּ *haqšībhū* ['attend', 'listen'] for one שִׁמְעוּ *šimeʿū*; or to read הִקָּבְצוּ *hiqqābheṣū* ['assemble'] without שִׁמְעוּ

šime'ū); and in this case, also, there is no need for emendation. In the first hemistich the word שִׁמְעוּ *šime'ū* is only part of the compound expression הִקָּבְצוּ וְשִׁמְעוּ *biqqābheṣū wešime'ū,* in which the primary idea is that of assembly, gathering, gathering for the purpose of hearing; in the second hemistich, the imperative שִׁמְעוּ *šime'ū* occurs alone, and the basic idea is that of listening. The same applies to our verse: the first time וּרְבוּ *ūrebhū* ['and multiply'] forms part of the compound expression פְּרוּ וּרְבוּ *perū ūrebhū* ['Be fruitful and multiply'], and signifies the raising up of seed, pro-creation; the second time it is used by itself, and its primary meaning is to increase numerically. The word וּרְדוּ *ūredhū* read by the Septuagint was copied here from i 28, and its sense is complete-ly foreign to the theme of our verse.

The intention to achieve alliteration is noticeable in this verse, in the repeated occurrence of the letter *Bēth* (possibly the letter *Pē'* also belongs to the scheme) : וְאַתֶּם פְּרוּ וּרְבוּ שִׁרְצוּ בָאָרֶץ וּרְבוּ בָהּ *we'attem Perū ureBHū šireṣū BHā'āreṣ ūreBHū BHāh* ['And you, be fruitful and multiply, bring forth abundantly on the earth and multiply in it'].

The conclusion of this paragraph corresponds to that of the eighth paragraph (viii 17).

ELEVENTH PARAGRAPH

THE DIVINE PROMISE TO FULFIL AND EXTEND THE COVENANT

8.   *Then God said / to Noah and to his sons with him, saying:*

9.   *'As for Me —*
     behold, I establish My covenant / through you
     and your descendants / after you,

10. *and with every living creature / that was with you,*
     the flying creatures, the cattle, / and every [other] *creature*
     of the earth / with you,

as many as came out of the ark, / even every creature of the
earth.

11. *I will establish My covenant / through you,*
   that never again shall all flesh be cut off / because of the
   waters of a flood,
   and never again shall there be a flood / to destroy the earth.'

This communication comes to extend the preceding one. At first
God confirmed the blessing that was bestowed upon Adam, and
assured its fulfilment in Noah and his sons; now He promises that
this benison will be realized in *all* their descendants, that is to say,
there will never again occur a universal cataclysm that will cut
off almost all their offspring, leaving only one family, as happened
in their days.

9. *As for Me —*] This parallels, as I have explained, the word
you in *v.* 7: *you* will be fruitful and multiply in security, and
I shall protect your lives. Compare further on, in the section of the
Circumcision: AS FOR ME, *behold, My covenant is with you* (xvii
4); and afterwards, AND AS FOR YOU, *you shall keep My covenant*
(ibid. *v.* 9).

Behold, I shall establish My covenant through you, etc.] For
the significance of this sentence and the nature of the covenant, see
above, my comments on vi 18. According to my conclusions there,
the covenant is a promise that they would be fertile and fill the
earth; here God reiterates the assurance given in the preceding
communication in order to extend it and include in it the future
generations. This extension will be expressly stated later on (*v.*
11), but it is already hinted at here in the expression, *and with
your descendants after you.* In this verse, and likewise in *v.* 11
(*I will establish My covenant through you*) and in *v.* 17 (*the
covenant which I established*), the Bible concludes the section with
words and concepts resembling those with which it began (vi 18:
But I will establish My covenant through you).

Through you [אִתְּכֶם *'ittᵉkhem,* literally, 'with you'] / The word
אִתְּכֶם *'ittᵉkhem* occurs four times in the paragraph, and each time
it comes at the end of its sentence, or at the end of a special part
of the sentence (in this verse, twice in *v.* 10, and once in *v.* 11);
in *v.* 8 we find אִתּוֹ *'ittō* ['with him']. Compare vi 18, viii 16–17.

There may be a word-play here on וְחִתְּכֶם *weḥittekhem* ['the dread of you'] in *v.* 2.

10. *And with every living creature, etc.*] Since no general destruction will come upon humanity, it follows that none will come upon the creatures either, as happened in the days of Noah. This promise is likewise implied in the expression *behold, I establish My covenant* of the preceding verse, for also to the creatures was the benison of fecundity granted when they were created: to the fish and the flying creatures expressly (i 22), and to the other species by implication (*ibid. v.* 25: *And God saw that it was good,* and whatever is good will, we may be sure, endure).

That was with you] That was with you in the ark and shared your lot; in the same way they are destined to share your fortune in the future.

The flying creatures, the cattle, and every [other] creature of the earth] After the general reference to *every living creature,* the details follow here in the usual way but with a difference of formulation, which also accords with normal practice. The purpose of the *Bēth* here is to explain and particularize.

As many as [מִכֹּל *mikkōl,* literally, 'from all'] *came out of the ark*] The prepositional *Mēm* has here the sense of *that is,* as above, vii 22, viii 17.

Even every [לְכֹל *lekhōl,* literally, 'to all'] *creature of the earth*] This expression is difficult. It is wanting in the Septuagint, and many modern exegetes delete it; but this method of solving difficulties is too easy. Interpretations have been suggested that connect the prepositional *Lāmedh* [of לְכֹל *lekhōl*] with the *Mēm* of מִכֹּל יֹצְאֵי הַתֵּבָה *mikkōl yōṣeʾē hattēbhā* ['as many as came out of the ark'] (the meaning being: 'from all the people who came out of the ark to every beast of the earth'; or 'both all the people who came out of the ark and all the beasts of the earth'), but they are unsatisfactory, because Biblical syntax does not permit such constructions. It has also been proposed to regard the expression under consideration as an addition for the purpose of generalization, as in xxiii 10: *of all* [לְכֹל *lekhōl*] *who went in at the gate of his city.* This explanation is more plausible, but there is still the difficulty that an almost identical phrase has already been used in our verse: וּבְכָל חַיַּת הָאָרֶץ *ūbhekhol ḥayyath hāʾāreṣ* [rendered: 'and every

131

[other] creature of the earth']. However, this repetition may be explained in the same way as the reiteration of the word וּרְבוּ *ūreḇḥū* ['and multiply'] in *v.* 7 (see *ibid.*), to wit, that the expression recurs in a different meaning. The first time it is connected with the words *the flying creatures, the cattle,* and means: all the other animals upon earth apart from the flying creatures and the cattle; here it is unrelated and has a general signification: all the living creatures upon earth.

11. *I will establish My covenant through you*] Here, at the end of the second Divine communication, the opening words are repeated in the same way as in the first communication. This repetition was particularly necessary after the interruption of the theme by the detailing of all those through whom God would establish His covenant.

That never again shall all flesh be cut off BECAUSE OF THE WATERS OF A FLOOD [מִמֵּי הַמַּבּוּל *mimmē hammabbūl*] / The words מִמֵּי הַמַּבּוּל *mimmē hammabbūl* [literally, 'from the waters of the flood'] are not to be construed, with many exegetes, as the *complement of the agent* after a passive verb. Such a construction is, indeed, quite usual in European languages, but is completely foreign to the Semitic tongues, which regard the passive as 'a verb whose agent is not named'. The expression מִמֵּי הַמַּבּוּל *mimmē hammabbūl* comes to indicate the cause or operative factor, as do the words with the prepositional suffix *Mēm* in the following sentences where there is no verb in the passive: AND RESULTING FROM [E. V. 'and with'] MY SONG [וּמִשִּׁירִי *ūmiššīrī*], *I give thanks unto Him* (Psa. xxviii 7); BECAUSE OF [E.V. 'At'] THY REBUKE [מִגַּעֲרָתְךָ *migga'ārāthekhā*], *O God of Jacob, both rider and horse lay dead* (ibid. lxxvi 6 [Hebrew, *v.* 7]); MAY THEY PERISH BECAUSE OF [E.V. 'at'] THE REBUKE OF [מִגַּעֲרַת *migga'ārath*] *Thy countenance* (*ibid.* lxxx 16 [Hebrew, *v.* 17]); BECAUSE OF [E.V. 'By'] THE BREATH OF [מִנִּשְׁמַת *minnišmath*] *God they perish,* AND ON ACCOUNT OF [E.V. 'by'] THE BLAST OF [וּמֵרוּחַ *ūmērūaḥ*] *His anger they are consumed* (Job iv 9); *and Thou dost terrify* ME BECAUSE OF [E.V. 'with'] *visions* [וּמֵחֶזְיוֹנוֹת *ūmēḥezyōnōth*] (*ibid.* vii 14).

All flesh] This phrase occurs here, in the penultimate paragraph, and several times again in the last paragraph (in *vv.* 15 [twice],

16, 17), in parallelism to the first two paragraphs, in which it appears four times (vi 12, 13, 17, 19).

And never again shall there be a flood] Not only shall all flesh not be cut off again as a result of the waters of a flood, but there will be no deluge in the world at all.

To destroy the earth] In this paragraph and in the concluding paragraph, which follows, we again find the stem שָׁחַת *šāḥath*, which has already been used several times in the first two paragraphs.

It is to this promise, which was given to Noah and his sons, that the words of the prophet apparently allude (Isa. liv 9): *For this is like the days of Noah to Me: as I swore that the waters of Noah should no more go over the earth.* Although the phrase *the waters of Noah* does not occur in our section, nor is an oath mentioned here, yet these elements may have existed in the ancient Israelite poetry relating to the Deluge (see the introduction to this section, pp. 24–26).

TWELFTH PARAGRAPH

THE SIGN OF THE COVENANT

12. *And God said,*
    'This is the sign of the covenant / which I make
    between Me and you / and every living creature / that is with you,
    for all generations:

13. *I have set My bow / in the cloud,*
    and it shall be a sign of the covenant / between Me and the earth.

14. *And it shall come to pass —*
    When I bring clouds / over the earth,
    and the bow is seen / in the clouds,

15. *I shall remember My covenant / which is between Me and you and every living creature / of all flesh;*

133

> *and the waters shall never again become a flood / to destroy*
>   *all flesh.*

16. *When the bow is / in the clouds,*
    I will look upon it / and remember the everlasting covenant
    between God / and every living creature
    of all flesh / that is upon the earth.'

17. *And God said to Noah,*
    'This is the sign of the covenant / which I have established
    between Me and all flesh / that is upon the earth.'

On the face of it, this paragraph appears to suffer from pleonasm; and the numerous repetitions of words and phrases make it difficult at first to grasp the tenor of thought and the connection between the verses. However, a certain wordiness is well suited to the formal conclusion of the section; and when we examine the verses carefully in detail, we can recognize the harmonious structure of the paragraph and the finished arrangement of the verses. Verse 12 introduces the theme of the paragraph: the institution of the sign of the covenant, which was to endure for ever between God and mankind and the animals on earth. Thereafter, the details are explained one by one. Verse 13 tells us that for the purpose of the sign the bow in the cloud is established *now*. In *vv.* 14–15, it is stated that it would be so not only now but also in the *future*: in time to come, too, when the bow would be seen in the cloud, it would serve as a sign and a reminder of the covenant. Verse 16 announces that the bow would fulfil this purpose not merely for a given period in the future, but *forever*. The last verse, *v.* 17, reverts to the theme with which the paragraph opens, after the pattern of the conclusion of the two preceding paragraphs, and gives to the entire section a formal ending.

The word *bow* occurs three times in connection with the word *cloud* (*v.* 13: *I set my bow in the cloud; v.* 14: *and the bow is seen in the cloud; v.* 16: *When the bow is in the clouds*). Three times we find the expression *every living creature* (*vv.* 12, 15, 16), and four times — in the last three verses — the term *all flesh*, indicating the universal application of the promise. Three times there appears the phrase *upon (over) the earth* (*vv.* 14, 16, 17), with which the paragraph and the section ends. The word *covenant,* which is common to the present and the preceding paragraphs and forms their principal theme, occurs seven times.

12. *This*] The object mentioned below, in *v.* 13. Possibly, however, the Bible implies that this announcement was made when the bow appeared in the cloud, and the word *this* points to it: this thing that you see in the sky. It should be noted that at this stage of the story we are at the beginning of the rainy season (viii 14).

The sign of the covenant] It is a sign and a reminder, so that you should not forget the covenant in the future. Likewise when God made a covenant with Abraham, a sign of the covenant was designated (xvii 11), and many of the expressions that appear here recur there. The individual covenant between the Lord and Israel corresponds to the general covenant between Him and all humanity.

Which I make [נֹתֵן *nōthēn*, literally, 'give'], etc.] This may be interpreted to mean: *the sign* that I establish (so the Septuagint understood it), or: *the covenant* that I establish. The verb נָתַן *nāthan* can be used for the institution of a sign, as in the next verse, and also for the making of a covenant, especially when there is no reciprocal obligation but only a unilateral assurance, as in the present instance and in Num. xxv 12: *Behold, I give to him My covenant of peace.* It is preferable to understand here, '*the covenant* which I make', since the expression *between Me and you* is better suited to a covenant than to a sign, and further on, in *v.* 15, it undoubtedly refers to a covenant. Furthermore, in *v.* 17, which parallels this verse, it is stated: *This is the sign of the covenant which I have established,* and the verb הֲקִים *bēqīm* ['established'] is appropriate only to a covenant, not to a sign. In the verb נָתַן *nāthan* in *v.* 13 is to be seen a word-play on its use here.

Every living creature] After all the multiform variations in the terms used to denote the different kinds of creatures, there occurs in this last paragraph, as though to mark the conclusion, the general expression *every living creature,* found in this verse and in *vv.* 15, 16 (it also occurs in the previous paragraph, *v.* 10, but there it appears as a general statement followed by the enumeration of details, and consequently it has the definite article).

FOR *all future* GENERATIONS [לְדֹרֹת *ledhōrōth*] / Towards the close of the section, Scripture employs again a word used in the opening verse (vi 9: בְּדֹרֹתָיו *bedhōrōthāw* ['in his generations']).

135

13. *My bow*] The story of the rainbow was, apparently, one of the episodes on which the ancient Israelite poetry concerning the Flood expatiated, but which were blurred and compressed in the Torah section so that the merest relic was left. The poetic saga may have related that after the Lord had used His bow to shoot arrows (that is, lightnings) at the Deluge storm, He hung it in the sky, intending not to use it again in this manner in the future. The Torah, in accordance with its usual practice, declined to accept the mythological portrayal of the Deity shooting arrows from His bow, and therefore retained only the final symbol, which is not in conflict with its concepts and principles. Indications of a more materialistic conception of the rainbow are to be found both among the Gentiles and the Israelites. But the Sumerian and Akkadian legends concerning the Flood, in so far as they are known to us, provide no parallel to our theme. Jensen conjectured that such a parallel may be found in the Epic of Gilgameš, which narrates that after the Deluge the goddess Ištar lifted up the pendants of lapis lazuli on her neck and swore that just as she would not forget her pendants so would she not forget those days; but this theory stands refuted at the very outset, since the two things compared are entirely different. However, parallels are to be found elsewhere. In the Babylonian Epic of Creation (vi 82 ff.) we are told that after Marduk's victory the bow that served him as a weapon in the battle was set in the sky and became a constellation. So, too, the pagan Arabs related of one of their gods that after discharging arrows from his bow, he set his bow in the cloud. There is no need to cite parallels from the myths of non-Semitic peoples, like the Indians, who regard the rainbow as Indra's war-bow. Needless to say, it is wholly superfluous to mention the beliefs of primitive peoples or the uncultured classes of our times in regard to the rainbow. Although these ideas can shed light on the pre-history of the concept, they cannot help us to understand the passage before us. More important is the fact that the Biblical prophets and poets, who are accustomed, as we have seen, to allude to the ancient Israelite epics, make many references to the bow and arrows of the Lord, which He uses when fighting against His foes. Particularly worthy of mention is the prayer of Habakkuk, which repeatedly alludes to ancient epic songs (see my Hebrew essay in *Keneseth,*

dedicated to the memory of H. N. Bialik, viii, pp. 121–142). It is stated there (Hab. iii 9): *Thou didst strip the sheath from Thy bow* [otherwise: *Thy bow is made quite bare*]*; and subsequently (*v.* 11): *at the light of Thy arrows as they sped.* According to some commentators the reference (*v.* 9) is actually to the Flood. Similar examples are to be found in other parts of the Bible, even if we attach no special importance in this regard to the words of Balaam (Num. xxiv 8: *and pierce through with his arrows*), which were possibly intended to reflect the thought of the Gentile diviner. In the Song of *Ha'ăzīnū* (Deut. xxxii 23) it is written: *I will spend my arrows upon them;* and again *ibid. v.* 42: *I will make My arrows drunk with blood.* In the Song of David (ii Sam. xxii 15; Psa. xviii 15) we read: *And he sent out arrows* (His arrows) *and scattered them.* Compare also Zech. ix 14; Psa. xxxviii 2 [Hebrew, *v.* 3]; lxiv 8; lxxvii 17 [Hebrew, *v.* 18]; cxliv 6; Job vi 4; Lam. ii 4; iii 12 (in Psa. vii 13, the reference is not to the bow of the Lord but to that of the wicked man). Although one may suppose that in some of these verses, especially in the later ones, only a figurative expression is intended, yet in the earliest passages there is apparently an allusion to a still earlier literary tradition that conceived the matter in a materialistic light. The ancient poem on the Flood must have contained, so far as we are able to surmise, similar expressions; in the prose account of the Torah there is no trace left of the rainbow except as a shining sign of grace and lovingkindness from Heaven, and as a symbol of the fatherly love of the Creator towards His creatures.

The ancient idea of the war-bow remained, at least in the folk memory, even when the early epic poetry had already been forgotten by Israel, and it assumed once again a literary form in the Midrashim. Thus, for example, we find in the Midrash Haggadol, Genesis, edited by Margulies, p. 185: 'The Holy One blessed be He ... punished the world with a bow, for it is written: *Thou didst strip the sheath from Thy bow*', etc.; and in Midrash Leqah Tob, Buber's edition, p. 48: '*I have set My bow in the cloud*: This refers to the waters of the Flood ... *when the bow is in the clouds, I shall see it:* when I bent My bow, I brought thereby a flood; but from now on I shall see it that it is not bent.'

I have set [נָתַתִּי *nāthattī*, the perfect, literally, 'I have given'] /

Many scholars have understood this expression in a present sense, as in xxiii 13: I GIVE [נָתַתִּי *nāthattī*] *the price of the field; accept it from me.* But this interpretation does not appear to be correct, for in the preceding verse it is stated: *which* I MAKE [אֲנִי נֹתֵן *'ănī nōthēn*, literally, 'I give'], and it seems that the text wished to distinguish between אֲנִי נֹתֵן *'ănī nōthēn* and נָתַתִּי *nāthattī*. The meaning is not that the bow was then created for the first time, but that at that time a new symbolic meaning was given to the bow. It is as though God declared to Noah and his sons: At the end of the Flood you doubtless saw the bow, which is normally seen in the clouds after rain, even as you see it at this moment; and just as the rainbow marked for you then the termination of your grievous experience, so shall it mark for you now and also in the future the assurance of the fulfilment of My covenant for your good.

In the cloud] In point of fact, the rainbow is not always seen in the cloud. A person sees it, as we know, when the sun shines behind him, that is to say, when the clouds no longer overcast the sun. If at the time there are clouds in the sky in front of the observer, then he sees the rainbow against the background of the clouds; but if it happens that there are no clouds on that side either, the rainbow is seen by him against the blue of the sky. Apparently the nexus between the words *bow* and *cloud* was traditional in the literary style of the Bible, as we see also in Ezekiel i 28: *Like the appearance of the bow that is in the cloud on the day of rain.* Once the tradition was established it remained, even though it does not always conform to the actuality.

And it shall be a sign of the covenant between Me and the earth] From now on the rainbow will be a sign of the covenant. So, too, it is written with reference to the covenant with the patriarch Abraham (Gen. xvii 11): *and it shall be a sign of the covenant between Me and you.*

14. *When I bring clouds over the earth, and the bow is seen in the clouds*] The verse is not to be interpreted, as many do: 'When I bring clouds over the earth, then the bow will be seen in the clouds', for not on every occasion when there are clouds is there a rainbow. The meaning is rather, as other commentators explain: 'When I bring clouds over the earth, and the bow is seen in the clouds, then *I will remember*, etc. (*v.* 15).

15. *I will remember,* etc.] According to Rashi, and also according to the usual exegesis of present-day commentators, the sense is: When I gather clouds over the earth in order to bring destruction upon the world, the rainbow will remind Me of My covenant, and I shall refrain from doing what I thought to do. This interpretation is difficult, for the rainbow does not appear until after the rain has ceased, and if its function is to remind God that the rain must not be allowed to continue a long time as it did in the days of Noah, the rainbow would come too late. In order to understand the purport of the passage, we must compare this verse and the succeeding statement (*I will remember . . . I will look upon it and remember the everlasting covenant,* etc.) with what we are told in Num. xv 39, in connection with another sign, the sign of the fringes: *that you may look upon it and remember all the commandments of the Lord, and do them.* There the thought is certainly not that immediately upon seeing the fringes a man will perform all the precepts of the Torah, but that since he will *constantly* look on the fringes, he will always remember the commandments and do them whenever the opportunity arises. Similarly here: since God will always see the bow in the cloud, He will ever remember His promise, and the thought will never enter His mind to bring a flood upon the world. And the sign will be of greater service to mankind than to God. The whole purpose of this third communication is to give confidence to Noah and his sons in the future. The fact that the Bible tells us here that God *announced* to them the sign implies that it is to them that the announcement is important. They will always see the sign, and this constant observation will be a sign and token of the promise of God, who remembers the covenant.

The expression of remembrance, which occurs in this verse and the next, corresponds to the one found at the beginning of the second part of our section (viii 1); see my annotations there and on the preceding verse.

And every living creature OF [־בְּ *be*, literally, 'in'] *all flesh*] See the notes to *v.* 12. The phrase commencing with the prepositional *Bēth* is explicative.

And the waters shall never again BECOME [יִהְיֶ֫ה *yihᵉye*] *a flood*] The waters, that is, the rain and the waters of the deep, will never

139

again be turned into a deluge (the verb יִהְיֶה *yiheye* is in the singular because it precedes the subject).

To destroy all flesh] — that is, in such a way that all flesh will be destroyed. Regarding the stem שָׁחַת *šaḥath,* see above, on *v.* 11.

16. *When the bow is in the clouds*] So it shall be constantly, for ever.

I will look upon it and remember the everlasting covenant] For the exposition of the subject, see on *v.* 15. The new point made by this verse lies in the word עוֹלָם *ʿōlām* ['ever', 'everlasting'],

17. *This*] — which I have already mentioned.

This verse repeats, with few changes and in shortened form, the exordium of the paragraph, following the pattern that we observed in the two preceding paragraphs. It forms a fitting conclusion to the entire section by reiterating its opening expressions (*the covenant which I have established* corresponds to vi 18: *But I shall establish My covenant through you;* the words *upon the earth* come at the end of the last verse here just as they do at the conclusion of the first paragraph), and by reaffirming the good tidings, to wit, the promise of life to all the creatures *that are upon the earth.*

SECTION TWO

THE SONS OF NOAH

CHAPTER IX, VERSE 18 — CHAPTER XI, VERSE 9

GENERAL INTRODUCTION

§ 1. *Delimitation of the Section.* The entire portion from ix 18 to xi 9 constitutes a single, unitary section, although it includes (after the two verses ix 18–19, which form the exordium of the entire section) three wholly unrelated themes, namely:

(a) The story of Noah's intoxication (ix 20–27), followed by a concluding passage on Noah's death (ix 28–29).

(b) The history of Noah's descendants (ch. x).

(c) The story of the Generation of Division (xi 1–9).

Although it is manifest that in the ancient tradition each of these three subjects was an independent theme and pursued its own course of development, yet in the Book before us they are all three linked together and have become a single unit that can no longer be dismembered.

The unmistakable sign that marks the unity of the section and determines its extent is the framework in which the Torah arranged the three topics mentioned. In the two opening verses (ix 18–19) it is stated that from the sons of Noah who went out of the ark *the whole earth* WAS PEOPLED [נָפְצָה *nāphᵉṣā*, literally, 'was scattered'], and in the last verse (xi 9) we are told: *and from there the Lord* SCATTERED THEM ABROAD [הֱפִיצָם *hēphîṣām*] *over the face of all the earth.* The exordium alludes to the main theme of the section, which is the dispersion of Noah's descendants in all parts of the earth; the continuation of the section proceeds to explain in detail the manner in which the dispersion was effected; and the last verse indicates it as the final outcome of the course of events.

From this it follows that it is not possible for us to understand these passages properly unless we pay attention to the inter-

141

connecting links between them and to the purport of the section as a whole. To study each of its themes as though it were an independent entity, as all the expositors are accustomed to do, is to close the way to full understanding of the text. It is, indeed, worth while making the attempt to trace the separate origin and the evolution of the subject matter of each part of our section in the ancient tradition preceding its composition; and we, too, shall do this in the introduction to each individual subsection. Without doubt there is much benefit to be derived from such an investigation, but we must not forget that the primary task of a commentator is to elucidate the text before him, and that the study of the sources and the stages of development that preceded this text is only a means to the fulfilment of his task.

Apart from the framework, which marks the opening and close of the section, as I have explained, there are other indications of its unity: some of these are internal, relating to the content; and some are external, appertaining to the form. Let us endeavour to understand each of these categories of evidence.

§ 2.   The theme of the division and dispersion of Noah's descendants is not only indicated at the beginning and at the end, as we have noted, but runs like a golden thread throughout the whole section, integrating all its parts into one organic whole. After the reference in the opening verses to the fact that from the three sons of Noah the inhabitants of the whole earth had sprung and spread abroad, comes the first narrative, the story of the intoxication of Noah, which portrays the special character of each of the three branches of mankind that stemmed from the three sons of Noah. This is followed by the second subsection, the genealogy of chapter x, which details the offspring of Noah's sons and tells how all the peoples of the earth evolved from them. Finally, there is the third part, the story of the Generation of Division, which explains how the languages of the various peoples became differentiated.

Wellhausen already pointed out, and most scholars have agreed, that there is a contradiction between the genealogy set forth in chapter x and the story of the Generation of Division: chapter x explains the existence of various peoples in the world as a result of natural genealogical development, without any allusion to mir-

142

acles and direct Divine interposition, whereas the story of the Division attributes the ethnic diversification of mankind to the direct intervention of the Lord, who suddenly changed the course of events in supernatural fashion. The two accounts are thus in conflict.

There can be no doubt that there are two distinct accounts here of different origin. But this fact does not yet impugn the unity of our section in its present form; conceivably the Torah utilized two different traditions in the composition of this section. It is possible that on the one hand the Torah took material for its construction from the tradition of the "wise men", who reflected on the relationship between the families of peoples and sought to establish their original unity on a genealogical basis; and on the other hand, it also derived material from the tradition current among the people at large, which explained the ramification of humanity in a dramatic and marvellous manner. There is no incongruity between these two parts of the section, for their purpose is not, as Wellhausen and his followers thought, to offer two different and contradictory explanations of a *single* phenomenon. On the contrary, the two accounts are complementary and necessary to each other. The pedigree of chapter x does not suffice to explain the existence of the various *tongues* in the world: it shows the genealogical relationship between the peoples, but this is not enough to account for the differences of language. Contrariwise, this chapter gives rise to a serious question. It states that all the peoples of the earth are the descendants of only three brothers, the sons of one man. Now normally brothers have one common language. How then is it possible to explain the fact that there are many different tongues in the world? The story of the Generation of Division provides an answer to this question. On the other hand, the story of the Generation of Division was inadequate by itself, because, although it explains why there are different languages in the world, it does not tell us why there exist precisely these particular languages belonging to these particular peoples. For the answer to this question we require chapter x.

Another point. The problem mentioned — to wit, the question of the existence of various languages — does not merely arise by implication from what is stated in chapter x. On the contrary, it is expressly alluded to in that chapter, in the expression *each with his*

143

own language or *by their languages,* which is repeated in connection with each one of the three branches of mankind (*vv.* 5, 20, 31). This phrase serves, as it were, to draw the attention of the reader to the problem, and to prepare him to peruse with curiosity what is related in the next chapter, which actually begins with a reference to language: *Now the whole earth had one speech and a single language.* This exordium comes, as it were, to tell us: It was, in truth, the case that all the persons mentioned in the preceding chapter, who were related to one another, spoke at first one language, but an event occurred that changed the position; and this is what happened.

The use of the different terms לָשׁוֹן *lāšōn* and שָׂפָה *śāphā* [both rendered 'language'] — the former in ch. x and the latter in ch. xi — is not to be regarded, with the adherents of the documentary hypothesis, as an indication of exact quotation from two sources that differ from each other in their style and vocabulary, one source using לָשׁוֹן *lāšōn* and the other שָׂפָה *śāphā*. Anyone holding this view shows that his feeling for Hebrew usage is imperfect. The nouns לָשׁוֹן *lāšōn* and שָׂפָה *śāphā* cannot always be interchanged; it would certainly have been impossible to say: לִשְׂפֹתָם *liśephōthām* instead of לִלְשֹׁנֹתָם *lilešōnōthām* ['by their languages']. The word שָׂפָה *śāphā* in the sense of a *spoken language* is used in Biblical Hebrew only in the singular. Nor would it have been possible to say אִישׁ לִשְׂפָתוֹ ' *îš liśephāthō* in place of אִישׁ לִלְשֹׁנוֹ ' *îš lilešōnō* ['each with his own language'], for two reasons: first, on account of the parallelism with the verses containing לִלְשֹׁנֹתָם *lilešōnōthām;* and secondly because an expression such as אִישׁ לִשְׂפָתוֹ ' *îš liśephāthō* would not have been clear in Hebrew and could have been construed in various ways. Whenever we find a concept of this kind in the Bible, it is expressed by לָשׁוֹן *lāšōn* and not by שָׂפָה *śāphā* (Esther i 22: *and to every people in its own language;* ibid. iii 12: *and every people in its own language;* ibid. viii 9: *and to every people in its language;* Nehemiah xiii 24: *but the language of each people* [in each of these instances לְשׁוֹ(ו)ן *lāšōn* is used]). One may perhaps add that in general, when there is no need to use both synonyms for the sake of parallelism, as in Isa. xxxiii 19 and Ezek. iii 5–6, Biblical Hebrew prefers the word שָׂפָה *śāphā* if the reference is to a given language considered by itself, not in relation to other tongues, and the word לְשׁוֹ(ן) *lāšōn*, when it is intended to express relationship and differentiation between languages. It will suffice to consider such passages as Isa. xix 18: *which speak* THE LANGUAGE OF [שְׂפַת *sephath*] *Canaan;* Zeph. iii 9: *Yea, at that time I will change the speech of the peoples to a pure* SPEECH [שָׂפָה *sāphā*]; Deut. xxviii 49: *a nation* WHOSE LANGUAGE [לְשֹׁנוֹ *lešōnō*] *you do not understand;* Jer. v 15: *a nation* WHOSE LANGUAGE [לְשׁוֹנוֹ *lešōnō*] *you do not understand;* so, too, Isa. xxviii 11: *by men of strange* LIPS [שָׂפָה *sāphā*] *and with an alien* TONGUE [לָשׁוֹן *lāšōn*]. The same obtains when the meaning of the word לְשֹׁנוֹת *lešōnōth* ['languages'] is transferred from the signification of 'various languages' to the sense of 'various peoples', as in Isa. lxvi 18, Zech. viii 23 (compare also the expression mentioned above, like לִלְשֹׁנֹתָם *lilešōnōthām,* אִישׁ לִלְשׁוֹנוֹ *îš lilešōnō,* עַם וָעָם כִּלְשׁוֹנוֹ *'am wā'ām kilešōnō* ['every people in its own language']. Now in Gen. xi 1–9, the only language of humanity prior to the dispersion is spoken of, when there were no other forms of speech. Hence it was right, according to the usage of Biblical Hebrew, that the word שָׂפָה *sāphā* should be used there, both when mention is made of its universality (v. 1: *one* SPEECH [שָׂפָה *sāphā*] *and a single language;* v. 6: *and they have all one* LANGUAGE [שָׂפָה *sāphā*]), and when the termination of its sole use is recorded (*v. 7: and there confuse* THEIR LANGUAGE [שְׂפָתָם *sephāthām*]; *v. 9: because there the Lord confused* THE LANGUAGE OF [שְׂפַת *sephath*] *all the earth*). Only in the last clause of *v. 7* (*that they may not understand one another's* SPEECH [שְׂפַת *sephath*]) the word לָשׁ *lāšōn* could have been used in place of שָׂפָה *sāphā,* but the parallelism and connection with the first part of the verse caused the word שָׂפָה *sāphā* to be preferred there, too.

This apart, there appears to be some link between the mighty deeds of Nimrod and the construction of the cities built by him (x 8–12), on the one hand, and what is related in chapter xi of the pride of the Generation of Division and the buildings that they erected, on the other.

It should also be pointed out that in each of the three parts of the section there is a reference to the idea of 'beginning': *Noah, the master of the earth, was the first* [literally, 'began'] *to plant a vineyard* (ix 20); *he was the first* [literally, 'began'] *to be a mighty man on earth* (x 8); *and this is only the beginning of what they will do* (xi 6).

§ 3. Further evidence of the internal nexus between the parts of our section is to be found in a number of details that appear incomprehensible, if we study each part as a separate entity, but are easily explicable if we treat the section as a unified whole.

One of these details is the expression *his youngest son* in ix 24. A variety of strange suggestions have been advanced in explanation of it, and in truth we cannot understand it, if we detach the story of Noah's drunkenness from its context. But if we regard the section as a single sequence, it provides us with the means of finding the correct interpretation, as we shall show later. Similarly, if we treat the story of the Generation of Division as an isolated narrative, it will not be easy for us to grasp instantly the connection between the land of Shinar mentioned at the commencement of the story and the name Babel that appears suddenly at the end. But if we read the whole section as one indivisible unit, and we recall that we read earlier (x 10) that *Babel* was the beginning of Nimrod's kingdom in the land of *Shinar,* it all becomes clear of its own accord, and the very words *in the land of Shinar* in xi 2 lead us to expect that in the continuation of the story *Babel* will be mentioned.

We have already seen in the previous paragraph that the expressions *each with his own language* and *by their languages* in chapter x (*vv.* 5, 20, 31) refer to the dispersion described in chapter xi, and it is hardly necessary to draw attention to the explicit reference in *v.* 25: *for in his days the earth was* DIVIDED.

A more important point. Noah's utterances concerning the future of Canaan, Shem and Japhet, especially the threefold reference to the status of Canaan as a slave (ix 25–27), appear to present an insoluble riddle. All kinds of forced and strange explanations of the verses have been put forward, and not one of them is acceptable. The reason for this is that the expositors sought to explain the story as an independent narrative. But we shall show later in our commentary that if we consider our whole section as a single sequence, and this sequence as an inseparable part of the entire Book of Genesis, we shall have no difficulty in understanding Noah's words simply and clearly; indeed the interpretation is so simple and clear that it is surprising that the commentators before me did not think of it.

§ 4. Let us now pass on to the external indications that testify, jointly with the framework, to the unity of our section.

A point that is not actually decisive, but may nevertheless be worthy of mention without our attributing to it undue importance, is the copulative *Wāw* at the beginning of chapter x (*And this is the history of the sons of Noah*), which connects this chapter with the one preceding. It is inconclusive evidence because, as we know, the copulative *Wāw* is often found even at the commencement of a book. However, the fact that this chapter opens with the copulative *Wāw* and the next section does not (xi 10: *This is the history of Shem*), is deserving of attention.

More important are the signs of numerical symmetry. We have already observed in the preceding sections, beginning with the story of Creation (Part I, pp. 12 ff.), that the words expressing the principal ideas of the section are usually repeated a given number of times — seven times or a multiple of seven. Now here the word אֶרֶץ *'ereṣ* ['earth', 'land'], which is the key word in this section whose aim is to describe how the descendants of Noah spread abroad over the face of the whole earth, occurs fourteen times in the section — twice times *seven*. Furthermore, it occurs precisely *seven* times in the account of the distribution of Noah's offspring and their division and dispersal (ix 19: *and from these the whole* EARTH *was peopled;* x 5: *From these the coastland peoples spread in their* LANDS; x 25: *the* EARTH *was divided;* x 32: *and from these the nations spread abroad on the* EARTH; xi 4: *lest we be scattered abroad upon the face of the whole* EARTH; xi 8: *So the Lord scattered them abroad from there over the face of all the* EARTH; xi 9: *and from there the Lord scattered them abroad over the face of all the* EARTH). If we dismember the section, this symmetry is destroyed.

Other important indications of the unity of the section are to be found in the verbal parallels between its parts; with these we shall deal in the course of our annotations.

§ 5. In the commentary that follows, each part of the section will be preceded by its own introduction.

OPENING VERSES OF SECTION

18. *The sons of Noah / who went forth from the ark were Shem, Ham, and Japheth. / Ham was the father of Canaan.*

19. *These three were the sons of Noah; / and from these the whole earth was peopled.*

18. *And the sons of Noah,* etc.] The object of this verse is not to tell us who the sons of Noah were, and those who have interpreted it in this way and consequently have assigned it to a different source from that of the preceding verses, which have already mentioned Shem, Ham and Japheth (v 32; vi 10; vii 13), have misunderstood it. This verse and the next come to underline the contrast between the small number of Noah's sons who left the ark — that is, who remained on the earth after the Flood — and the great multitude of the earth's inhabitants subsequently, and to tell us that nevertheless this vast population came into being only through the descendants of these three men. Similarly the Bible, at the beginning of the Book of Exodus, lists the sons of Jacob in full, and states the exiguous total of the members of their households, in order to emphasize that from such a small group the whole people of Israel arose, *so that the land was filled with them.*

Who went forth from the ark] These three only of the 'younger' generation were saved from the waters of the Deluge and were privileged to leave their place of refuge when the cataclysm had passed, and on these three alone rested all hope for the continued life of humanity. These words recall to our minds the terrible catastrophe that was described in the preceding section, and enable us to see, as it were, the world-wide emptiness existing outside the ark. They also provide a verbal parallel to the conclusion of the previous section (ix 10: *went forth from the ark*).

Shem, Ham and Japheth] — only these, mentioned here by name; none other.

Ham was the father of Canaan] A preliminary announcement is made here in accordance with the established principle of Biblical narrative style, in order that the reader should be able to understand what will subsequently be told of Canaan in the story of Noah's intoxication. On this subject see my observations in the introduction to that story, § 3.

19. *These three were the sons of Noah*] They were only three, no more.

And from these the whole earth was peopled] Although they were only three, they succeeded in raising up descendants in such large numbers that from them there went forth and spread abroad all the people of the earth (this is the significance of the expression *the whole earth* in this verse and in xi 1), and by their dispersion they were able to fill the earth, in accordance with the blessing bestowed upon them by God (ix 1): *Be fruitful and multiply, and fill the earth.* There is thus a thematic connection between the present section and the one preceding, apart from the verbal link through the word הָאָרֶץ *hā'āreṣ*.

A. THE STORY OF NOAH'S INTOXICATION

(IX 20–29)

INTRODUCTION

§ 1. THE PURPOSE of this narrative in its present form is to characterize, from the viewpoint of Israel's Torah, the three branches of mankind that are descended from the three sons of Noah, and to illustrate their attributes by reference to the personality of their primogenitors. To the *sons of Shem* belongs the spiritual merit that they, or at least their great men, preserved the knowledge of *YHWH* (*v.* 26: *Blessed be YHWH, the God of Shem*), who guided them in the paths of moral righteousness. This knowledge was handed down in the course of the generations to Abraham, who proclaimed it to the world and dedicated thereto his life and the lives of his sons and spiritual heirs. The *sons of Ham* — especially those of them who came in direct contact with the children of Israel, namely, the Egyptians and Canaanites — acted in sexual matters in accordance with customs that the Israelite conscience regarded as utterly abominable. Not without reason does the section on Forbidden Relations begin with these words (Lev. xviii 3): *You shall not do as they do in the land of Egypt, where*

you dwelt, and you shall not do as they do in the land of Canaan,
to which I am bringing you. You shall not walk in their statutes.
Nor is it stated without cause at the end of the section (*vv.* 24 ff.) :
Do not defile yourselves by any of these things, for by all these
the nations I am casting out before you defiled themselves; and the
land became defiled, so that I punished its iniquity, and the land
vomited out its inhabitants. But you shall keep My statutes and My
ordinances and do none of these abominations, either the native or
the stranger who sojourns among you (for all of these abominations
the men of the land did, who were before you, so that the land be-
came defiled); lest the land vomit you out, when you defile it, as it
vomited out the nation that was before you. As for the *sons of*
Japheth, who were not so well known to the Israelites, it was sufficient, in their case, to indicate negative qualities: on the one hand
they did not attain to the knowledge of *YHWH* as did the sons of
Shem, but only to a general conception of the Godhead (in *v.* 27,
God enlarge Japheth, the name אֱלֹהִים *'Elōhīm* ['God'] occurs and
not the personal name *YHWH,* as in *v.* 26 in connection with
Shem), and on the other hand, they did not practise morally reprehensible customs like the sons of Ham, but were comparable in
this respect to the sons of Shem.

All these characteristics of the three branches of humanity are
presented to us by the narrative as though they were embodied —
and forecast — in the different personalities of the three eponyms.
§ 2. It is in truth difficult to determine what was the original form
of the narrative concerning the three sons of Noah in the tradition
preceding the Torah. But it may be surmised that at first the story
about Ham's deed had a coarser and uglier character than the
Biblical tale. From the writings of Philo Byblius we learn that there
was current among the Canaanites a legend regarding one of their
gods — El-Kronos ['Ηλος Κρόνος] — who approached his father
and with the knife in his hand perpetrated an act that prevented
him from begetting any more children. Similar legends are found
in great number in the mythology of oriental peoples and the
Greeks, and there is no need to cite many examples. It may be
that the original tradition from which our narrative emanated
described an episode of this nature or possibly an even more sordid
act. The view has been advanced that the Torah narrative itself

150

included such an incident at first, but that subsequently the account was abridged (see, for instance, the commentary of Holzinger or that of Gunkel). So, too, the Talmudic sages understood the story (see B. Sanhedrin 70a: 'Rab and Samuel [differ], one maintaining that he castrated him, and the other that he abused him sexually'), and in like vein Ibn Ezra comments on *v*. 24: 'Scripture has not revealed what was done.' Although it is possible that the recollection of an ancient tale about an extremely vile deed survived among the Israelites throughout the generations, and that it is reflected in rabbinic legends, yet this is not the meaning of the Pentateuchal story according to its simple sense. The Torah slurs over the shameful aspect of the ancient story, reducing it to minimal proportions. There were a number of reasons for this:

(a)   It was not right to attribute to one who merited to be delivered from the waters of the Flood so disgusting an act.

(b)   In general, it was not fitting to include in the Pentateuch an episode so abhorrent — far more repulsive, in fact, than the incident of the daughters of Lot (who, in the ultimate analysis, acted in good faith), and even worse than that of Er and Onan.

(c)   It was worth while teaching that even conduct like that portrayed in the present narrative was something that the sensitive Israelite conscience found shocking and regarded as an unforgivable sin.

No evidence can be adduced from the expression, *and [Ham] ... saw the nakedness of his father* (*v*. 22), which is found elsewhere in the Pentateuch in connection with actual sexual relations (Lev. xx 17: *If a man takes his sister, a daughter of his father or a daughter of his mother, and* SEES HER NAKEDNESS, *and* SHE SEES HIS NAKEDNESS, *it is a shameful thing* etc.), for of Shem and Japheth it is said, in contradistinction to Ham's action: *their faces were turned away,* AND THEY DID NOT SEE THEIR FATHER'S NAKEDNESS (*v*. 23), from which we may infer, conversely, that Ham's sin consisted of seeing only. Furthermore, the statement (*ibid.*), *and covered the nakedness of their father,* supports this interpretation: if the covering was an adequate remedy, it follows that the misdemeanour was confined to seeing. And it is the seeing itself, the looking, that is accounted by the refined sensitivity of the Israelite as something disgusting, especially when it is associated, as it is here, with an affront to the dignity of one's father. This is also the case in the aforementioned verse of the Book of Leviticus: even the seeing, the looking with unclean intent, is in itself a shameful thing when it disgraces the family relationship between brother and sister. It is also worth while comparing, in order to understand the Israelite attitude to these matters and to the Gentile practices in relation to them, Habakkuk's declaration in chapter ii 15, which is likewise connected with drunknness: *Woe to him who makes his neighbours drink, that put your venom thereto and make him drunken also, that you may look on their nakedness.'* [the translation is based on the version of the Jewish Publication Society of America]. The prophet speaks there of the Babylonians, and according to Gen. x 10 Babel [i. e. Babylon] was the beginning of the kingdom of Nimrod the son of Cush, the son of Ham; possibly his intention was to allude to what is stated here in Genesis.

Nor is any proof to be adduced from the clause in *v. 24, and knew what his youngest son had* DONE *to him,* that the words refer to an actual *deed.* At most one may regard it as a relic of the ancient tradition. But even this supposition is unnecessary. The seeing itself and the conversation in which Ham *told* the story *to his two brothers outside,* that is to say, the derision he brought upon his father and the unchaste talk — these things are in themselves forbidden acts. Since these deeds dishonoured the father, even the words *to him* after the verb *had done* are understandable.

Hence, irrespective of the content of the ancient tradition preceding the Torah, we must not read into the Pentateuchal narrative more than it actually states, taking the words at their face value.

The primary sin of Ham was his transgression against sexual morality, the disrespect shown to his father being only an aggravation of the wrong. The Canaanites were not reputed to be guilty of offences against paternal honour. On the contrary, from the Ugaritic epic of Danel and Aqhat, which lists the commandments that a son has to fulfil towards his father, we learn that the Canaanites included among these precepts also the duty of holding the father's hand when he was in his cups ('takes him by the hand when he is drunk, carries him when he is filled with wine'). But the Canaanites were suspect in the eyes of the Israelites, as we noted from the section on Forbidden Relations, of sexual offences against relatives.

§ 3.   The exegetes have experienced great difficulty in explaining the curse pronounced on Canaan, for they find it hard to comprehend why Canaan should be cursed for a sin that not he, but his father, committed. Numerous solutions of various kinds have been proposed, and they may be divided into three categories:

(a)   The first type comprises explanations that seek to justify the transference of the punishment from the father to the son. Thus, for example, according to one of the opinions expressed in rabbinic literature, Canaan was cursed in his father's stead because his father had already been vouchsafed God's benison (ix 1), and a curse cannot rest where blessing has been bestowed (Bereshith Rabba xxxvi 7). Other sages take the view that the curse fell on Canaan in accordance with the law of retaliation: Ham prevented his father from raising up a fourth son, hence his fourth son was cursed (Bereshith Rabba, *loc. cit.*); or, put differently: Ham, who was the youngest son of Noah, sinned against his father; hence he was punished by the curse set upon his youngest son (Delitzsch and others).

(b)   The second class includes the interpretations of those who hold that although the name of Canaan is explicitly mentioned, the reference is not really to Canaan but to his father. Thus, for instance, R. Saadia Gaon considers that the words *cursed be Canaan* are to be understood as though the verse read, *cursed be the father of Canaan*. Koenig conjectures that at first *Ham* was the actual reading of the text, but subsequently the name was changed to conform to the fact that the Canaanites were subjugated by the Israelites. In this way, it seems, the passage was understood by the redactors of several recensions of the Septuagint, which substituted the name of Ham for that of Canaan.

(c)   There is still a third group: solutions based on the assumption that according to the purport of the text, or of its source, Canaan himself was the transgressor, or at least was an accessory to his father's iniquity. This supposition, too, is already found in traditional Jewish literature. According to one of the interpretations in Bereshith Rabba (*loc. cit.*), Canaan saw and told Ham. Other haggadic passages attribute to Canaan the disgraceful act alluded to above (see, for example, Pirke Rabbi Eliezer, xxiii, and Zohar Ḥadash, Venice edition, 1663, p. 35 b; and compare Ibn Ezra on *v.* 22: 'The text does not reveal what was done, but the perpetrator of the deed was Canaan. It happened thus: Ham saw and did not cover him [Noah] as did his brothers; he only made the matter known, and Canaan heard. But what he did we do not know'). This line of exegesis, with individual variations of interpretation, is followed by many commentators in modern times. Ilgen in his day suggested that we should read in *v.* 22: וַיַּרְא חָם כְּנַעַן *wayyar' Ḥām Kᵉna'an,* and he naively thought that these Hebrew words could bear the meaning that Ham showed the thing to Canaan. In Wellhausen's opinion the original form of the narrative spoke of three sons of Noah — Shem, Japheth and *Canaan,* and it was the latter, the youngest of them, who sinned against his father; only, one of the editors altered *v.* 18 and added, in *v.* 22, the words *Ham the father of.* Many exegetes — for instance Budde and Gunkel — agreed with this view; others were in partial agreement with it, for example, Dillmann, who thought it possible that in the original narrative Canaan was the offender, but not that Shem and Japheth were his brothers. Others, again, express other views.

It is difficult to find a satisfactory solution among these explanations. Some of them are fanciful interpretations that do not accord with the natural sense of the text, and others are arbitrary conjectures without any basis. However, there is no need to explain anything. If we understand the verses correctly, there is no problem, and the whole thing is very simple.

Noah's utterance, in which he curses Canaan and speaks of his servitude to Shem and Japheth, is not directed against the man Canaan, the son of Ham, but against the Canaanite *people,* the descendants of Canaan many generation later, who were as far removed from their ancestor Canaan as they were from Ham, his father. This is not a case, therefore, of a son being punished for his father's sin: the perspective is much wider. Even these later scions are not punished for the transgression of their ancient ancestor. As we pointed out already in the preceding subsection, Ham simply represents here the Canaanites who were known to the Israelites, and his actions merely symbolize the practices of the

154

children of Canaan. There is no other possible interpretation of the expression *the father of Canaan* (we shall deal with the signification of the word אֲבִי *'ăbhī* ['father of'] later in the introduction to chapter x). The Canaanites were to suffer the curse and the bondage not because of the sins of Ham, but because they themselves acted like Ham, because of their own transgressions, which resembled those attributed to Ham in this allegory. To which subjugation Scripture is referring and how it is related particularly to sins such as those of Ham, we shall elucidate later in our commentary.

§ 4. Noah's pronouncement provides us with the first example in the Pentateuch of utterances of benison and curse from man to man (Lamech's utterance in v 29 is not a blessing bestowed on his son, but an expression of good wishes to all humanity); hence it is worth while devoting a few lines here to the question of the value attributed by the Torah to pronouncements of this kind.

In the ancient East there was current the belief, based on the concept of the magic power of the spoken word, that blessings and curses, and particularly curses, once uttered, act automatically and are fulfilled of their own accord, as it were, unless another force opposes and annuls them. This explains the important place occupied in Eastern religions, and especially in the cults of the Mesopotamian peoples and the Hittites, by the magical incantations of the priests, whose object was to nullify the power of the anathemas pronounced by one of the gods or a human being. The belief in the power of blessing and curse existed among the Israelites, too, not only in the Biblical period but also in Talmudic times (see, for instance, B. Megillah 15a; B. Baba Qamma 93a), and it continues to our own day (it will suffice to draw attention to the custom of 'the dissolution of curses'). In the Bible we find traces of this belief not only in the cited statements of Gentiles — for instance, in the words of the king of Moab, who believed in the magic power of Balaam's imprecations (Num. xxii 6: *for I know that he whom you bless is blessed, and he whom you curse is cursed*), but also in the utterances of Israelites. For example, Micah's mother, who had previously cursed the one who stole a sum of money from her, on hearing that the thief was her son, instantly hastened to nullify the power of the curse by a blessing: *Blessed be my son by the Lord* (Judges xvii 2). Similarly, to quote another example, when Jacob was afraid lest his father curse him, if he should come before him instead of his elder brother, Rebekah immediately said to him: *Upon me be your curse, my son* (Gen. xxvii 13), in order to remove the effect of the curse from her son onto herself. But these are only the remarks of individual Israelites, and the Bible simply relates the stories and reflects the beliefs current among the people, which do not, however, accord with Israel's true faith. The sublime religion of Israel cannot acquiesce in such a conception. In the view of Israel's Torah, it is impossible to imagine that a man's word should have the power to effect anything without God's will, for only from the Lord do evil and good issue. Human blessings are, according to the Torah, no more than wishes and prayers that God may be willing to do this or that. So, too, human imprecations, in so far as they are not iniquitous, are, in the ultimate analysis, but prayers that God may act in a given way. The Lord, needless to say, may not grant the request of the person that blesses or curses, and He may or may not act according to his wish; it all depends on the Divine will (compare Psa. cix 28: *Let them curse, but do Thou bless! When they arise they shall be put to shame, but Thy servant shall rejoice*).

The majority of contemporary exegetes, it is true, are inclined to attribute to the Torah itself the belief in the magic power of blessing and curse, but those who hold these views have not distinguished between folk beliefs and the concepts of the Torah, and have failed to understand the passages properly. Not only the antithesis between the popular cult and the basic principles of the Pentateuch but also the wording of the blessings and curses to which the Torah attaches importance rebuts this view. In particular, two aspects of the formulation call for attention: (a) the verbs appear mostly in the jussive (shortened form of the imperfect or the like), which expresses a desire or request, a petition or prayer; (b) the good or evil deed is attributed mostly to God himself (for example, Gen. xxvii 28, in the benediction of Isaac: *May God give you,* etc.). It is clear from this that in such cases the one who blesses or curses is only making a supplication to God.

This is not the place to extend our study beyond the confines of our section and to discuss in detail the other Biblical blessings and curses (see concerning these what I have written in my Hebrew article 'Blessing and Curse', published in the *Encyclopaedia Biblica* [Hebrew]); it will suffice to examine specifically what is stated here concerning Noah's pronouncement. According to the view prevailing today (see, for instance, the commentary of Gunkel), the purpose of the passage is to explain that the subjugation of Canaan by Shem and Japheth was due to the fact that Noah had cursed him in ancient times and his imprecation acted magically, creating and shaping the events. But this cannot be the intention of the Torah. It is inconceivable that the Torah, which is imbued with perfect faith in the absolute dominion of God in the world, should come to tell us that because certain words fell from the lips of Noah in a moment of anger, the Lord of the universe was compelled to tolerate the occurrence of given events that were not in accord with His will, or were even in conflict therewith and militated against His original intention, to the point of allowing calamity to befall innocent people as a result of the magical power of those words. In this instance, likewise, the phrasing is not in keeping with this conception; and the action (*v.* 27) is dependent on God's will: *God enlarge Japheth;* and the verbs occur in the jussive form: יַפְתְּ *yapht* ['enlarge'] is jussive, and similarly יְהִי *yᵉhī* ['let ... be'], which is found twice, in *v.* 26 and in *v.* 27, is jussive. The form יִשְׁכֹּן *yiškōn* (*v.* 27) can, taken by itself, be either the jussive or the regular imperfect; but since it is parallel to יְהִי *yᵉhī*, it also, undoubtedly, has a jussive sense. Regarding the verb יְהְיֶה *yihᵉye* in *v.* 25, this is the form of the jussive in *Lāmedh-Hē'* verbs when they occur in a pause or, as here, immediately before a pause (see Gesenius–Kautzsch, § 109a, note 2). The meaning of the text can be only this, that the wholly righteous man made supplication that God should execute righteous judgement and deal with each one according to his deserts (and also with the descendants of Ham, who behave like their ancestors), and since the request was just and accorded with the will of the Judge of the whole earth, He granted it.

§ 5. The connection between the planting of the vineyard by Noah and the mythological stories recounted by various peoples in regard to the origin of wine, we shall discuss in our annotations to *v.* 20.

§ 6. A detailed *Bibliography* on this narrative will be given at the end of the volume, as stated above, p. 47 (see p. 285).

FIRST PARAGRAPH

THE INCIDENT

20. *Noah, the master of the earth, was the first / to plant a vineyard.*

21. *And he drank of the wine, and became drunk, / and lay uncovered in his tent.*

22. *And Ham, the father of Canaan, saw / his father's nakedness, and told his two brothers / outside.*

23. *Then Shem and Japheth took / a garment, laid it / upon both their shoulders, and walked backward / and covered their father's nakedness; their faces were turned away, / and they did not see their father's nakedness.*

20. *Noah . . . was the first* [וַיָּחֶל *wayyāḥel*, literally, 'began'] / We have here another parallel to the preceding section, where we find, although in a different signification, וַיָּחֶל עוֹד *wayyāḥel ʿōdh* ['He waited again'] (viii 10), and afterwards וַיִּיָּחֶל עוֹד *wayyiyyāḥel ʿōdh* ['Then he waited again'] (*ibid. v.* 12). Perhaps the form וַיָּחֶל *wayyāḥel* is used in *v.* 10 instead of וַיִּיָּחֶל *wayyiyyāḥel* in order to emphasize this verbal parallelism. Here, of course, וַיָּחֶל *wayyāḥel* has the meaning of *he began.* In this sense the verb occurs again, as we have pointed out in the introduction, in the other two parts of this section (x 8: HE WAS THE FIRST [הֵחֵל *hēḥēl*] *on earth to be a mighty man;* xi 6: *and this is only* THE BEGINNING [הַחִלָּם *haḥillām*] *of what they will do*); in this instance it is an internal link, and not merely an external verbal correspondence.

The verse does not come to tell us that Noah began to be a 'man of the earth', as several expositors have understood it. Other scholars have already pointed out that the verb הֵחֵל *hēḥēl*, or in later Hebrew הִתְחִיל *hithḥil* [both verbs signify 'he began'], can be followed by the participle, but not by a noun, and in any case it cannot have the definite article as in the present instance (אִישׁ הָאֲדָמָה *'īš hā'ǎdhāmā*, 'the man of the earth'). The correct interpretation is: Noah, the man of the earth, was the first [literally, began'] to plant a vineyard (Naḥmanides).

The master of the earth [אִישׁ הָאֲדָמָה *'īš hā'ǎdhāmā*, literally, 'the man of the earth'] / As a rule the Hebrew phrase is interpreted to mean: עוֹבֵד הָאֲדָמָה *'ōbhēdh hā'ǎdhāmā* ['tiller of the soil']. But this is not possible, for two reasons:

(a) In the term עוֹבֵד הָאֲדָמָה *'ōbhēdh hā'ǎdhāmā*, the key word is עוֹבֵד *'ōbhēdh* ['worker', 'tiller'], whereas here it is wanting. Although it is possible to say אִישׁ מִלְחָמָה *'īš milḥāmā* ['man of war'], since the word מִלְחָמָה *milḥāmā* ['war'] expresses the idea in its entirety, yet the word אֲדָמָה *'ǎdhāmā* alone is insufficient to convey the concept of עֲבוֹדַת הָאֲדָמָה *'ǎbhōdath hā'ǎdhāmā* ['tilling of the soil'].

(b) The word אֲדָמָה *'ǎdhāmā* does indeed denote at times cultivated ground specifically, but not necessarily so; at other times it simply means *earth* in general. It will be enough to cite verses like Gen. xii 3: *in you all the families of the* EARTH *['ǎdhāmā] will be blessed*, which corresponds to Gen. xviii 18: *in him all the nations of the* EARTH *[הָאָרֶץ hā'āreṣ] shall be blessed;* and there are many similar passages. It is necessary, therefore, to explain the phrase אִישׁ הָאֲדָמָה *'īš hā'ǎdhāmā* differently.

When Noah was born, Lamech his father, according to the explanation of his name given above (v 29), said: *This one shall bring us comfort from our labour and from the toil of our hands arising from the* GROUND *[אֲדָמָה 'ǎdhāmā], which the Lord has cursed.* We expect, therefore, to be told of the fulfilment of this wish, for otherwise why did Scripture make a point of quoting Lamech's words? Nor is the general statement (viii 21) that the Lord would not curse the ground any more sufficient; we still need some specific reference to Noah's personality in relation to the ground and the abrogation of the curse that rests upon it (*This one shall bring us comfort ... arising from* THE GROUND, *which the Lord has cursed*). This reference we find here. After the Deluge Noah became lord over the whole earth (Rashi: 'lord of the earth'), for his family was the only one

159

left of all the families of the earth, and he, as head of this family, was the head of the entire earth. Now this was the curse laid upon the ground (Gen. iii 17–19), that of its own accord it would bring forth only thorns and thistles, and as a result of man's hard work it would provide him with sufficient grain of the field to live on, but no more. At this juncture, on account of Noah's merit, the curse was set aside, and the earth not only brought forth enough produce for the sustenance of mankind, but also wine that rejoiced their hearts (in Psa. civ 15: *and wine to gladden the heart of man;* compare Jud. ix 13). This achievement was due to Noah, who was now אִישׁ הָאֲדָמָה *'īš hā'ădhāmā,* sovereign of the earth.

To plant a vineyard] It may be that the beginning of viticulture and the making of wine occupied an important place in the ancient epic tradition, but it is incorrect to say, following the view of many exegetes, that the passage intends to record here interesting information relative to the history of civilization. In the narrative as we have it, this detail is only the starting-point of the main theme, namely, Noah's utterances. If we are to see in this introductory episode also a secondary purpose, we may surmise that the intention is to oppose the mythological concepts that attribute the origin of wine-making to some god or demi-god: the Bible informs us that this, too, was only a human invention. Compare my remarks on a similar matter in Part I, pp. 187 ff. Be this as it may, it is interesting to note that the original home of the vine was apparently in Armenia and the neighbouring regions, and this accords with what was stated earlier about the place where Noah and his sons left the ark (see my notes to viii 4, pp. 103ff.).

In the Mesopotamian tradition, in so far as it is known to us today, the discovery of wine-making was not a *post-diluvian* achievement. On the contrary, in the Gilgameš Epic it is related that during the time when the ship was being built Utnapištim gave the workmen wine to drink in abundant measure (Tablet xi, lines 72–73). But an interesting parallel, to which insufficient attention has been given hitherto, is to be discerned between our narrative concerning the planting of Noah's vineyard after he had been saved from the waters of the Flood and the Greek tradition about Deucalion, the hero of the Deluge, and his connection with the myth of Dionysus and the introduction of wine-making (on these Greek legends see now W. Borgeaud's observations in *Museum Helveticum,* iv, 1947, pp. 240–249). Possibly this tradition emanated from the countries of the East. The resemblance to the Biblical story will become even more arresting when we consider later on another parallel between the Hellenic legends regarding Deucalion and Amphictyon his son and the history of the sons of Noah recorded in the next chapter.

21. *And he drank of the wine, and became drunk, and lay uncovered in his tent*] The whole incident is related with extreme brevity — with the fewest words possible — since it is only a prelude to the main topic. Moreover, the nature of the story precludes a detailed description.

And lay uncovered] — during the sleep that overcame him as a result of his drunkenness; compare below (*v.* 24) : *When Noah awoke.*

His tent [אָהֳלֹה *'ohŏlō(h)*] / Note the archaic spelling of the pronominal suffix with *Hē'*. This spelling is still found at times even in the Masoretic text, especially in short words like עִירֹה *'irō(h)* ['his foal'], סוּתֹה *sūthō(h)* ['his vesture'], נֻחֹה *nūḥō(h)* [literally, 'his resting'], לֵחֹה *lēḥō(h)* ['his natural force'], קִצֹּה *qiṣṣō(h)* [literally, 'his end'], and a number of times כֻּלֹּה *kullō(h)* [literally, 'all of it']. The word אָהֳלֹה *'ohŏlō(h)* is written thus also in other passages (Gen. xii 8; xiii 3; xxxv 21).

22. *And Ham . . . saw, etc.*] Here, too, as in the preceding verse, the Bible is brief for the same reasons, and gives us no details of Ham's transgression. This brevity raises a question, with which the Talmudic sages, the medieval commentators and also modern exegetes have concerned themselves, namely: What was the nature of Ham's sin? I have discussed this question in detail above, § 2, pp. 150 ff. There is no need to go over the ground again here.

The father of Canaan] It was already stated earlier (*v.* 18) that Ham was the father of Canaan. Here the Bible mentions the fact again, at the moment of the deed, because it is in this act that the similarity between Ham and the children of Canaan, who are suspected by the Israelites of improper conduct in their sexual life, became manifest. See on all this my remarks in the introduction, § 1, pp. 149 f.

161

His father's nakedness] — since he was uncovered and was lying bare.

And told his two brothers outside] He told his brothers outside what he had seen within the tent, and the narration itself was a disgraceful thing, since he committed an offence not only against his father's honour by making him an object of derision, but also against the dictates of chastity.

23. In this verse the style becomes more expansive and detailed. Here proper and honourable conduct is spoken of; hence it is not desirable to shorten the narration.

Then Shem and Japheth took] From this sentence the Talmudic sages deduced (Bereshith Rabba, xxxvi 6) that Shem took the lead in performing the good deed, and this may be the actual sense of the verse, which puts Shem before Japheth (but see my note on *v.* 24 regarding the method of listing the names). But this inference cannot find support in the employment of the singular form וַיִּקַּח *wayyiqqaḥ* [literally, 'and he took'] instead of וַיִּקְחוּ *wayyiqᵉḥū* [literally, 'and they took'], for the use of the singular of the verb before two subjects is a common grammatical feature requiring no special reason. It will suffice to cite, for example, Gen. xi 29: *And Abram and Nahor* TOOK [וַיִּקַּח *wayyiqqaḥ*] *wives.*

A garment [הַשִּׂמְלָה *haśśimlā*, literally, 'the garment'] / The definite article here serves only to express 'general definition', in accordance with established Biblical usage. The meaning is: the particular garment that they took; compare Gen. xiv 13: *Then* ONE WHO HAD ESCAPED [literally, *'the* escaped one'] *came*, that is, the particular fugitive that came.

Laid it on both their shoulders] The repetition of Šin or Śin several times in succession clearly shows that alliteration was intended here: וַיִּקַּח שֵׁם וָיֶפֶת אֶת הַשִּׂמְלָה וַיָּשִׂימוּ עַל שְׁכֶם שְׁנֵיהֶם *wayyiqqaḥ Šēm wāyepheth 'eth haśśimlā wayyāśīmū 'al šᵉkhem šᵉnēhem* ['Then Shem and Japheth took a garment, laid it upon both their shoulders']. Similar alliteration may also be intended in *v.* 21: וַיֵּשְׁתְּ מִן הַיַּיִן וַיִּשְׁכָּר *wayyēšt min hayyayin wayyiškār* ['And he drank of the wine, and became drunk'].

And walked backward, etc.] At this point the style assumes an almost poetic form, and shows signs of parallelism, as is clearly to be seen from the way I have arranged the members of the

162

verse above. The clause *and walked backward* is paralleled by the clause *their faces were turned away;* the words *and they did not see their father's nakedness* correspond to the hemistich *and covered their father's nakedness.* The expression *their father's nakedness,* which occurs here twice, echoes the words *his father's nakedness* in *v.* 22; this threefold use of the phrase serves to emphasize it. The details of the story have to be understood as follows: When they approached the tent and entered it, *they walked backward,* that means, not in the direction of their faces but of their backs, and when they drew near to their father, they cast the garment that was on their shoulders over him, and in this way *they covered his nakedness;* also at the moment when they covered him they turned their *faces backwards,* that is to say, they turned their heads away and looked behind them so as not to gaze on their father until they had finished covering him. Thus *they did not see their father's nakedness.*

They did not see] — in antithesis to what was stated above (*v.* 22): *And Ham . . . saw,* etc.

SECOND PARAGRAPH

BLESSING AND CURSE

24. *When Noah awoke from his wine / and knew*
    what his youngest son had done to him,

25. *he said,*
    'Cursed be Canaan; / a slave of slaves / shall he be to his
    brothers.'

26. *He also said,*
    'Blessed be YHWH, / the God of Shem;
    and let Canaan be / his slave.

27. *God enlarge Japheth, / and let him dwell in the tents of Shem;*
    and let Canaan be / his slave.'

24. *When Noah awoke from his wine*] — that is, from the sleep and the prostration of body and mind brought on by the wine.

163

The restoration of a drunken person to normal vigour is used as a simile by the Psalmist (Psa. lxxviii 65): *Then the Lord awoke as from sleep, like a mighty man* RECOVERING FROM WINE [compare the version of *The Jewish Publication Society of America*].

And knew] We are not told how he knew, and it is superfluous to attempt to determine by guessing what the Bible does not state, since it was of no importance to its purpose.

Had done to him] There is a noticeable tendency here not only towards brevity but also to employ chaste language. In such matters a slight allusion suffices. On the use of the verb עָשָׂה *'āśā* ['had done'] in this verse, see above, the introduction, p. 152.

His youngest son] The commentators have found this detail very difficult, for in general it would seem that the usual order in which the sons were listed in the Bible — Shem, Ham and Japheth — represented the order of seniority of the three brothers, and accordingly Ham was the middle one; and if Scripture wished to indicate another chronological order, this was not the proper place to do so incidentally. Various suggestions have been put forward to resolve the difficulty, but none is satisfactory. The interpretation of the word קָטָן *qāṭān* [literally, 'small', 'young'] in a comparative sense, that is, younger than Shem (Septuagint; Vulgate) does not conform to Hebrew usage; to give it the connotation of 'unworthy' (Bereshith Rabba xxxvi 7; see Rashi) does not accord with the simple meaning of the text; the conjecture that the reference here is to the youngest son of Ham, that is, to Canaan (Ibn Ezra and others) is based on a misunderstanding of the real meaning of the narrative (see the introduction); the theory that the verse emanates from a different source from that which gave the order as Shem, Ham and Japheth (the view of many modern exegetes) does not solve the problem in the existing text. Other suggested explanations are even more difficult.

But if we study the passage carefully, and particularly if we do not separate this story from the other parts of the section, the difficulty falls away. First of all it should be noted that the order in which the names of brothers are mentioned does not establish the order of their birth. It is written, for example, in Gen. xxv 9: *Isaac and Ishmael his sons buried him,* although Ishmael was born before Isaac. Similarly, in the list of Jacob's sons given at the beginning of the Book of Exodus, the brothers are not enumerated in the order of their birth, but the sons of the wives precede the sons of the handmaids. In the continuation of our section — actually in the genealogy of Noah's sons — Japheth comes first and thereafter Ham and at the end Shem (the reason for this we shall see later). We thus observe that there are different methods of drawing up lists; and one of them may be governed by the general usage of the language, which prefers to place short words before long ones. This is a fundamental rule in Akkadian, and it holds good in Hebrew, too, in numerous instances. We say, for example חֵן וָחֶסֶד *ḥēn waḥesedh* ['grace and favour'], not חֶסֶד וָחֵן *ḥesedh wāḥēn;* חֶסֶד וְרַחֲמִים *ḥesedh werahămīm* ['steadfast love and mercy'], not רַחֲמִים וָחֶסֶד *raḥămīm wāḥesedh;* similarly חֹק וּמִשְׁפָּט *ḥōq ūmišpāṭ* ['a statute and an ordinance'], דַּל וְאֶבְיוֹן *dal weʾebhyōn* ['weak and needy'] יוֹם וָלַיְלָה *yōm wālaylā* ['day and night'], and many more examples of the same kind. This may account for the normal Biblical order, Shem, Ham and Japheth, but this sequence does not imply that Shem was the oldest and Japheth the youngest of them. The order of their birth the Torah tells us by a combination of various data. Further on (x 21), Shem is described as *the brother of Japheth the eldest,* which, as I shall explain *ad locum,* is a term commonly used in the ancient system of fratriarchy or headship of the brother, which required the brothers to be designated in relation to their first-born brother. This passage, therefore establishes that Japheth was the eldest; and our verse, which calls Ham *the youngest son* of Noah, informs us that Ham was the third and that Shem was consequently the second. As for the argument, mentioned earlier, that this was not the right place to give this information casually, it may be answered that possibly the word הַקָּטָן *haqqāṭān* [rendered: 'the youngest'], whose primary meaning is certainly *the least in years,* contains also another nuance (which Midrashic exegesis treated as the principal sense), to wit, an allusion to his moral degradation; and it was fitting that precisely in the story of the incident that shows Ham's turpitude, reference should be made to the fact that he was *the least* of the brothers.

Later it will be seen that on the basis of this interpretation we can explain a chronological detail that is otherwise difficult to understand, namely, the date *two years after the flood* (xi 10).

25. *He said, Cursed be Canaan*] Here we are confronted with a difficult problem: why does Noah *curse Canaan* on account of *Ham's* sin? See on this question, on the various proposals advanced to solve it, and on the simple way, which I consider to be correct, of elucidating the subject, my remarks in the introduction to this narrative, § 3, pp. 153–155.

A slave of slaves shall he be to his brothers] The meaning is not that he would be a slave to his brothers' slaves, but that he would be an inferior and despised slave of his brothers. The phrase *slave of slaves* expresses a single concept only (compare the observations of N. H. Tur-Sinai on phrases of this kind in many of his works and most recently in his Hebrew book *Hallāšōn weHassēpher*, p. 284). This is evidenced here by the verb יִהְיֶה *yiheye* ['shall he be'], which serves to separate the expression *slave of slaves* from *to his brothers* and to indicate that the *Lāmedh* ['to'] prefixed to אֶחָיו *'ehāw* ['his brothers'] does not merely connect the latter to the word *slaves* but to the entire phrase *slave of slaves*.

To his brothers] These brothers are not, as many have held (for example, B. Jacob), the brothers of Canaan who are mentioned later (x 6), nor Shem and Japheth, the brothers of Ham (Dillmann). The name Canaan does not denote here an individual but the Canaanite people, and his brothers are the other nations in general. Subsequently it will be explained to whom in particular the Bible is referring.

A poetic rhythm is discernible in Noah's words (2: 2: 2): אָרוּר כְּנַעַן / עֶבֶד עֲבָדִים / יִהְיֶה לְאֶחָיו *'ārūr Kenaʿan* / *'ebhedh 'ābhādhīm yiheye le'ehāw* ['Cursed be Canaan / a slave of slaves / shall he be to his brothers'].

26. *He also said* [וַיֹּאמֶר *wayyōmer*] / This verb is repeated here [see *v.* 25] in order to separate the curse from the blessing.

Blessed be YHWH, the God of Shem] The formula *blessed be* [בָּרוּךְ *bārūkh*] *YHWH,* in the Bible connotes thanksgiving and praise to the Lord who performed a beneficent act (see, for instance, Gen. xxiv 27; Exod. xviii 10; and so forth). Our verse is to be understood in the same way: Thanksgiving and praise be to *YHWH* who guided Shem in the good way and taught him to conduct himself with decency and all other virtues. The textual

amendments suggested (Graetz: בָּרֵךְ ה' אָהֳלֵי שֵׁם *bārēkh YHWH
'oḫŏlē Šēm* ['Bless, O Lord, the tents of Shem']; Budde: בָּרוּךְ ה'
שֵׁם *berukh YHWH Šēm* ['Blessed of the Lord be Shem']) are not
amendments but corruptions. Concerning the Bible's intention to
emphasize the knowledge of *YHWH* that was preserved among
the children of Shem, see the introduction, § 1, pp. 149–150.

And let Canaan be his [לָמוֹ *lāmō*, literally, 'to him'] *slave*]
The word לָמוֹ *lāmō* can signify both 'to him' and 'to them'; but
the difference between these two senses does not affect the meaning
here, since in any case the reference is not specifically to Noah's
son Shem but to his descendants. The same applies to the identical
clause that occurs in *v.* 27 in connection with Japheth.

Commentators are very much divided in their views concerning
the actual event or circumstances to which the Bible refers when
it speaks of the subjugation of Canaan by Shem and Japheth.
Gunkel, who thinks that Noah's words preserve relics of an ancient
tradition, sees in Canaan's subjection by Shem an allusion to the
invasion of the areas of the land of the Canaanites (understood in
a very broad sense of the term) by Aramaean and Hebrew tribes in
the second half of the second millenium B.C.E., and in his enslavement by Japheth a reference to one of the migrations of the northern
peoples in the same — or approximately the same — period. Others
(Wellhausen and many who hold identical or similar views) think
that the reference is to the conquest of the Canaanites by the Israelite
tribes, the sons of Shem (this is also the Jewish traditional interpretation, which regards Noah's utterance as a kind of prophecy),
and by the Philistines, who are considered here as sons of Japheth.
Other exegetes again have advanced various other theories, the
latest being Bertholet, who is of the opinion that the blessing on
Japheth was added in the Hellenistic period and that it alludes to
Alexander the Great and the Diadochi. The complexity of conjecture and suggestions is so great that in despair B. Jacob concluded
that Noah's curse was only a threat, and that possibly Scripture
did not have in mind an actual event.

However, all the involved discussions and bizarre solutions are
superfluous. The whole difficulty arises from the fact that the
commentators have wrenched the verses from their context and
have endeavoured to explain them in isolation without reference to

167

their literary setting — the Haggadists in their way, interpreting each sentence separately; and the modern scholars in their way, breaking up the text piecemeal. If we have regard to the plain sense of the verses and their continuation, the passage can be elucidated without difficulty.

Here it is stated that Canaan would be a slave to Shem, that means that the children of Canaan would be in bondage to the children of Shem. Now further on, in chapter x (*v.* 22), we are told who the children of Shem are, and that the first of them is *Elam*. In the same chapter (*v.* 19) the borders of the Canaanites are defined, and they are said to extend *in the direction of* SODOM, GOMORRAH, ADMAH *and* ZEBOIIM, *as far as Lasha*, that is to say, that all these cities were included in the territory of the Canaanites (see my commentary *ad locum*). These cities — Sodom, Gomorrah, Admah and Zeboiim — are again listed together in chapter xiv, where the relations between the kings of the *Canaanite* cities and Chedorlaomer, king of *Elam*, are described. Now the relationship was that *they had served Chedorlaomer* (xiv 4), that is, the children of *Canaan* served him who ruled over the first of the peoples of the children of *Shem. They had served* [עָבְדוּ *'ābhedhū*] — exactly what we are told here: *and let Canaan be his* SLAVE [עֶבֶד *'ebhedh*]. There can be no doubt that it is to this historic episode that our verse refers. Nay more, later on we are also informed (xiii 13; xviii 20 f.; xix 1 f.) of the wickedness of the people of Sodom and Gomorrah, and of their particular sins (xix 5), which belong to the same category of offences as that committed by Ham, *the father of Canaan* — the very sin that the ancient tradition possibly attributed to Ham, as we noted in the introduction. The connection between the passages is thus clear.

It will further be shown immediately below that the next verse, which deals with Canaan's servitude to Japheth, can be satisfactorily explained in the same way.

The rhythm of the blessing in this verse is 2:2//2:2, as I have indicated above, p. 163, in the arrangement of the members of the verse.

27. [*God*] *enlarge* [יַפְתְּ *yapht*] / Both the ancients and the moderns have explained this word in the sense of 'make wide' on the basis of the Aramaic usage (compare also Prov. xx 19: *therefore*

meddle not with him that OPENETH WIDE [פֹּתֶה *pōthe*] *his lips,* in parallelism with *revealeth secrets*), and this appears to be the correct interpretation. The word does not allude to any particular occurrence, but is a general wish for success (compare Gen. xxvi 22: *For now the Lord has made room for us,* and similar phrases), that finds expression in the verb פָּתָה *pāthā* in order to achieve a play on the name יֶפֶת *Yepheth* [Japheth]. It would seem that the primary form of the name, following the original pattern of the Segholate nouns, was יַפְתְּ *Yapht,* exactly like the form of the verb.

God [אֱלֹהִים ʾ*Elōhīm*] / On the use of this name here, in place of *YHWH,* which is found in *v.* 26, see p. 150.

And let him dwell in the tents of Shem] The traditional exposition, which takes the subject of the verb יִשְׁכֹּן *yiškōn* ['let him dwell'] to be God, does not accord with the simple meaning of the verse. According to the plain sense of the words, the subject can only be Japheth. But it is difficult to agree with the exegetes who see in this sentence an expression of Messianic hope and the acceptance of the God of Israel by the children of Japheth. The correct interpretation has to be sought in the direction of our explanation of the preceding verse. Among the allies and confederates of Chedorlaomer king of Elam there is mentioned (xiv 1, 9) Tidal king of *Goiim* [גּוֹיִם *Gōyīm*]. This strange expression can only be explained on the basis of what is stated in chapter x (*v.* 5) with regard to the sons of Japheth, from whom *the coastland* PEOPLES [הַגּוֹיִם *haggōyīm*] *spread.* The name *Goiim* denotes, therefore, a section of the sons of Japheth; and since Tidal king of *Goiim* was the confederate of Chedorlaomer king of Elam, who was of the sons of Shem, and went forth with him to help him in his war, it is possible to say of him and of his men, who belonged to the sons of Japheth, that they dwelt in the *tents of Shem,* precisely as it is stated of Abram in the same chapter, xiv (*v.* 13): *who was* DWELLING *by the oaks of Mamre the Amorite, brother of Eshcol and of Aner; these were the* ALLIES *of Abram.* Noah blesses Japheth to the effect that just as he was privileged to be a partner of Shem in a virtuous deed, so may it be granted to his descendants to be associates and allies of the sons of Shem, whose status is the highest, and to dwell with them in their tents.

And let Canaan be his slave] See my remarks above on the
identical clause in the preceding verse. According to the narrative
in chapter xiv, Tidal king of Goiim, who belonged to the sons of
Japheth, was one of the kings who reimposed the yoke of servitude
upon the Canaanite cities in the Jordan plain.

The poetic rhythm of this verse, as can clearly be seen from the
way I have arranged its parts in the Hebrew, is 3:3/ /2:2.

CONCLUDING VERSES

DEATH OF NOAH

28. *And Noah lived / after the flood*
    three hundred years / and fifty years.

29. *And all the days of Noah were / nine hundred years / and*
    fifty years;
    and he died.

Till now the Torah spoke of Noah and his sons together; after
this it is the history of the sons of Noah alone that will be
related. Hence these two verses come at this point to bid farewell
to Noah and to tell us how he departed from the world. In the
same way, the passing of Terah (xi 32) is mentioned before the
stories about Abraham; so, too, Abraham's death is recorded before
the histories of Ishmael and Isaac, and the death of Isaac (xxxv
28–29) before the narratives of Esau and Jacob.

The wording is similar to — almost identical with — that
employed in chapter v. It differs from it in this respect: the
dividing line between the two periods of Noah's life is not,
as in the earlier passages, the birth of the first-born son, but
the Deluge, this being the principal event in Noah's life, as
in the life of ancient humanity as a whole. Nor do we find here
the formula used in chapter v, *and beget sons and daughters;* this
agrees with what has been stated earlier (*v.* 19), that only from
his three sons — Shem, Ham and Japheth — was the whole earth
peopled.

28. *After the flood*] The exegetes have devoted considerable
discussion to the question whether this expression signifies after the
commencement or the termination of the Deluge. As a rule, it is
true, *after* is used only to indicate the time following the completion
of something. But here it is difficult to interpret it thus, for if
Noah lived 350 years after the Flood had run its course completely,
that is, after the waters had dried from the face of the earth on
the twenty-seventh day of the second month of the six hundred
and first year of his life, Noah would have attained, at the end of
his days, the age of 951, not just 950 years. On the other hand,
it is difficult to interpret *after the flood* to mean after the *beginning*
of the Deluge. In order to understand the matter, we must distinguish between two different uses of the phrase in question. When
it refers to the new period of human history, in contradistinction
to what happened *before* the Flood (like the Akkadian *arku abûbi.*
in contrast to *lam abûbi*), it undoubtedly means after the end of the
catastrophe. But when the expression fixes the starting-point of a
short period of time, as in xi 10 (*two years after the flood*), or of
a relatively short interval of time, as here, then it means subsequent
to the termination of the rain that came down forty days (in
accordance with the unmistakable connotation of the word *flood*
in vii 17: *And the flood continued forty days upon the earth*), that
is, after the twenty-seventh day of the third month of the six
hundredth year of Noah's life. Understood thus, all is clear.

Three hundred years and fifty years] We have already shown
(Part I, pp. 257 ff.) that the chronology of the Book of Genesis is
in general founded on two principles: (a) the *sexagesimal* system,
which was commonly used in the ancient East; (b) the addition
of *seven* or multiples of *seven* to the round numbers appertaining
to the sexagesimal system. This is also the case here. Before the
Deluge Noah lived to the age of 600 years, to wit, ten times 60,
and after it he was granted 350 additional years, that is, fifty
times seven.

29. In this verse the formula employed is identical with that used
in chapter v.

And . . . were [וַיְהִי *wayᵉhī*, literally, 'was'] / In the Samaritan
Pentateuch, and likewise in a number of MSS and old editions of
the Hebrew Scriptures (among others also MSS of Aaron ben

Asher and his school) the reading is: וַיְהִיוּ *wayyihᵉyū* ['and . . . were']. Both forms are possible.

Nine hundred years and fifty years] Thus he also reached an age approximating to that of most of the ancient patriarchs listed in chapter v.

And he died] When his time came, he died like all other people. According to the Mesopotamian myths, the gods raised the hero of the Flood to the status of a deity and endowed him with eternal life. The Torah is absolutely opposed to any such idea.

From now on, since Noah has departed from the world, he no longer appears in the Torah narrative, and the continuation of the passage speaks only of what happened subsequently to his descendants.

B. THE HISTORY OF THE SONS OF NOAH
(x 1 — 3 2)

INTRODUCTION

§ 1. THE AIM of this chapter is to show in detail how the fact alluded to in general terms in the opening verses of the section came about, namely, that from the three sons of Noah the whole earth was peopled, and from their offspring all the families of the world were formed.

Once again the Torah differs here fundamentally from the traditions of the Gentiles, who could not imagine the rise of a new humanity after the Deluge by a natural process. In the Epic of Atraḥasis we are told that seven males and seven females were created from fourteen lumps of clay by means of magic incantations and acts of the god Ea and the goddess Mama or Mami. In the same way the Greek tradition about Deucalion related that after the Flood men were formed from the stones that Deucalion threw behind him, and women from the stones that Pyrrha his wife cast behind her. The Pentateuch speaks only of natural procreation.

§ 2. Almost the entire content of the chapter is recapitulated, in nearly identical form, in i Chronicles i 4–23. The latter, however, does not represent an independent parallel account to our chapter but only an excerpt, with a few changes, taken from our chapter. The differences are as follows:

(a) The author of Chronicles, who at the beginning of his book was interested only in genealogies, copied from our passage only the genealogical material proper, omitting the opening and closing sentences of the chapter and also of its paragraphs (*vv.* 1,5, the second half of *v.* 18, *vv.* 19–20, 21, 30–32), as well as the statements here concerning Nimrod that come after the words *in the earth* (*vv.* 9–12).

(b) The spelling of some words is full [with a *Wāw*] in Chronicles and defective in Genesis (Chronicles i 7: וְרוֹדָנִים *werō(w)dhānīm* ['and the Rodanim']; *v.* 10: נִמְרוֹד *Nimrō(w)dh* [Nimrod], גִּבּוֹר *gibbō(w)r* ['mighty man']; *v.* 13: צִידוֹן *Ṣīdhō(w)n* [Sidon]).

(c) The two words וְסַבְתָּה *wesabhtā(h)* ['and Sabta'] וְרַעְמָה *wera'mā*(h) ['and Raama'] have in Chronicles (*v.* 9) an *'Āleph* at the end instead of the *Hē'* appearing in *v.* 7 here.

(d) Instead of the spelling לוּדִים *Lūdhīm* [Ludim], which we find here, in *v.* 13, the text in Chronicle i 11 (according to most MSS and editions) reads לודיים *lwdyym* as the *Kethībh* and לוּדִים *Lūdhīm* as the *Qrē*.

(e) In our chapter (*v.* 4) we have וְתַרְשִׁישׁ *wetharšīš* ['and Tarshish']; in Chronicles (*v.* 7) וְתַרְשִׁישָׁה *wetharšīšā(h)*, with locative *Hē'* but without locative signification.

(f) The *Wāw copulative* is missing in Chronicles (*v.* 8) before בְּנֵי חָם *benē Ḥām* ['The sons of Ham'] and before פּוּט *Pūṭ* [Put].

(g) The names of the sons of Aram (Gen. x 23) appear in Chronicles (i 17) as a continuation of the table of the sons of Shem (וְעוּץ *we'ūṣ* ['and Uz'], with *Wāw copulative*, etc.).

(h) Differences in the forms of the names: instead of רִיפַת *Rīphath* [Riphath] דֹּדָנִים *Dōdhānīm* [Dodanim], מַשׁ *Maš* [Mash], עוֹבָל *'Obhal* [Obal], listed here (*vv.* 3, 4, 23, 28), we find in Chronicles, at least in some of the MSS and editions, the names דִּיפַת *Dīphath* [Diphath], רוֹדָנִים *Rō(w)dhānīm* [Rodanim], מֶשֶׁךְ *Mešekh* [Meshech], עֵיבָל *'Ebhal* [Ebal].

The first divergency is due to the difference in character of the two books; the discrepancies in (b)–(f) concern external forms only; to the differences enumerated in (g)–(h) we shall revert in the continuation of the commentary. We shall likewise deal in our annotations with the variant readings in the Samaritan Pentateuch and the Septuagint.

§ 3. This is one of the chapters that commentators and other scholars have discussed at great length, and an entire literature has been created around it. But most of the contributions to the subject have not advanced our understanding of it to any great degree. Even if it is possible to justify to a certain extent the name *Table of Nations, Völkertafel* and the like by which the chapter is usually called, it is difficult to agree with all the views flowing from this designation.

According to the prevailing opinion in Biblical scholarship, we have here a kind of 'scientific' attempt, as it were, to explain the origin of the peoples of the world and to present an ethnographical classification of all sections of mankind. Gunkel, for instance, senses in this chapter, 'a spirit of erudition' (*Geist der Gelehrsamkeit*) and sees in it 'a first step in Ethnography' (*ein erster Anfang der Ethnographie*). If this were indeed the intention of Scripture, this attempt was certainly a primitive experiment, naïve and valueless. But if we endeavour to understand the text properly, we shall see that this is not its purpose. This chapter does not come to teach us ethnology, just as the first section of Genesis does not purport to instruct us in geoglogy or palaeontology or any other sciences. We must be careful not to introduce some of our own thoughts into the passage and imagine that our chapter is founded on concepts similar to those of our own period, such as racial propinquity, linguistic relationship, geographical position, historical associations and the like.

It is true that the Torah used, as will be explained later, the knowledge of the international 'Sages', who gathered reports about varied and distant peoples from the tales of travellers and merchants, but it had no speculative aim in mind, and it did not seek to convey to its readers information for its own sake. The Bible culled from that material what was necessary to the implementation of its general programme, and the notices about the peoples are not its central purpose, but only a means to attain it.

174

Its real purpose is different. When our chapter seeks to explain how the whole earth became peopled through the three sons of Noah, it has a threefold aim: (a) to show that Divine Providence is reflected in the distribution of the nations over the face of the earth not less than in other acts of the world's creation and administration; (b) to determine relationship between the people of Israel and the other peoples; (c) to teach the unity of post-diluvian humanity, which, like antediluvian mankind, was wholly descended from one pair of human beings. Let us dwell for a while on each of these three points.

§ 4. In order to show the working of Divine Providence in the dispersion of the peoples of the earth, the Bible depicts this dispersion in a harmonious form that is distinguished and symbolized by the numerical symmetry prevailing throughout the chapter. The planned pattern of the dispersal of humanity serves here as proof that the settlement of mankind in the world did not occur haphazardly, according to the chance circumstances of greater or less fecundity in one or another family, but took place according to a preconceived Divine plan, the implementation of which proceeded without humanity's being aware of it.

The numerical symmetry is discernible both in the over-all aspect of the chapter and in its details. Regarding the chapter as a whole, it is well known that the Jewish and Christian exegetical tradition found in it seventy or seventy two nations. It would seem that tradition fathomed the true meaning of the text, for it is in keeping with the customary practice obtaining in the ancient East generally, and among the Israelites in particular, of using the number seventy — seven times ten — for the purpose of indicating the abundance of children of a family blessed with fertility. Thus, for example, according to the concepts of the Canaanites concerning the origin and genealogy of the deities in their pantheon, the family of the gods — the sons of El and the sons of Asherah — comprised seventy souls (*seventy sons of Asherah* in the Ugaritic Tablet II AB, vi, 46). We do not actually possess a list of the names of the seventy gods, and possibly there existed records that differed from one another in some particulars, except for the total of seventy, which remained unchanged. This usage was also to be found among the Israelites. The number of the sons of Jacob who went down to Egypt

175

was fixed at seventy persons (Gen. xlvi 27; Exod. i 5; Deut. x 22);
and although there are some divergences between the list in Gen.
xlvi and other Biblical lists, and an element of doubt attaches to some
of the details of the calculation, the total seventy is considered the
essential factor from which there can be no deviation. In order
to arrive at this figure, Joseph and his sons, who were already
in Egypt, are included; and to prevent a reduction of the number
through the death of Er and Onan in the land of Canaan, Hezron
and Hamul are substituted for them (I have discussed all this
in my Hebrew essay 'The story of Tamar and Judah' in the J. M.
Simḥoni Memorial Volume of *Ṣiyyūnīm,* Berlin 1929, pp. 96 f.).
Possibly it was also intended that the roll of families in
Num. xxvi should aggregate seventy, at least approximately, as a
round figure; actually only sixty five families are enumerated there,
but this is near to seventy, and if we add the families of the Levites
mentioned in chapter iii, which were not incorporated in chapter
xxvi, we shall arrive at seventy less one. Similarly, the Book of
Judges (viii 30; ix 2) speaks of the seventy sons of Gideon, and
this figure is still adhered to even when it is subsequently stated
(*ibid.* ix 5) that one of them slew his brothers, *seventy men,* and
yet another of them, Jotham, remained alive for he hid himself.
This shows that the number seventy is not exact, but serves,
according to the traditional system, to indicate a numerically ideal
family. In the same way, in ii Kings x 1, 6, 7, reference is made
to the seventy sons of Ahab. Even the Canaanite tradition concerning the seventy sons of El and Asherah has a sequel in Israel's
literature. The expression בְּנֵי אֵל *benē* '*El* ['sons of El'], as we
have already noted (Part I, pp. 291 ff.), was inherited by the
Israelites from the Canaanites, and received among the former the
connotation of angels, members of God's household. Now Jewish
tradition has likewise fixed the number of angels surrounding the
Divine throne precisely at seventy. In view of all this, if we find
in our chapter, too, that the descendants of Shem, Ham and Japheth
total exactly seventy (see on this below), we must not regard this
figure as a mere coincidence but as an additional example of the
aforementioned use of the traditional number seventy. The family
of the children of Noah is depicted as perfect in the number of its
sons, and all mankind, which comprises the seventy nations that

issued from these sons, is represented as an ideal creation in the number of its part. Nor may we suppose that the sum of seventy peoples is the result of later redaction, for the Ugaritic parallels prove that the system is old.

In keeping with this interpretation is the statement in the song הַאֲזִינוּ Haʾăzīnū ['Give ear'] (Deut. xxxii 8): *When the Most High gave to the nations their inheritance, when He separated the sons of men, He fixed the bounds of the peoples according to the number of the sons of Israel* (certain ancient versions read: *according to the number of the sons of ʾEl* ['God']; see on this further on). The connection between this verse and our chapter becomes quite clear from the parallelism observable in the use of expressions common to both — not only of general terms like *nations* and *bounds* [or *borders*], but also of a characteristic word such as the stem פָּרַד *pāradh* ['separate']. This verse may therefore be regarded as ancient evidence that our chapter was understood in the manner indicated: the number of the peoples of the world is seventy like that of the children of Israel. This also applies to the reading, *according to the number of the sons of ʾEl,* which is found in the Septuagint, Symmachus and the Vulgate (in Targum, Pseudo-Jonathan [or Palestine Targum]both readings are reflected); also the *sons of ʾEl,* that is to say, the angels who surround the Throne of Glory and likewise serve as the guardian angels of the nations, were considered to number seventy.

However, it would seem that the names mentioned in this chapter, apart from those of Noah and his three sons, which are not, of course, to be counted with the eponyms of the peoples, come to seventy one and not precisely seventy. But we have already seen that the number seventy may be used inexactly, and one more or less is not material. Moreover, it appears that Nimrod has to be deducted from the total, since he is not mentioned as a nation but as an *individual* who ruled over many cities; and if we omit him, there remain exactly seventy (others have suggested that the Philistines or Joktan should be left out, but without adequate reason).

Nor is it to be objected that the number seventy is not expressly mentioned in the text, for commonly the numerical symmetry is not explicitly stressed, and only the careful reader discovers it as a

177

result of his study. We have observed this in all the preceding sections, especially in the 'book of the history of Adam'.

The numerical harmony is discernible, as stated, also in the details of our chapter. Other numbers, too, are very prominent there, although they are not expressly mentioned: *seven,* which, as we know, is the number of perfection, and *twelve.* The latter, likewise, when it appertains to peoples or tribes, indicates perfection, for the peoples and tribes of antiquity were accustomed, both in the East and in the West, to unite in amphictyonic councils or leagues of twelve branches. The union of the twelve tribes is only one example of this system. We observe, moreover, that the total remains unchanged even when the composition is altered. If Joseph is reckoned as one tribe, then the tribe of Levi is also counted; but if the sons of Joseph are regarded as two tribes, then the Levites are excluded. Similarly, we find in the Bible twelve princes of Ishmael (Gen. xvii 20; xxv 13–16), twelve sons of Nahor (*ibid.* xxii 20–24) and two lists of chiefs of Edom, which appear to be based essentially on the number twelve. The first (*ibid.* xxxvi 15–18) actually contains thirteen names, but the chief of Amalek (who is descended from the son of Eliphaz by his concubine) was added to the basic group of twelve chiefs; and the second (*ibid. vv.* 40–43) comprises eleven names, partly different from those given in the first, but this list likewise rests on a basic organisation of twelve chiefs, only one of them for some reason disappeared or left the league. If we may add to this roll the name Zepho, which is found in the Septuagint in place of Iram, then in this case, too, there will be exactly twelve in all.

In this connection it is worth noting that the Greek tradition attributed the founding of the Amphictyonic Council of Delphi, which comprised precisely twelve tribes, to Amphictyon, the son of Deucalion, the hero of the Deluge, thus providing an interesting parallel to our chapter, which attributes many confederations of twelve peoples or tribes to the descendants of Noah after the Flood.

Let us now examine how the names are arranged in our chapter, and we shall see that the numbers *seven* and *twelve* predominate therein. Japheth has *seven* sons (Gomer, Magog, Madai, Javan, Tubal, Meshech and Tiras), and his grandsons also number *seven*

(Ashkenaz, Riphath, Togarmah, Elishah, Tarshish, Kittim and Dodanim); in all, *fourteen*. In the pedigree of the sons of Ham, the sons and grandsons of Cush are *seven* (Seba, Havilah, Sabtah, Raamah, Sabteca, Sheba, Dedan); the sons of Egypt are *seven* (Ludim, Anamim, Lehabim, Naphtuhim, Pathrusim, Casluhim, Caphtorim), to whom have been added the Philistines, who were descended from the Casluhim; Canaan's sons total *twelve* (Sidon, Heth, the Jebusites, the Amorites, the Girgashites, the Hivites, the Arkites, the Sinites, the Arvadites, the Zemarites, the Hamathites, the Canaanites [see the commentary below]). Thus altogether the sons of Ham number: Cush and his sons and grandsons, *eight;* Egypt and his seven sons and the Philistines, *nine;* Put, having no sons, *one;* the tribes of the Canaanites, *twelve;* in all, *thirty*. The sons and grandsons of Shem, up to Peleg, are *twelve;* the sons of Joktan are *thirteen,* and with Joktan *fourteen* — twice times seven. All told, the sons of Shem are *twenty-six*. Thus all the sons of Shem and Ham and Japheth mentioned in the chapter come to: 14+30+26=70. On the variant readings of the Septuagint, which do not disturb the numerical symmetry and do not change the total, see below, the commentary on *v.* 31.

A note should possibly be added on the number of times that characteristic words occur in the chapter. The most typical word (וּ)בְנֵי *(ū)beᵉnē* ['(and) sons of'] is found *seven* times in the first part, *vv.* 1–7, and another *seven* in the last part, from *v.* 20 to the end; in all, fourteen times. If we add to these the other terms that are characteristic of a genealogy, אֲבִי *'ăbhī* ['the father of'], בָּנִים *bānīm* ['sons'], תּוֹלְדוֹת *tōleᵉdhōth* ['generations of', 'history of'] and the forms of the verb יָלַד *yāladh,* we obtain twenty-eight — four times *seven*. Possibly this is not fortuitous. But certainly the sum total of the peoples and the detailed numbers of their families are not coincidental.

Thus the Bible indicates the perfection of humanity by its numerical harmony, and it is not Scripture's intention to cite the names of *all* the peoples seriatim. Those who conclude *a priori* that our chapter purports to present a *complete* ethnic list, and as a result of this premise discover a number of omissions, since in truth the list is incomplete, have failed to understand the chapter properly. It explicitly declares that its aim is not to mention *all* the peoples. It states, for example, in *v.* 5 with regard to the sons of Japheth: *From these spread the coastland peoples in their lands, each with his own language, by their families, in their nations,* that means to say, that there were many other nations in the world who traced their descent to Japheth, but there was no need to detail their names. Similar expressions are subsequently used with reference to the sons of Ham (*v.* 20), the sons of Shem (*v.* 31), and the sons of Noah as a whole (*v.* 32). The Torah was concerned only to complete the number of seventy names, and to incorporate therein the names of the principal nations that were near to Israel, or were in some way connected with the Israelites, or were in some manner known to them.

§ 5.   This brings us to the second of the three subjects whose treatment we considered to be the primary purpose of the chapter, to wit, the question of the relationship between Israel and the other peoples. Before the following chapters tell the story of the patriarchs of Israel and their relations with the Canaanites, the Philistines and other peoples, it was fitting that these peoples should be introduced to the reader and their place among the families of the earth indicated. It was likewise necessary to determine at the outset the border of the Canaanites (*v.* 19), that is to say, the boundaries of the land that was destined to be promised to Abraham and his descendants (xii 7). It was also essential to prepare the ground now for what would subsequently be said in *v.* 8 of the song *Ha'ăzīnū* ['Give ear' Deut. xxxii], which we have quoted earlier (further on, too, we shall find evidence of close ties between the Book of Genesis and the Book of Deuteronomy). There the fact is stressed that the number of nations corresponds to the number of the children of Israel (or, according to another reading, to the number of the sons of God ['*El*], the guardian angels of the nations, in contradistinction to the Lord, who Himself watches over Israel). The general harmony in the history of the world is paralleled by the particular harmony prevailing in Israel's history. Seventy peoples on the one side, seventy sons and seventy families on the other. The people of Israel occupies in the plans of the Divine Providence a place resembling, on a small scale, that of all mankind; it is a small-scale world, a microcosm similar in form to the macrocosm.

180

The third point implied in the text is clear: the new humanity that came into being after the Deluge was also unitary, like the one that preceded the Flood; it, too, was descended in its entirety from one human pair; thus all peoples are brothers. This concept serves as the foundation of the prophetic promise for the end of days that *nation shall not lift up sword against nation, neither shall they learn war any more* — a promise that is quoted already by Isaiah and Micah as an ancient tradition in Israel.

§ 6. In order to understand the chapter correctly, we must realize in what sense the nouns אָב *'ābh* ['father'] and בֵּן *bēn* ['son'] and the verb יָלַד *yāladh* ['bear', 'beget'] are used therein. From passages like *v.* 4, which lists as בְּנֵי־יָוָן *'benē' Yāwān* ['"sons" of Javan'] first Elishah and Tarshish, which are unquestionably geographical terms, and afterwards the Kittim and Dodanim, whose plural forms show them to be peoples or tribes, it is manifest that the word בֵּן is not used here in its normal and simple signification. The same applies to the verb יָלַד *yāladh* in sentences like *v.* 13 f.: *and Egypt* יָלַד *yāladh the Ludim and Anamim and Lehabim*, etc. Egypt is the name of a people or land, and the other names are designations of peoples; hence, undoubtedly the meaning of the verb יָלַד *yāladh* in this passage is not the same as in verses like, *Hearken to your father who* BEGOT YOU [יְלָדֶךָ *yelādhekha*] (Prov. xxiii 22). Similarly, we read later on in *v.* 15 f.: *And Canaan* יָלַד *yāladh Sidon, his first born, and Heth and the Jebusites, and the Amorites, and the Girgashites*, etc. Sidon is the name of a city, and the following names belong to peoples or tribes. Without doubt the genealogical terms in our chapter are employed in figurative senses. Words used in such metaphorical connotations are found in great number in the genealogical lists of the Book of Chronicles. There it is said, for example, that Shobal was the father of Kiriath-jearim (i Chron. ii 50), or that Salma was the father of Bethlehem (*ibid. v.* 51), or that the sons of Salma were Bethlehem, the Netophathites etc. (*ibid. v.* 54), and so forth. It is clear, therefore, that in these verses of Chronicles the 'father' of a given city is its founder, or the one who rebuilt it, or the eponym to whom the tribe dwelling there traces its descent; and his 'sons' are not actually *sons*, but are called sons only metaphorically. Outside the confines of the people of Israel we also

181

find such linguistic usages. For instance, on the coins of Sidon this city is termed the 'mother' of other Phoenician cities or settlements, including Tyre (*lṣdn 'm kkb 'p' kt ṣr*), and on the coins of Tyre, the latter is called the 'mother' of the Sidonians (*lṣr 'm ṣdnm*); compare ii Sam. xx 19; *a city and a mother in Israel.* In this way we must understand in our chapter the terms *father, son, begot.* Nor should we be surprised at the fact that in this chapter the boundaries between an *individual* and a *tribe* (or *people*) and a *city* (or *state*) are blurred. The scholars who attribute to this chapter naive and primitive conceptions, as though it intended to tell us that a man named Egypt begot a man called Ludim and a man called Anamim and other people with similar names, or that a person called Canaan begot a man called Sidon and a man called Heth and a man named the Jebusite and the like, fail to understand the nomenclature of the passage.

In this way it is possible to understand the duplication of the names Havilah and Sheba, which occur twice in the chapter, the first time among the sons and grandsons of Cush, and subsequently among the sons of Joktan (the name Ludim in *v.* 13 may denote a different people from Lud in *v.* 22). Although one man can have only one father, a tribe may be composed of different elements, and in such instances the Bible apparently intends to indicate that these tribes comprised some ethnic elements pertaining to Cush and others belonging to Joktan, like the Manahathites mentioned in Chronicles, half of whom were assigned to Shobal (i Chron. ii 52; compare Gen. xxxvi 23) and half to Salma (i Chron. ii 54). Needless to say, the two different elements are counted as two in the total of seventy nations.

§ 7. According to the prevailing Documentary Hypothesis the chapter is not homogeneous, but is *an amalgam of fragments, some culled from source J and others derived from source P, apart from later interpolations.* This is the dominant view since Wellhausen (previously, opinions were divided as to whether to attribute the chapter to J or E or P). As a rule scholars assign to P *vv.* 1a, 2–7, 20, 22–23, 31–32, and the rest to J (according to Pfeiffer to S), except for a few verses or fragments of verses that are regarded as later additions.

But actually the fact that the structure of the chapter shows clear signs of numerical symmetry both in its general framework and in its details, as we have learnt from our investigation in § 4, proves beyond doubt that the entire chapter is a unitary composition and not the product of the chance piecing together of various excerpts and later insertions. Hence, we might have been justified in forgoing any discussion of the reasons that led to the above-mentioned dissection of the chapter. However, in order to discharge our duty fully, let us examine the arguments and test them one by one.

The reasons, as Gunkel summarizes them in his commentary, are as follows:

(1) There is a double exordium to the history of the sons of Shem, *v.* 21 on the one side and *v.* 22 on the other; there is also a twofold introduction to the entire 'Table' — ix 18a–19 on the one hand, and x 1a on the other.

(2) The names Sheba and Havilah occur twice (*v.* 7 and *vv.* 28–29).

(3) The character of some verses is quite different from that of others: dry lists of names occur in one part, whilst in another we hear the echo of ancient legends concerning Nimrod.

(4) Nimrod the son of Cush, who is spoken of in *vv.* 8–12, is not mentioned among the sons of Cush in *v.* 7.

(5) In several verses there are noticeable characteristics peculiar to the style of P: words like תּוֹלְדוֹת *tōledhōth* ['generations', 'history'] or לְמִשְׁפְּחוֹתָם *lemišpehōthām* ['by their families']; the use of the explicative *Beth;* opening and closing formulae like *This is the history, The sons of, And sons of, These are the sons of.*

(6) In other verses there are discernible stylistic pecularities exclusive to J: the verb יָלַד *yāladh* in the sense of הוֹלִיד *hōlīdh* and examples of it in passive conjugations (*v.* 1, וַיִּוָּלְדוּ *wayyiwwāledhū* ['were born']; *vv.* 21, 25; יֻלַּד *yulladh* ['were (was) born']; the occurrence of the Tetragrammaton twice in *v.* 9; נָפֹצוּ *naphōṣū* ['were spread abroad'] in *v.* 18; בֹּאֲכָה *bō'ăkhā* ['in the direction of'] in *vv.* 19, 30.

Regarding these arguments, it should be noted:

(1) There is a special introduction to the history of the sons of Shem in *v.* 21, apart from the usual opening formula of *v.* 22, on account of the particular importance of Shem, the father of all the sons of Israel. But the earlier exordium, ix 18–19, does not

belong to our chapter, and can be linked to our chapter only arbitrarily in order to declare subsequently that there is a redundant duplication here.

(2)   The difficulty represented by the repetition of the names Sheba and Havilah is not solved by the distribution of the verses between the different documents. The conjecture that the text is composite only transfers the problem from the responsibility of the author to that of the editor, and in so far as the latter is concerned the difficulty remains unresolved. I have already indicated in the previous subdivision [§ 6] how the duplication is to be correctly explained.

(3)   The introduction of material from the ancient legends into 'dry' lists is common in the ancient East; it will suffice to mention the numerous examples of mythological material interpolated in the Sumerian King List. See my remarks on this subject in Part I, pp. 188 f.

(4)   In *v.* 7 are mentioned the *peoples* that claim descent from Cush, whereas in *vv.* 8–12 Nimrod is spoken of as a notable *individual* of the sons of Cush; it is self-understood that the name of a *person* could not be included in a list of *peoples*.

(5)   The view that words like תּוֹלְדוֹת *tōlᵉdhōth* or לְמִשְׁפְּחוֹתָם *lᵉmišpᵉḥōthām* or a particle like the explicative *Bēth*, or formulae like 'This is the history of', '(And) the sons of so-and-so', 'These are the sons of so-and-so' were restricted to a given writer or to a group of writers, and might not be used by other authors or groups, cannot be considered a serious contention save by those who forget that the Biblical writers spoke and wrote Hebrew as a living language and had full command of it in all its aspects, and *a fortiori* were cognizant of simple expressions like these.

(6)   The same is true of phrases that are regarded as peculiar to source J. The reason for the occurrence of the Tetragrammaton instead of אֱלֹהִים *'Elōhīm in v.* 9 I shall explain in my commentary to that verse. On the employment of the verb יָלַד *yāladh* in the sense of הוֹלִיד *hōlīdh* ['beget'], I have written at length in my Italian work *La Questione della Genesi*, pp. 102–104, and in my Hebrew book *The Documentary Hypothesis* (English translation, pp. 43–47). There I have shown that the use of this verb in the *Qal* or *Hiphʿīl* is governed by the laws of Biblical Hebrew and

184

Hebraic style in general, and is not limited to any particular author or source. In similar vein I wrote with regard to the word בֹּאֲכָה *bō'ăkhā* in *La Questione della Genesi*, pp. 148–149. Since I have published my observations on this word only in Italian, I shall revert here to an interesting point, namely, that of the five examples of this word in the Book of Genesis one is found in a paragraph that is attributed as a whole to source P, and the adherents of the documentary theory delete this verse from the passage on the very ground that it contains this word, which they wish to assign to J exclusively. This is the method of the Procrustean bed; it seeks by force to render the explicit evidence of the text null and void. Thus we see that not one of the reasons advanced in favour of the said dissection of the chapter is able to stand the test of criticism.

§ 8. *The sources of the chapter* are not therefore documents of the type of P or J or the like, from which fragments were extracted mechanically. Without doubt the material was derived from different sources, but the whole variegated content was smelted down into a single mass by the fire of literary creation, as silver is smelted in a crucible, and it is no longer possible to discern in the work before us each of the various elements that have become amalgamated in it, just as in the waters of the Jordan that pour into the Dead Sea one cannot distinguish between the waters that came from the Yarmuk or the Jabbok or the other tributaries. However, even if it is not possible to distinguish and separate everything with precision, it is at least possible to discern a few of the source types. One of these is the tradition of the exponents of 'Wisdom', which is itself compounded of various elements, including information gathered in the circles of the Canaanite merchants. The parallels between our chapter and the Book of Ezekiel, and especially the lament on Tyre, which details the trading centres of the Tyrians, and is based, as B. Maisler [Mazar] has recently proved, on Phoenician documents, enables us, as we shall show in detail in the continuation of our section, to recognize these sources of the chapter. Another kind of material emanates from epic poetry, the ancient heroic poesy. Just as in the Sumerian King List there are often interpolated, among the official data concerning the names of kings, the cities of their kingdoms and the length of their reigns, notices about the valorous deeds of the most famous monarchs, drawn from the epic poetry of Mesopotamia, so there are introduced here references to the mighty acts of Nimrod from an epos that spoke of him and his deeds at length. In the commentary we shall deal fully with these allusions — the form in which they appear, and the character, content and distinctive features of the ancient poem on Nimrod — as far as it will be possible to elucidate them.

§ 9. This is not the place to discuss the *age* of the chapter's *composition*. This question is an inseparable part of the general problem of the date of the Book of Genesis, and the proper place for examining the subject will be the Introduction to the entire Book, which I shall prepare later, *Deo volente* *. Here it will suffice to make one general observation, to wit, that the knowledge we have gained about the ancient world from the documents that have been discovered and published in recent years point to an earlier rather than a later date for the composition of our chapter. Peoples about whom, till a little while ago, we had knowledge only from late sources are now known to us from older documents, and hence the mention of them in our chapter cannot be regarded as evidence of the late date of its composition or final redaction. It also contains a number of details that can be properly understood only on the assumption that its date is early. We shall deal with some of these indications later in our notes. The treatment of the problem in its entirety is best reserved, as I have stated, for the introductory volume *.

§ 10. It is desirable to add a few more prefatory observations regarding the correct method, as I see it, to be adopted in the interpretation of this chapter.

Most commentators, thinking that the intention of the text is to explain the ethnographic divisions of mankind, have devoted their main efforts to attempts to identify the peoples mentioned. It was quite easy to advance theories in this regard, but it was very difficult in most cases to achieve any degree of probability. In the vast store of ethnic and geographical names preserved in the documents and literatures of the Eastern and Classical peoples,

---

* Unfortunately, the author died before he was able to write the Introduction.

it was no problem for any scholar to find for every name in our chapter a number of more or less similar names; he had only to choose. Nor was the choice always made with adequate care; some did not pay sufficient attention to phonetic principles and were content with some similarity in the sound of the names, and others did not hesitate to emend and change the form of the Scriptural names in order to achieve closer approximation to their suggestions. Consequently the attempts at identification grew increasingly numerous, and the material that accumulated in commentaries and dissertations on this chapter was unending. But many of these attempted explanations are mere conjectures, and not a few were disproved recently by the extension of our knowledge of the ancient world. Yet even in our present state of knowledge, despite all the endeavours of a number of exegetes to identify the names, much still remains unclear.

In my view (which I shall endeavour to prove in the continuation of my commentary) some details of the Table were obscure from the very outset, and the Bible's intention in including them was merely to make certain vague allusions and nothing more — to refer generally, as it were, to distant peoples a faint echo of whose names only had reached the Israelites, without any precise information about their character or the places of their habitation. These names served the Torah only as material for the building of a given structure, and as a means of expressing a certain idea. To elucidate the structure that Scripture wished to build, and the thought that it desired to convey, is the primary task, if I am not mistaken, of the commentator.

Consequently, I shall not assign greater importance to the problem of identifying the names than it deserves. I shall content myself with mentioning the explanations that have probability, mostly without naming the expositors, who will be cited later in the bibliography; only occasionally, when I see some specific reason for it, shall I include a passing reference to less likely proposals. Of the names that are indeterminate, I shall simply state that we have no means of identifying them. The reader who is interested in the detailed history of the research into the problems of identification, will be able to find the requisite information in other commentaries or in monographs on the subject that I shall list in the bibliography. Although this investigation is instrinsically valuable, it is not in my opinion of primary importance in the exegesis of the chapter. The principal and most vital problems connected with the understanding of this chapter are of a different kind, and my predecessors among the commentators have not paid attention to them. These are, as I have stated, the questions relating to the structure of the chapter and its general and detailed aims. It is chiefly to these problems that I shall devote myself in my annotations, just as I have already devoted to them most of the subsections of the introduction.

§ 11. The *bibliography* will be given, as I have previously indicated, at the end of the volume, p. 286.

THE RUBRIC

CHAPTER X

1.   *And this is the history of the sons of Noah.*

1.   *And this* [וְאֵלֶּה *we'ēlle*] *is the history,* etc.] The *Wāw* of וְאֵלֶּה *we'ēlle* serves as a link with the end of the preceding narrative of this section. Noah passed away, but his sons and grandsons remained alive and founded a new human race that filled the earth, as we were told in the previous narrative: *These three were the sons of Noah; and from these the whole earth was peopled.* In the *preceding section* and in the *next section,* the superscription comes to indicate a new theme, and it contains the words אֵלֶּה תּוֹלְדֹת *'ēlle tōledhōth* ['This is the history'] without *Wāw.* Compare, in *vv.* 2–4, בְּנֵי *benē* ['sons of'] at the beginning of the paragraph, and subsequently וּבְנֵי *ūbhenē* ['and sons of'] in the continuation thereof; so, too, further on in our chapter.

INTRODUCTORY WORDS

[1. continued]   *Shem, Ham and Japheth;*
  and sons were born to them / after the flood.

Shem, Ham and Japheth] These names are not, as many exegetes suppose, in apposition to the expression *sons of Noah;* for if this were the intention, the word order would have been reversed, thus: And this is the history of Shem, Ham and Japheth, the sons of Noah. It is likewise difficult to agree with the interpretation of those who construe the sentence as follows: And these are the תּוֹלָדוֹת *tōlādhōth* [literally, 'generations'; rendered: 'history'] of the sons of Noah, to wit, Shem, Ham and Japheth. For Shem, Ham and Japheth were not the *tōlādhōth of the sons* of Noah, but only the *sons* of Noah. The correct way of understanding the verse is to regard the three names as standing alone (just as at the beginning of the Book of Chronicles we find: Adam, Sheth, Enosh, etc.), and forming, as it were, a list of the first generation after the Deluge.

And sons were born to them after the flood] Although there were only three when they left the ark, sons were born to them afterwards, and the number of human beings multiplied.

After the flood] In the section of the Deluge only their wives are mentioned, not their sons; in order to elucidate the matter the verse expressly explains that sons were born to them only after the Flood.

The expression *after the flood* constitutes another link with the end of the preceding chapter (ix 28: *And Noah lived after the flood*).

DESCENDANTS OF JAPHETH

2. *The sons of Japheth:*
    Gomer, and Magog and Madai and Javan, and Tubal and
    Meshech and Tiras.

3. *And the sons of Gomer:*
    Ashkenaz, and Riphath and Togarmah.

4. *And the sons of Javan:*
    Elishah and Tarshish, / Kittim and Dodanim.

5. *From these spread / the coastland peoples in their lands,*
    each one with his own language, / by their families, in their
    nations.

2. *The sons of Japheth*] Japheth was regarded as the eldest of the
sons of Noah, as we saw above in the commentary to ix 24; hence
the list of his generations comes first. On the meaning of the word
sons, which denotes not actual sons but nations who claim kinship
with Japheth, see the introduction to this chapter, § 6, pp. 181 f.
Not all of these peoples can be identified with certainty, but, as far
as it is possible to judge, they have this in common that they all
lived in the lands of the North.

Gomer] This people, which is listed here before Magog, is
mentioned in Ezekiel xxxviii 6, as one of the confederates of *Gog,*
of the land of *Magog.* Apparently they are identical with the
Cimmerians (Κιμμέριοι) alluded to by the Greeks, and may have
belonged to the same stock as the Scythians. They dwelt at first
north of the Black Sea, but after a time they migrated to Asia
Minor, and, under the name of *Gimirraya,* they are mentioned in
Assyrian inscriptions as living there.

And Magog] This is the name of the land or people of Gog in
Ezekiel xxxviii 2, and xxxix 6. Regarding the identification of
Magog, as of Gog, numerous suggestions of various kinds have
been made, but they all encounter many difficulties, and it is
impossible to decide between them. In any case, it seems that Magog
belongs to the group of Scythian peoples (on the Scythians see

190

further the notes to *v.* 3). Recent researches have shown that in the area inhabited by the Israelites the existence of the Cimmerians and Scythians was known at a much earlier period than was previously supposed.

And Madai] This is the well-known people that dwelt east of Assyria and is mentioned in the Bible a number of times. As far back as the dynasty of Akkad, Median soldiers were mentioned by the name of *Umman Manda* (the second half of the third millenium B.C.E.). Their usual name in the Assyrian documents is *Madaya*, which corresponds to the Hebrew name. In the inscriptions on the fall of Nineveh into the hands of Babylon and Media, the ancient name Umman Manda reappears.

And Javan] This is the tribe of the Ionians, one of the tribes of the stock that we are accustomed to call collectively the Hellenic race. Ionian settlers founded twelve settlements in the western part of Asia Minor. The view has been advanced that this name existed in the form *ym'an* in the Ugaritic writings, but this is doubtful.

And Tubal and Meshech] These two peoples are always mentioned together in the Bible (Ezek. xxvii 13; xxxii 26; xxxviii 2–3; xxxix 1). In Isa. lxvi 19, *Tubal* occurs next to *Javan*, but before them mention is made of מֹשְׁכֵי קֶשֶׁת *mōšekhē qešeth* ['who draw the bow'], which is an allusion to *Meshech,* and in the Septuagint we actually find Meshech (in Psa. cxx 5 *Meshech* is not definitely to be identified with the peoples referred to here; and in i Chronicles i 17 *and Meshech* occurs in error for *and Mash*).

In the Assyrian inscriptions, too, the land of *Tabâl* is mentioned next to the land of *Mušku* or *Musku,* and apparently they were near to the land of *ḥlkh* (Cilicia of the Greeks) in Asia Minor. Herodotus also places the two peoples Μόσχοι and Τιβαρίνοί (or Τιβαροί) in juxtaposition. In his time they seemed to have lived in a more northern region, on the southern shore of the Black Sea. On the vowel *u/o* in the Assyrian and Greek forms of the name מֶשֶׁךְ *Mešekh* ['Meshech'], compare the form מוֹשֶׁךְ *Mōšekh* in the Samaritan Pentateuch and Μόσοχ in the Septuagint.

And Tiras] It has been suggested that they are to be identified with the people mentioned in the Egyptian documents by the name of *Twrwš'* or *Tywr'š',* who invaded Egypt at the end of the thirteenth and the beginning of the twelfth centuries B.C.E. (They

191

are perhaps the Τυρσηνοί of the Greeks, that is, the Etruscans).
But the matter is uncertain.

On all these peoples see also my remarks at the end of my
annotations on *v.* 4.

3. *And the sons of Gomer*] — that is, peoples who were considered to be branches of the Gomer race, or were connected with
it in some way.

Ashkenaz] It appears that this name denotes the inhabitants of
the country called *Ašguza* or *Iškuza* in Assyrian inscriptions, and
that they are the Scythians (see above, on Gomer). In Jer. li 27,
the kingdoms of Ararat, Minni and Ashkenaz are invited to attack
Babylon — from the north, of course.

And Riphath] The name cannot be identified. Several conjectures
have been made, but they are improbable. In the usual editions of
i Chronicles i 6, we find *Diphath*, with a *Dāleth;* but in a number
of MSS and early editions, and likewise in the Septuagint and
Vulgate, the word is also written with a *Rēš* in Chronicles as here.

And Togarmah] In Hittite writings there occurs the name of
the district and city *Tagarma, Tegaram(m)a,* (also *Takarama*),
and from the history of the Hittite king Muršiliš II (fourteenth
century B.C.E.) it appears that this district was north of the road
between Haran and Carchemish. This seems to be Togarmah of the
Bible. In Ezek. xxxviii 6, mention is made of *Beth-togarmah from
the uttermost parts of the north* as one of the allies of Gog; and
in Ezek. xxvii 14, Beth-togarmah is included among the peoples
who maintain trading relations with Tyre.

Also with regard to the sons of Gomer see my remarks at the
end of the annotations to *v.* 4.

4. *And the sons of Javan*] On the meaning of the words *and the
sons of* see above, on *vv.* 2, 3.

Elishah and Tarshish, Kittim and Dodanim] These names are
arranged in two pairs, the two names in each pair being connected
by a copulative *Wāw,* but there is no such link between the pairs.
The first two words, which have no plural ending, are geographical
designations. The second two, which have a plural termination, are
ethnic appellations.

Elishah] Apparently it is identical with *Alašiya* of Akkadian
and Hittite inscriptions (the gentilic name *'alty* is found in Ugaritic

writings), that is, the island of Cyprus or a part of it. The latest archaeological discoveries testify to the existence of Greek settlements in Cyprus already in the fifteenth and fourteenth centuries B.C.E., if not earlier still; it is to one of these colonies that our text refers. Other identifications of Elishah are unlikely. *The coasts of Elishah* are also mentioned in Ezekiel xxvii 7.

And Tarshish] The reference apparently is to a Greek settlement in a region where subsequently a Phoenician colony by this name was founded — possibly the famous Tarshish in Spain (Ταρτησσός), whose fortress was built, according to Herodotus, by the Phocaeans of Ionia; or perhaps another Phoenician settlement by this name in Sardinia (see Albright, *BASOR*, 83, October 1941, 21–22). The establishment of Phoenician colonies in the islands of the Mediterranean is considered today to have begun much earlier than was estimated by scholars a few decades ago. The name is mentioned a number of times in the Bible.

Kittim] It seems to have been another Hellenic settlement in the island of Cyprus, apart from the one referred to above, called Elishah. There, too, there was later founded a Phoenician colony, known as *kty* or *kt* (in Greek Κίτιον or Κέττιον, today Larnaka). The name Kittim occurs several times in Scripture, having at times a wider signification.

And Dodanim] In i Chron. i 7, according to some MSS and the editions: *And Rodanim*. In this verse, too, the Samaritan Recension reads *Rēš* instead of the initial *Dāleth*. The inhabitants of the island of Rhodes (already in the Septuagint, Ῥόδιοι), may be intended. Other conjectures are implausible. In Rhodes, too, as in Cyprus, we know today of ancient Greek colonies.

For the understanding of these verses, 2–4, the parallels between them and the Book of Ezekiel are very important; it is of value, therefore, to discuss the matter in detail. In the prophecy concerning Gog, the prophet turns to *Gog of the land of* MAGOG, *the chief prince of* MESHECH *and* TUBAL (xxxviii 2–3; xxxix 1), and among the confederates of Gog he counts GOMER *and all his hordes,* BETH-TOGARMAH *from the uttermost parts of the north with all his hordes* (xxxviii 6), and in the continuation he mentions also *the merchants of* TARSHISH (*v.* 13). In the dirge over Tyre (Ezekiel xxvii), among the peoples that have mercantile relations with Tyre, reference is made to the inhabitants of *the coasts of Elishah* (*v.* 7), *Tarshish* (*v.* 12), and again in juxtaposition in one verse (*v.* 13), *Javan, Tubal and Meshech,* and immediately afterwards (*v.* 14) *Beth-togarmah.* It is further written in Ezekiel xxxii 26, in the description of Sheol: MESHECH AND TUBAL *are there, and all their multitude.* Without doubt there is some connection between Ezekiel's prophecy and our chapter (see also below). Now we know today, from the parallels between the Book of Ezekiel and the Ugaritic inscriptions, that Ezekiel was well-versed in Canaanite culture and traditions (Daniel [דָּנִאֵל *Dāniʾēl*], whom he mentions in chapter xiv together with Noah and Job, and again in chapter xxviii, in his address to the prince of Tyre, is not, it seems, Daniel [דָּנִיֵּאל *Daniyyēʾl*] the hero of the Biblical book that bears his name, but *dnʾil* of the Ugaritic epic). Recently B. Maisler [now, Mazar] showed in a lecture that he delivered at the World Congress of Jewish Studies (summer, 1947) that the details about international trade found in the lament of Tyre are based on Phoenician, that is, Canaanite documents. It is permissible, therefore, to surmise that, on the basis of the information that the Phoenician merchants acquired in their contacts with the peoples of distant lands, there was created and spread in the land of Canaan, and accepted also in the circle of the 'Sages' in Israel, an established tradition concerning the names of the peoples inhabiting the northern countries and those claiming kinship with them.

This tradition is reflected, apparently, both in our chapter and in the Book of Ezekiel. It is impossible to suppose that Ezekiel's statements are dependent solely on our chapter, for they contain more information than we find here, for instance, the names of nations that are not mentioned in our chapter, and details of the characteristics of the peoples and their trade, to which there is not the slightest reference in our passage. Of course, the knowledge of the Israelites regarding the more remote races was only of a general and vague nature — mostly names and nothing more. In the prophecy on Gog, the intention of the prophet, it would appear, was only to allude to very distant peoples, the mere mention of whose names aroused terror and dread for the very reason that they were unknown, and assumed in the imagination of the people a mythical character. So, too, these verses of the Torah refer only in a general and indefinite way to races in far away countries. As I stated in the introduction, the purpose of this chapter is to show the perfect harmony that marks the genesis of the families of the earth in accordance with the preconceived design of God, and not to furnish us with 'scientific' ethnographic data. If someone portrays for the general reading public the majestic splendour of the heavens filled with shining stars on a bright night, he may mention in the course of his description the names of a few stars by way of illustration, but he would not expect that the ordinary reader would have a thorough understanding of the nature of these stars and their position in the heavenly constellations, or that his remarks would serve him as a lesson in astronomy. Such, too, was the purpose of these verses, and also of several of the succeeding verses in mentioning names of peoples far removed from the habitation and the knowledge of the children of Israel. The Bible is content to record the names of the peoples, but has no intention of giving us information about their character and country; and we must not seek to discover in Scripture more than it purposes to tell its readers.

5. *From these spread,* etc.] This is the end of the paragraph; it corresponds to the closing sentences of the two following paragraphs (*vv.* 20, 31), which are essentially similar to it, differing from it only in the changing and modification of a few words in accordance with the usual stylistic canon (see further below). From this it is clear that the words *from these* do not refer, as many have held, solely to the sons of Javan but to all the sons of Japheth collectively, just as in *v.* 32 the sentence, *From these spread abroad* etc., alludes to all the families of the sons of Noah taken together. The paragraph-ending in our verse (*v.* 5) comes to tell us that those named do not represent *all* the nations that stemmed from the sons of Japheth, but only the principal peoples, and from them spread various other races whom it is unnecessary to detail.

Spread [נִפְרְדוּ *niphreᵈhū,* literally, 'were separated, divided'] / Compare Gen. ii 10: *and from there* IT DIVIDED [יִפָּרֵד *yippārēdh*] *and became four branch-streams.* Just as the river that went forth from Eden divided — that means, split and became ramified — into four branch-streams, even so from the aforementioned offspring of

Japheth there branched out many more different nations. Compare also Deut. xxxii 8: *when He* SEPARATED [בְּהַפְרִידוֹ *b^ehaphrīdhō*] *the sons of men.*

The coastland peoples [אִיֵּי הַגּוֹיִם *'iyyē haggōyīm*, literally, 'the isles [coastlands] of the nations'] / The meaning is: 'the peoples of the coastlands of the nations', just as further on (xi 1) כָל־הָאָרֶץ *khol hā'āreṣ* [literally, 'all the earth'] signifies all human beings upon the earth. The reference is not only to the islands but to all the lands bordering the Mediterranean on the west and the north. The word אִיִּים *'iyyīm* ['islands'] denotes in general all countries adjoining the sea, like the rabbinic phrase מְדִינַת הַיָּם *m^edhīnath hayyām* ['maritime province or country', i. e. a distant country overseas].

In their lands, each one with his own language, by their families, in their nations] These are all distributive expressions: From these spread abroad the peoples of the coastlands of the nations, each one in his own land, each one speaking his own language, each one divided into his families, each one organized according to his own political system. These distributive terms recur with a few changes, as I have mentioned, in the concluding sentences of the following paragraphs (*v.* 20: *by their families, by their languages, in their lands, in their nations;* and almost the identical wording is found in *v.* 31, the only divergence being the last word לְגוֹיֵהֶם *l^eghōyēhem* [literally, 'to their nations'] in place of בְּגוֹיֵהֶם *b^eghōyēhem* [literally, 'in their nations']. Similar expressions are used also at the end of the entire chapter with reference to all the sons of Noah (*v.* 32: *according to their genealogies in their nations*).

The number of the peoples mentioned in this paragraph is fourteen — twice times seven: seven sons of Japheth and seven grandsons. On the significance of the number *seven* and of the other numbers in this chapter, see above, in the introduction, pp. 175 f.

SCOND PARAGRAPH

DESCENDANTS OF HAM

6. *And the sons of Ham:*
   Cush, and Egypt, and Put, and Canaan.

7. *And the sons of Cush:*
   Seba, and Havilah, and Sabtah, and Raamah, and Sabteca.
   And the sons of Raamah:
   Sheba and Dedan.

8. *And Cush —*
   begot Nimrod:
   he was the first / to be a mighty man on earth.

9. *He was a mighty hunter / before the Lord;*
   therefore it is said,
   'Like Nimrod a mighty hunter / before the Lord.'

10. *And the beginning of his kingdom was / Babylon,*
    and Erech, and Accad, and Calneh / in the land of Shinar.

11. *From that land / he went to Assyria,*
    and built Nineveh, / and Rehoboth-ir and Calah,

12. *and Resen between Nineveh and Calah; / that is the great*
    city.

13. *And Egypt —*
    begot Ludim, and Ananim, and Lehabim, and
14. *Naphtuhim, //* *and Pathrusim, and Casluhim (whence*
    came the Philistines) and Caphtorim.

15. *And Canaan —*
16. *begot Sidon his first-born, and Heth, // and the*
17. *Jebusites, and the Amorites and the Girgashites, // and the*
18. *Hivites, and the Arkites, and the Sinites, // and the*
    Arvadites, and the Zamarites, and the Hamathites; and
    afterward the families of the Canaanites spread abroad.

---

* The two strokes indicate the beginning of a verse; one stroke, here
as elesewhere, marks the caesura.

19. *And the territory of the Canaanites extended / from Sidon,*
   until you come to Gerar, / as far as Gaza:
   until you come to Sidon, and Gommorrah, and Admah and
      Zeboiim, / as far as Lasha.
20. *These are the sons of Ham,*
   by their families, by their languages / in their lands, in their
      nations.

6. *And the sons of Ham*] After the genealogy of the sons of
Japheth, the oldest of the sons of Noah, the Bible gives us the
pedigree of the sons of Ham, the third son, in order to leave to the
end — as the climax — Shem, who, although the middle one in
order of birth, was the most important of them, since he was
the primogenitor of the people of Israel. The Torah first completes
the genealogy of Japheth and Ham so as to dispose of the subject
and avoid the need to revert to it later; whereas the account of
Shem's offspring, who are central to the narrative, will continue
in the subsequent chapters. In accordance with this principle, the
descendants of Ishmael are listed first (xxv 12–18), so that the
Bible may proceed afterwards to the history of Isaac's children, who
are the more important (xxv 19 ff.); similarly the roll of Esau's
sons (chapter xxxvi) precedes that of Jacob (xxxvii 2 ff.).

Cush and Egypt and Put and Canaan] Here, too, the names are
divided into two pairs as in *v.* 4. In each of the two pairs, a short
name comes first followed by a longer one, in accordance with
the rule that I have explained above, p. 165. In i Chron. i 8, the
division into pairs is even more palpable because of the omission
of the copulative *Wāw* before *Put;* see a similar example in *v.* 4
of our chapter.

Cush] It is difficult to identify this Cush with the well-known
people of Cush, who dwelt south of Egypt, or with the Cassites who
ruled for a long time over southern Mesopotamia in the second half
of the second millenium B.C.E. More probably the reference is to
the west Semitic tribes called *Kwšw* in the Egyptian Execration
Texts, second series, which belong to the second half of the
nineteenth century B.C.E. Apparently, these tribes lived south of
the land of Israel or Transjordania, and in the course of time were
absorbed among the Midianites (compare the *Cushite* woman in
Num. xii 1, and *Cushan* in parallelism to Midian in Hab. iii 7).

And Egypt] Here the reference is undoubtedly to the well-known country of Egypt, and not as many exegetes have thought, to the tribe *Muṣri,* who lived south of the land of Canaan, or to *Muṣri* of Asia Minor. It is not feasible that no mention should be made in this chapter of a people so important in the history of Israel as the people of Egypt.

And Put] The name is mentioned several times in the Bible, but it is impossible to identify it. Many scholars have thought it to be the land called in Egyptian *Pwnt,* apparently in West Africa. But it is difficult to accept that *Ṭēth* in Hebrew should take the place of the feminine termination *Tāw.* Possibly the reference is to the land of *Putāyā* mentioned in the list of the conquests of Darius I; it is apparently Cyrenaica in North Africa.

And Canaan] This name denotes here the whole group of peoples inhabiting the country called later in the Bible the *land of Canaan* — the land that was destined to become the land of Israel (xii 7; compare below xi 31). In *vv.* 15–19 we shall be told in detail who are the people comprised by the name Canaan, and from there it will be clear that *Canaan* is used here in its widest connotation.

7. *And the sons of Cush: Seba,* etc.] All the names of the sons of Cush are those of Arabian tribes, or Arabian places, apparently in North Arabia. The attempts made to identify them exactly are mere conjectures, and it is unnecessary to consider them in detail.

Sheba] It is known as the name of an important kingdom in South Arabia, but at first the people of Sheba dwelt in North Arabia, and it seems that they did not migrate to the south till the eighth century B.C.E.

And Dedan] — apparently al-ʿUlā in North Arabia, a very important trading centre.

Many of the peoples recorded in these verses (6–7) are mentioned also in other passages of the Bible, especially in Ezekiel. See on this point my remarks at the end of the annotations to *v.* 4. With reference to *Sheba* and *Dedan* in Gen. xxv 3, see my commentary *ad locum,* when it is published. *

* Owing to the author's demise, this section of the Commentary was not written.

8. This verse and the verses following, as far as *v.* 12 (inclusive), form a parenthetic note on Nimrod and his deeds.

And Cush begot Nimrod] Above already there appeared a list of the sons of Cush and of Raamah the son of Cush, that is to say, a list of peoples who claimed descent from Cush. Here the Bible comes to give us additional particulars concerning a renowned *man* (not *people*) of the sons of Cush. Possibly the verse does not imply that this person was a direct offspring of Cush and his wife, but that he belonged to one of the peoples known as the 'sons' of Cush. Since the term 'sons' was till now used in the sense of peoples, and in the present verse a particular individual is referred to, it was appropriate to introduce a variation in the phrasing here; hence the verb יָלַד *yāladh,* which is more suited to the theme, is employed at this point. The subject precedes the verb, in accordance with the principle we discussed in our notes to i 2 (Part I, p. 21), as though to say: As for Cush mentioned earlier, it should also be added that he was the father of Nimrod etc.

Nimrod] It appears that Nimrod was a famous ancient hero, and was a popular subject of Israelite epic poetry. One may conjecture that here, in the second part of *v.* 8 and in the first part of *v.* 9, as well as in *vv.* 10–12, several lines of an epic devoted to Nimrod are quoted — perhaps an excerpt from the very opening lines which indicated at the outset, in accordance with the customary practice in epic poetry, the subject of the poem. In the continuation of the poem, in so far as we can surmise, a detailed account was given of his mighty deeds in hunting beasts and monsters, of his military expeditions and conquests in the lands of Babylon and Assyria, and of the cities he built. The poem may have reflected memories of the wars and conquests of the 'Amorites' in Babylon and Assyria. We know that successive invasions of the 'Amorites' brought about the destruction of the kingdom of Sumer and Akkad at the beginning of the second millenium B.C.E. The city of Babylon became, apparently about the nineteenth century, the capital of an 'Amorite' kingdom, and near the end of that century, the city of Asshur, the capital of the kingdom of Assyria, fell into the hands of an 'Amorite' conqueror. In the Akkadian language these conquerors were called Amurru (Amorites), and the name embraces a group of nations that are termed today West Semitic. The Cushite tribes in the southern part of the country belonged specifically to the West Semitic peoples (although the term 'Semitic', which is commonly used in present-day science, was, as we know, coined on the basis of this chapter in Genesis, it does not fit exactly the group of peoples described here as sons of Shem; the Canaanites, for example are classified by modern scholarship as Semitic peoples, although they are here listed among the sons of Ham). We have already noted earlier (p. 185) that such quotations introduced from epic poetry into registers of important personages are likewise found in Mesopotamian writings. We also discussed above (p. 146) the connection between what is here related concerning Nimrod and the story of the Generation of Division at the beginning of chapter xi.

He was the first to be a mighty man on earth] It appears that the epic poem related that in the post-diluvian period Nimrod was the first that began to perform wondrous deeds of valour.

9. *He was a mighty hunter*] The mighty fighters showed their prowess by hunting fearsome animals and terrifying monsters; it is enough to mention the deeds of Gilgameš and his friend Enkidu.

Before the Lord ['ה *YHWH*] / When *YHWH* looked upon the earth and the acts of mankind, the heroic acts of Nimrod stood out with particular prominence before His eyes. Compare Gen. vi 11: *Now the earth was corrupt before* אֱלֹהִים ’*Elōhīm;* and Jonah iii 3: *Now Nineveh was a great city unto* אֱלֹהִים ’*Elōhīm* [E.V. 'an exceeding great city']. The Tetragrammaton occurs here because the epic poem from which these verses are cited was a purely Israelite work. On the use of the name אֱלֹהִים ’*Elōhīm* in vi 11, and in the section of the Flood generally, see above, p. 35 f. As for the expression in Jonah iii 3 ['a great city unto אֱלֹהִים ’*Elōhīm*], it seems to belong to the same type of expression as חִתַּת אֱלֹהִים *ḥittath* ’*Elōhīm* [Gen. xxxv 5: 'a terror from God', i.e. a great terror]; חֶרְדַּת אֱלֹהִים *ḥerdath* ’*Elōhīm* [i Sam. xiv 15: 'a panic from God', i.e. a great panic]; נַפְתּוּלֵי אֱלֹהִים *naphtūlē* ’*Elōhīm* [Gen. xxx 8; 'wrestlings of God', i.e. mighty wrestlings]; אַרְזֵי אֵל ’*arzē* ’*El* [Psa. lxxx 10 (Hebrew, *v.* 11) 'the cedars of God', i.e. mighty cedars]; הַרְרֵי אֵל *harerē* ’*El* [Psa. xxxvi 7: 'mountains of God', i.e. mighty mountains], and the like, which prefer the generic names of the deity.

Therefore it is said, etc.] A popular proverb is quoted here that was widely current in Israel, and was based on the words of an epic poem in praise of Nimrod. When people wanted to pay the highest tribute to anyone for his prowess in the chase, they used to say of him that he was *like Nimrod, a mighty hunter before the Lord.* 10. *And the beginning of his kingdom was Babel,* etc.] — that is to say, his first conquests, which laid the foundation of his kingdom, comprised these cities and their environs. See my observations above (*v.* 8) on the conquests of the 'Amorites'.

Babylon] The well-known city in South Mesopotamia, which became the centre of an extensive empire in the days of its first dynasty, the 'Amorite' dynasty, due chiefly, to Ḥammurabi, the greatest of the kings of this line.

And Erech] This is the city of Gilgameš (*Unuk* in Sumerian, *Uruk* in Akkadian). Today the name of the place is *Warka,* about two hundred kilometre south-east of Babylon. In the Sumerian King List it is mentioned as one of the first royal cities after the Deluge, and Gilgameš is listed there third in the series of kings who ruled over it. It was captured by Ḥammurabi and annexed to his domains. Reference is made to the siege of Erech by the 'Amorites' in the Sumerian tale about *Lugalbanda* and *Emmerkar.*

And Akkad] — a city in the northern area of Babylonia, situated beside the ancient course of the Euphrates. Its exact site has not yet been definitely determined. It was the centre of the great empire founded by Sargon I in the twenty-fourth century B.C.E., and fell under the pressure of the barbarian Gutaeans in the twenty-second century. This city also formed a part of the empire of Ḥammurabi.

And Calneh] There is no city by this name known to us in Mesopotamia. The Calneh of Amos vi 2 (or Calno in Isa. x 9) is another town, in North Syria. Various explanations of the word have been advanced. Among others, there is the view that the reference is to the city of Nippur (so already in B. Yoma 10a), the basis for it being the strange conjecture that the ideogram ENLIL KI was read erroneously KI-ENLIL. Others hold that it is not the name of a city, and that the Masoretic vocalization must be changed; thus, for instance, Poebel (1942) proposed: וְכָל-נָוֶה *wᵉkhol nāwe* ['every habitation']; and Albright (1944): וְכֻלָּנָה

w^ekhullānā ['and all of them']. It is not possible to decide between them.

In the land of Shinar [שִׁנְעָר *Sinʿār*] / — Akkadian *Sanḫaru,* and in Egyptian *Sngr* (apparently the *ʿAyin* was originally *Ġayin,* غ). Although this name denotes, in so far as we can judge, a region north-west of Babylonia, in Israelite literature it is used in a wider signification and includes also the land of Babylon; see, for example, below, xi 2, 9; Daniel i 2.

11. *From that land he went to Assyria*] Some have interpreted the Hebrew to mean: Assyria went forth from that land; and others: From that land Nimrod went forth to Assyria. The second interpretation appears more probable, because after reading the previous verse about the *beginning* of Nimrod's kingdom, we expect to be told something about the sequel to this beginning. Compare my remarks above, in my notes to *v.* 8, regarding the conquests of the 'Amorites'. On the basis of this explanation and my aforementioned conjecture, we can well understand the parallelism between *the land of Assyria* and the *land of Nimrod* in Micah v 5.

And built] The word may be understood in the sense of initial building or founding; or it can have the meaning of rebuilding something after it had been destroyed, a connotation that the verb has in several passages of the Bible and in the Mesha inscription.

Nineveh] This is the famous city on the River Tigris, which was, after the city of Ashur, the principal city of the kingdom of Assyria.

And Rehoboth-ir] This may be the Hebrew form of *Rêbit Ninâ,* one of the suburbs of Nineveh, on the northeastern side of the city.

And Calah] — one of the important cities of Assyria; *Kalḫu* in Assyrian. Its ruins are to be found today in a place called now, on the strength of this verse, Tel-Nimrud, which is south of Nineveh.

12. *And Resen*] The site of this city has not yet been determined. The Akkadian form of the name may be indicated by another town, *Risnu,* which was situated in Southern Mesopotamia.

That is the great city] The rabbinic sages already rightly noted: 'One cannot tell whether Nineveh or Resen was described as the great city; but since it is written: *Now Nineveh was an exceeding*

203

great city of three days' journey (Jonah iii 3), it follows that Nineveh is referred to as the great city' (B. Yoma 10a). The meaning would seem to be that the gigantic built-up area of the great city of Nineveh stretched as far as, and included, Resen.

13. *And Egypt begot,* etc.] The names here are of peoples, and not of persons, such as the name of the individual in *v.* 8; hence it was possible to have used in this case, too, as in the first paragraph and at the beginning of this paragraph, the phrase, *and the sons of.* But since in *v.* 8 there occurs the formula *And Cush begot,* it has given rise, by attraction, to a similar expression in our verse, which parallels *v.* 8. It should also be noted that this construction, which places the subject before the verb, is employed here, as in *v.* 8, in order to draw attention once again to the 'father', who is mentioned earlier, as though to say: And as for Egypt, it may be added that he begot Ludim, etc. Generally speaking, we find 'and the sons of so-and-so' when it is intended to emphasize the name of the sons, and 'so-and-so begot' when the intention is to stress the name of the father.

The names in *vv.* 13–14 denote certain sections of the Egyptian population, Egyptian colonies outside the land of Egypt, and other settlements that were to some degree dependent on Egypt. They are listed here in order to indicate the genealogy of the Philistines and Caphtorim, who will be mentioned later. Reference is made to the Philistines in the history of the Patriarchs and also in the Book of Exodus (xiii 17: *the land of the Philistines;* xv 14:; *the inhabitants of Philistia;* xxiii 31: *the sea of the Philistines*); and to the Caphtorim in Deut. ii 23, in a section closely connected with the Book of Genesis, as I have shown in my book *La Questione della Genesi,* pp. 365–374.

From this register it is clear that the use of gentilic names of this kind as proper names without the definite article is not restricted to the names פְּלִשְׁתִּים *Pelištīm* ['Philistines'] and כַּפְתֹּרִים *Kaphtōrīm* ['Caphtorim'], as is stated in the *Hebrew Grammar* of Gesenius-Kautzsch, § 125e. It is apparently a fundamental rule in Hebrew that gentilic names like these in the *plural* can be used either as common nouns, in which case they take the definite article; or as proper names, and then they cannot take the definite article. Compare also i Sam. v 3: *And when the* PEOPLE OF ASHDOD

[אַשְׁדּוֹדִים *'Ašdōdhīm*] *rose early the next day.* In the singular these nouns serve only as appellatives; see *vv.* 16–19.

The order of the names here follows the principle that we discussed earlier (p. 165): first comes the shortest word, לוּדִים *Lūdhīm* ['Ludim'], which has two stem-consonants (the quiescent *Wāw*, which was not written in the ancient spelling, is not, of course, to be counted); this is followed by words of three stem-consonants, עֲנָמִים *'Anāmīm* [Anamim] and לְהָבִים *Lᵉhābhīm* [Leha-bim], and finally names with four radicals, נַפְתֻּחִים *Naphtūḥim* [Naphtuhim] and פַּתְרֻסִים *Pathrūsīm* [Pathrusim], etc.

Ludim] This verse apart, we find in the Bible only the collective name לוּד *Lūdh* [Lud] in the singular. The reference, it seems, is to the people called by the Greeks Λύδιοι (it is superfluous to mention other conjectures that are improbable), who lived in Asia Minor. From Jer. xlvi 9 and Ezek. xxx 5 we learn that the Israelites knew the Ludim at that time as bowmen who served in the Egyptian forces. Hence they are listed here among the peoples related to Egypt. The *Lud* mentioned later (*v.* 22) among the sons of Shem may be a different people; see *ibid.*

Anamim] Various identifications of this people have been suggested, mostly without adequate foundation. Worth noting is Albright's theory (*JPOS,* I [1921], p. 191–192), that the reference is to the inhabitants of the region that was subsequently called Cyrenaica, after the chief city Cyrene, in North Africa.

Lehabim] Perhaps they are the Lybians, who dwelt in Lybia in North Africa, on the shores of the Mediterranean Sea, between Egypt and Cyrenaica. For the form of the word, with added *Hē',* compare the Ugaritic plural *bhtm,* which is equivalent to the Hebrew בָּתִּים *bāttīm* ['houses'], from the stem בית *byt.*

Naphtuhim] Various explanations of the name, based on an Egyptian derivation, have been suggested. The most likely is the view that it denotes the inhabitants of Lower Egypt, on the strength of an Egyptian expression that means 'the north-land'.

14. *Pathrusim*] The inhabitants of Pathros (Isa. xi 11; Jer. xliv 1, 15; Ezek. xxix 14; xxx 14), which is apparently Upper Egypt.

Casluhim] This word is also in doubt. Many scholars have supposed that it denotes the region round the mountain called by the Greeks Κάσιον ὄρος (Mount Casius) between the coast of Egypt and that of Canaan. More probably it refers to the area of the city of Scylacé (Σκυλάκη) in Asia Minor (see below, on the *Philistines*). It need cause us no surprise that the Bible reverts to a region near the land of the Ludim, who had been mentioned first, because the order of the names is not based on geographical but on totally different considerations, as I have indicated in the commentary on *v.* 13.

Whence came the Philistines] Apparently the Philistines are to be identified, according to Albright (*JPOS*, I [1921], p. 57), with the pre-Hellenic population whom the Greeks called the Pelasgians (Πελασγοί). The statement here that the Philistines came from Casluhim accords with the reference in Herodotus to the Pelasgians, who dwelt in Scylacé (I, 57: καὶ τῶν ... Σκυλάκην Πελασγῶν οἰκησάντων ['or those Pelasgians again who founded ... Scylacé']; see the note above on Casluhim).

However, there are two objections to the identification. The first is that from other parts of Scripture it is evident that according to the tradition current among the Israelites the original home of the Philistines was the island of Caphtor (Jer. xlvii 4; Amos ix 7: compare Deut. ii 23, and, since Caphtor is Crete, as we shall see below, also Ezek. xxv 16 and Zeph. ii 5). Various harmonistic attempts have been made to reconcile the conflicting passages; for example, that of Naḥmanides, who conjectures that Casluhim is the name of a particular city in the land of Caphtor; or that of Delitzsch, who surmises that at first immigrants from Casluhim settled in Philistia and thereafter came settlers from Caphtor; or that of Dillmann, who advances the theory that the first migration of the Philistines to the region of their settlement in Canaan took place *via* the Egyptian coast, especially along that part of the coastland that, according to one view, was called Casluhim (see above, on this name). But all these conjectures are far-fetched. Naḥmanides' theory has nothing to support it, whilst the hypotheses of Delitzsch and Dillmann do not really solve the difficulty, since both Casluhim in our verse and Caphtor in the aforementioned passages are mentioned as the *only* place of origin of the Philistines (moreover, it is impossible to understand the expression 'came [literally, 'went forth'] from Casluhim' in the sense of '*passed through* Casluhim', as Dillmann suggests). The majority of later exegetes hold that the whole clause, *whence came the Philistines,* should be transferred to the end of the verse, after *Caphtorim,* or that it should be regarded as a marginal note, appertaining to the name Caphtorim, that was interpolated into the text in the wrong place. But this method of exegesis is equally unsatisfactory; textual harmonization by force — by arbitrary change of wording — fails of its purpose.

The second difficulty is this: both here and later on in the stories of the Patriarchs and in several passages of the Book of Exodus, which we have already cited above, mention is made of the Philistines in an early period of history, whereas, on the other hand, there is reason to believe that the settlement of the Philistines on the coast of Canaan did not take place till after the Israelite conquests. In the Egyptian monuments referring to the invasion of 'the sea peoples', the Philistines are first mentioned in the time of Rameses III, in the beginning of the twelfth century B.C.E., and it seems that only after the attack on Egypt had been repelled, did these Philistines settle on the Canaanite coast by agreement with the Egyptian government, which sought to remove thereby the danger from its own borders. Hence, most scholars hold that all that is stated concerning the Philistines in Genesis and Exodus is purely anachronistic — a description of ancient events in accordance with the later situation obtaining in the period in which the passages were written.

But this interpretation is also difficult. Although it is possible to regard an expression like *the way of the land of the Philistines* (Exod. xiii 17) as an anachronism, that is to say, to assume that this route was called by its subsequent name, just as we are told that Abraham pursued his enemies *as far as Dan* (Gen. xiv 14); yet it is difficult to believe that the actual narratives depicting the relationship between Abraham and Isaac and the Philistines, as well as their background, are mere figments of the imagination. Some time ago (1921), Albright advanced the theory that the Philistines in the time of the Patriarchs were not actually Philistines but Cherethites or Caphtorim (see below); and only in a later formulation of the passage were they called Philistines — a more 'modern' name than the archaic terms Cretan or Caphtorim, and capable of serving as a synonym for them, since the Pelasgo-

Philistines also came to the shores of Canaan from Caphtor, after living in that island for many generations. Nevertheless, it is not easy to understand why the Bible abandoned the correct name and used a synonym.

Recently (1944; see the Bibliography below) my pupil, Y. M. Grintz, put forward a new theory that simultaneously solves the two problems — both the first and the second. His conjecture appears to me plausible. He points out that the Philistines in the period of the Patriarchs differed from those who came after the settlement of the Israelites in a number of respects. They lived in different areas: the former dwelt in the Negeb, between Kadesh and Shur (Gen. xx 1), and the latter on the coast, at Gaza, Ashkelon, Ashdod, Ekron and Gath. Their political systems were also dissimilar: in the time of the Patriarchs, the king of the Philistines is mentioned, whilst in the later epoch, the five lords of the Philistines are spoken of, and if there is any reference to a king, he is king of one city only. There were likewise divergences in their economic and social life: the Philistines in the days of the Partiarchs were shepherds and husbandmen; but the state of the Philistine lords has a military character. They differed, too, in their attitude to the Israelites: the Patriarchs made a covenant of peace with the Philistines, whereas the lords of the Philistines and their subjects were the sworn foes of Israel. On the strength of all these differences, Grintz comes to the conclusion that the Philistines in the days of the Patriarchs were not the same as those who were governed by the lords. He postulates three successive waves of immigration and settlement. The earliest was that of Pelasgo-Philistine tribes who came from Casluhim, and settled in the region of the Negeb; they are the Philistines mentioned in the days of the Patriarchs and at the time of the Exodus from Egypt. The second was that of the Caphtorim who originated from Caphtor and made their abode south of Gaza (see below). The third was that of the Pelasgo-Philistines who arrived in the twelfth century, in the period of Ramses III, after staying for a period in Caphtor, and they established themselves on the coastland and founded there the state of the five lords of the Philistines.

Caphtorim] (In Egyptian *K f t y w;* they are the inhabitants of the island of Caphtor — that is, Crete — in Akkadian *Kaptara,* in

Ugaritic *K p t r*). Possibly they are included here among the sons of Egypt on account of the connection between them and the Egyptian state; or the reference may be to Cretan settlers in Egypt (see Grintz, *Tarbiz*, xvii [1946], pp. 38–39). The Caphtorim mentioned in Deut. ii 23 are in Albright's view (*J P O S*, I [1921], pp. 187–194) Cretans who emigrated from Crete and settled south of Gaza as a military colony in the service of Egypt, perhaps already in the days of the Hyksos, or subsequently during the Eighteenth Dynasty (the sixteenth century B.C.E.). Conceivably our verse refers to them. On the tradition that regards Caphtor as the original home of the Philistines, who are likewise called *Cherethites* or *nation of Cherethites*, see above.

15. *And Canaan begot*, etc.] On this formula see above, the annotations to *v.* 13.

The purpose of this list is not to tell us that a racial kinship existed between the peoples and tribes enumerated therein, but only to indicate who were the inhabitants of the country called in the Torah, *the land of Canaan,* and thereby define the boundaries of the land that was assigned to the children of Israel.

Sidon] — the celebrated Phoenician city. It is known that the Phoenicians themselves, as well as the Poeni of Carthage, considered themselves Canaanites (Χνᾶ in the writings of Philo of Byblus and Stephen of Byzantium). On a Laodicean coin we find the inscription: 'To Laodicea a mother-city of Canaan'.

His first-born] The eponym of Sidon was thus termed on account of the particular importance of Sidon among the Phoenician cities. This thought finds expression in another form on a Sidonian coin that describes Sidon as the *mother* of Phoenician cities and colonies (*ṣdn 'm kkb 'p' kt ṣr* ['Sidon the mother-city of Carthage, Joppa(?), Citium, Tyre']).

Heth] The reference is not to the great kingdom of the Hittites in Asia Minor, but to Hittite settlements that were multiplying within the borders of the land of Canaan. Later on we are told that Abraham came in contact with the sons of Heth in Hebron (xxiii), and that Esau took two wives of the daughters of Heth (xxvi 34); of these women it is stated that they were *of the daughters of Heth* ... OF THE DAUGHTERS OF THE LAND (xxvii 46), or OF THE DAUGHTERS OF CANAAN (xxxvi 2, where,

THE HISTORY OF THE SONS OF NOAH

however, the father of one of them is called a *Hivite* and not a
Hittite). Of the other Biblical passages that mention the Hittites
or particular Hittite persons there is no need to speak here. But
it is worth while mentioning Ezekiel xvi 3: *Thus says the Lord
God to Jerusalem: Your origin and your birth are of the land of
the Canaanites; your father was an Amorite, and your mother a
Hittite;* and *ibid. v.* 45: *Your mother was a Hittite and your father
an Amorite.*

16. *The Jebusites*] — the citizens of Jerusalem and the surrounding region. They, too, were not apparently of 'Canaanite' stock,
but of another race — Hurrian or Hittite. This and the succeeding
names are in the singular with a collective signification; and since
they have not yet lost the character of general appellatives, they
take the definite article.

The Amorites] The name designates here, it seems, the in-
habitants of the mountainous region on both sides of the Jordan.
According to N. H. Tur-Sinai, they are the giants, the Rephaim.
On Ezek. xvi 3, 45, see above, under *Heth*.

The prevailing view today that the name Amorites occurs in
many Biblical passages as the designation of all the inhabitants
of the country collectively, and that this usage is an unmistakable
indication of source E, cannot stand the test of serious criticism,
as I have shown in *La Questione della Genesi*, pp. 123–132, as
a result of an exact and detailed examination of the passages
concerned. This is not the place to recapitulate the whole of that
discussion, which extends in my Italian work over ten full pages.
In our verse it is self-evident that *the Amorites* referred to are
only a given section of the population. In any case, in the continuation of my commentary on the Book of Genesis I shall have
the opportunity to deal with the matter specifically *.

The Girgashites] They are apparently the people called *Karkisa*,
allies of the Hittites. This people lived in Asia Minor, near to the
Hittites, and it seems that from among them, too, settlers came
to the land of Canaan. The connection between the Girgashites
and the famous Phoenician colony Carthage, in North Africa, to

---

* Owing to the author's demise, this section of the Commentary was
not written.

which rabbinic legends about the migration of the Girgashites to Africa allude, may be based only on the resemblance between the two names. It is nevertheless a fact that in the inscriptions of Carthage (Nos. 343, 365, 448, in N. Slouschz's *Thesaurus of Phoenician Inscriptions* [Hebrew]) there occur the names *Grgš* and *Grgšm*.

17. *The Hivites*] — people of Hivite stock. Cities belonging to this tribe in the land of Canaan are mentioned a number of times in the Bible, beginning with Shechem the son of Hamor (Gen. xxxiv 2). In the Septuagint this name is often interchanged with that of the *Hittites* or *Horites*.

The Arkites] — the inhabitants of the city of *'Arqa* in the Lebanon.

The Sinites] — perhaps the inhabitants of *Sin(na)*, which is near to 'Arqa.

18. *The Arvadites*] — the inhabitants of the city of Arvad ['Arwad] and the adjacent territory. The city was noted for its fleet and maritime trade. It was situated on a small island near the mainland (a distance of about three kilometres), north of the mouth of the River El-Kebir. In the Amarna letters, it is called *Arwada*, in the Hittite inscriptions *Yaruwaddas*, in Assyrian and Babylonian documents *Armada, Aruda,* etc.; today its name is *Ru'âd*.

The Zemarites] — apparently the citizens of the town called *Ṣumur* in the Amarna letters; *Ṣimirra* in the Assyrian tablets. It is north of 'Arqa.

The Hamathites] It is difficult to determine if the citizens of one of the cities called Hamath are intended, and, if so, of which one. It is best to regard the name as referring, in accordance with the general trend in these verses (see further below), to the central point of the northern border of the Promised Land, which is designated in many passages by the words לְבוֹא חֲמָת *lebhō' Ḥāmāth* ['the entrance (i.e. approach) to Hamath']; it is apparently the place called today, *Labwe,* in northern Coele-Syria (on this identification and on the topographical questions relating to the northern boundary, see the Hebrew article by B. Maisler [Mazar] in *Bulletin of the Jewish Palestine Exploration Society,* xii [1946], pp. 91–102).

211

And afterward the families of the Canaanites spread abroad] — that is to say, that subsequently, in the course of time, there were formed other settlements — offshoots of the first — that were called by the generic name *Canaanite*, and will be referred to later by this very name, beginning with xii 6. If we understand the text thus, and count these Canaanites as a single unit among the 'sons' of the eponym Canaan, we have the customary total of twelve units (see above, the introduction).

The verb נָפֹצוּ *nāphōṣū* ['spread abroad'] parallels the various forms of this verb that occur above (ix 19), and several times later on in the story of the Generation of Division.

19. *And the territory of Canaanites extended, etc.*] The commentators have found great difficulty in interpreting this verse; and it appears that they were unable to grasp its true meaning because they failed to pay attention to its primary purpose, which is to delimit at this stage the boundaries of the land of Canaan, which was subsequently to be promised, as we shall learn, to Israel. Only by taking this fact into account are we able to understand the passage properly; it does not furnish us with objective geographic information, purely for learning's sake, but forms a link in the chain of interconnected sections of which the Book of Genesis is composed. Here and in other passages, the boundaries are demarcated (particularly worthy of note is Num. xxxiv 1–12: *the land of Canaan according to the borders thereof,* etc.) in conformity with the boundaries of the Egyptian province called Canaan.

From Sidon] In the same way as the genealogy began with Sidon (*v.* 15), so the demarcation of the borders commences with Sidon, which is the northern boundary. It is clear that the reference is not to the *city* of Sidon itself, but to the *land* of Phoenicia, since places north of the city of Sidon have already been mentioned, for instance, Arvad and others. How far Phoenicia extended according to this view can be inferred from the name *Hamathites* in *v.* 17, which points, as we have stated, to the central location in the ideal boundaries of the land of Israel on the northern side. This is known as לְבוֹא חֲמָת *lebbō' Hămāth* ['the entrance (i.e. approach) to Hamath'] (compare also Jos. xiii 5, Jud. iii 3), which is about seventy kilometres north of Damascus. In the story of Abraham's military expedition it is stated that he came *to Hobah, which is on the left hand* (that is, north) *of Damascus* (Gen. xiv 15; see my commentary *ad locum,* when it is published *).

Uutil you come [בֹּאֲכָה *bō'ăkhā(h)*] *to Gerar, as far as Gaza*] The word בֹּאֲכָה *bō'ăkhā(h),* here and in the second part of the verse, is usually understood to mean 'in the direction of': in the direction of Gerar—that is, toward the south-west —the territory of the Canaanites reached as far as Gaza, and in the direction of Sodom and Gomorrah, etc. — that is, toward the south-east — it extended as far as Lasha. But this appears to be incorrect. The word בֹּאֲכָה *bōă'khā(h)* is only a shorter form of the phrase עַד בֹּאֲכָה *'ădh bōă'khā(h),* or with fuller spelling, עַד בֹּוֲאכָה *'ădh bō[w]ăkhā(h),* which indicates not only the direction, but also—and principally—the final point of the action or situation. It will suffice to mention verses like Jud. vi 4: *and destroyed the produce of the earth,* TILL YOU COME [עַד בֹּאֲךָ *'ădh bō'ăkhā*] *unto Gaza*: or i Kings xviii 46: *and ran before Ahab,* TILL YOU COME [עַד בֹּאֲכָה *'ădh bō'ăkhā(h)*] *to Jezreel.* Sometimes the word occurs without עַד *'ădh* ['till', 'until'] preceding it, not only in cases where, as in this verse, עַד *'ădh* is used to indicate an additional place, but even when this is not the case, as for example, in *v.* 30 of our chapter: UNTIL YOU COME [בֹּאֲכָה *bō'ăkhā(h)*] *to Sephar, the hill country of the east;* or in Gen. xiii 10: *that it was well watered everywhere, before the Lord destroyed Sodom and Gomorrah, like the garden of the Lord, like the land of Egypt,* TILL YOU COME [בֹּאֲכָה *bō'ăkhā(h)*] *to Zoar.* Similarly here: in the interior of the land the territory of the Canaanites extended to the point where you come to Gerar, and incorporated that city; and on the coast it reached as far as, and included, Gaza, the last station on the way to Egypt (south of Gaza were located, as we stated, the Caphtorim, who were in the service of the Egyptian kingdom). Although the Philistines had settled in Gerar and its environs and held dominion over the region, the title to it of the Canaanites, the former owners of the land, was not thereby voided; nor was that of the children of Israel who were destined to inherit their rights, according to the solemn declaration in Exod. vi 4: *I also established My covenant with them* (the Patri-

---

* This section of the Commentary was never written owing to the author's untimely demise.

archs), *to give them the land of Canaan, the land in which they dwelt as sojourners.* It is particularly with regard to Gerar and the land of the Philistines that it is stressed again and again that Abraham *sojourned* there (Gen. xx 1: *and he* SOJOURNED *in Gerar;* xxi 34: *And Abrahm* SOJOURNED *many days in the land of the Philistines*). Of Isaac it is written that, when he was in Gerar, he was told by the Almighty (xxvi 3): *SOJOURN in this land, and I will be with you, and will bless you; for to you and to your descendants I will give all these lands;* and again (*v.* 4): *and I will give to your descendants all these lands.* Moreover, we must pay attention to the memorials to Israel's God that were set up in the land by Abraham (xxi 33: *And Abraham planted a tamarisk tree in Beer-sheba, and called there on the name of the Lord, the Everlasting God*) and by Isaac (xxvi 25: *So he built an altar there and called upon the name of the Lord*); and likewise to the digging of the wells there and to the stubborn determination to retain ownership of them (xxi 25–32; xxvi 15–33), and also to Isaac's agricultural work there (xxvi 12). Furthermore, this verse is in exact accord, as will clearly be seen in the following lines, to what is related of Abraham in the continuation of the Book.

The identification of the site of the city of Gerar is disputed. But there is no need for us to become involved in this dispute, since the name Gerar does not denote here the *city* itself but the whole land of Gerar, that is to say, the district bordering on Egypt (Grintz, *Tarbiz,* xix [1948], p. 64).

Till you come to Sodom, and Gomorrah, and Admah and Zeboiim, as far as Lasha] Here, too, the conventional interpretation is not to be followed, to wit, 'in the direction of Sodom and Gomorrah' etc.; the sense is: as far as, that is, incorporating the region of these four cities (collectively the names indicate the entire area, and are used as a single, unitary term), and thence unto Lasha, including that city. The four cities are the cities of the Plain, which are near to the Dead Sea. The determination of their sites, whether to the north or south of the Dead Sea, is a complicated problem; we shall deal with this question in the continuation of our commentary on the Book of Genesis *. The

* Owing to the author's demise, this section of the Commentary was not written.

present verse, which tells us that the border of the Canaanites reached thus far, supports the view that the cities were to the south, for presumably the entire plain was included in the territory. Our text adds that the border extended still farther as far as Lasha. This city is not otherwise known to us, and it is not possible to identify it. The conjectures made in this regard are without foundation, and the emendations that have likewise been suggested (Leshem, Laish, La'ash, Zoar) are even less well founded, Apparently the reference is to a place situated at the extreme limit of the area, beyond Zoar. It follows from the subsequent description (xiii 10) : *like the garden of the Lord, like the land of Egypt, till you come to Zoar,* that the fruitful region extended as far as Zoar; and it would seem that the Canaanite occupation continued still further, up to a place called *Lasha,* which may have been located at the edge of the wilderness. The Bible indicates here the extreme eastern point, bordering the desert, just as the first half of the verse specifies the farthest point on the west, on the coast.

All this is in agreement with subsequent statements in Genesis. In the story of Lot's separation from Abraham it is said (xiii 10–12) : *And Lot lifted up his eyes, and* SAW *all the plain of the Jordan, that it was well watered everywhere, before the Lord destroyed Sodom and Gomorrah ... So Lot chose for himself all the plain of the Jordan ... and Lot dwelt among the cities of the Plain, and moved his tent as far as Sodom.* Thus prior to their separation from each other, both Abraham and Lot were at a point from which it was possible to *see* the cities of the Plain; and after their separation the Lord said to Abraham (*ibid. vv.* 14–15) : *Lift up your eyes and* LOOK *from the place where you are, northward and southward and eastward and westward; for all the land which you* SEE *I will give to you and to your descendants for ever.* This proves that the cities of the Plain, which could be *seen* from the locality where Abraham was, formed part of the Promised Land. It is further stated in chapter fourteen that Abraham defeated the kings of the east after they had conquered Sodom and the other cities of the Plain; hence the right of possession that they had acquired by their conquests was transferred to Abraham as a result of his victory, and remained an ideal right of ownership of this area (although the cities themselves were overturned and des-

215

troyed) vested in Abraham and his descendants for all generations.

The connection between the cities of the Plain in the east and the land of Gerar in the west is also a feature of the stories about Abraham, just as it is in this verse. Thus it is stated later on (xx 1): *From there Abraham journeyed towards the territory of the Negeb . . . and he sojourned in Gerar* — 'From there', that is, from a place near to the cities of the Plain, whence it was possible to see them (xix 28: *and he* LOOKED DOWN *toward Sodom and Gomorrah and toward all the land of the Plain, and* BEHELD, *and lo, the smoke of the land went up like the smoke of a furnace*). From this point, the end of the eastern boundary, Abraham passed on to sojourn in Gerar, the western extremity of the territory, and thereby he established the rights of his descendants to the whole land in which he sojourned, from end to end.

20. *These are the sons of Ham,* etc.] On the expressions in this verse see the annotations to *v.* 6.

This paragraph is also based on the numbers *seven* and *twelve*. The sons and grandsons of Cush are *seven;* the sons of Egypt are *seven;* and the peoples or tribes listed as sons of Canaan are *twelve,* as we have noted.

THIRD PARAGRAPH

THE DESCENDANTS OF SHEM

21. *And unto Shem, / to him also were children born, —*
 the father of all the children of Eber, / the brother of Japheth, the eldest.

22. *The sons of Shem:*
 Elam, and Asshur, and Arpachshad, and Lud, and Aram.

23. *And the sons of Aram:*
 Uz, and Hul, and Gether, and Mash.

24. *And Arpachshad / begot Shelah;*
 And Shelah / begot Eber.

216

25. *And to Eber / were born two sons:*
    the name of one was Peleg ['Division']; for in his days was
        the earth divided;
    and his brother's name / was Joktan.

26. *And Joktan —*
        begot Almodad, and Sheleph, and Hazarmaveth, and
27. *Jerah; //* and Hadoram, and Uzal, and Diklah; //*
28. *and Obal, and Abimael, and Sheba; //*
29. *and Ophir, and Havilah, and Jobab;*
    all these were the sons of Joktan.

30. *And their territory extended / from Mesha,*
    until you came to Sepharah, / the mountain of the east.

31. *These are the sons of Shem,*
    by their families, by their languages, / in their lands, by their
        nations.

21. *And unto Shem, to him also were children born*] The children
of Shem are mentioned last, as we have noted, because they are the
most important for the history of the people of Israel, and because
the rest of the Book of Genesis will deal with the history of
the sons of Shem, and thereafter the Torah will speak of the children of Israel, who are descended from Shem's sons. On this method
of arranging the genealogies, see above, the notes to *v.* 6.

Because of the exceptional importance of Shem, the Bible was
not content with a simple phrase, like 'And the sons of Shem',
for the preamble to the paragraph, in the style of the formula
found above, *The sons of Japheth, And the sons of Ham.* Instead,
the roll of the sons of Shem is prefaced by this complete verse,
which serves as a formal introduction, mentioning together with
Shem's name all his other designations.

The father of all the children of Eber] — that is to say, the
primogenitor of all the peoples comprised by the term *children of
Eber* or *Hebrews,* who include the children of Israel.

The appellation *Hebrew* — also in the plural *Hebrews* — occurs

---

* The two strokes indicate the beginning of a verse; one stroke, here
as elsewhere, marks the caesura.

217

in the Bible specifically as a name given to the children of Israel and their ancestors by Gentiles, or as one by which they call themselves when they converse with non-Israelites (Gen. xiv 13: *Abram the Hebrew* — vis-à-vis the fugitive; so, too, a number of times in the tales of Joseph and in the account of the Israelites in Egypt, as well as in Jonah i 9). This is not the place to discuss the complicated question of the relationship between the designation *Hebrew* and the terms *Ḥabiru* or *Ḥapiru* in Akkadian and the similar appellatives (with initial *ʿAyin* followed by *Pē* instead of *Bēth*) in Egyptian and Ugaritic. These designations found in non-Israelite languages denote a particular class of people in the society of the ancient East.

The brother of Japheth, the eldest [אֲחִי יֶפֶת הַגָּדוֹל *ʾăḥi Yepheth haggādhōl*] / The Hebrew does not mean: the eldest brother of Japheth, but the brother of Japheth, who was the eldest, the first-born. It is a designation of Shem and part of his name, according to the ancient system of fratriarchy or the hegemony of the eldest brother. According to this system people are called after the first-born brother, just as in the state of patriarchy, or the hegemony of the father, they are called after the father (so-and-so the son of so-and-so). Traces of this social order are discernible in various Scriptural passages (see, for example, Gen. xxii 21: *Uz the first-born and Buz his brother;* xxviii 9: *Mahalath the daughter of Ishmael Abraham's son, the sister of Nebaioth;* Exod. vi 23: *Elisheba, the daughter of Amminadab, the sister of Nahshon;* xv 20: *Miriam, the prophetess, the sister of Aaron;* and the like. Compare below, *v.* 25: *and his brother's name was Joktan*).

22. *Elam*] — the well-known people that dwelt east of Babylon. The fact that this people was not a Semitic people according to present-day concepts presents no difficulty. The identification with *ʿamw* of the Egyptian sources, suggested by some scholars (e.g. Reubeni) is not possible.

The Torah puts Elam at the head of the other sons of Shem in order to give him special prominence and thus enable us more easily to understand the allusion in Noah's words: *and let Canaan be his slave* (ix 26), in accordance with my explanation *ad locum*.

And Asshur] — the well-known people who dwelt north of Babylon.

218

And Arpachshad] In chapter xi (*vv.* 10–13), Arpachshad is referred to as an individual, and so, too, perhaps later on in this chapter (*v.* 24); but here, in the list of peoples, the name indicates the people that traced its genealogy back to Arpachshad as its 'ancestor'. The identity of the people is in doubt. The conjectures that have been put forward in this respect — for example, that אַרְפַּכְשַׁד *'Arpakhšadh* [Arpachshad] is a composite word incorporating the name כֶּשֶׂד *Keśedh*, from which it is inferred that the reference is to the כַּשְׂדִּים *Kaśdīm* [Chaldeans]; or the theory that the name denotes the district of the city of *Arrapḫa* (Kirkuk, today), which is near Nuzi, east of the city of Ashur — are mere suppositions.

And Lud] Its identification is difficult. Apparently, it is not the same as Ludim in the list of the sons of Egypt (*v.* 13). *Lubdu* of the Assyrians has been suggested, which seems to have been situated on the banks of the upper Tigris. There is no means of deciding.

And Aram] A number of tribes were called Arameans; they led a nomadic life for a long time in the middle of the 'Fertile Crescent', and after they had settled down in permanent habitations they attained political importance. Their exodus from Kir, mentioned in Amos ix 7, is connected apparently with one of the late migrations. Aramean tribes bear this name in the Assyrian documents from the twelfth century B.C.E. onwards; but they were doubtless already to be found in the vicinity a long time earlier.

23. *And the sons of Aram*] In i Chron. i 17 (apart from one MS that was emended in accordance with our verse), the words *And the sons of Aram* are omitted, and the name *Uz* is preceded by *Wāw* copulative. According to this reading, all the persons named in our verse are sons of Shem; but from the association of *Uz* with *Aram* in Gen. xxii 21 it appears that the omission is a scribal error, due to the copyist's eye slipping from *Aram* to *Aram*, and his adding thereafter the *Wāw* copulative.

Uz and Hul and Gether and Mash] It is difficult to identify these peoples. These are not names of Aramean settlements known to us from historical documents, and it would seem that the situation obtaining in a very early period is reflected here. *Uz* is not, apparently, the Edomite Uz (Job. i 1; Lamentations iv 21). On the identification of *Hul* and *Gether* nothing can be said. In the case of

219

Mash, too, it is difficult to decide. It has, indeed, been conjectured that it represents the mountain called by the Greeks Μάσιον ὄρος, in northern Mesopotamia, or the mountains *Māšu* mentioned in the Gilgameš Epic (Tablet ix, col. ii, lines 1—2; and col. iv, lines 40—41), which are perhaps the Lebanon and Anti-Lebanon; but all this is dubious. In place of וָמַשׁ *wā-Maš*, the Samaritan Pentateuch reads ומשא *w-Mš'*; but apparently this reading is an error based on the name מֵשָׁא *Mēšā'* [Mesha] in *v.* 30. In i Chron. i 17 (except for a few MSS) we find וָמֶשֶׁךְ *wā-Mešekh* ['and Meshech'] and so, too, in the Septuagint both here and in Chronicles. In this instance, likewise, the reading is to be regarded as a mistake occasioned by the name Meshech in *v.* 2.

The connection between the genealogy of the sons of Aram detailed here and that of the sons of Nahor given in Gen. xxii 20 f., which contains the names *Uz* and *Aram*, and also *Maacah*, known as an Aramean tribe, we shall discuss when we come to these passages.

24. *And Arpachshad begot Shelah; and Shelah begot Eber*] Here, too, as in the greater part of the chapter, the line of demarcation between the birth of children and the rise of peoples is blurred, but in this verse the former concept is somewhat more pronounced, since all three names occurring in it also appear in chapter xi (*vv.* 10–17) as the names of individuals. Hence the Bible prefers here the expression *begot*, just as it chose it, for a similar reason, in *v.* 8; and in the same way as there, in the second paragraph, this verb continued to be used subsequently, so its use continues in this paragraph.

The Septuagint reads: 'And Arpachshad begot Kenan, and Kenan begot Shelah', paralleling the pedigree of the sons of Sheth in chapter v. Similarly the Book of Jubilees speaks of Kenan the son of Arpachshad. But this appears to be a later interpolation. See below, on *v.* 31.

Shelah] Attempts have been made to explain the name as that of a place, or a deity, or as a common noun that became a proper name; but these are only surmises without any foundation in fact.

Eber] See above, on *v.* 21.

25. *And to Eber were born two sons*] In this instance, too, the text becomes more expansive, as it did in *v.* 21, on account of the

special importance of Eber in relation to all those who were called after him, *sons of Eber.*

Peleg] Possibly this is the name of a place near the junction of the Chaboras and the Euphrates, Φάλγα of the Greeks.

For in his days was the earth divided] The statement is somewhat obscure. When a child is born, he may be called after an event that occurs at the time of his birth; but how is it possible to name him after something that has still to happen *in his days,* that is to say, in the course of his lifetime? Furthermore, all that happened in his time happened also in the days of many other people, and it is not something confined to him. Conceivably the meaning is that the name Peleg, which was given to the boy for one reason or another at the time of his birth, fitted him and corresponded to the history of his time, as events subsequently proved, *for in his days the earth was divided.* In this way it is possible to understand many other examples of name etymologies.

And his brother's name was Joktan] Regarding the system of fratriarchy — that is, the subordination of the brothers to their first-born brother (Peleg is mentioned as the eldest in xi 16) — see above, on *v.* 21. On *Joktan* and his sons, compare *Jokshan,* mentioned in Gen. xxv 2–3, as the son of Abraham and Ketura, and as the father of *Sheba* and *Dedan.* In our annotations to that passage we shall deal with the relationship between the two lists. *

26–29. *And Joktan begot*] The use of begot in *v.* 24, for the reason given there, and also in *v.* 25, led by attraction to its use in the continuation of our paragraph.

The names of Joktan's sons seem to be Arabian. Most of them can be explained on the basis of Arabic dialects, whilst several of them correspond to names of Arabian places or tribes. So far as is known, most of them belong to South Arabia, but it should be borne in mind that the tribes used to wander from place to place, and it is possible that in an earlier period than that to which the information in our possession belongs, they lived in other areas of Arabia (see also above, on Sheba, in the notes to *v.* 7). On the duplication of the names *Sheba* and *Havilah,* which occur also in *v.* 7, see my remarks in the introduction, p. 182.

* This section of the Commentary was never written owing to the demise of the author.

Various conjectures have been advanced regarding each of the names, but there is no need to enter here into details. I shall mention only the more probable suggestions.

Almodad] This name is apparently composed of the Arabic definite article *al* and the word *modad*, 'friend'. Other suggestions, based on vowel changes, are improbable.

Sheleph] The word has been identified with *Šilph*, the designation of a district in Yemen, and also *Šalph* or *Šulph,* the name of a Yemenite tribe. Possibly the name *Šlp* is to be read on an ostracon discovered a short time ago in Elat (Driver, *BASOR,* No. 90 [April 1943], p. 34.).

Hazarmaveth] corresponds exactly to the well-known name *Ḥaḍramaut* or *Ḥaḍramut,* a district of South Arabia.

Jerah] This is the appellation of the moon god, who was particularly revered by the Arabs.

27. *Hadoram*] The signification of this name seems to be: 'The god Hadh is exalted'. A similar name has been found in South Arabia.

Uzal [אוּזָל *'Uzāl*] / In the Samaritan Pentateuch איזל *'yzl* (similarly in the Septuagint: Αἰζήλ)· According to a late tradition, Arabian and Jewish, this was the designation of the city Sanʿā, the capital of Yemen.

Diklah] It means 'date-palm', also in Arabic.

28. *Obal*[עוֹבָל *'Obhāl*] / (In the Samaritan Pentateuch עיבל *ʿybl,* and so, too, in i Chron. i 22). Perhaps it corresponds to *ʿAbil,* the name of a district and of several localities in Yemen.

Abimael] It is explained, on the basis of the South Arabian dialect, in which the particle *ma* is used for emphasis as in Akkadian, to mean: 'My father, verily he is god'.

Sheba] See above, on v. 7.

29. *Ophir*] It is doubtful if there is any connection between this Ophir and the land of Ophir, the gold-producing country. Nevertheless it is interesting to note that also the name *Havilah,* which immediately follows, is the name of a land from which gold was obtained (Gen. ii 11).

Havilah] It has been identified with the names of a number of places occupied by Arab tribes, but it is difficult to decide which is correct.

Jobab] It has been suggested that this word is connected with

Yuhaybib, a tribe in Southern Arabia; and even more far-fetched conjectures still have been advanced.

All these were the sons of Joktan] — a concluding formula after the long list of names. It is needed to make clear to whom the possessive pronoun *their* in the following verse refers.

30. *And their territory,* etc.] Here, as in *v.* 19, the limits of the land of the sons of Joktan are given. מוֹשָׁבָם *mōšābhām* [literally, 'dwelling'; rendered: 'territory'], that is, the area in which these tribes wandered from place to place.

From Mesha until you come to Sepharah] It is difficult to identify these places, and all the conjectures in this regard are questionable. We can only say this: apparently the name *Mesha* designates the most western point, perhaps a place near the Red Sea, and Sepharah a place in Eastern Arabia (קֶדֶם *qedhem* [see next note] means *east* [not 'ancient']). Whether these sites were in the north or south it is impossible to determine.

The mountain of the east [הַר הַקֶּדֶם *har haqqedhem*] / This is not a third geographical point, as many have supposed. Had this been the case, the wording, in accordance with *v.* 19, would have been: 'until you come to Sepharah, as far as [עַד *'adh*] the mountain of the east.' *The mountain of the east* is in apposition to *Sepharah,* the meaning being: Sepharah, which is the mountain of the east; or, perhaps, Sepharah, which is in the mountain of the east. הַר הַקֶּדֶם *har haqqedhem,* that is, the eastern mountain, is a general term and may denote many different mountains, just as the expressions קֶדֶם *qedhem* ['east'] or אֶרֶץ קֶדֶם *'ereṣ qedhem* ['land of the east'], or אֶרֶץ בְּנֵי קֶדֶם *'ereṣ benē qedhem* ['land of the children of the east'] may signify various countries in the east. Even if we succeed in determining what is meant by *ḳdm* in the tale of the Egyptian Sinuhe, and what the term *the eastern mountains* in the story of Balaam [Num. xxiii 7] denotes, we still cannot draw any conclusion in regard to the *mountain of the east* in our verse. Be this as it may, it is worth noting that with reference to the sons of Abraham's concubines, whom we have already mentioned in connection with the parallel *Joktan — Jokshan,* it is stated (Gen. xxv 6): *he sent them away . . . eastward to the east country.* We shall revert to this subject in our commentary to chapter xxv *.

* This section was never written owing to the demise of the author.

31. *These are the sons of Shem, etc.*] This is the end of the paragraph. On its form see above, on *v.* 5.

In the structure of this paragraph, too, the numbers *seven* and *twelve* occur. According to the recension of the Masorah, the descendants of Shem, up to Peleg, number *twelve*. With the name of Joktan, Peleg's brother, a new roll begins, that of the Arab tribes, to wit, Joktan and his brothers — in all *fourteen,* twice times *seven.* In the Septuagint, however, which adds Kenan the son of Arpachshad before Shelah, and omits Obal from the sons of Joktan, the numbers are reversed: there are *fourteen* descendants of Shem up to and including Joktan, and *twelve* sons of Joktan.

CONCLUSION OF CHAPTER

32. *These are the families of Noah / according to their histories, in their nations;*
and from these the nations spread abroad on the earth / after the flood.

32. *These are the families of the sons of Noah, etc.*] Just as the end of each of the three paragraphs of this chapter is marked by a concluding formula, so the entire chapter closes with a similar concluding sentence. The terminology of this verse (*families, histories, in their nations*) resembles that of the other concluding verses. Furthermore, the expression *and from these ... spread abroad* is like the wording at the end of the first paragraph (*v.* 5: *from these spread*). Here we have בָּאָרֶץ *bāʾāreṣ* ['on the earth'] and not בְּאַרְצֹתָם *beʾarṣōthām* ['in their lands'], as in the other endings, because there the reference is to the respective countries of the various peoples, and here the earth in its entirety is intended.

At the same time, this concluding sentence parallels the introductory formula of the chapter and the exordium to the whole section. Here it is written: *These are the families of the sons of Noah,* corresponding to the opening sentence of our chapter (x 1): *And this is the history of the sons of Noah;* and the structure of this verse resembles that of the second sentence of the exordium of the section (ix 19): *These three were the sons of Noah; and from these the whole earth was peopled.* In the last-mentioned passage, the Bible indicated the theme in general terms; in our verse, after we have been given a detailed description of the subject, this concluding formula comes to emphasize that what was stated earlier was fulfilled. All this apart, the phrase *after the flood,* with which our verse closes, establishes a parallelism with the end of the opening verse of the chapter (x 1), and likewise with the conclusion of the preceding narrative (ix 28), as well as the last words of the verse that heads the next section (xi 10).

C. THE STORY OF THE GENERATION OF DIVISION
(XI 1–9)

INTRODUCTION

§1. THIS NARRATIVE, as we saw earlier (pp. 142 ff.), constitutes, as it were, the completion and sequel of the history of the sons of Noah in chapter x, explaining how it came about that the peoples of the world, although they all originated from one family, speak different languages. However, it is not the primary aim of the story here to provide an answer to an academic question concerning the existence of various languages. Although originally an aetiological account, yet it has been given a place among the Peutateuchal sections not for a purely aetiological purpose. By incorporating it within the framework of its narratives, the Torah seeks to inculcate two ethico-religious lessons: (a) that boastful pride in material power is considered sinful in God's eyes; (b) that the Lord's purpose endures for ever, and that every plan that He formulates is inevitably implemented despite all the efforts and devices of men to nullify it. The later Haggadah enlarged the content of the story and depicted an attempt by human beings to rise in actual revolt against the Lord and storm heaven, but this does not represent the real meaning of the text; it would therefore be superfluous for us to deal with the legend in our book.

§ 2.   Although the construction of the tower occupies an important place in the narrative, it is not the main subject. The principal theme is the dispersion of mankind over the face of the whole earth, a matter that God purposed and that was ultimately fulfilled in accordance with the Divine will, notwithstanding human attempts to obstruct it. The tower is only a detail in the episode — part of the gigantic city that men sought to build in order to achieve their goal. Not without reason, therefore, does the end of the story refer only to the suspension of the building of the city but not of the construction of the tower (*v.* 8: *and they left off building the city*). Hence I did not put at the head of this narrative the usual title 'The Tower of Babel' or 'The building of the Tower of Babel'; I used instead the expression customarily employed in Jewish literature, 'The Story of the Generation of Division', which best fits the intention and the content of the text.

§ 3.   Despite the fact that the background of the story is Mesopotamian, there is no parallel to it in the Mesopotamian writings, as there is to the accounts of Creation and the Flood and to many other matters in the early sections of the Book of Genesis. Some scholars have, it is true, suggested that the narrative represents a redaction of Mesopotamian material, but this view is pure conjecture. Thus, for example, Galling holds that to begin with there existed a Babylonian tale that boasted of the building of the city and the tower, and that later an Assyrian recension was made, which did indeed portray the construction of the tower as a work pleasing in the sight of the gods, but regarded the building of the city of Babylon as an act directed against Assyria and consequently as displeasing to the deities, who impeded its execution. Not long ago (1947), too, a similar theory was put forward, which is also based on the premise that there existed a Mesopotamian text that has not survived. It is the theory of Kraeling, who is of the opinion that both in the account of Berossus and in the Biblical narrative there are discernible traces of a Mesopotamian recension of the story of the Deluge that differs from those known to us hitherto. The main purpose of this version was not, in his view, the rescue of Ziusudra but the return of his companions after the Deluge to the city of Babylon, the rebuilding of its ruins, and the renewal of human culture in restored Babylon on the basis of the ancient wisdom that was preserved in the books hidden in Sippara. But it is obvious that these theories and others like them are unsatisfactory, since they depend on imaginary documents that do not exist in fact.

But there is no need for conjectures, nor should it cause surprise that our story lacks parallels. It is impossible for such parallels to be found among the neighbouring nations, since the narrative is essentially a protest against the concepts and ideas of these peoples. There is no question here of partial opposition restricted to given points, such as we observed in the previous sections; the entire theme is a counterblast. This is not merely a new Israelite recension, a redaction of the traditional material of the ancient East in keeping with Israel's ethos; it represents a polarically opposite attitude to that of the pagan peoples. We have before us a kind of satire on what appeared to be a thing of beauty and glory in the eyes of the Babylonians, a parody of their customary assertions and narrations. The possibility of parallels existing in Babylonian literature is thus excluded.

It is, indeed, feasible that the Torah made use of an ancient poem on the building of the city of Babylon and its tower, but, if so, it was a poem that was of Israelite origin. Nor was it necessarily an epic poem, but one of a different kind, whose nature and content we shall endeavour to understand later on. The truly Israelite character of the source explains *inter alia* an important feature of our narrative, namely, the fact that the Tetragrammaton, which is the specific designation of Israel's God, and not '*Elōhīm*, which is also applicable to Gentile deities, is used.

§ 4. In each of the great cities of Mesopotamia, especially in every city that was considered holy and called *maḥāzu*, the temples of the gods were its glory and splendour; and the tower that arose from the temple area was its supreme glory and splendour. The tower, which was called *ziqquratu*, was built in terraces — that is, storeys — each of which was smaller than the one below it in length and breadth. The number of storeys was not fixed; some had few — three or four — and some had as many as seven. The most important and celebrated among the towers was that of the temple of Marduk in the city of Babylon. In the precincts of this magnificent sanctuary, known as *E-sag-ila* ('The house whose head is raised up'), there rose, alongside the shrines of the gods, the lofty tower called *E-temen-an-ki,* that is, 'House of the foundation of heaven and earth'. As far as it is possible to judge from an Akkadian description that has reached us in a copy, made in the third century B.C.E., that is not altogether clear, as well as from a portrayal by the Greek writer Herodotus, it seems that this tower consisted of seven storeys, apart from the dwelling of Marduk, which was erected on the seventh storey; its total height was one stadium (approximately ninety metres), which was also the measurement of the length and breadth of the lowest storey. On the details of the structure of Etemenanki, in regard to which scholars are not agreed, and generally for all that is known today about this tower, see the two comprehensive and instructive articles that recently appeared in the Dutch publication *Ex Oriente Lux, 1945–1948, Jaarbericht No. 10 van het Vooraziatisch-Egyptisch Genootschap,* one by Boehl on the city of Babylon generally (pp. 491–525), and one by Busink dealing specifically with the Ziqqurat (pp. 526–536).

When the Babylonian temple and its tower were first built we do not know for certain; apparently they were erected in the period of Ḥammurabi (eighteenth to seventeenth century B.C.E.). So proud and boastful of their splendid buildings were the Babylonians of that period that they attributed them to the gods. In the Babylonian Epic of Creation it is stated that after Marduk's victory over Tiamat, the Anunnaki deities built in heaven, in his honour, the celestial Babylon and within it the heavenly Esagila and its tower (Tablet vi, lines 56–64); and then Marduk built for himself, after the pattern of the sanctuary on high, his temple below, Esagila of Babylon (*loc. cit.* 114–115). The temple and tower were destroyed many times in the course of the years, and they were also rebuilt a number of times; among those known to have restored their ruins and beautified their structure were Esarhaddon king of Assyria (seventh century B.C.E.) and Nebuchadnezzar II king of Babylon, the destroyer of Jerusalem (sixth century).

Of the high tower only the merest fragment, a portion of the lowest storey, remains, and even this was buried beneath heaps of debris until the expedition of *Die deutsche Orient-Gesellschaft,* which excavated the ruins of Babylon (1889–1917), uncovered it.

Even this relic tends to leave on the observer an amazing impression of a colossal structure. Not without reason was the Tower of Babylon regarded as one of the wonders of the world.

There can be no doubt that the Biblical story refers specifically to the city of Babylon and to the ziqqurat *Etemenanki* therein; it is expressly stated in the Bible (*v.* 9): *Therefore its name* (that is, of the city mentioned at the end of the preceding verse) *was called Babel* [Babylon]. Actually there were in the *land* of Babylon many other ziqqurats, and one of them (that of the temple of Nebo in the city of Borsippa, which is near Babylon) survived in part through the years, and many of those who saw it, or knew of its existence, thought that this was the very tower of the Biblical narrative. This was the view of the Talmudic sages (B. San. 109a) and also of several contemporary scholars. But now that the remains of *Etemenanki* have been excavated, all agree that this was the tower referred to by Scripture.

I have already indicated earlier how overweening was the boastful pride of the Babylonians in regard to their city, temple and ziqqurat. Our narrative regards all this vaunting and conceit with a smile, as it were, and possibly such was the attitude already of the earlier Israelite poem. The poem and the prose story were composed apparently at a time when the city and tower were mounds of ruins. One may surmise that they were written after the fall of the First Babylonian Dynasty and the destruction of Babylon by the Hittites. This destruction took place in the middle of the sixteenth century B.C.E., and several centuries passed before they began to rebuild the city. Needless to say, during that period the children of Israel remembered the vainglorious bragging of the Babylonians with derision, and it is probable that at this period the Israelites composed satiric poems on the building of the city and its tower. 'You, children of Babylon' — in this, or similar, vein ran the thoughts of the Israelites — 'you called your city Babel — *Bâb-ili*, "Gate of god", or *Bâb-ilâni* "Gate of the gods" — and your tower you designated "House of the foundation of heaven and earth". You desired that the top of your tower should be in *heaven* (expressions of this kind are actually found in the Babylonian inscriptions in regard to the structure of the tower; we shall revert to them in the commentary), and you did not know that God alone, not a human being, can determine where the "Gate of God" is; nor did you realize that *the* HEAVENS *are the heavens of the Lord,* and only *the earth hath He given to the children of men.* You did not understand that, even if you were to raise the summit of your ziqqurat ever so high, you would not be nearer to Him than when you stand upon the ground; nor did you comprehend that He who in truth dwells in heaven, if He wishes to take a close look at your lofty tower, must needs *come down* (see the annotations on this below). You did not consider the fact that you lack strong and durable material, that the nature of your country compels you to use *bricks* for *stone* and *asphalt* for *mortar,* and hence you could not hope that your buildings would long endure. Your intention was to build for yourselves a gigantic city that would contain all mankind and you forgot that it was God's will to fill the whole earth with human settlements, and that God's plan would surely be realized. Now you have ceased building your city and it lies desolate and in ruins, and the ziqqurat that you built in its midst is only rubble. You were proud of your power, but you should have known that it is forbidden to man to exalt himself, for only the Lord is truly exalted, and the pride of man is regarded by Him as iniquity that leads to his downfall and degradation — a punishment befitting the crime. For this reason your city, which you wished to make into a unified and unique centre for all the peoples of the world, a city in which all tongues were spoken, lies in ruins. On account of this, your dominion was shattered and your families were scattered over the face of the whole earth. Behold, how fitting is the name that you have given to your city! It is true that in *your* language it expresses glory and pride, but in *our* idiom it sounds as though it connoted confusion — the confusion of tongues heard therein, which caused its destruction and the dispersion of its inhabitants in every direction.'

Such thoughts may have found expression in Israel's poems when Babylon lay in ruins after her defeat at the hands of the Hittites, and the same ideas are reflected in the Biblical story of the Generation of Division.

§ 5.   Possibly there are allusions to this subject in Zeph. iii 9–11. It is stated there: *Yea, at that time I will change the speech of the peoples to a pure speech, that all of them may call on the name of the Lord and serve Him with one accord. From beyond the rivers of Ethiopia My suppliants, the daughter of My dispersed ones, shall bring My offering. . . for them I will remove from your midst your proudly exultant ones, and you shall no longer be haughty in My holy mountain.* The prophet describes the situation in the end of days as the antithesis of the Generation of Division. On account of the pride and arrogance of mankind, the Lord, in ancient days, did away with the *one language* that they had, and confused their tongues; but in the end of days, when the proud will be brought low (this is the central idea of the Book of Zephaniah), the Lord will *change* the situation: in the days of the Generation of Division no one understood the speech of his fellow, and the peoples were divided from one another by their languages, but at that time, in the future, all the *peoples* will once again have only one tongue, a *pure speech* understood by each one of them (it means, of course, ideas shared by all humanity), so that all of them may accept the yoke of the Lord's kingdom and serve Him with one accord, united not by their opposition to His will but in fulfilling it. Even in the obscure phrase *My suppliants, the daughter of My dispersed ones* one may see an allusion to the *dispersion* of the peoples, who, although they were scattered of old over the face of the whole earth in accordance with the Divine will, because they were haughty and insolent, would yet in time to come, after their pride had been humbled, once more be gathered together spiritually by the Lord in His service, and they would all be united in His worship and make *supplication* to Him and bring their offering in His sanctuary in Jerusalem. In this worship would participate even the most distant of them like *Cush* (the reference here, unlike that of Genesis ch. x, is to Ethiopia, which is situated south of Egypt, as an example of one of the remotest races; compare Zeph. ii 12), and even those further away still, those who dwell *beyond the rivers of Ethiopia.* All this would be possible because the Lord would then remove from mankind *the proudly exultant ones,* and men *would no longer be haughty* in His sight.

It is impossible to decide if the prophet had in mind the Pentateuchal account or an earlier poetic tradition, or both together. Be this as it may, the allusion to our theme is amply clear.

§ 6. In this short narrative we have a fine example of Biblical literary art. It comprises two paragraphs, of almost equal size, that constitute an antithetic parallel to each other in form and content The first begins with a reference to the situation that existed at the outset (*v.* 1), and thereafter describes what men proceeded to do (*vv.* 2–4). The second recounts what the Lord did (*vv.* 5–8), and concludes with a reference to the position created at the end of the episode (*v.* 9). The contrast between the initial and final situations is emphasized also by the antithesis in the wording. In *v.* 1 we read: *Now the whole earth had one language*; and in *v.* 9: *because there the Lord confused the language of all the earth.* Similarly the contrast between the human attempt to perpetuate the original situation and the Divine action that brought to fruition what God had planned in the beginning is stressed by successive parallels, mostly antithetic, between the first paragraph and the second. In *v.* 1 we find *one language,* and in *v.* 6, *one language;* in *v.* 3, *and they said to one another,* and in *v.* 7, *that they may not understand one another's speech;* in *vv.* 3–4, COME, *let us make bricks. . .* COME, *let us build ourselves a city,* and in *v.* 7, COME, *let us go down, and there confuse their language.* We are told in *v.* 4 that men wished to reach by means of their structure, to THE HEAVENS, and in *v.* 7, *that the Lord* CAME DOWN *from* HEAVEN to frustrate their plan; it is written in *v.* 4, *and let us make a* NAME *for ourselves,* and in *v.* 9, *Therefore its* NAME *was called Babel;* at the end of the first paragraph it is stated, *lest we be scattered abroad upon the face of the whole earth,* and at the conclusion of the second, *So the Lord scattered them abroad from there over the face of all the earth . . . and from there the Lord scattered them abroad over the face of all the earth.*

This apart, we hear a constantly recurring melody in the passage, a kind of *leit-motif,* which accompanies the narrative almost from beginning to end, and reaches its climax in the explanation of the name *Babel;* it is the sound of the letters *Bēth* [b bh], *Lāmedh* [l], *Nūn* [n], which occur repeatedly in close association. In *v.* 3 : הָבָה נִלְבְּנָה לְבֵנִים *hābhā nilbenā lebhēnīm* ['Come, let us make bricks']; and thereafter, *ibid.*: לָהֶם הַלְּבֵנָה לְאָבֶן *lāhem hallebhēnā leʼābhen* ['they had brick for stone']; *v.* 4: הָבָה נִבְנֶה לָנוּ *hābhā nibhne lānū* ['Come, let us build ourselves']; *v.* 5: בָּנוּ בְּנֵי *bānū benē* ['the sons (of men) had built']; *v.* 7: וְנָבְלָה

wᵉnābhᵉlā ['let us confuse']; v. 8: וַיַּחְדְּלוּ לִבְנֹת wayyaḥdᵉlū libhnōth ['and they left off building']; v. 9: בָּבֶל Bābhel ['Babel', 'Babylon'] —בָּלַל bālal ['confused'].

Nay, more. Other interesting contributions to the musical quality of the narrative inhere in other features that are in keeping with the taste and methods of oriental literary style. These are:

(1) Instances of alliteration, particularly noticeable in the recurrence of Sīn or Šīn, for example: בְּאֶרֶץ שִׁנְעָר וַיֵּשְׁבוּ שָׁם bᵉʾereṣ Šinʿār wayyēšᵉbhū šām ['in the land of Shinar and settled there'] (v. 2); וְרֹאשׁוֹ בַשָּׁמַיִם וְנַעֲשֶׂה לָּנוּ שֵׁם wᵉrōʾšō bhaššāmayim wᵉnaʿăśe lanū šēm ['with its top in the heavens, and let us make a name for ourselves'] (v. 4); שָׁם שְׂפָתָם אֲשֶׁר לֹא יִשְׁמְעוּ אִישׁ שְׂפַת רֵעֵהוּ šām śᵉphāthām ʾăšer lōʾ yišmᵉʿū ʾīš śᵉphath rēʿēhū ['there (confuse) their language, that they may not understand one another's speech'] (v. 7); שְׁמָהּ šᵉmāh ['its name'] — שָׁם šām ['there'] — שְׂפַת śᵉphath ['the language of'] —וּמִשָּׁם ūmiššām ['from there'] (v. 9); or marked by the repetition of Lāmedh: אֶל רֵעֵהוּ הָבָה נִלְבְּנָה לְבֵנִים 'el rēʿēhū וְנִשְׂרְפָה לִשְׂרֵפָה וַתְּהִי לָהֶם הַלְּבֵנָה לְאָבֶן וְהַחֵמָר הָיָה לָהֶם לַחֹמֶר hābhā nilbᵉnā lᵉbhēnīm wᵉniśrᵉphā liśᵉrēphā wattᵉhī lāhem hallᵉbhēnā lᵉʾābhen wᵉhaḥēmār hāyā lahem laḥōmer ['to another, "Come, let us make bricks, and burn them thoroughly." And they had brick for stone, and asphalt for mortar'] (v. 3); לָּנוּ עִיר וּמִגְדָּל lānū ʿīr ūmigdāl ['unto ourselves a city, and a tower'] (v. 4); לָּנוּ שֵׁם פֶּן נָפוּץ עַל פְּנֵי כָל הָאָרֶץ lānū šēm pen nāphūṣ ʿal pᵉnē khol hāʾāreṣ ['a name for ourselves, lest we be scattered abroad upon the face of the whole earth'] (ibid.); לְכֻלָּם וְזֶה הַחִלָּם לַעֲשׂוֹת lᵉkhullām wᵉze haḥillām laʿăśōth ['they have all (one language); and this is only the beginning of what they will do'] (v. 6); וְעַתָּה לֹא יִבָּצֵר מֵהֶם כֹּל אֲשֶׁר יָזְמוּ לַעֲשׂוֹת wᵉʿattā lōʾ yibbāṣēr mēhem kōl ʾăšer yāzᵉmū laʿăśōth ['and nothing that they propose to do will now be impossible for them'] (ibid.); ...עַל פְּנֵי כָל הָאָרֶץ ʿal pᵉnē khol hāʾāreṣ ... וַיַּחְדְּלוּ לִבְנֹת wayyaḥdᵉlū libhnōth ['over the face of all the earth, and they left off building'] (v. 8); עַל כֵּן קָרָא שְׁמָהּ בָּבֶל כִּי שָׁם בָּלַל ה' שְׂפַת כָּל הָאָרֶץ...עַל פְּנֵי כָל הָאָרֶץ ʿal kēn qārāʾ šᵉmāh Bābhel ki šām bālal YHWH śᵉphath kol hāʾāreṣ ... ʿal pᵉnē kol hāʾāreṣ ['Therefore its name was called Babel, because there the Lord confused the language of all the earth ... over the face of all the earth'] (v. 9).

(2)   Examples of paronomasia, like נִלְבְּנָה לְבֵנִים *nilbenā lebhēnīm* ['let us make bricks'] (*v.* 3); וְנִשְׂרְפָה לִשְׂרֵפָה *wenisrephā liserēphā* ['and burn them thoroughly'] (*ibid.*).

(3)   The word-play, which occurs three times, between the verb פּוּץ *pūṣ* ['be scattered'] and the phrase פְּנֵי כָל הָאָרֶץ *penē khol hā'āreṣ* ['the face of all the earth'], whose initial and final letters constitute the chief consonants of the verb; see *v.* 4: פֶּן נָפוּץ עַל פְּנֵי כָל הָאָרֶץ *pen nāphūṣ 'al penē khol hā'āreṣ* ['lest we be scattered abroad upon the face of the whole earth'] (the words פֶּן — פְּנֵי *pen — penē* should also be noted); *v.* 8: וַיָּפֶץ ה' אֹתָם מִשָּׁם עַל פְּנֵי כָל הָאָרֶץ *wayyāpheṣ YHWH 'ōthām miššām 'al penē khol hā'āreṣ* ['So the Lord scattered them abroad from there over the face of all the earth']; *v.* 9: וּמִשָּׁם הֱפִיצָם ה' עַל פְּנֵי כָל הָאָרֶץ *ūmiššām hĕphīṣām YHWH 'al penē kol hā'āreṣ* ['and from there the Lord scattered them abroad over the face of all the earth'].

(4)   Other word-plays, like הַלְּבֵנָה לְאָבֶן *hallebhēnā le'ābhen* ['brick for stone'] (*v.* 3); וְהַחֵמָר הָיָה לָהֶם לַחֹמֶר *wehaḥēmār hāyā lāhem laḥōmer* ['and they had asphalt for mortar'] (*ibid.*); בָּנוּ בְּנֵי *bānū benē* ['the sons of (men) had built'] (*v.* 5).

(5)   The recurrence of similar words in close association: שָׂפָה אַחַת וּדְבָרִים אֲחָדִים *sāphā 'aḥath ūdhebhārīm 'ăḥādhīm* ['one speech and a single language'] (*v.* 1); עַם אֶחָד וְשָׂפָה אַחַת *'am 'eḥādh wesāphā 'aḥath* ['one people, and... one language'] (*v.* 6); or the repeated use of such words in the course of the narrative: שָׂפָה *sāphā* ['language'], שְׂפַת *sephath* ['language', 'speech' of], שְׂפָתָם *sephāthām* ['their language'] — five times; כָּל הָאָרֶץ *kol hā'āreṣ* ['the whole (all) the earth'] — three times; שֵׁם *šēm* ['name'] or שָׁם *šām* ['there'] (here, too, there is a play of words) — seven times.

§ 7.   The adherents of the documentary theory attribute this narrative to source J, since it contains the Tetragrammaton and not *'Elōhīm* (how the use of the Tetragrammaton is to be correctly explained, in accordance with our method of exegesis, we have already seen above); nevertheless many (though not all) hold that the story is not unitary, but may be resolved into two strata of J.

Among the suggested modes of division, which differ in method and detail, particular interest attaches to that of Gunkel, which is based on acute and thoroughgoing analysis. The existence of two sources is indicated, according to this scholar, by the following facts:

(1)   There is a contradiction between *v.* 5, which declares: *And the Lord* CAME DOWN *to see the city and the tower,* and *v.* 7, wherein the Lord says: COME, LET US GO DOWN, as though He had not previously descended.

(2)   The aim of the sons of men is at first expressed in the words: *and let us make a name for ourselves,* whereas in the continuation of the verse a different purpose is stated: *lest we be scattered abroad upon the face of the whole earth.*

(3)   After we had been told that the sons of men were scattered abroad over the face of the whole earth, it was obvious that they had left off building the city; it was superfluous, therefore, to state this explicitly in *v.* 8.

(4)   In *v.* 9 the clause *and from there the Lord scattered them abroad over the face of all the earth* is parallel to the preceding clause *because there the Lord confused the language of all the earth,* and one of them is redundant.

(5)   Similarly in *v.* 3 the sentence *Come, let us make bricks, and burn them thoroughly* corresponds to the sentence *And they had brick for stone and asphalt for mortar;* one of them is, accordingly, unnecessary.

(6)   The motif of the building of the city parallels that of the building of the tower, and each one suffices in itself.

On the basis of all these considerations Gunkel came to the conclusion that originally two recensions of the story existed, the recension of the city (*Stadtrezension*) and that of the tower (*Turmrezension*), and the present text was formed by the amalgamation of fragments from both versions. The form of the narrative in the two editions, according to Gunkel, was a follows:

THE CITY-RECENSION: *And the whole earth had one speech and a single vocabulary. And they said to one another, 'Come, let us make bricks and burn them thoroughly.' And they said, 'Come, let us build ourselves a city and make for ourselves a name.' And the Lord said, 'Behold it is one people, and all of one language. Come, let us go down and confound there their language, so that they may not understand one another's speech.' So they ceased to build the city. Therefore is its name called 'Babel', for there the Lord confused the speech of the whole earth.*

THE TOWER-RECENSION: *And when they broke up from the east, they found a plain in the land of Shinar, and settled there. And they had brick for stone and asphalt for mortar. [And they said, 'Come, let us build ourselves]* a tower, with its top in the heavens, lest we be scattered over the face of the whole earth.' And the Lord came down to see the tower which the sons of men had built. [And the Lord said:] 'This is but the beginning of their enterprise, and now nothing that they purpose to do will be impossible for them.' So the Lord scattered them from there over the face of the whole earth. [Therefore was its name called ... for] from there the Lord dispersed them over the face of all the earth.*

It is unnecessary to enter into elaborate arguments in order to show that no intelligent Hebrew writer would have produced such insipid texts. It is also obvious that it is impossible to begin a story with the words *And when they broke up from the east*, without first mentioning the people to whom 'they' refers (in the narrative before us it is explicitly stated, *the whole earth*, that is, all the people of the earth). It is likewise clear that in *v.* 6 the words הֵן *hēn* ['Behold'] — וְעַתָּה *weʻattā* ['and now'] cannot be separated, since they are normally linked together in the Biblical idiom, the former (הֵן *hēn* or הִנֵּה *hinnē*) indicating to begin with the existing facts, and the latter (וְעַתָּה *weʻatta*) stating the conclusions to be drawn from these facts (see above, Part I, p. 172). Furthermore, the ending, *Therefore was its name called Babel* etc., cannot be properly comprehended unless mention of the *land of Shinar* (*v.* 2) preceded it.

After pointing out, in the previous sub-section, the beauty and harmonious structure of the story in its present form, it is perhaps superfluous to examine in detail the reasons advanced for partitioning it between two sources. However, since the majority of scholars, even if they do not agree in every particular, give serious consideration to this analysis of the sources, we must add a few words about the value of these arguments.

First, with regard to the two motifs, that of the city and that of the tower. Even among those who do not accept Gunkel's division of the sources, there are some who hold that the two motifs were

236

initially separate. Thus, for example, Staerk, who is of the opinion, nevertheless, that the two motifs were united not through the work of a redactor but as a result of the tradition's inner development.

However, the entire principle of detaching the two themes is intrinsically unsound. Several scholars — like Dombart, for instance, in his book *Der Babylonische Turm* — have rightly pointed out that the city and tower were closely-linked features in the architectural designs of the Babylonians. There is also another argument, simpler and more decisive, to wit, that our narrative cannot be understood without both themes. We cannot envisage the tower as an isolated structure in an absolute wilderness, as a watchmen's lookout or military fortress, without a city around it; a tower whose top reaches, as it were, to heaven is unmistakably an urban edifice. If, moreover, its purpose is to serve as the rallying-point of a great multitude, it requires *a fortiori* an inhabited city to accommodate all these people. On the other hand, the mere building of a city is not an act of arrogance liable to cause the intervention of the Deity to frustrate it; only if the plan includes a building such as the tower, which is intended to prevent the widespread dispersion willed by God, is the Divine action against the implementation of the scheme comprehensible. Furthermore, those who separate the two motifs have failed to understand the Hebrew expression *city and tower*. This phrase does not mean *a city plus a tower* but *a city in the midst of which was a tower,* just as in Gen. xxxviii 1, the phrase 'to a certain Adullamite *and his name Hirah*' [so literally] means 'to a certain Adullamite *whose name was Hirah*'. Nor have we to seek our evidence afar; immediately after *and a tower* come the words *and* [rendered: 'with'] *its top in the heavens;* just as the top is inseparable from the tower and forms an integral part of it, even so is the tower an indivisible part of the city. Hence it is not surprising that after *vv.* 4–5 Scripture makes no further mention of the tower (Gressman, for instance, expresses surprise at this in his work *The Tower of Babel,* p. 2); the tower is included in the concept of the city, and every time *city* is mentioned the tower is also implied.

As for the discrepancies and duplications that, as we have seen, are found in our narrative, they do not represent serious problems, with the possible exception of one, namely, the coming down of the Lord, which is mentioned twice. With this difficulty we shall deal later in our commentary, and we shall see that this too can easily be explained. The other problems are not really problems. The sentence *Come, let us make bricks, and burn them thoroughly* has not yet informed us that the bricks were to be used for construction; consequently it is not redundant to add *and they had brick for stone* etc. On the words of the sons of men *and let us make a name for ourselves,* which do not indicate a purpose other than that of preventing dispersion over the face of the earth, see my notes below. In *v.* 8, even after it had been stated that the sons of men were scattered over the face of the earth, it was not superfluous to tell us that they had ceased to build the city: this point is the climax of the whole story, and even though it is self-understood, it was proper to give emphatic expression to it. So, too, in *v.* 9 it was not enough to declare that the languages had been confused, but it was necessary to add that mankind were dispersed; nor would it have sufficed to speak of the dispersion only without mentioning that its cause was the confusion of tongues.

From all this it is clear that there is no reason for doubting the unity of our story.

§ 8. *Bibliography.* In the case also of the story of the Generation of Division and of the Tower, as on all that has preceded, the relevant book-list will be given at the end of the volume, pp. 286 ff.

FIRST PARAGRAPH

MANY ARE THE PLANS IN THE MIND OF
A MAN

CHAPTER XI

1. *Now the whole earth had / one speech / and a single language.*

2. *And as men wandered about in the east, / they found a plain in the land of Shinar / and settled there.*

3. *And they said to one another,*
   'Come, let us make bricks, / and burn them thoroughly.'
   And they had brick as stone, / and asphalt as mortar.

4. *Then they said,*
   'Come, let us build ourselves a city, / and a tower with its
      top in the heavens,
   and let us make a name for ourselves, / lest we be scattered
      abroad over the face of the whole earth.'

1. *The whole earth*] — that is, all the inhabitants of the earth (compare ix 19), for they then formed a single family (*one people*, v. 6) and they dwelt in one place.

Now . . . one speech [literally, 'Now . . . was one speech'] / — that is, they spoke one speech. On the construction of the sentence, compare Exod. xvii 12: *so his hands were steady* [literally, 'steadiness']; Psa. cix 4: *even as I make prayer* [literally, 'I am prayer']; *ibid.*, cxx 7: *I am for peace* [literally, 'I am peace']; and many similar examples.

And a single language [literally, 'and single words'] / Various explanations have been suggested: they come with one plan (Rashi); the words of the sage and the fool were alike, not as now when there are to be found in every language words that not all who speak that tongue can understand (Ibn Ezra); the same words and the same expressions (Dillmann); a limited vocabulary (Ehrlich); and still other interpretations. But they are all forced. The correct explanation is that we have here a simple parallelism, the same thought reiterated in different terms. *Words* is synonymous in this verse with *speech*. Similarly we read in Ezek. iii 6: *many peoples of foreign* SPEECH *and a hard tongue, whose* LANGUAGE [literally, 'words'] *you cannot understand*, which corresponds to what is written here (*v.* 7): *that they may not understand one another's* SPEECH. Since the noun *words* means *language*, that is, it signifies a singular concept although its grammatical form is plural, the adjective qualifying it, אֲחָדִים *’ăḥādhīm* ['single'], although in the plural, has a singular signification. Thus the meaning of the phrase *single words* is *one language, one tongue*, just as the expression אֱלֹהִים חַיִּים *’Elōhīm ḥayyīm* [plural] (Deut. v 23; i Sam. xvii 26, 36; Jer. x 10; xxiii 36) connotes *living God* [singular],

239

and the phrase אֱלֹהִים קְדֹשִׁים ʾElōhīm qedhōšīm [plural] (Jos. xxiv 19) signifies *holy God* [singular]. In order to simplify the matter, Hebrew uses as a rule the name ʾEl instead of ʾElōhīm, when it is accompanied by an adjective, as I have demonstrated in my study of the name ʾEl (*La Questione della Genesi*, pp. 66–67).

2. *And as men wandered about* [נָסְעָם nosʿām] *in the east* [מִקֶּדֶם miqqedhem] / According to Rashi: when they went forth from the land of the east in which they dwelt; this is also the first explanation of Gunkel. Jacob renders: when they journeyed eastwards; and Kraeling now gives a similar interpretation: when they left the place where the ark rested, going towards the east, to the site of Babylon. It is better, however, to understand נָסְעָם nosʿām [literally, 'their journeying'] in the sense of 'wandering', that is, as they wandered about (compare below, xii 9: *And Abram journeyed on, still going toward the Negeb* [Dillmann]), and מִקֶּדֶם miqqedhem [literally, 'from the east'] to mean 'from the קֶדֶם qedhem side, on the eastern side (of the land of Israel)', that is, in the countries of the east.

The expression *in the east* at the beginning of this narrative serves as a verbal link with the end of chapter x (*v*. 30: *mountain of the east*).

They found a plain [בִּקְעָה biqʿā] / In the course of their wanderings they found by chance a plain suitable for settlement. Here בִּקְעָה biqʿā [often rendered: 'valley'] signifies 'a plain' (compare Ibn Ezra). The city of Babylon was situated, as we know, in a wide plain (πεδίον μέγα ['great plain'], Herodotus calls it; likewise Strabo, πεδίον).

In the land of Shinar] See above, the notes to x 10.

And settled there] — at first as nomad shepherds.

3. *Come, let us make bricks*, etc.] In contemporary exegesis it is usually held that Scripture alludes here to the invention of bricks and their use for building. But this view does not accord with the text. One who says, 'Come, let us make bricks' already knows that bricks are in existence. Moreover, both the Mesopotamian and Biblical traditions tell of cities existing before the Deluge, and undoubtedly they refer to cities in which bricks played an important part in their building. The mention of the making of the bricks serves only as a preamble to the work of construction; compare

240

the passage in the Babylonian Epic of Creation dealing with the building of the celestial Babylon (Tablet vi, lines 58–61): 'The Anunnaki carried the basket on their shoulders; for a year they made bricks, and when the second year came, they raised high the head of Esagila, over against the Ocean, and they built the tower upon the Ocean' [see, also, the translation in *ANET*, pp. 68–69]. Similarly, it seems, the intention of our passage is to tell us that after the Flood had destroyed all the cities and structures, men lived at first the life of nomads and tent-dwellers (compare *his tent* in ix 21; and *the tents of Shem*, ibid., *v.* 27), but in the course of time, when they found a suitable plain where to build a city, they thought: It would be well for us to take up the handicraft of our fathers and revive the manufacture of bricks and the construction of buildings as the generation that preceded us used to do.

And burn them THOROUGHLY [נִשְׂרְפָה לִשְׂרֵפָה *niśrephā liśerēphā*, literally, 'and burn to a burning'] / The object of the verb *burn* is *bricks*, as though it had been written, *and burn them to a burning*, only the pronoun representing the object may be omitted, as we find above (ix 23: *Then Shem and Japheth took a garment, laid* [*it*] *upon both their shoulders* [the pronoun 'it' is missing in the Hebrew]. Here there was a special reason for the absence of the pronoun, namely, the intention to give added emphasis to the paronomasia (found in our clause as well as in the preceding, נִלְבְּנָה לְבֵנִים *nilbenā lebhēnīm* ['let us make bricks']) through the like endings of the two words [נִשְׂרְפָה לִשְׂרֵפָה *niśrephā liśerēphā*].

Thoroughly [literally, 'to a burning'] / — that is, that it should become wholly transformed into a burnt object.

And they had brick for stone, etc.] The irony in the words is manifest: Behold the things that formed the object of their boasting and self-glorification — buildings of bricks, which stand today and tomorrow are in ruins; the poor creatures did not even have hard stone for building such as we have in the land of Israel, and which we bind together with mortar! This note corresponds to the facts, for this in truth was the method of building in the plain of Babylon, which lacks stone but is rich in clay suitable for brick-making, and in asphalt, which can be used in place of cement. The Babylonians used mortar only for the interior parts of the buildings, and any one looking from outside saw only bricks and asphalt.

241

This appeared surprising to those who, like the Israelites and also the Greeks, who likewise stress this point in their descriptions, were unacquainted with this method of construction.

And they had . . .] וַתְּהִי – הָיָה *wattᵉhī* (imperfect with Wāw consecutive) — *hāyā* (perfect), literally, 'and was — was'] / This use of parallelism between the 'imperfect' and the 'perfect' of the same stem, I discussed earlier (Part I, p. 27), and I dealt with a similar Ugaritic usage in my Hebrew article 'Biblical and Canaanite Literature' in *Tarbiz*, xiv (1943), pp. 9–10.

As stone — as mortar] The text does not say *instead* of stone, *instead* of mortar, but actually *as* stone, *as* mortar. They did not realize — so the Bible informs us in its ironic note — that they were using substitutes; they valued the bricks as though they were actually stone, and the asphalt as though it were indeed mortar.

There are many word-plays in this verse; see the introduction on this point.

4. *Then* [literally, 'and'] *they said, 'Come, let us build'*, etc.] The repetition of the words *And they said* and *Come*, exactly as they occur in the previous verse, indicates a second stage in the plans of the children of men. At first they erected small and humble buildings: thereafter they became more ambitious and wished to build for themselves grandiose structures.

A city and a tower] The city, as it is expressly stated in *v.* 9, is Babylon; and the tower is *Etemenanki*, the famous ziqqurat in the temple of Marduk in Babylon. See my remarks on the subject above, in the introduction, pp. 227 ff.

With its top in the heavens] Already in the Sumerian name of the tower (*Etemenanki*, 'House of the foundation of heaven and earth') there is an allusion to heaven; and in many Babylonian texts, such as building inscriptions and various hymns, it is said of the one who built or repaired the ziqqurat that *he lifted up its head to the heavens* or *like the heavens*. Compare also: Deut. i 28: *the cities are great and fortified up to heaven*.

And let us make a name for ourselves] — for the future, for generations to come, on account of these splendid edifices. In the continuation of the story it is stated, with bitter satire, that in truth they succeeded in making a *name* for themselves (*v.* 9: *Therefore its* NAME *was called Babel*), but only a name of derogatory significance, alluding to the confusion of tongues in their midst.

Most modern expositors consider that the Bible implies that the ambition to win fame in the world is one of the things that God dislikes. But this is not true, for among the blessings bestowed upon Abraham is included also that of renown: *and I will make your name great* (Gen. xii 2). It is likewise incorrect to suppose that the 'making of a name' is mentioned here as the reason for building the city and the tower — a different motive from that stated thereafter, *lest we be scattered abroad* etc. The enunciation of the objective begins only with the word *lest*, and the sentence *and let us make for ourselves a name* comes, as it were, in brackets, thus: Let us build ourselves a city and a tower with its top in the heavens (and thereby we shall make a name for ourselves), so that we may not be scattered abroad etc.

Lest we be scattered abroad] Earlier (ix 1) it was stated that God said to Noah and his sons, *and fill the earth*. But the people of the Generation of Division did not wish this; they desired to remain all together in one place. To this end, in order that they should not be dispersed, as was liable to happen if each of them were to consider only his own interests, they decided to build for themselves, by cooperative endeavour, a great city, a kind of central habitation and meeting-place for all of them, in which there was to be a high tower, which could be seen from afar, as a sign-post of their point of assembly.

The whole earth] The expression that occurs at the beginning of the paragraph is repeated here at the end, but in a different sense; in the opening sentence it means *all mankind,* here it signifies *all the countries of the world.*

SECOND PARAGRAPH

IT IS THE PURPOSE OF THE LORD THAT WILL BE ESTABLISHED

5. *But the Lord came down / to see the city and the tower,*
   which the sons of men were building.

6. *And the Lord said,*
   'Behold, they are one people, / and they have all one language;
   and this — is only the beginning of what they will do;
   and now nothing will prove too hard for them / of all that
      they purpose to do.

7. *Come, let us go down, / and there confuse their language,*
   that they may not understand / one another's speech.'

8. *So the Lord scattered them abroad from there / over the face*
      of the whole earth,
   and they ceased to build the city.

9. *Therefore its name was called Babel [Babylon] / because*
      there the Lord confused the language of the whole earth;
   and from there the Lord scattered them abroad / over the face
      of the whole earth.

5. *But* [the Hebrew letter *Wāw;* literally, 'and'] *the Lord came down*] The *Wāw* here is antithetic: They [the sons of men] might plan as they wished, *but* the Lord came down and put their plans to nought. This 'coming down' does not mean that God descended in order to find out what was happening, which is the view of many commentators, who see in the passage a primitive conception of the Deity, as though God does not know what He does not see with His eyes. On the contrary, if we say that He came down to view the city and the tower that the sons of men had built, it follows that He was already aware of what had taken place. The expression *came down* is only one of the corporeal phrases commonly found in the Pentateuch, and it means that God, as a righteous Judge, wished to investigate the matter thoroughly. As I have explained in the introduction, there is a satiric allusion here: they imagined that the top of their tower would reach the heavens, but in God's sight their gigantic structure was only the

244

work of pigmies, a terrestrial not a celestial enterprise, and if He that dwells in heaven wished to take a close look at it, He had to descend from heaven to earth.

A city and a tower] These words connect the last verse of the first paragraph with the first verse of the second paragraph.

Which . . . were building [perfect tense] / — that is, which they had begun to build.

Sons of men] — in contradistinction to the Lord. Their undertaking is merely that of mortals; only He, the Lord of the universe, is eternal. Possibly here, too, one may detect a note of irony directed against the belief of the Babylonians, who attributed the structure to the god Marduk.

On the word-play בָּנוּ – בְּנֵי *bānū — bᵉnē* ['built — sons of'], see the introduction, p. 232.

6. *Behold, they are one people*] Behold, there is here before Me a single, homogeneous people.

And they have all one language] Hence it is easy for them to work together. The words *one language* form a parallelism with the initial sentence of the first paragraph.

And this is only the beginning of what they will do, etc.] They have already succeeded in what they have started to do; from this initial success it is clear that if they continue their work they will be able to carry out their plan.

And now] This is the opening word of the conclusion to be drawn from the premise, which begins with the word *Behold* (see Part I, p. 172, and the introduction here, p. 236).

Will not prove too hard [יִבָּצֵר *yibbāṣēr;* literally, 'be cut off', 'be withheld'] *for them*] — that is, it will not be beyond their capacities.

Of all that they purpose to do] — that is, the building of the city and the tower (not, of course, *with its head* actually *in the heavens*). Compare Job xlii 2: *and that no purpose can be withholden from Thee.* The word לַעֲשׂוֹת *laᶜăśōth* ['to do'] at the end of the verse echoes the preceding לַעֲשׂוֹת *laᶜăśōth* ['will do']. The inauguration of their work is seen as an earnest of the completion of the enterprise, and what they *have done* shows what they *will do,* if they are not halted.

7. *Come, let us go down*] They said, 'Come, let us make bricks',

'Come, let us build', and I say, 'Come, let us go down' (see Rashi and many later exegetes). The plural forms 'let us go down', 'let us confuse', are to be explained in much the same way as 'let us make man' (Part I, pp. 55 f.). Here, too, the correct interpretation is that it is the plural of exhortation.

There is an apparent discrepancy between this verse, which tells us that the Lord said, *Come, let us go down,* and the earlier statement in *v.* 5 that *the Lord came down.* The dissection of the narrative into two strata does not resolve the difficulty, for it is still a matter of surprise that the redactor should have left the incongruity in his revised recension. In order to find a solution to the problem a number of varied and fantastic suggestions have been advanced, such as, that the Bible refers to a gradual descent, to begin with up to a certain distance — to the point at which the structure would be visible, or as far as the top of the tower — and subsequently down to the earth; or that in the original form of the tale, the subject of *came down* was not the Lord but one of His angels; or that after *v.* 5 a paragraph, which related that the Lord returned and ascended again to heaven, has been omitted; or that we should read, *But the Lord saw* instead of *But the Lord came down to see.* But not one of these interpretations seems plausible. It is also difficult to agree with Ibn Ezra, who, in accordance with his usual method of exposition in such cases (for example, in Gen. ii 8 he interprets 'and [the Lord God] planted' to mean 'had planted'), understands the verb וַיֹּאמֶר *wayyōmer* ['and said'] in *v.* 6 to refer to a time anterior to that of the verb וַיֵּרֶד *wayyēredh* ['and went down'] in *v.* 5, the meaning being: and the Lord had already said to the angels before He came down. In Biblical Hebrew the pluperfect is not expressed in this way, although the translator into European languages may find it convenient at times to employ the pluperfect in his rendering. In Biblical narrative style it is impossible for a series of verbs like וַיֵּרֶד...וַיֹּאמֶר *wayyēredh ... wayyō'mer* [literally, 'and came down ... and said'] to mean: He came down ... and had already said. The correct way of understanding the passages is to compare it with similar instances where וַיֹּאמֶר *wayyō'mer* ['and said'] is used not in the signification of actual speech but of thought, and not of thought preceding the action described earlier, but of reflection that took place at the same time as the action. To take an example: it is written in Gen. xxvi 22: *so he called its name Rehoboth* ['Broad Places' or 'Room'], *saying, 'For now the Lord has made room for us, and we shall be fruitful in the land';* that means to say, Isaac called the name of the well Rehoboth, thinking: For now the Lord has made room etc. So, too, in Exod. ii 10: *and she named him Moses, for she said, 'Because I drew him out of the water',* that is to say, she gave him this name, reflecting: Because I drew him out of the water. This is also the case here: *But the Lord came down . . .* thinking: *Behold, they are one people* etc.; therefore, *Come, let us go down* — it is desirable that I go down.

It may also be added that the expression 'came down' may have been the customary way of indicating the intervention of God in human affairs, for the Canaanites already used this or a similar idiom (in the Ugaritic Tablet I K, lines 35–36: *wbḥlmh 'il yrd,* which means: 'and in his [i.e. King Keret's] dream El came down'). Wherever we find customary and stereotyped phrases in the literary tradition we need not concern ourselves too much with their literal meaning.

And there confuse their language] In this way we shall destroy the prerequisite that assures the success of their work.

On the repeated occurrence of the adverb שָׁם *šām* ['there'] in this narrative, even where it seems redundant, as in the present case, and on the word-play between it and שֵׁם *šēm* ['name'], see the introduction above, p. 234.

That they may not understand [literally, 'that they shall not hear'] / — that is, in a way that they shall not comprehend.

The Bible does not tell us expressly that the Lord's decision to confuse the language of mankind was carried out. But it is self-understood that it was implemented; such omissions are not uncommon in analogous episodes, whether told in epic poetry or in narrative prose.

8. *So the Lord scattered them abroad from there*] — as He had originally planned, contrary to the wishes of the sons of men when they said, *lest we be scattered.* A similar example occurs in Exod. i 10: Pharaoh said of the Israelites, *lest they multiply,* and immediately afterwards, in *v.* 12, it is written *But the more they*

247

were oppressed, THE MORE THEY MULTIPLIED *and the more they spread abroad*, as though to say: Pharaoh said, *lest they multiply*, but the Lord said, *they would multiply the more*; and as the Lord willed so it was.

All the earth] Here the phrase is used in its second signification: all the countries of the world.

And they ceased to build the city] Thus the city was left forsaken and in ruins; it is unnecessary to add that *a fortiori* they gave up building the tower. In the Samaritan Pentateuch and in the Septuagint the tower is also mentioned here; it is an attempt by these recensions, in accordance with their customary practice, to harmonize the Biblical passage. Since the very next words are: *Therefore its name was called*, it is manifest that the city alone is mentioned here.

9. *Therefore its name was called*] — that is, the name of the city that they had begun to build but did not complete.

Babel [Babylon] / This is the name that they achieved. They had said: *and let us make a name for ourselves*, that is, a name of glory; but they were destined to be given an inglorious name, or one that can be so interpreted.

Because there the Lord confused, etc.] Although the name Babel means in Babylonian 'Gate of god', here it has a pejorative connotation. We must not assume the verse to mean that the city was actually given a name — especially a derisive one — on the basis of Hebrew etymology. Its intention is to say mockingly: How befitting for her is this name, which in our tongue is a designation signifying confusion!

THE LANGUAGE OF [שְׂפַת *sephath*] *the whole earth*] Here, at the close of the story, the wording of the opening sentence is unmistakably reiterated: *Now the whole earth had one* SPEECH [שָׂפָה *sāphā*]; and the expression *the whole earth* has the identical meaning here as there.

And from there the Lord scattered them abroad over the face of the whole earth] — a solemn ending to the narrative; as the Lord desired so it was.

Over the face of the whole earth] Again the phrase *the whole earth* of the first verse recurs — three times in the last two verses, each time at the end of a clause; and twice in these two verses we find the phrase *over the face of the whole earth,* which likewise concludes the first paragraph. Thus the two paragraphs end with the same words but in antithetic contexts: the first passage closes with the expression of the desire of the sons of men *not to be dispersed over the face of all the earth,* and the second concludes with the fulfilment of the Lord's desire *to disperse them over the face of the whole earth.*

The phrase *the whole earth* is used in the last verse in both its significations: the first time it means *all mankind* and the second time, *all the countries of the earth.* There is biting mockery in this: they willed to become, and remain, *the whole earth,* but the Lord willed that *they should be dispersed over the face of the whole earth,* and their will was nullified before God's.

SECTION THREE

THE HISTORY OF THE DESCENDANTS
OF SHEM

CHAPTER XI, 10–32

INTRODUCTION

§ 1. ALL THE sections of the Book of Genesis that we have
read so far have presented us with stories and records concerning
the history of humanity as a whole, in order to provide the requisite
introduction and background to the principal theme of the Book,
namely, the saga of the ancestors of the people of Israel. Now
we approach the main subject; the horizon contracts and interest
is centred on the chronicle of one family.

But this contraction and focalization of interest takes place gradually, and the present section, the story of the descendants of Shem,
marks a transition from the extensive area of the history of
mankind, to the specific sphere of the account of an elect family.
Out of the three branches of mankind spoken of in chapter x that
of the sons of Shem is chosen here — the one from which the
progenitor of the Israelite people will be descended — and we are
given the genealogy of this branch, through successive generations,
in a form similar to that found in chapter v, which details the
pedigree of the antediluvian world patriarchs. And just as in
chapter v the genealogy in the tenth generation reaches Noah, the
father of the new, post-diluvian humanity, so here the pedigree in
the tenth generation gives us Abram-Abraham, the founder of the
Israelite microcosm, which parallels the macrocosm of all mankind.
The last paragraph of the section serves as another point of transition, this time from the record of the offspring of Shem collectively
to the sections that deal specifically with the biography of Abraham.

§ 2. The system of notices in this section resembles that of chapter
v, but is not identical with it in all its details. Here as there, the
Bible gives the following data about each generation: the father's

250

name; his age at the time of the birth of his son; the first-
born's name; the number of years that the father lived after
the birth of the eldest son; a general reference to his other
sons and daughters. In the same way as in chapter v all three sons
of Noah are mentioned at the end, and not his first-born only,
so here at the close of the genealogy mention is made of the three
sons of Terah. However, there are also divergences between the
two sections. The main difference is the absence in this section of
anything corresponding to the last verse of each paragraph in
chapter v, which records the total years of the father's life and
concludes with the words *and he died* (or, in the paragraph of
Enoch, an expression of similar signification). Only in the case of
Terah, who has special importance, Scripture reverts to the fuller
form and expands it even more. In the Samaritan Recension of the
Pentateuch, every paragraph contains the total years as in chapter v,
but this is obviously a later addition, in accordance with the
established practice of the Samaritan Pentateuch, which, as we have
noted, is accustomed to alter the wording of passages with a view
to harmonizing them. Be this as it may, even the difference in the
Masoretic text between the two genealogies is only an external
variation — nothing more than a shortening of the formulation —
for the reader can easily add up the figures and arrive at the year
of death. Other minor changes of form — for instance, those
of *v.* 10, in connection with Shem's age at the time of Arpachshad's
birth, or in *vv.* 12, 14 (*and Arpachshad* LIVED [חַי *ḥay*], *and Shelah*
LIVED [חַי *ḥay*] — we shall discuss in the commentary.

Also here, just as in chapter x (and in agreement with the Book
of Jubilees), the Septuagint adds *Kenan* between Arpachshad and
Shelah. Certain scholars suppose that this was the original form of
the text, since it brings the number of generations from Shem to
Terah up to ten; and even among those who disagree with this
view, some surmise that a link needed to complete this number is
missing in the Masoretic text. But this conjecture is wrong; the
tenth generation is not that of Terah but of Abraham, and the
mention of Kenan is not part of the original text, but a later
interpolation of no value.

As regards the chronological discrepancies between the Masoretic
text and the other recensions, see below, § 4.

§ 3. *The geographical background* of this genealogy is undoubtedly *Mesopotamia,* at least in the later generations. This is clearly to be inferred not only from the mention of the Mesopotamian cities, Ur of the Chaldees and Haran [*Ḥarran*] in *vv.* 28, 31, 32, but also from the fact that several of the names of the persons recorded here are known to us as the names of places in Mesopotamia; it is, indeed, a common feature of the history of the Orient for the names of individuals, or of families and tribes, to be substituted for geographical designations and *vice versa.* The name *Peleg,* as we have already observed (in the annotation to x 25) corresponds to the name of a city on the middle Euphrates. If it is doubtful whether there is a geographical parallel to *Reu,* there is no doubt with regard to the subsequent names. *Serug* [שְׂרוּג *Serūgh*] corresponds to *Sarûgi* in the Assyrian inscriptions, which designates a district and city in the vicinity of Ḥarran, called by the Arabs سروج *Sarûj* and by the Syrians *Serug* [or *Sarug*]. *Nahor* was the name of an important city near Ḥarran (compare *the city of Nahor* in Gen. xxiv 10), the centre of the civic and economic life of the area, just as Ḥarran was the centre of the worship of Sin, the moon-god. It is often mentioned by the name of *Naḫur* in the documents of Mari (nineteenth and eighteenth centuries B.C.E.), in the Cappadocian tablets (belonging to the same period), in Assyrian inscriptions (fourteenth century) and others: and by the name *Til Naḫiri,* with adaptation to Assyrian vocalization, in later Assyrian records. There is also a geographical parallel to the name *Terah* in *Til Turaḫi,* which is likewise mentioned in Assyrian sources (ninth century) as a place in the neighbourhood of Ḥarran.

The names of the ancestors of these generations are thus closely linked with the land of Mesopotamia, particularly with Northern Mesopotamia. Although the reference to Ur of the Chaldees in *vv.* 28, 31 takes us over to Southern Mesopotamia, we shall deal with this point later, in our commentary to *v.* 28.

§ 4. *Chronology.* Also in this section dealing with the history of the sons of Shem there recur most of the chronological problems that have already occupied our attention in connection with chapter v. My earlier observations on these questions (Part I, pp. 251–254) apply equally to this section. I shall not, therefore, discuss again the problems themselves, or the question of the parallel Mesopotamian texts, or the conjectures of contemporary scholars, or even the method of resolving these difficulties that I consider to be correct; for all these things the reader in studying this section is referred to the introduction in Part I, *loc. cit.* Here I shall only deal with those matters that pertain specifically to our section. In order to facilitate the study of its chronology, I shall arrange in tabular form the figures given in the section, and I shall indicate in square brackets also the numbers that are not expressly recorded but clearly emerge from the data before us. Following is the table:

	Age at birth of first son	Remaining years	Total
Shem	100	500	[600]
Arpachshad	35	403	[438]
Shelah	30	403	[433]
Eber	34	430	[464]
Peleg	30	209	[239]
Reu	32	207	[239]
Serug	30	200	[230]
Nahor	29	119	[148]
Terah	70	[135]	205

We have here the continuation of the chronology of chapter v; there we find recorded data on the antediluvian period, and here data relative to the post-diluvian period. In our very first verse (*v.* 10) there is expressly mentioned the phrase *after the flood,* which frequently occurs, as we have seen, also in the Mesopotamian tradition. In the latter, too, exactly as in the Israelite tradition, the Flood is regarded as the boundary line between two epochs in human history, which are differentiated *inter alia* by the divergent human life-span in each. According to the Mesopotamian tradition, the kings who reigned before the Deluge enjoyed fabulous longevity, each one living myriads of years, whereas the post-diluvian kings, although they also lived long, did not attain to the ages of their predecessors, nor even approximate to them. If we examine the list of kings belonging to the first dynasty of Kish, which comes immediately after the Flood in the Sumerian King List and comprises two series, one before *Etana* and one after, we observe a sudden decline in the longevity of the monarchs; even the first ruler of the earlier series reigns for only 12,000 years. The decline continues thereafter almost progressively, though not without a few rises in certain instances. Not even one of the remaining kings of this series reigns longer than 960 years. Etana, who heads the second list and is pre-eminent in his deeds of might and valour, which are linked with the mythology of the gods, reigns 1500 years (according to another reading 1560), and his successors do not as a rule exceed 900 years of kingship. Only two of them live longer and rule 1200 years, whilst one, whose life is short, attains to only 140 years of sovereignty. After the first dynasty of Kish comes the first dynasty of Uruk, in which the ages of the kings decline again, almost in ordered progression (only *Lugalbanda*, the illustrious hero, is vouchsafed exceeding long life and is king for 1200 years), until the last kings, who are on the throne for only a few decades or even less than one decade.

Likewise in the Biblical tradition there is noticeable after the Flood a sudden decrease in the length of human life. In chapter v we are told that the antediluvian world patriarchs first begot sons at a very advanced age, and in most instances they lived over 900 years. Here, in our section, much more modest figures are recorded. The age at which the first son is born is fixed, starting from Arpachshad, round about the thirtieth year, and also the figures for the life-span of the respective patriarchs fall far below those of chapter v. Shem, already, the son of Noah, who is the intermediary link between the two periods, does not reach the age of his ancestors; he lives only to 600 years; and after him there is an almost graduated decrease in the length of life. In the first three generations after Shem the patriarchs live to a little over 400 years (464, 433, 438); in the three succeeding generations the life-span of the patriarchs is somewhat over 200 years; after them Nahor the son of Serug lives only a few years over 140. Terah his son, who is particularly important in as much as he is the father of Abraham, once again exceeds the limit of 200 years, just as Eber, who likewise enjoys special importance in that he is the eponym of the Hebrews and marks the fourteenth generation from Adam, the seventh after the seventh, lives somewhat longer than his predecessors.

Thus in their general orientation, the Biblical and Mesopotamian chronological traditions agree. In both, the measure of human life

suffers an amazing contraction after the Deluge; in both, the decrease continues progressively or nearly so; and in both a few
individuals of special significance form exceptions to the rule, and
live longer than their ancestors. But there are important differences
between the two traditions; they are divergences that we have
already encountered in chapter v. In the same way as in that chapter
the Torah scaled down the ages of the antediluvian patriarchs, and,
in place of the myriads of years that we find in the Mesopotamian
tradition, it left only figures of less than one thousand, so in the
present passage, in the history of the sons of Shem, we are given
much lower figures than are cited in the Sumerian list of post-
diluvian kings. Similarly in this section, as in chapter v, the Torah
negated by its silence all the mythological elements that find a
place in the chronological records of Mesopotamia also in connection
with the post-diluvian generations. Here, too, as in the earlier
chapter, the heads of the generations are ordinary human beings,
not royalty; according to the Torah no kingship in the world came
down from heaven, as the Mesopotamian peoples imagined; and
there are no individuals belonging to a race of divine kings appointed to have dominion over the rest of mankind. The persons
listed here are important only in this respect, that they are the
ancestors of the Israelite nation, and guardians of the tradition
of the knowledge of the Lord, the God of Shem. Their genealogy
is given here for the purpose of teaching us the works of Providence, which watches carefully over the continuation of this
knowledge in the midst of Shem, and their superiority is entirely
of a spiritual nature, not one of power and domination over the
rest of humanity.

Also in the details of the figures a parallelism is discernible
between what is here recorded and the data provided by the Mesopotamian tradition. The reader will, I trust, forgive me for devoting
to this subject about two pages of dry, analytical calculations.

After the Flood, too, the basic elements of the chronology are the
same as those that we found in connection with the antediluvian
generations both in the Pentateuch and in the Mesopotamian tradition: primarily the *sexagesimal system,* augmented by the use of the
numbers *seven* or *multiples of seven.* In the aforementioned register
of the kings of the first dynasty of Kish, only numbers based on

255

the sexagesimal system appear; for example, 1200, 960, 900, 840, 720, 600. Even those that at first appear to break this rule are not really exceptions, if we only bear in mind the unit of five years, which comprises *sixty* months; for example: 625 years, that is, 600 years plus five units of sixty months; 305 years, that is, half 600 years and another unit of 60 months; 140 years, that is *seventy* units of twenty four months. The total years of the dynasty (how the sum total is arrived at it is impossible to tell because of the impaired condition of the texts) is expressed in terms of six *šar* ($6 \times 3,600 = 21,600$ years), four *nēr* ($4 \times 600 = 2,400$ years), eight *šuš* ($8 \times 60 = 480$ years) and thirty years ($\frac{60}{2}$), plus another three months and three and a half days, that is to say, with the addition of half of *six* in the number of months and half of *seven* in the number of days (on such additions of half the basic numbers, see my remarks in the *Ginzberg Jubilee Volume*, New York 1946, Hebrew Section, p. 388, note 21).

In a similar manner the figures in our section are to be explained:
(1)   The years of Shem are 600, a *nēr* in the sexagesimal system, and it is divisible into 100 years (or twenty units of sixty months) before the birth of Arpachshad, and 500 years (one hundred such units) after it.

(2)   From Arpachshad to Nahor, the age of the patriarchs at the time of the birth of the first son is fixed, as we have stated, round about thirty, that is, half a unit of sixty years, or six units of sixty months. In three cases it is exactly thirty, and in four instances it is slightly more or less, namely, $+ 5$, $+ 4$, $+ 2$, $- 1$, making an algebraic total of $+ 10$ years, that is, two units of sixty months. In the generation of Terah, the age rises again and reaches *seventy* years — fourteen units of sixty months.

(3)   The sum total of the ages of the patriarchs prior to the birth of the first-born amounts, in the whole of the section, to 390, that is, 6×60 plus half of 60.

(4)   The fundamental number in the years following the birth of the eldest son is, in the three generations after Shem, 400 years, that is, two thirds of 600 years, or eighty units of sixty months. To this basic figure there is added twice a half of 6 and once a half of 60, in all 36 or 6×6. In the three succeeding generations the essential period is 200 years, that is, a third of 600, or 40 units

of 60 months. In the last of these generations, the number appears without any addition, and in the other cases there is an increment, once of 9 and once of 7 years. In the generation of Nahor the son of Serug the basic number is 120, that is twice 60, less one year (*a hundred and twenty years* represent the maximum span of normal human life; see my note to vi 3). The algebraic total of the additions and subtractions from Peleg to Nahor the son of Serug (+ 9 + 7 — 1) is + 15 years, that is, three units of sixty months.

(5)   Apart from these notes, which concern mainly the place of the figures in the general structure of the section and the connection between them, a few more observations of a like nature have still to be made on the specific numbers pertaining to each of the patriarchs separately, and also on their ages at the time of their death, which are not expressly mentioned in the text. We shall discuss all this in the course of our annotations; see particularly our remarks on the figures relating to Terah and to Nahor his father.

Doubtless the year of birth of each of the heads of the generations is stated in order to enable us to calculate the length of time that elapsed between the Deluge and the principal events that took place subsequently. What events are alluded to and the precise calculation intended by the Bible are not explicitly stated; hence the various views on the subject have multiplied endlessly. Having already mentioned in Part I the most important of them, I shall not recapitulate them here. To me it appears that this section seeks to fix the length of the period between the Flood and Abraham's immigration to the land of Canaan, which may be regarded as the initial stage in the creation of the people of Israel. The reckoning is very simple. Arpachshad, the eldest son of Shem, was born *two years* after the Deluge. To this number — two years — must be added the succeeding figures for the years elapsing between each birth and the next, namely, 35 + 30 + 34 + 30 + 32 + 30 + 29 + 70, plus the 75 years of Abraham's age when he went up to the land of Canaan (xii 4); we then arrive at the total of 367. The customary practice of using a round figure based on the *sexagesimal system,* to which *seven* is added, may clearly be discerned in this number: 360 — that is, 6×60 — plus 7. Possibly there is, at the same time, another allusion here, which is also quite simple, namely, that from the year of Arpachshad's birth to the time of Abraham's immigration 365 years passed, corresponding to the number of days in the solar year. The numerical symmetry is intended to convey the lesson that all is in Heaven's hands, and human events are not dependent on the accident of the birth of a given person at a given time, or on his travelling at a specific time from one place to another, but they are ordered in accordance with the plans that Divine Providence designed and decided upon from the beginning.

The simplicity of this reckoning — 367 years since the Flood, or 365 years from the birth of Arpachshad to Abraham's arrival in Canaan — shows that the suggestions put forward by other scholars on the basis of involved calculations are incorrect. By complicating the subject and working out a multiplicity of sums, it is possible to discover in the text whatever we wish, for the figures are flexible and can be made to fit all sorts of numerical combinations and to serve all kinds of constructions that may occur to each and every exegete.

In this section too, as in chapter v, the chronology in the Samaritan recension differs from that of the Masorah, and the chronology of the Septuagint diverges from both. In the Samaritan Pentateuch, the ages of the patriarchs at the time of the birth of the first son, from Arpachshad to Serug, exceed those of the Masoretic text by a hundred years; contrariwise, the figures for the years of their life after the birth of the eldest son are a century less (in the case of Eber only sixty years). In the case of Nahor, there is a discrepancy of fifty years: fifty more before the birth of Terah, and fifty less after it. The age of Terah, when his eldest son was born, is the same as that given in the Masoretic text, but the total years of his life come to only 145. In the Septuagint there are many divergences between the various MSS, especially among those found recently. In most cases, the father's age at the birth of his first-born is identical with that of the Samaritan recension (in some MSS the age of Nahor exceeds that given in the Samaritan Pentateuch by a hundred years), whilst the figures for the years lived after the birth of the eldest son are the same as in the Masoretic text only for Peleg, Reu and Serug; in the remaining generations they differ both from the Samaritan and Masoretic figures, and some of them also vary in the different MSS. For Kenan, who is interpolated in the Septuagint between Arpachshad and Shelah, the numbers of the years given are identical with those of Shelah.

Much has been written on these divergences, and many proposals have been put forward to explain them and to determine which of the versions is to be preferred. However, it seems that in regard to this section, too, we have to arrive at similar conclusions to those that I set forth in connection with the discrepancies in chapter v. The chronological parallelism between the Masoretic text and the ancient Mesopotamian system shows that the Masoretic text is the original one, and that the differences in the other recensions are only later emendations. It is possible to explain these variations in the light of the familiar tendency in the Samaritan Pentateuch and in the Septuagint to adopt orderly schemes. The raising of the age at which the eldest son is born to the patriarchs serves to obviate our surprise at its sudden and drastic decrease. The differences in the number of years lived after the birth of the first son produce a gradual and systematic diminution of the length of life from Shem the son of Noah to Terah (in the Samaritan recension: 600, 438, 433, 404, 239, 239, 230, 148, 145; and in the Septuagint, according to the MSS that appear more reliable in this respect: 600, 535, 460, 460, 404, 339, 339, 330, 304, 205). The reduction of Terah's life-span to 145 years in the Samaritan Pentateuch is intended also to avoid any chronological difficulty that might otherwise have been felt. Abraham's departure from Ḥarran, which is related in the next section, took place, according to the Masoretic text, before Terah's death, which is recorded here in *v.* 32; for if Terah attained the age of 205, he would still have been alive when Abraham was seventy-five (xii 4), in which case the order of the Biblical passages would not conform to the chronological order.

Actually such conformity is not necessary, and the Masoretic reading can well be explained as we shall show later on. However, the Samaritan recension endeavoured, as usual, to give the text an easier and simpler form. The Samaritan chronology makes Terah die precisely in the seventy-fifth year of Abram's life, if we consider Abram to be his eldest son, who was born when his father was seventy; this makes it possible to regard the event recorded in xii 1 to have happened after that referred to in xi 32.

§ 5. *Bibliography.* For this section, as for those preceding, the bibliography will be given at the end of the volume (p. 287).

RUBRIC OF SECTION

10. *This is the history of Shem.*

10. *This is the history*] On this introductory formula, without the *Wāw* copulative, see my remarks in the commentary on x 1.

FIRST PARAGRAPH

SHEM

[10. continued] *When Shem was a hundred years old, / he begot Arpachshad*
two years after the flood.

11. *And Shem lived / after he begot Arpachshad*
five hundred years, / and begot sons and daughters.

Shem] The text repeats the last word of the superscription, as in the history of Noah (vi 9), the history of Terah (below, *v.* 27) and the history of Isaac (xxv 19).

A hundred years old] — twenty units of sixty months. Shem, the ancestor of Abraham, is like Abraham also in this respect, that his eldest son was born to him when he was a hundred years old, the age at which Abraham's first son by Sarah was born. On the numbers comprised in the section and on the connection between them see the introduction, § 4, pp. 252 ff.

He begot Arpachshad] See above, on x 22.

Two years after the flood] The commentators have found these words extremely difficult, for it is written earlier (v 32): *And Noah was five hundred years old; and Noah begot Shem, Ham and Japheth;* thereafter it is stated that he was six hundred years old at the commencement of the Deluge (vii 6, 11), and six hundred and one when the episode of the Flood came to an end and the ground became dry (viii 13–14). Hence it seems difficult to understand how Shem could have been one hundred years old two years after the Deluge. Many forced and complicated explanations of the difficulty have been advanced, but there is no need for such interpretations, since the entire problem is capable of quite simple elucidation. The statement in v 32 means that when Noah was five hundred years old, his first son was born to him (see Part I, p. 290, and compare *v.* 26 in this section). Now, as we showed in our note to ix 24, Shem was the second son of Noah. If we assume that he was born two years after the eldest son (a plausible conjecture when we bear in mind the common practice in eastern countries for a woman to suckle her son for twenty-four months), Noah was five hundred and two years old when Shem was born to him and Shem was ninety-eight in the six hundredth year of Noah's life, when the waters of the Flood came down upon the earth. Since we have already demonstrated in our commentary to ix 28 that the phrase *after the flood,* when it is used to indicate an exact period of time, does not mean after the termination of the entire event — that is, when the water had dried from off the earth — but after the cessation of the rain, which came down for forty days (compare vii 17: *And the* FLOOD *was forty days upon the earth*), then it follows that Shem was actually one hundred years old when two years had elapsed after the Deluge, that is, after the twenty-seventh day of the third month of the six hundredth year of Noah's life.

11. *Five hundred years*] — a hundred units of sixty months. In all Shem lived to 600 years, Noah's age before the Flood. This represents a unit called *nēr,* in Mesopotamia, which equals ten *šuš.*

SECOND PARAGRAPH

ARPACHSHAD

12. *Now Arpachsad lived / five and thirty years, and begot Shelah.*

13. *And Arpachshad lived / after he begot Shelah*
three years / and four hundred years,
and begot sons and daughters.

12. *Now Arpachshad lived*] In view of the fact that the preceding
paragraph does not conclude with a verse giving the total years of
Shem's life, in accordance with the system of chapter v, Arpachshad's name comes here very soon after its previous mention; hence,
in conformity with customary Hebrew diction in such cases (see
Part I, p. 21, on *As for the earth it was without form or life*), the
wording of our text (the subject preceding the predicate) is
וְאַרְפַּכְשַׁד חַי *weʾArpachshad ḥay* [ʾand A. lived'] and not וַיְחִי אַרְפַּכְשַׁד
wayeḥi ʾArpachšad [literally, 'and lived A.], as though to say: As
for Arpachshad, mentioned above, this was his age when his eldest
son was born.

Five and thirty years] — seven units of sixty months.

Shelah] See above, on x 24.

13. *Three years and four hundred years*] To the basic figure 400,
which is common to all three generations after Shem, there are
added here three years, the half of 6, which contain 36 months
(6×6). The total length of Arpachshad's life is 438 years; thus
the fundamental number of 400 years has been augmented by
456 months ($360 + 60 + 36$).

THIRD PARAGRAPH

SHELAH

14. *Now Shelah lived / thirty years,*
And begot Eber.

15. *And Shelah lived / after he begot Eber*
three years / and four hundred years,
and begot sons and daughters.

14. *Now Shelah lived*] On the order of the words in the sentence,
see *v.* 12.

Thirty years] This is the basic figure for the age of the patriarchs at which the eldest son was born, that is, six units of 60 months, or half a unit of sixty years.

Eber] See above, on x 24.

15. *Three years and four hundred years*] — as in *v.* 13. The total years of Shelah's life are 433; thus to the fundamental age of 400 years have been added 396 months (360 + 36).

FOURTH PARAGRAPH

EBER

16. *When Eber had lived / four and thirty years,*
    he begot Peleg.

17. *And Eber lived / after he begot Peleg*
    thirty years / and four hundred years,
    and begot sons and daughters.

16. *When Eber had lived* [וַיְחִי עֵבֶר *wayᵉḥī ʿEbber,* literally, 'And lived E.'] / Here, too, it was possible to write, after the manner of the two preceding paragraphs, וְעֵבֶר חַי *weʿEbber ḥay* ['And E. lived']; but since three verses had already begun with the word וַיְחִי *wayᵉḥī,* they attracted the form וַיְחִי *wayᵉḥī* at the beginning of the sentence here and also in the succeeding paragraphs as far as the ninth.

Four and thirty years] On the addition of four years to the basic number thirty in relation to the other additions, see the introduction, p. 256.

Peleg] See above, on x 25.

17. *Thirty years and four hundred years*] The basic figure of 400 has been augmented by thirty years, half of a unit of 60 years or six units of 60 months. The total age of Eber is 464 years; the fundamental number of 400 has been increased by a unit of 60 years plus the aforementioned addition of 4 years.

FIFTH PARAGRAPH

PELEG

18. *When Peleg had lived / thirty years,*
    he begot Reu.

19. *And Peleg lived / after he begot Reu*
    nine years / and two hundred years,
    and begot sons and daughters.

18. *Thirty years*] — as in *v.* 14; the exact basic figure.
    Reu] see above [§ 3].

19. *Nine years and two hundred years*] The fundamental age for these three generations, 200 years, has been increased by nine years; on the connection between this addition and the other increments, see the introduction, pp. 256 f. The total length of Peleg's life was 239 — the basic figure of 200 plus 36 years and 36 months.

SIXTH PARAGRAPH

REU

20. *When Reu had lived / two and thirty years,*
    he begot Serug.

21. *And Reu lived / after he begot Serug*
    seven years / and two hundred years
    and begot sons and daughters.

20. *Two and thirty years*] Regarding the relationship between the two years added to the basic age and the other additions, see the introduction, p. 256.

Serug] On this name as a geographical designation, see the introduction, p. 252.

21. *Seven years and two hundred years*] The fundamental figure has been augmented by seven; on the total of 239 years, see note on *v.* 19.

SEVENTH PARAGRAPH

SERUG

22. *When Serug had lived / thirty years,*
he begot Nahor.

23. *And Serug lived / after he begot Nahor*
two hundred years / and begot sons and daughter.

22. *Thirty years*] — as in *v.* 14 and *v.* 18, the exact basic number.
Nahor] On this name as a geographical term, see the introduction, p. 252.
23. *Two hundred years*] — the fundamental age precisely.

EIGHTH PARAGRAPH

NAHOR

24. *When Nahor had lived / nine and twenty years,*
he begot Terah.

25. *And Nahor lived / after he begot Terah*
nineteen years / and a hundred years
and begot sons and daughters.

24. *Nine and twenty years*] — the basic figure less one year.
Another such reduction occurs in *v.* 25.
Terah] On Terah see the two following paragraphs.
25. *Nineteen years and a hundred years*] — two units of 60 years
minus, once again, one year. The contraction of human life reaches
in this generation its nadir; Nahor quickly begets children, and
quickly leaves the world. The days of his life total only 148 years.
His ancestor Shem, the son of Noah, lived 600 years, a complete
nēr, but he does not attain even to one quarter of this life-span.
His son Terah, however, since he is privileged to raise up so
eminent a son as Abraham, is also vouchsafed to rise from the low
ebb to which human life-expectation had sunk and to live much
longer than his father.

NINTH PARAGRAPH

TERAH

26. When Terah had lived / seventy years,
he begot Abram, Nahor and Haran.

26. *Terah*] On the name of a locality corresponding to this word, see the introduction, p. 252. In view of the fact that this place was near to Ḥarran, and Terah is mentioned in connection with Ur and Ḥarran, two important centres of the worship of the moon-god, it appears that the view that the name *Terah* is related to the word יָרֵחַ *yārēaḥ* ['moon'] and has some association with the worship of the moon is to be accepted.

In the Ugaritic epic on Keret, as well as in other Ugaritic writings, the word *trḫ* is found several times. The first scholar to publish Ugaritic texts, Virolleaud, and other savants who followed in his footsteps, thought that the Ugaritic tradition contained a reference to wars between the sons of Terah, who invaded the land of Canaan, and the native inhabitants of the land. But it is now clear that the word *trḫ* in Ugaritic is not the name of a man but signifies the giving of the marriage price (מֹהַר *mōhar*) and marriage, and has no connection with Terah, Abraham's father.

Seventy years] After the measure of human life had shrunk in the generation of Nahor, it grew larger again in Terah's generation. Although many generations had begotten their first sons round about the thirtieth year, and Nahor had became the father of his first-born even one year before he attained the age of thirty, now, in Terah's generation, the age of paternity rose once more and reverted to the position obtaining in the antediluvian generations. This was indicative of the special importance and the exceptional vitality of this generation and its offspring. And it is precisely the number *seventy*, ten times *seven*, that denotes a state of perfection; thus the meaning of the verse is that the three sons of Terah were born only when Terah, their father, had attained to the full development of his personality.

He begot Abram, Nahor and Haran] This time reference is not made to the first-born only but to all the sons of Terah, just as earlier (v 32) the three sons of Noah are listed. The purpose is to tell us that this generation is not just an ordinary link in the genealogical chain, like the preceding generations, but one of intrinsic and outstanding significance. Not only Abram but also his brothers, it seems, were well-known figures in the subsequent Israelite tradition; they are due, moreover, to play a part in the narratives of the Bible. Hence it was fitting that the three of them should be mentioned here.

Needless to say, the verse does not mean that they were triplets born in the seventieth year of Terah's life, but that, in conformity with the correct interpretation of v 32, the eldest was born in this year and later the others came into the world.

Abram] It is not explicitly stated that he was the first-born, but since Scripture contains no contrary indication such as we found in the case of Shem the son of Noah, we may conclude that the Bible intends us to understand that he was the first-born, and that he was born when his father Terah was seventy years old.

The name אַבְרָם *'Abhrām* [Abram] (compare the form אֲבִירָם *'Abhīrām* [Abiram]) may be interpreted in various ways: (1) exalted father; (2) the father of the exalted one; (3) the father is exalted; (4) my father is exalted; (5) the father was exalted; (6) my father was exalted; (7) he is exalted through his relationship to his father, that is, he came from a noble family. According to explanations 3–6, the 'father' can be the human parent or the Heavenly Father. In the cuneiform inscriptions of Dilbat (nineteenth century B.C.E.) there occurs the name *Abamrama;* if this name is West Semitic, it can be explained in accordance with the last interpretation: 'he is exalted through his relationship to his father.' If it is Akkadian, the signification may be: 'he loved the Father'; according to this etymology it is possible to regard the description of Abraham as the friend [lover] of the Lord (Isa. xli 8; ii Chr. xx 7) as an interpretation of the name. On the form Abraham, which is used from xvii 5 onwards, see the notes *ad locum.* *

Nahor] The fact that he is called after his father's father, in accordance with the papponymic system, ** does not indicate that he

---

* This section of the Commentary was never written owing to the demise of the author.

** The system of naming a child after the grandfather.

is the first-born. On the contrary, the tradition may wish to indicate thereby that it was the second son who continued to cherish the family heritage of idolatry, not the first. The second son, whose name was identical with that of his paternal grandfather, was like his grandfather and never liberated himself from his spiritual legacy; whereas the first, Abram, introduced an important and noble innovation in the life of the family, and became *the exalted father* [אַב רָם 'abh–rām] of the new humanity.

Of the sons of Nahor, the son of Terah, mention is made later (xxii 20–24); we shall discuss the problems connected with his genealogy in our notes to this passage. *

Haran] The name is derived apparently from הָר *Hār*, a Divine name or epithet, with the termination ן— — *ān*, which is a common feature of West Semitic names. The conjecture that it is a variation of the name of the city Ḥarran is improbable. According to Maisler [Mazar, now] (*Lešonenu*, xv [1947], pp. 43–44), the name of the city Beth-haran in the land of Moab (Num. xxxii 36; Jos. xiii 27: *Beth-haram*) may be connected with the name of Haran the father of Lot and the progenitor of the children of Moab.

TENTH PARAGRAPH

THE HISTORY OF TERAH

27. *Now this is the history of Terah.*
Terah begot Abram, / Nahor and Haran;
and Haran begot Lot.

28. *And Haran died / in the lifetime of his father Terah*
in the land of his kindred, / in Ur of the Chaldees.

29. *And Abram and Nahor took / unto them wives:*
the name of Abram's wife was Sarai; / and the name of
Nahor's wife, Milcah,
the daughter of Haran, / the father of Milcah, and the father
of Iscah.

* This section of the Commentary was never written owing to the demise of the author.

30. *Now Sarai was barren; / she had no child.*

31. *And Terah took Abram his son, / and Lot son of Haran, his grandson,*
and Sarai his daughter-in-law, / his son Abram's wife;
and they went forth with them from Ur of the Chaldees, / to go into the land of Canaan;
and they came unto Haran, / and dwelt there.

32. *And the days of Terah were / five years and two hundred years;*
and Terah died in Haran.

Just as the sons of Shem are outstanding among the offspring of Noah, and therefore have a special section to themselves, so within the group of Shem's descendants the sons of Terah are pre-eminent, and in consequence a separate paragraph is devoted to them at the end of the section, which is longer and more detailed than those preceding. It gathers from the ample storehouse of ancient tradition about the family of the Patriarchs the information required by the reader in order to acquaint himself with the lineage, culture and religion of this family, and in order to understand in the light of this knowledge the nature of the original contribution that Abram-Abraham made to religious life, as well as to identify his relatives, who were subsequently to be mentioned in the continuation of the stories concerning him and his descendants. This information is conveyed with artistic grace, in a simple and almost casual manner, without emphasizing their importance, which eventually becomes clear to the reader of its own accord, as he peruses the subsequent sections.

Contemporary exegetes, who have paid attention only to the external differences between the form of this paragraph and that of the preceding paragraphs, and have made no attempt to penetrate its inner content or to understand its purpose and aim, have decided that it contains elements from a different source. They assign the previous paragraphs to P, whereas this paragraph they divide between P and J. Most commentators attribute to P *vv.* 26–27, 31–32, and to J *vv.* 28–30; but there are considerable divergences of opinion in regard to the detailed analysis of the elements derived from the two sources and the arguments on which the dissection is based. The reasons advanced are chiefly concerned with language and style; words and expressions regarded as belonging specifically either to J or to P are considered foreign to the vocabulary and phraseology of the other of the two documents. I dealt with all this at length and in detail in an essay on this passage that I published in *GSAI,* New Series, I (1925–26), pp. 194–215, in which I arrived at the conclusion that there is no reason to divide the paragraph between two sources, nor to separate it from the preceding text. It would be quite superfluous for me to repeat here what I stated in the aforementioned essay in the course of my examination of the arguments advanced in favour of the composite character of the paragraph. For one who knows Hebrew as his mother tongue it is unnecessary, for example, to prove at length that a word like עֲקָרָה *'aqārā* ['barren'], or a formula like 'the name of the one was so-and-so and the name of the other was so-and-so', is not the exclusive property of any particular Hebrew writer or of a given group of Hebrew writers, and that the use of these expressions is not forbidden to other Hebrew authors. It will suffice here to give a brief resumé of the exposition of the paragraph that I gave in my article. As a corollary of my exegesis, the unity of the paragraph and its connection with the other parts of the section will also be demonstrated.

27. *Now* [literally, 'And'] *this is the history of Terah*] The formula *this is the history* is the customary preamble to the most important genealogies. It is preceded by *Wāw* copulative, because this paragraph is connected with the preceding paragraphs, and its subject-matter is a continuation of theirs. In the same way as the entire section marks the transition from the history of mankind as a whole to the story of the Patriarchs of Israel, so this paragraph serves as a special bridge between the account of the sons of Shem collectively and the story of Israel's patriarchs.

Terah begot, etc.] The formal phrase *Now this is the history of Terah* necessitated the renewed mention of the three sons. This is not a redundant duplication but an unavoidable repetition arising from the customary stylistic scheme. Even Terah's name, which occurs at the end of the superscription is reiterated at the beginning of the genealogy in accordance with the usage that we observed above in *v.* 10 and in other passages that we cited in our annotations

270

to that verse. If we were to formulate the account in modern idiom, we should write approximately as follows: This, then, is the history of Terah; first of all Terah begot, as we stated earlier, Abram, Nahor and Haran; thereafter Haran begot Lot, and after that etc.

And Haran begot Lot] The Bible mentions here only the offspring of the third son and not of his brothers, for two reasons: (1) that the third son died before his father Terah (*v.* 28), and only the son of the former remained to take his place; from the two verses 27–28 taken together we gain the information necessary to our understanding of the subsequent history of the patriarchal family, to wit, that the family tree headed by Terah had three branches: Abram, Nahor, Lot; (2) that for the time being neither Abram (*v.* 30) nor Nahor (xxii 20–24) had children.

Lot] It is difficult to determine the meaning of this name. The suggestions advanced to connect it with Lotan the Horite (Gen. xxxvi 20, 22, 29), or with the Egyptian word *Rṯnw,* which denotes the inhabitants of the land of Canaan, or with Lud the son of Shem (Gen. x 22), are mere conjectures without probability.

28. *And Haran died in the lifetime* [literally, 'upon the face of'] *of his father Terah*] The Bible says little about the death of Haran. Possibly detailed traditions were current about the untimely death of Haran, *upon the face of his father Terah,* that is, still in his father's lifetime, and about its causes and circumstances. The Torah was content with a brief allusion to the subject here, to the extent required to elucidate Lot's position in the family. It may be that the Midrashic tales about Haran and his death preserve some vestiges of the ancient tradition, but obviously we are not in a position to come to any detailed conclusions.

In the land of his kindred in Ur of the Chaldees] Since Scripture is due to tell us later (in *v.* 31) that most of Terah's family left their country, it stresses here that Haran died before this exodus, whilst he was still in his native land. After the general expression *in the land of his kindred,* comes the particular specification, *in Ur of the Chaldees,* to indicate the exact place; compare Gen. xlviii 7: *Rachel to my sorrow died in the land of Canaan on the way, when there was still some distance to go to Ephrath.* 'Ur of the Chaldees' is undoubtedly the name of a city. The explanation of the word *Ur* [אוּר *'Ur*] as *fire,* given in a number of Midrashim, is

271

not its true meaning; and the attempt of several expositions to interpret the word as an appellative has proved abortive (the Septuagint
already has: χώρα, that is, 'land'; many medieval commentators
translate: 'plain'; some modern scholars render: 'mountain'; and
so forth). In regard to the identity of the city called here Ur of the
Chaldees there was till recently considerable diversity of opinion.
In B. Baba Bathra 91a it is stated in R. Hisda's name: 'the small
side of Kuthi is Ur of the Chaldees' [see commentaries s. עִיבְרָא
זְעִירָא 'ibbrā' ze'īrā'; cf. Jastrow s.v.]; similarly Jewish commentators and Arab geographers of the Middle Ages were of opinion
that Ur of the Chaldees is Cutha, near Babylon. In modern times
various identifications have been suggested: *Urarṭu* (that is,
Ararat); *Urhâi* (that is, Edessa, north-west of Ḥarran); Erech (see
above, on x 10); Mari (on the middle Euphrates); Arbela (south-
east of Nineveh); Ur (Southern Mesopotamia, south of Erech);
and so forth. Today, especially after the brilliant results of
Sir Leonard Woolley's excavations (1922–1933) in Tel 'el-
Muqayyar, the site of the ancient Ur, all agree that the Biblical Ur
of the Chaldees is none other than this famous city, which was one
of the most important centres of Sumerian culture and apparently
reached the zenith of its political power and economic efflorescence
at the end of the third millenium and the beginning of the
second millenium B.C.E. The addition of *Chaldees* to the name
Ur (that is, 'Ur of the Chaldees') may perhaps be explained
on the assumption that the inhabitants of Canaan were accustomed
to join to the name of this city the general designation of the
district in which it was situated, and in which there wandered
about, at least from the beginning of the second millenium,
Chaldean tribes — West Semitic desert-dwellers. Commencing
with the eleventh century, the Chaldean tribes exerted strong
pressure against Ur, and possibly the composite name 'Ur of the
Chaldees' does not antedate this situation, and does not belong to
the period of which the Bible speaks here; but the city was thus
called in anticipation of its ultimate designation; compare the
statement in Gen. xiv 14 that Abram pursued the eastern kings *as
far as Dan,* that is, as far as the place that was subsequently named
Dan as a result of the conquests of the tribe of Dan.

The mention of Ur of the Chaldees in this paragraph raises

272

several doubts. First, many of the names of the scions and the sires of the family point, as we have seen, to Northern Mesopotamia, whereas Ur of the Chaldees lies in the south, and there is not the slightest allusion to their having migrated from the north to the south. And another point: Nahor the son of Terah and his family are referred to, in chapter xxiv, as inhabitants of the city of Haran in the north, but it is nowhere stated that they left Ur of the Chaldees for Haran. Of Abram it is, in truth, related in *v.* 31 that he went forth together with his father Terah from Ur of the Chaldees to Haran, and similarly we are told in the section of the 'Covenant between the Sacrificial Pieces' (Gen. xv 7) that the Lord said to him: *I am the Lord who brought you from Ur of the Chaldees* (and on this authority the point is reiterated in Nehemia ix 7); yet when Abram was commanded to go forth from Haran, he was enjoined: *Go* FROM YOUR COUNTRY AND YOUR KINDRED *and your father's house* (xii 1); and when he sent his servant, the oldest of his house, he said to him: *but you will go* TO MY COUNTRY AND TO MY KINDRED (xxiv 4), as though he really originated from Haran and not from Ur of the Chaldees. All this appears at first sight very difficult.

The division of the text according to sources does not remove the difficulties, as is evident from the diversity of opinions among the adherents of this exegetical method. One view maintains that P (*v.* 31) makes Ur of the Chaldees the home of the Patriarchs, whereas J places their abode in Haran. Now here, in *v.* 28, which, like chapter xxiv, belongs to J, the words *Ur of the Chaldees* are only an interpolation from P. Since chapter xv is also attributed to J, the supporters of the documentary theory are constrained to delete therefrom *v.* 7, which again mentions Ur of the Chaldees as Abram's country of origin. Others hold that even according to P the patriarchs dwelt only in Haran, and that both in this verse and in *v.* 31, which is assigned to P, the reference to Ur of the Chaldees has been added later, in the same way as in ch. xv. Others distinguish two strata of J; according to the one source, the earlier of the two, the patriarchs dwelt in the north, and according to the second, the later document, Ur of the Chaldees was the place of their abode. There are still other conjectures; but all these dissections serve only to increase the confusion.

The matter, however, can be explained quite simply, if we understand the word מוֹלֶדֶת *mōledheth* [usually rendered: 'birthplace'] correctly. In the vast majority of the passages in which this word occurs (I have cited them all in my aforementioned essay in *GSAI*, p. 206) it is clear from the context, and sometimes also from the parallelism, that the word signifies 'the circle of relatives, the family.' It will suffice to mention, for example, Gen. xliii 7: *The man questioned us carefully about ourselves and* OUR KINDRED [מוֹלַדְתֵּנוּ *mōladhtēnū*], *saying, '*IS YOUR FATHER STILL ALIVE? HAVE YOU ANOTHER BROTHER?*'; ibid.* xlviii 6: AND THE OFFSPRING [מוֹלַדְתְּךָ *mōladht*ekhā] BORN TO YOU *after them shall be yours;* Esther viii 6: *For how can I endure to see the calamity that is coming to* MY PEOPLE? *Or how can I endure to see the destruction of* MY KINDRED [מוֹלַדְתִּי *mōladhtī*]*? Since this is the signification of מוֹלֶדֶת *mōledheth*, the meaning of the expression אֶרֶץ מוֹלֶדֶת *'ereṣ* ['the land of'] *mōledheth* (or אֶרֶץ וּמוֹלֶדֶת *'ereṣ ūmōledheth* ['land and *mōledheth*'], which is only a single concept, hendiadys) must be: the land in which the circle of relations dwells. It has not the modern connotation of the word מוֹלֶדֶת ['native land']. To the man who wanders about from country to country, the place in which he happened to be born, because his father and mother chanced to be there on the day of his birth, has not the same importance as our *birth-place* has for us. After he and his family have gone from there, he has no further connection with the place. Hence, after the whole family of Terah had left Ur of the Chaldees for Haran, and all its ties with the former place were severed, the land of Haran could be referred to as 'the land of Abram's kindred' or 'his land and kindred' when the Lord spoke to him, and even when he mentioned it himself in the course of his sojourning in the land of Canaan, far from his family and the house of his father, who had remained in Haran. Proof of the correctness of this interpretation can be found in the synonyms of the term אֶרֶץ (וּ)מוֹלֶדֶת *'ereṣ (ū)mōledheth* that are used in association with it, or as variants in its stead, in chapter xxiv (*v.* 27: *the house of my master's kinsmen; v.* 40: *from my kindred and my father's house; v.* 41: *my kindred*). Thus there is no contradiction at all between the passages that indicate Ur of the Chaldees as the original home of Abram and those that afterwards refer to the land of Haran as his native land. The problem of his brother Nahor, of whom it was not specifically stated that he left Ur of the Chaldees, we shall discuss later on, in our annotations to *v.* 31, where we shall show that even in his case there is no discrepancy between the Scriptural texts. As for our verse — *v.* 28 — we must bear in mind that the words *in the land of his kindred, in Ur of the Chaldees* refer only to the time of Haran's death, and provide no evidence with regard to the preceding period. When Haran died, his whole family-circle lived in Ur of the Chaldees, and consequently this country was at the time *the land of his kindred,* in the same way as the land of Haran was subsequently the land of Abram's kindred. It is more than possible that the ancient tradition related, in conformity with the testimony of the geographical names, which resemble those of the patriarchs of the family, that these sojourned at first in Northern Mesopotamia, in the neighbourhood of Haran, and that from there they went forth in the course of their wanderings and finally reached Ur of the Chaldees; but the Torah, which cites here from the current tradition only the details essential to its purpose and nothing more, was not concerned to mention the original abode of these patriarchs, because it was of no importance to its theme proper. Accordingly, the migration to Haran mentioned in *v.* 31 really marks the return of the family to its original home. The fact that Ur and Haran were the chief centres of the cult of the moon-god Sin, and consequently were linked together by firm and permanent ties, serves to explain the movements from one to the other.

29. *And Abram and Nahor took unto them wives*] The Bible does not tell us whether these marriage preceded Haran's death or *vice versa*. The order of the passages provides no chronological evidence. The Torah is silent in regard to the date, since it was not necessary to its purpose.

The name of Abram's wife, etc.] The name of Haran's wife is not given, because there is no further mention of her in the rest of the narrative, and consequently the reader has no need to know her name. It is enough for him to be told that Haran left a son after him named Lot. But the wives of Abram and Nahor are to be mentioned again in the succeeding sections, and therefore their names are recorded in this paragraph, which serves to introduce all the members of the family and to set before us all the preliminary details necessary to the proper understanding of what will be related later.

Sarai] Later her name will be changed to *Sarah* (xvii 15). These are only variant forms of the same name (in Ugaritic writings י- -*y* is a common termination in feminine nouns). The signification of the word is clear: 'princess', 'chieftainess', or, in the Akkadian language, 'queen'. Perhaps this name was also connected, like Terah's, with the Mesopotamian worship of the hosts of heaven, *Šarrat* (that is, 'queen') being one of the Akkadian designations of Ištar, the goddess of the planet Venus.

Scripture does not tell us the name of Sarai's father. Later (xx 12) it is related that Abram said to Abimelech that she was the daughter of his father but not of his mother, and hence he could marry her according to the custom prevailing before the Pentateuchal prohibition. Most commentators think that the verse implies that this was actually the case. But this is difficult, for it is not stated here that Sarai was Terah's daughter, but, on the contrary, in *v.* 31 she is called the *daughter-in-law* of Terah. According to the haggadic interpretation, Sarai is Iscah the daugther of Haran the son of Terah, and Abraham called her *the daughter of my father* on the principle that grandchildren are accounted as children; but this exposition is not in accord with the simple meaning of the text. More probable is the explanation of Ibn Ezra, that Abraham's intention was merely to find an excuse in answer to Abimelech.

Milcah [*Milkā*] / This is the archaic form of the appellative מַלְכָּה *malkā* ['queen'], which remained preserved in the proper name; also the masculine form *milk-* occurs in the Amarna letters as a component of proper names in the ancient Canaanite language. Possibly the name Milkā is likewise connected with the worship of the heavenly hosts: *malkat-* (apparently in the sense of *counsellor* [fem.]) was one of the Akkadian titles of Ištar. Similarly there are a number of references in the Book of Jeremiah (vii 18; xliv 17–19, 25) to Ištar under the designation מְלֶכֶת הַשָּׁמַיִם *mᵉlekheth haššāmayim* [E. V. 'queen of heaven'], the vocalization being emended [from מַלְכַּת *malkath*] in order to convey a derogatory sense [the vowels are those of the word מְלָאכֶת *mᵉle'kheth* ('the work of'), implying that Ištar was not divine but created].

276

The daughter of Haran, the father of Milcah and the father of Iscah] Here, too, the Bible gives the impression that these worthies were well known to the Israelites, and that the ancient tradition related more about them than is stated here. Most of the commentators regard this Haran to be Terah's son; but if this were so, it is difficult to understand why Scripture tells us that he was *the father of Milcah and the father of Iscah,* without also mentioning Lot, Haran's male child. It seems more likely that this was another Haran. Perhaps Nahor's wife was known in the tradition as *Milcah the daughter of Haran,* and to prevent the reader's mistaking this Haran for Terah's son, the Bible identified him by the designation *the father of Milcah and the father of Iscah,* as though to say: he is not Haran father of Lot, or, after the manner of the Arabic *kunya* ['a surname of relationship' (Lane)], Father-of-Lot Haran, who was mentioned earlier, but another Haran, who had no sons but daughters, and they were Milcah and Iscah.

Iscah] She is not mentioned elsewhere in the Bible, and we do not know what the tradition related of her. Her identification with Sarai is only a late haggadic interpretation. Nor is the meaning of the name quite clear. Perhaps it may be explained on the basis of the expression לֹא יִיסָךְ *lō ʾyīsākh* ['it shall not be poured'] (Exod. xxx 32), as an allusion to the fragrance of the perfumed oil of anointing — a pretty name for a woman.

30. *Now Sarai was barren*] Milcah, too, was barren for many years, as one may deduce from the words *she also* in Gen. xxii 20. But it was fitting to note at this stage that Sarai had no sons, in order to underline Abram's merit, to wit, that he believed in the Lord who had promised him (xii 2): *and I will make you a great nation.* We can understand the greatness of his faith only if we are previously aware that he has no children, his wife being barren. But the barrenness of Milcah is of no importance to our theme, and is therefore not referred to by Scripture. Later the children of Milcah are mentioned when the Torah prepares the reader for the story of Rebekah's marriage to Isaac by providing him with detailed information about her lineage.

31. *And Terah took,* etc.] This is a stereotyped Biblical formula. When Scripture wishes to tell us that someone left, with all his family, the place where he was living, in order to settle elsewhere

or sojourn there for a long time, it employs the following phraseology: So-and-so (the head of the family) took so-and-so
(members of his family) and such-and-such possession (for
example, his cattle and his beasts and his goods, and the like), and
he went etc. So it is written here of Terah; and so it is also stated
of Abram (xii 5): *And Abram took Sarai his wife, and Lot his
brother's son, and all their possessions which they had gathered,
and the persons that they had gotten in Haran; and they set forth
to go to the land of Canaan*, etc.; similarly in the case of Esau
(xxxvi 6): *Then Esau took his wives, his sons, his daughters, and
all the members of his household, his cattle, all his beasts, and all
his property which he had acquired in the land of Canaan; and he
went*, etc.; and likewise of Jacob and his sons it is said (xlvi 6):
*They also took their cattle and their goods, which they had gained
in the land of Canaan, and came into Egypt, Jacob and all his
offspring with him.* Those who accept the documentary hypothesis
regard this formula as the peculiar characteristic of P, which is
difficult even according to their own theory, for similar expressions
are found in Exod. xviii 2–4 (*Now Jethro, Moses' father-in-law,
had taken Zipporah, Moses' wife, after he had sent her away, and
her two sons*, etc.), which they assign to E; furthermore, the
narrative form cannot be dissociated from that of the imperative,
which is found in Gen. xix 15 (*take your wife and your two
daughters*, etc.), which is attributed to J. The truth is that the
formula used in such circumstances belongs to the ancient literary
tradition of Canaan, as we learn from the writings of Ugarit. In
the Ugaritic epic of Baal, the god of heaven, who makes the wind
to blow and the rain to come down, it is related that Mot, the
god of Sheol, sent a threatening message to his brother Baal, telling
him through his [Baal's] messengers that he would soon slay him
and force him and all that he had to go down to him in Sheol.
Following are his actual words (Tablet I* AB, v, 6–13): 'But thou,
take thy clouds, thy winds, thy chariots and thy rains; with thee
thy seven attendants and thine eight boars; with thee *Pdry*
daughter of *Ar;* with thee *Ttly* daughter of *Rb* (the wives of
Baal); then set thy face within the caves of *Knkny'*, etc. [com-
pare *ANET*, p. 139]. In another Ugaritic tablet (BH, i, 17–22)
there occur, in similar form, the words of El, the father of

the gods, when he banishes the handmaid of his wife Asherah. The phraseology was thus bequeathed, together with the entire store of the ancient literary tradition, by the Canaanites to the children of Israel — not, of course, to a particular author or to a specific group of writers, but equally to all the writers of Israel.

Abram his son] The fact that Nahor is not mentioned here would appear to be a difficulty. A few MSS of the Septuagint have after *Abram* the words, καὶ τὸν Ναχώρ ('and Nahor'); but this is obviously an addition made by the scribes in order to remove the difficulty, for after Nahor's name, *his son* remains in the singular. The reading in the Samaritan Pentateuch is: 'and Abram his son and Sarai and Milcah his daughters-in-law, the wife of Abram, and Nahor his sons'; the awkwardness of the diction shows that this is not the original text. The exponents of the documentary hypothesis endeavour to solve the problem by pointing out that P, to whom they attribute this verse, does not subsequently allude to Nahor's stay in Haran. But the problem remains, even in so far as P is concerned. Nahor is mentioned, along with the other brothers, in *vv.* 26–27, which are assigned to P; the Torah should therefore have told us here what happened to him, just as it tells us what befell his brothers. If his father had brought him out of Ur of the Chaldees with him, his name should have been included among the other emigrants; and if he alone remained behind, we should have been informed of this. Apparently the difficulty has to be solved in another way, as we shall explain later.

And Lot son of Haran, his grandson [literally, 'his son's son'] / The translators and commentators have failed to understand the construction of this expression properly. Many, beginning with the Septuagint, have rendered the text: καὶ τὸν Λὼτ υἱὸν Ἀρράν, υἱὸν τοῦ υἱοῦ αὐτοῦ ; *und Lot, Sohn Harans, seines Sohnes Sohn; — and Lot, the son of Haran, his son's son.* But after specifying that he was the *son of Haran* there was no point in adding the general statement that he was Terah's *son's son*. If the intention was to indicate the exact relationship of Lot to Terah, it would have sufficed to state: 'and Lot the son of Haran, his son.' Some have added in their translations an explicative word, thus: 'and Lot the son of Haran, *namely*, his son's son'; but the original text contains no such word. Others, again, have given a free rendering, for example: *und Lot, seines Sohnes Haran Sohn* ['and Lot, his son Haran's son'] (Gunkel); or: *und Lot, den Sohn seines Sohnes Haran* ['and Lot, son of his son Haran'] (Koenig); and the like. But these free translations do not fit the original text and indicate that the translators did not understand it. The truth is that the phrase *son of his son* here denotes only a single, unified concept, and means, *his grandson,* as we find in Phoenician inscriptions: *so-and-so the son of so-and-so, the son of the son of so-and-so,* in other words: so-and-so the son of so-and-so and the grandson of so-and-so (similarly in Akkadian the compound word *binbini* means *grandson*). The expression *Lot son of Haran* is simply the full name of Lot; accordingly, the meaning of the text is: and Lot-son-of-Haran, his grandson.

And they went forth with them [וַיֵּצְאוּ אִתָּם *wayyēṣeʾū ʾittām*] / This also appears to be difficult: who went forth with whom? Many scholars emend the text on the basis of the Samaritan Pentateuch, the Septuagint and the Vulgate: וַיּוֹצֵא אֹתָם *wayyōṣēʾ ʾōthām* ['and he brought them forth']; others, following the Syriac Version, read: וַיֵּצֵא אִתָּם *wayyēṣē, ʾittām* ['and he went forth with them']; and others, again, conjecture: וַיֵּצְאוּ אִתּוֹ *wayyēṣeʾū ʾittō* [and they went forth with him']. But none of these emendations are plausible: the first, because it would have been incorrect to say that Terah brought forth his household without stating that he also went forth; the second, because Terah was the head and leader of the family, and consequently it was not he who went with them but they who went with him; the third, because Terah also went forth and he, too, is included in the subject of the verb *went forth,* and therefore it was not possible to add *with him* after *they went forth,* for the same reason as it is not found in the similar verse, xii 5.

In order to understand the sentence, we must consider the comparable verse, xii 5. The similarity between the two passages, not only in formulation but also in regard to the proper names and the other expressions used, indicates an inner relationship between them, and comes, as it were, to tell us that already before they left Haran, and even whilst the family was still in Ur of the Chaldees, Abram, Sarai and Lot were closely associated and constituted a specific group within the general circle of the family. It is not without reason that the words *to go into the land of Canaan* occur in our verse as well as there. Apparently the import of our verse is that quite at an early stage, when they were still dwelling in Ur of the Chaldees, Abram, Sarai and Lot planned to go to the land of Canaan, and they influenced Terah and the other members of the family to such an extent that they all went with them with the intention of travelling together to their destination. They proceeded *via* the 'Fertile Crescent', and on coming, in the middle of their journey, to Haran, they stayed there and did not continue their travels. Only Abram's group, after a time, resumed their journey and reached their original goal, as we are told in the opening verses of chapter xii.

Accordingly, the sense of the verse is as follows: And Terah, the head of the family, took his son Abram, and Sarai and Lot, whose ties with Abram were particularly close, and all the members of the family *went forth with them* — that is, with Abram, Sarai and Lot — *to go with them,* in accordance with their plan, to the land of Canaan, but when they reached Haran they settled there. The expression *and they went forth with them,* which at first seemed difficult, is thus easily explained. Even the omission of explicit reference to Nahor and Milcah is understandable in the light of this interpretation: they are included, like all the other members of Terah's house, in the indefinite subject of the verb *went forth.* There was no need to mention them all individually, since the rest of the narrative is not concerned with them but with Abram, Sarai and Lot exclusively; only the names of these, the heroes of the next sections and the promoters of the migration, are specifically mentioned.

To go into the land of Canaan] See my remarks above, on the clause *and they went forth with them.* Influenced by Abram and his circle, Terah and the other members of the family also felt an inner urge — yet not sufficiently strong or clear — in the spiritual direction towards which Abram was set with all his heart and soul. But they did not succeed in overcoming completely the attraction of idol worship and were unable to abandon the world of paganism; they did, in truth, set out on the journey, but stopped in the middle of the way. Of Abraham and his company, too, it is said (xii 5), *and they went forth to go into the land of Canaan,* just as it is stated here, but there the verse goes on to say: *and into the land of Canaan they came,* that is to say, they carried out their intention, whereas here it is stated: *and they came unto Haran, and dwelt there.*

32. *And the days of Terah were five years and two hundred years*] Up to Nahor the father of Terah, the length of life of the heads of the generations decreases steadily, but when we reach the generation of Terah, who was privileged to be the father of Abram, we observe once more a rise in the graph of human life. We have likewise noted in the Mesopotamian tradition an extension of the life of the more important personages. Longevity is indicative of special merit and especial importance.

But there was a definite limit to Terah's life, namely, the time of Rebekah's marriage to Isaac. The story of this union (ch. xxiv) shows us Bethuel the son of Nahor at the head of the family, and makes no mention of Terah at all; hence, according to tradition, Terah was no longer alive. Now Isaac, who was born when his father Abraham was 100 years old (xxi 5) and his grandfather Terah was 170, married Rebekah when he was 40 (xxv 20). In view of the fact that in the history of the Patriarchs, as we have seen earlier (Part I, pp. 259 f.), the Biblical chronology employs chiefly units of five years, the Bible states here that Terah died when he was 205 years old, that is to say, when Isaac was 35, five years before his marriage. These dates also accord with the numerical symmetry, which is a common feature of these passages, in two other respects, to wit:

(a) When Abram separated from his father, his age was 75 (xii 4); when his son Isaac was born to him he was 100 (xxi 5), and when he passed away he was 175 years (xxv 7). His life is consequently divided into three periods: the first period, with his father; the third, with Isaac; the middle stage, without his father and without Isaac. The length of the first period and of the last are equal, whilst the middle phase is a third of the others, thus: 75+25+75.

(b) Terah was 145 (75 + 70) when Abram left his house; thus the last period of his life, after Abram had separated from him, was 60 — the basic unit of the sexagesimal system of chronology.

On the length of Terah's life according to the Samaritan recension, see my observation above, in the introduction, p. 259.

And Terah died in Haran] Throughout his life, he did not find the strength to continue his journey and reach the goal that he originally had in mind under his son's influence. Although he made an effort to get away from the centre of the moon-cult in Ur of the Chaldees, yet when he came to another city dedicated to this worship — to Haran — he did not succeed in freeing himself from the spell of idolatry, and stayed there. Where he halted he also died.

Chronologically, Terah's death took place after what is narrated in the coming chapters; but Scripture mentions it here, in accordance with its usual practice, in order to complete all that it had to say about Terah, and to pass on thereafter to the story of Abram without interruption or the need to revert again to what happened to his father. From now on, Abram-Abraham will be the central figure of the text.

The bibliography up to the year 1934 is listed in my Italian work *La Questione della Genesi,* where the reader will find it without difficulty. It was my intention originally to give also in this volume, in conjunction with each section, complete, detailed bibliographical information, as far as this was possible, from the year 1934 onward, and to include therein even articles dispersed among the scientific periodicals of those years, as I did in my book *From Adam to Noah.* However, seeing that to date (May 1949), regular access to the University Library and to other big libraries in Jerusalem has not been restored, I can only add to the literature I have cited in the course of this volume a few notes that may serve as a guide to the reader who wishes to delve more deeply into the questions connected with the chapters discussed. *

First Section: THE FLOOD

On the conjectures advanced for the division of the section between the different sources (P, J and others), and on the reasons for and against this analysis, I have cited the bibliography up to 1934 in my aforementioned Italian work, in the references given above, p. 35.

Regarding the question of the relationship between the Biblical narrative of the Deluge and the parallel legends of the ancient East, the reader can now refer to A. Heidel's compendious work [1] and to the Hebrew essay of T. Fish [2]. On the Epic of Gilgameš, in particular, note should be taken of the monumental edition of Thompson [3], and among the recent studies dealing with the text

* No attempt has been made to bring the bibliography up to date, since it is felt that this is a task that only the author, had he lived, could properly have performed *(Translator).*

[1] A. Heidel, *The Gilgamesh Epic and Old Testament Parallels,* Chicago 1946.

[2] T. Fish, *'Hōmer mesōpōṭāmī ʿal ʾōdhōth hammabbūl',* Melilah i (1944), pp. 142–151. The author, apparently, wrote his essay in English; the Hebrew translation is inaccurate.

[3] R. Campbell Thompson, *The Epic of Gilgamesh,* Oxford 1930.

in detail, attention should be given to the investigations of Kramer [4] and Oppenheim [5]. Other articles on the relationship between the Scriptural and parallel accounts of the Flood mentioned above are cited in note [6]. For the comparative study of the Eastern and Greek traditions of the Flood, the essay of W. Borgeaud, whom I have mentioned above, p. 161, should be consulted. New views on the traditions relating to the Deluge have recently been put forward by E. G. Kraeling in several articles [7].

On 'the sign of the Covenant' see N. H. Tur-Sinai, "*Othōth* ['signs'] in the Bible and in the Lachish Letters'[8].

Second Section: THE SONS OF NOAH

A. *The Story of Noah's Intoxication*

See the aforementioned essays of Borgeaud and Kraeling. On the parallels to the story of Ham, see now the latest article by Güterbock [9]. Regarding the blessing and curse of Noah, see my Hebrew article 'Blessing and Curse' in the Encyclopaedia Biblica (Hebrew) and the bibliography given there.

---

[4] S. N. Kramer, 'The Epic of Gilgamesh and Its Sumerian Sources: A Study in Literary Evolution', *JAOS*, lxiv (1944), pp. 7–23, 83.

[5] A. L. Oppenheim, 'Mesopotamian Mythology', II. *Orientalia*, N. S. 17 (1948) [on the Flood, specifically, see pp. 51–55].

[6] E. E. Boughey, 'An Ancient Egyptian Flood Legend?' *Journal of the Manchester Egyptian and Oriental Society,* xix (1935), pp. 27–31.

J. H. Schoneveld, *De oorsprong van het bijbelsche Zondvloeverhaal,* Groningen 1938.

A. C. Custance, 'The Flood Traditions and the Bible', *Bibliotheca Sacra,* xcvi (1939), pp. 412–427.

G. Contenau, *Le Déluge babylonien; Ishtar aux Enfers; La tour de Babel,* Paris 1941.

[7] E. G. Kraeling, 'The Significance and Origin of Gen. vi 1–4, *JNES*, vi (1947), pp. 193–208. — *idem.* 'The Earliest Hebrew Flood Story', *JBL*, lxvi (1947), pp. 279–293 — *idem.* 'Xisouthros, Deucalion and the Flood Traditions', *JAOS*, lxvii (1947), pp. 177–183.

[8] *Tarbiz* xx (1949) = Jubilee Volume presented to J. N. Epstein on the occasion of his Seventieth Birthday, Jerusalem 1950, pp. 49–57 [Hebrew].

[9] H. G. Güterbock, 'The Hittite Version of the Hurrian Kumarbi Myths: Oriental Forerunners of Hesiod', *AJA,* lii (1948), pp. 123–134.

B. *The History of the Sons of Noah*

On the arrangement of the chapter and its relationship to the story of the Generation of Division, see *La Questione*, pp. 102–106, 203–205. In regard to detailed points, bibliographical information up to the year 1932 is given in A. Reubeni's book [10]; see on this work the critical review of W. F. Albright [11]. Since I am confining myself to a brief bibliography here, I cannot list in full the considerable number of more recent books that I consulted for my introduction and commentary. I shall mention only the essay of Dhorme on the descendants of Japheth [12] and the Hebrew articles of Grintz [13]. I shall also indicate here, with a view to supplementing my references to the subjects in the commentary, the publications in which the suggested identification of Cush (p. 198) [14] and Calneh (p. 202) [15] that I have cited appeared. Other bibliographical details I have included in the text of the book.

C. *The Story of the Generation of Division*

To the bibliography, up to 1934, given in *La Questione*, pp. 359–365, a few more studies should be added [16]. In regard to the

[10] A. Reubeni, *Shem Ham and Japhet, The Peaples of the Bible, their Racial Connections and Place in History*, Tel-Aviv 1932 [Hebrew, English Summary].

[11] *Kirjath Sepher*, vol. x No. 1 (1933), pp. 28–29 [Hebrew].

[12] E. Dhorme, 'Les peuples issus de Japhet d'après le chapitre X de la Genèse', *Syria*, xiii (1932), pp. 28–29.

[13] I. M. Grintz, 'Hap-Pelištîm bi-Gerār wehap-Pelištîm šel ḥôph hayyām. *Studies in Memory of Moses Schorr*. New York 1945, pp. 96–112. — *idem.*, 'Hā'awwîm wehā-'Amālēqî; 'A'mîm, 'Elāmîm', *Tarbiz*, xvi (1945), pp. 163–168. — *idem.* ''Aliyyath hap-Pelištîm hāri'šônîm bakkethôbhôth', *ibid.*, xvii (1946), pp. 32–42; xix (1948), p. 64. — *idem.*, 'Benē Miṣrayim', *Sinai*, xii (1949), pp. 2–17.

[14] First see W. F. Albright, *BASOR*, 83, p. 34, n. 8. Note thereafter also the remarks of B. Maisler [now, Mazar] in his article 'Palestine at the Time of the Middle Kingdom', *Bulletin No. 1 des études historiques juives* (= *Revue de l'histoire juive en Egypte*, No. 1), Cairo 1946, pp. 37–38, 59.

[15] A. Poebel, *JNES*, i (1942), p. 256, n. 17; W. F. Albright, *ibid.*, iii (1944), pp. 254–255; A. S. Yahuda, *JBL*, lxv (1946), pp. 325–326.

[16] G. Martiny, 'Der Turm zu Babel', *Forsch. u. Fortschr.*, x (1934), pp. 30–31. — A. Brock-Utne, 'Gen. xi 9 im Lichte der Kulturgeschichte des

Mesopotamian towers generally, see L. H. Vincent's article [17] and the literature cited there. For a detailed description of the ziggurat Etemenanki, the reader is referred to the two articles I have mentioned on p. 228; both of them contain a comprehensive bibliography.

Third Section: THE HISTORY OF THE DESCENDANTS OF SHEM

On the chronology, see my essay in the *Louis Ginzburg Jubilee Volume,* Hebrew Section, pp. 381–390, and R. H. Pfeiffer's work, *Introduction to the Old Testament,* pp. 200–205; and compare the data in the Mesopotamian sources in Jacobsen, *op. cit.* [18]. For the names of the heads of the generations and the geographical problems, see the article by R. de Vaux on 'Les Patriarches Hébreux et les Découvertes Modernes' [19], which comprises a detailed bibliography. On the last paragraph, see my article on the subject in Italian [20], and the literature cited there.

nahen Orients', *ARW,* xxxii (1935), pp. 293–310. — O. E. Ravn, 'Der Turm zu Babel; eine exegetische Studie ueber Gen. xi 1–9', *ZDMG,* xci (1937), pp. 352–372. — A. H. de Boer, 'Genesis xi 1–9: een vertaling met aanteekeningen in een opmerking over de beteekenis', *NTbS,* xxiv (1941), pp. 304–309.

[17] *RB,* liii (1946), pp. 403–440.
[18] *The Sumerian King List,* Chicago 1939, pp. 76–85.
[19] *RB,* lv (1948), pp. 321–326.
[20] *GSAI* N. S. i (1925–1926), pp. 193–215.

APPENDIX

A fragment of
PART THREE

ABRAHAM AND THE PROMISED LAND
A Commentary on Genesis XII–XVII *

---

* The author died in the course of his work on this part of the com
mentary (*See Translator's Foreword*).

מ. ד. קאסוטו: אברהם וארץ היעוד

*First published posthumously in Hebrew
as an appendix to 'From Noah to Abraham',
Jerusalem 1953,
and reprinted in the edition
of 1959*

First English edition, Jerusalem 1964

GENERAL INTRODUCTION TO THE
PENTATEUCHAL STORIES ABOUT ABRAHAM

§ 1.   The preceding sections dealt with matters appertaining to all humanity. Now, after the transition paragraph at the end of pericope Noah (xi 27–32), the life histories of Israel's Patriarchs become the central theme; and first of all attention is focussed on the primogenitor of the nation, Abram-Abraham.

§ 2.   According to the genealogy in Gen. xi, Abram belongs to the tenth generation of the line of Shem the son of Noah. Just as in the tenth generation after Adam there arose Noah, a wholly righteous man who was privileged to become the father of the new humanity after the Flood, so in the tenth generation after Noah, Abram was born, the chosen of the Lord, who was to become the father of a spiritually renewed mankind. And even as Noah was granted, on his own behalf and on behalf of his children, the blessing, *Be fruitful and multiply, and fill the earth* (ix 1), which confirmed and realized in him and in his offspring the benison bestowed upon the first man (i 28: *Be fruitful and multiply, and fill the earth*), so Abram-Abraham was vouchsafed the blessing of fertility (xvii 2–6), apart from the special spiritual benisons that were promised to him and his offspring after him.

§ 3.   In view of the fact that these sections have an Israelitic, and not a universal content, there are, of course, no parallels to be found to their subject-matter in the literatures of the neighbouring peoples, such as were discovered in the case of the preceding sections. The story of Creation, of the Garden of Eden, the 'histories' of the earliest generations of mankind, the account of the Flood, and the like — these are all themes in which other peoples were also interested, weaving many tales around them and recording them in their writings; but the biographies of the Israelite partiarchs were of concern, in antiquity, to Israel only. Nevertheless, even for the comprehension of these sections the documents surviving from the ancient East that were recently discovered are of value. They help us to understand better not only the general geographic and historical background of the Bible narratives concerning Abraham and his family, but also the environment into which these stories transport us. Thus, for example, the documents recovered

in great numbers from the Mesopotamian archives, particularly at Mari and Nuzu, give us a diversified and detailed picture of the social life in Mesopotamia, the first homeland of Israel's ancestors, especially in the first half of the second millenium B.C.E., which is the epoch of the Patriarchs. We must always take a glance at the surviving records of the neighbouring peoples wherever they can be instructive for the fuller understanding of these Scriptural sections.
§ 4.   But we must beware of hasty conjectures that find in the extra-Biblical sources actual references to the Patriarchs in person. Two such theories have been advanced — one in ancient and the other in modern times — and both are without foundation.

The first of these occurs in Josephus' work *Contra Apionem*. He states that there is an allusion to Abraham in the writings of the Babylonian author Berossus; the latter tells of a man who lived in the tenth generation after the Deluge, who was distinguished by his wisdom and by his knowledge of astronomy and the other sciences. It is difficult to agree with Josephus in this matter. He sought to prove, on account of his apologetic tendency, that the Gentile peoples also acknowledged the greatness of the first Patriarch; but objectively one cannot find in the words of Berossus what Josephus discovered in them. The only parallel is provided by the importance attached to the series of ten generations, thus affording another illustration of the love of numerical symmetry that was common both to Israel and to the environment from which the ancestors of Israel came.

The second conjecture of this nature, which was put forward in modern times, is that of Virolleaud and other scholars, who saw in certain sentences of the Ugaritic writings an allusion to the immigration of the Terahites into the land of Canaan. As I indicated in my commentary on xi 26 (see p. 266), Virolleaud thought that the word *trḫ*, found in the Epic of Keret, was the name of Abraham's father Terah, and that the military movement described in the epic was none other than that of the Terahites invading Canaan. Virolleaud further discovered references in Ugaritic poems to the names of Israelite tribes and to the places where the invaders clashed with the inhabitants of the land. There was no lack of scholars who concurred in Virolleaud's view, but today it is clear that this theory is incorrect, and that *trḫ* in the Ugaritic texts is simply a term for the giving of the mohar ['marriage price'] and marriage, and that these records contain no reference to the tribes of Israel nor to battles waged for the conquest of the land of Canaan.

As far as we know today, there is no evidence of a non-Israelite tradition relating specifically to the immigration of the children of Terah, and to their settlement in Canaan. We have, in this regard, the Israelite tradition alone.

§ 5. The Torah does not reproduce all that the tradition current in Israel used to tell of the first Patriarch of the nation and his milieu. In the Pentateuchal account itself there are still discernible allusions to various topics that are not expressly narrated therein. We have already observed above (xi 28) a reference to the death of Haran in the lifetime of his father Terah, and thereafter (*ibid.* v. 29) an allusion to Haran, the father of Milcah and the father of Iscah; and in my commentary to these verses I noted (see pp. 271, 277) that possibly there existed among the Israelites detailed traditions concerning the untimely passing of Haran, Abram's brother, and its causes and circumstances, and so, too, with regard to Haran the father of Milcah and Iscah — apparently a different person, whose name was identical with that of Abram's brother — as well as his two daughters. The Torah, however, contented itself with such brief references as were necessary to the elucidation of the relationship between the members of Abram's family, and did not elaborate the things that were not essential to its purpose. Similar allusions will also be found later; for instance, the mention of Damascus-Eliezer * (xv 2). It is possible that in the material cited in the pseudepigrapha and Midrashim some remnants of the ancient tradition have been preserved, but we have no means of determining the matter in detail.

Out of the store of traditions that used to be related among the Israelites concerning Abram-Abraham, the Torah selected the material that was best suited to its plan and aims, gave this material a form consonant with its own spirit, and fitted it, in characteristic

---

* Hebrew: דַּמֶּשֶׂק אֱלִיעֶזֶר *Dammeśeq* ʾ*Eliʿezer*. The author regarded the two words as a compound name, like Jerubbaal-Gideon (Jud. viii 35) or Tubal-cain (Gen. iv 22), and conjectured that Damascus-Eliezer may have been considered the eponymic founder of Damascus; see *Encyclopaedia Biblica* (Hebrew), ii, col. 676. — *Translator.*

manner, into a general literary structure that is harmonious and complete. The perfected form of this structure does not support the view espoused by most modern exegetes, who regard the text as the accidental product of the combination of a number of fragments from various sources that are cited word for word and joined together by a complicated process of repeated redactions. This theory and the problem of the sources of the narratives in general we shall discuss later. Here we must consider the arrangement and interconnection of the stories in the existing form of the text.

The material is set out with numerical symmetry based on the numbers seven and ten, and the theme develops progressively stage by stage. Abraham is put to repeated tests, which amount to ten in all. Although these are not, if we follow the simple meaning of Scripture, identical with the tests enumerated in the haggadic expositions of the Rabbis, yet the total is undoubtedly the same even according to the objective interpretation of the text, and the number continues the system that assigned ten generations for the period between Adam and Noah, and ten, again, for that between Noah and Abraham. The first ordeal is preceded by a Divine promise to Abraham of a general nature, and after each trial he receives consolation in the form of a renewed assurance by God, or of a specific act for his benefit. Thus there is fashioned a chain of alternating light and shade, in continuing succession, until the last and most sublime promise, which is given to Abraham at the end of the final and severest ordeal — that of the offering of Isaac.

The trials are as follows:

(1) The first, which Abram had to undergo immediately after the promise contained in the Lord's communion with him in Haran, was his migration from his country and his kindred and his father's house to a new land, unknown to him. He believed in the promise and stood the test successfully (xii 1–4); consequently, the second promise was given him, namely, that he would possess this land in place of his native country (xii 7).

(2) After he had passed through the whole of Canaan, and had taken, as it were, ideal possession of it, the act of acquisition being symbolized by the altars that he built to the Lord in the land, he was forthwith compelled to leave the country on account of the famine and to go down to Egypt, and there Sarai his wife found

herself in danger. But the Lord protected her, and Abram returned in peace with all his family to the site of the altar that he had erected near Bethel (xii 10 — xiii 4).

(3)   The land did not suffice for both him and Lot his brother's son, and he was compelled to separate from Lot and to reconcile himself to forgo, for the sake of peace, a portion of the land; but Lot chose an area that did not belong to Canaan proper, and the Lord again promised the entire land to Abram, as well as a large offspring to replace his nephew, who had left him (xiii 5–18).

(4)   In order to rescue Lot, Abram was forced to risk a hard fight against the eastern kings, but the Lord delivered [מִגֵּן *miggēn*] his foes into his hand (ch. xiv), and then assured him that He was his 'shield' [מָגֵן *māghēn*], and confirmed and even enlarged and elaborated still further the promises in regard to the acquisition of the land and the abundance of his descendants (ch. xv).

(5)   When Hagar was about to give birth to his first-born, this son was in danger of being taken from him because of family strife. But the danger passed (ch. xvi), and the Lord assured him that a multitude of nations would issue from him, not only by his first son but also by his second son, whom Sarah would bear unto him, and in this son the covenant of the Lord would be fulfilled (ch. xvii).

(6)   Again Abram was tested by the commandment of circumcision, and he stood the test (ch. xvii), after which he was privileged to be visited by the three 'men', and the promise concerning the birth of his chosen son was confirmed and explained to him and to Sarah (xviii 1–15).

(7)   Once again Lot was in jeopardy on account of the wickedness of his neighbours; but this peril also passed, and Lot was saved for Abraham's sake (xviii 17–xix 28).

(8)   At the very time that the birth of Isaac is drawing near, Abraham's wife finds herself again in danger at the hands of Abimelech king of Gerar, but from this peril, too, she is delivered, and Isaac is born in peace (xx 1–xxi 7).

(9)   The birth of Isaac led to the departure of his first-born, but he was solaced by the covenant he made with his neighbours and the building of a new sanctuary at Beer-sheba and the proclamation there of the Lord's name (xxi 8–34).

295

(10) In the end came the supreme trial, the offering of Isaac. Abraham withstood even this terrible ordeal, and received on account of it the most sublime blessings and the most comprehensive assurances, which include and sum up all that had been promised him previously.

When we consider the details of this list, we observe an unmistakable progression in the successive tests, and in many instances a certain correspondence between the trial and the benison or consolation that followed.

Note should also be taken of the chiastic parallelism between the ten episodes. The last trial corresponds to the first (*Go from your country* etc.; *and go to the land of Moriah* etc.; in the former passage there is the command to leave his father, in the latter to bid farwell to his son; in both episodes the blessings and promises are similar in content and in phrasing). The penultimate two tests parallel the pair of tests following the first (in the earlier trials Sarai is in danger from Pharaoh, and Lot goes away; in the later ordeals Sarah's peril stems from Abimelech, and Hagar and Ishmael depart; in both sets of tests a sanctuary is founded and the name of the Lord is proclaimed). The seventh episode corresponds to the fourth (in both Lot is in jeopardy and is saved). Similarly, the sixth trial parallels the fifth (both appertain to Ishmael and Isaac).

The Divine communications of benison and promise to Abram-Abraham are seven:

(1) The first, which he received at Haran (xii 2–3), comprises seven expressions of blessing (the details we shall discuss in the continuation of our commentary).

(2) The second (xii 7: *To your descendants I will give this land*) briefly explains and specifies two important points in the first promise, namely, enduring offspring and possession of the land.

(3) The third (xiii 14–17) further expands and elucidates the promise of the land and confirms that of the offspring.

(4) The fourth, the theophany in connection with the Covenant between the Sacrificial Pieces (ch. xv), extends and clarifies the promise of children and fixes the time for the acquisition of the land.

(5) The fifth (ch. xvii, the section of Circumcision) contains the good tidings that not one nation alone but a multitude of nations will come forth from Abram, and that the covenant of the Lord will find particular realization in the son that Sarah will bear unto him.

(6) The sixth (ch. xviii) brings the news that in another year Sarah would give birth to this son.

(7) The seventh, more comprehensive and exalted than all the previous communications, was vouchsafed Abraham after the attempted sacrifice of Isaac (xxii 16–18) and contains once again, like the first, seven expressions of benison.

All this shows clearly how out of the material selected from the store of ancient tradition concerning Abraham a homogeneous narrative was created in the text before us, integrated and harmoniously arranged in all its parts and details.

§ 6. Contemporary scholars have devoted much attention to the historicity of the Torah stories about the Patriarchs, including those dealing with Abraham. The mythological interpretation of I. Goldziher (1876) and J. Popper (1879), which has long been out of date and rejected, regarded the Patriarchs as symbols of the forces of nature, and the tales about them as nature myths. According to this view, Abraham represented the אַב 'abh ['father'] רָם rām ['exalted'], that is, the actual heavens, or more especially the sky at night. Others thought that the figure of Abraham was that of a god, or demigod, who had been demoted to human level and had become among the Israelites the progenitor of the nation. This is the common basis of the various views held by Nöldeke, Lagarde, Stade, Meyer, Weil and others, who picture the original character of Abraham in various ways, to wit, as one of the holy men and heroes of Edomite or Calebite Hebron, or as one of the Nabatean gods, Dū-Šara (that is, 'the Husband of Sarah'), or as the particular deity of a particular tribe, which was subsequently named after him, or some similar conjecture. The theory has also been advanced that the stories about Abraham are borrowed from Egyptian mythology (Voelter), or that they are connected with the Mesopotamian myths relating to the moon and its worship (Winckler, Jeremias), since the two cities Ur and Haran, from which Abraham migrated, were centres of the lunar cult, and the name of Terah, Abraham's father, points to the moon, and the name of Sarah and Milcah, the wife and sister-in-law of Abraham, may be titles of the moon-goddess, and the number of Abraham's 318 trained men corresponds to the number of days in the year on which the moon is visible, and so forth.

Many scholars consider the narratives of the Patriarchs to be symbolizations of tribal histories, and in certain instances this is quite evident, for example, in the episodes depicting the relations between Jacob and Esau; but in regard to Abraham it is difficult to accept this view, since the name Abraham does not occur as the name of a tribe or people, with the possible exception of a solitary instance in Micah vii 20. According to the interpretation of Gunkel and Gressmann, most of the stories about the Patriarchs are only myths belonging to the type of folk-tale that is transmitted from place to place. In the case of the Israelites these legends were attached to names commonly found among them, and in the course of time their heroes came to be regarded as patriarchs of the people. This line of exposition has also not been accepted by the majority of exegetes, because motifs of the kind found in folk-legends are present to only a small extent in the patriarchal narratives, whilst the names Abraham, Isaac and Jacob were, particularly among the Israelites, not common in the period of antiquity.

The feature common to the views of most scholars till a few years ago was the assumption that the narratives of the Patriarchs were composed in a much later period than that in which the Patriarchs lived, and that they underwent repeated changes before they were crystallized in their present form; consequently, it was held, they cannot preserve reliable historical information. But all these conjectures have become obsolete today. The ancient documents discovered in recent times in Mesopotamia (see above, § 3) have enabled us to familiarize ourselves with the Mesopotamian society of the first half of the second millenium B.C.E., to know its customs and conditions of life, and we find that the background of the patriarchal narratives of the Book of Genesis is precisely the same as that which emerges before us from those texts. We shall deal with this subject in detail in the continuation of our commentary; here it will suffice to point briefly to a few examples. The relationship between Abraham and Damascus-Eliezer, for instance, becomes perfectly clear in the light of the customs that are reflected in the documents of Nuzu; and the act of Abraham's wife in giving him her handmaid in order to be built up by her can be explained not only on the basis of several clauses in the Code of Hammurabi, but particularly by reference to other documents from Nuzu. In general, the entire cultural, social, ethnographic and linguistic setting of the narratives in Genesis concerning Abraham corresponds to what we learn from the texts of the ancient East belonging to the first half of the second millenium B.C.E. Needless to say, it was not possible for the Israelites of a later epoch to compose literary works that would so faithfully reflect the conditions of earlier generations, which were doubtless unknown to them. This enables us to assess the antiquity of the narratives and the historic value of their main content.

§ 7.   However, the Torah does not narrate its stories for the purpose of teaching us antiquities. Its aim is not to record history for its own sake, in the scientific sense of the term, or to chronicle the exact manner in which certain events happened. Its goal is more exalted, namely, the religious and national education of the people of Israel, and to this end it employs traditional material. Hence the Pentateuch did not incorporate in its sections the entire fund of narrative that tradition had stored up relative to Abraham (see above, § 5), but merely a part of it. Only those tales were included from which religious or national instruction could be derived. In particular, Scripture's motive was to teach: (a) how Abraham came to know his Creator, and to devote himself to His service, and how he was chosen as the bearer of the covenant that the Lord made with him, so that he might establish a new religious society that would transcend the level of idolatry prevailing in his days, and that he might guide his children and children's children to keep the way of the Lord and do righteousness and justice (compare xviii 19); (b)   how Abraham received Divine promises concerning the future of his descendants, their increase in number without end, and the acquisition of the land of Canaan as their everlasting possession; (c) how the events of Abraham's life paralleled the destiny of the people of Israel, in the sense that the experiences of the sires prefigured those of the scions; and how the reader may conclude from this that the history of the Israelites was not the result of

299

chance, but the execution of plans that were predetermined from the beginning by God's will and were foreshadowed from the first in the events that befell the primogenitor of the people. In the continuation of our commentary it will be fully explained how the intention to inculcate these doctrines can be discerned in the details of the stories, and that the narratives are so worded as to convey Scripture's motive to the reader.

SECTION ONE

ABRAM COMES TO THE LAND OF CANAAN

CHAPTER XII, 1–9

INTRODUCTION

§ 1. THIS SECTION tells of the event that marked the turning-point in Abraham's life. By the Lord's command Abraham left his land and his kindred and his father's house in Haran, and went up to the land of Canaan; there the Lord assured him that this land would be given to his descendants, and, in keeping with this promise, Abram traversed the whole land of Canaan, from north to south, as though to symbolize thereby the ideal conquest, so to speak, of the whole area promised to him and to his children after him; and in two important places he built altars unto the Lord, a token of the sanctification of the land to the Lord and to His worship for generations to come.

§ 2. The Israelite tradition, which finds explicit expression at the end of the Book of Joshua (xxiv 2; compare *ibid. vv.* 14–15), related that idolatry was practised in the house of Terah, Abraham's father: *Your fathers lived of old beyond the Euphrates, Terah, the father of Abraham and of Nahor; and they served other gods. But* — Joshua continues in the name of the Lord (*ibid. v.* 3) — *then I took your father Abraham from beyond the River and led him through all the land of Canaan.* This accords with the story of our section, which begins with the words of the Lord to Abram: *Go from your country and your kindred,* etc. The meaning is that Abram succeeded in rising above the idolatrous notions of his environment, recognizing ה' *YHWH* [usually rendered: 'Lord'] as *God Most High, Maker of heaven and earth* (xiv 22), and hearing in the recesses of his soul the voice of the Lord, who communed with him (of the name אֵל שַׁדַּי *'El Šadday* [E. V. 'God Almighty'] we shall speak later). From the blessing that Noah bestowed upon

301

Shem is to be inferred, as we have already observed, that according to the Israelite tradition the knowledge of the Lord was preserved among the descendants of Shem, or at least among the élite of them. In the light of our narrative, Abram alone was associated with this religious chain of tradition, in contrast to the rest of his family, who did not belong to the elect few that acknowledged the Lord, and consequently he was enjoined to separate himself from them and to devote himself to the service of the Lord in a new land appointed for this purpose.

§ 3. Abram's journey to Canaan with his household, family and slaves, as well as the persons they had gotten in Haran, who thus formed a kind of branch-group or tribe of nomads, falls within the historic framework of the migrations of peoples and tribes who entered the land of Canaan and Syria in the first half of the second millenium B.C.E., namely, Hurrian tribes, who came from the mountainous region of the North, and various West Semitic tribes. It seems probable that among these Semitic tribes were to be found elements appertaining to a body of people called *Ḥapiru* in Akkadian, '*pr.w* in Egyptian, '*prm* in Ugaritic; this name does not denote, it appears, a specific people, but a social category, a class of foreign origin who were living in an alien environment, and who sometimes served as slaves or hired soldiers or the like. The question whether this name can possibly be identified with that of the עִבְרִים *'Ibhrīm* ['Hebrews'] or בְּנֵי עֵבֶר *benē 'Ebher* ['children of Eber'] is highly complicated, but the objection that used to be considered the most formidable against the identification, namely, the difference between the letter *Bēth* in the word עִבְרִי *'Ibhrī* ['Hebrew'] and the letter *Pē'*, which is also found in the Canaanite idiom of Ugarit, is easily answered by taking into account the influence of the adjoining letter *Rēš;* it is a fact that the Ugaritic word '*rpt* corresponds to the Hebrew עֲרָבוֹת *'ărābhōth* ['clouds'; compare Psa. lxviii 5 (E.V. 4)]. Be this as it may, it appears that the name under discussion, like the Biblical term 'children of Eber' (compare x 21), denotes a very broad-based class, in which Abram and his offspring formed only a single group. They are called Hebrews particularly when they are found in an environment of foreigners, for example, in Egypt (many times at the end of Genesis and in Exodus), or among the Philistines (several times in i Samuel), or in the company of the mariners sailing to Tarshish (Jonah i 9), and it is Abram in particular who is termed 'the Hebrew' in relation to the inhabitants of Canaan (xiv 13).

The essential difference between the immigration into Canaan of the other groups and that of Abram's company consisted in this, that the cause of the latter's migration was not, or was not solely, economic, social or political, but was primarily religious, and its aim was the founding of a new faith; therein lies its unique significance.

It is true that Scripture does not expressly state for what purpose Abram was commanded to go forth from his land and kindred; hence several scholars, like Gunkel, thought that the original meaning of our section was not that Abram was bidden to go from there with the specific intention of detaching him from the pagan environment; in their opinion this conception arose in a later epoch. But what the Bible does not say expressly it indicates by inference. It is a characteristic of these narratives (and Gunkel himself realized it in a general way) not to describe the thoughts and feelings of the *dramatis personae,* but only to record their deeds, and to inform the reader through the narration of events of the ideas and sentiments that prompted their actions. In the present instance, the building of the altars by Abram in the land of Canaan immediately after his immigration, symbolizes, as I have already noted earlier, the dedication of the land to the Lord and to His service. From this we clearly learn the purpose, according to the Torah, of Abram's settlement in Canaan.

§ 4. The Bible tells us nothing about Abram's itinerary from Haran to the land of Canaan. The ancient tradition, apparently, described it in some detail: how the patriarch went journeying from place to place until he arrived at Damascus (see the end of the annotation on xii 5), and thence to Northern Canaan. But, since all these details were of no importance to the Torah's aim, Scripture does not mention them. Nevertheless, traces of them are still discernible in the reference to Damascus-Eliezer (xv 2), which points to Abram's passage through Damascus and to his relations with its inhabitants.

§ 5. Details of Abram's travels are given only in respect to the last and most important stages, namely, his wanderings in Canaan itself. These raise three questions: What was the Bible's intention in furnishing us with these particulars and in delimiting Abram's journeys in the land of Canaan in the manner it does: first as far as the neighbourhood of Shechem, thence up to the environs of Bethel, and finally from there to the Negeb? Why was the area of the land divided thereby into three regions: one extending from the northern border to Shechem, the second from Shechem as far as Bethel, and the third from Bethel to the southern boundary? And why is it that it was at these particular stations — in the vicinity of Shechem and of Bethel — that Abram built altars unto the Lord ?

In seeking the answer to these questions, we should first note the fact that it is these stopping-places and this division of the country that are mentioned again in similar form in the account of Jacob's travels after his return from Paddan-aram. Although he did not enter from the north but from the north-east, yet he also came first to the place of Shechem (xxxiii 18): *And Jacob came safely to the city of Shechem, which is in the land of Canaan, on his way from Paddan-aram; and he camped before the city*, etc. After the story of Dinah, and the conquest of Shechem by her brothers Simeon and Levi, we are told in chapter xxxv (*v.* 1): *God said to Jacob, 'Arise, go up to Bethel, and dwell there'*, etc., and thereafter (*v.* 6): *And Jacob came to Luz (that is, Bethel), which is in the land of Canaan, he and all the people who were with him.* He, too, continues his journey southward and comes as far as Hebron (xxxv 27) and Beer-Sheba (xlvi 1). And like his grandfather, he also builds altars to the Lord in the localities of Shechem and Bethel (xxxiii 20: *There he erected an altar and called it El-Elohe-Israel* [that is, 'God, the God of Israel']; xxxv 7: *and there he built an altar, and called the place El-bethel* [that is, 'God of Bethel']). Thus he likewise passes through the land and conquers it, as it were, ideally in the name of the Lord (apart from the actual conquest of Shechem by his sons), and he, too, erects upon it altars, tokens of this ideal conquest. Just as the altar-tokens of Abram serve to divide the land into three regions, each south of the other, so do the altar-tokens of Jacob, which were set up at the same sites. And just as Abraham bought for the full price a specific place in the land — the field of Machpelah near Hebron — so also Jacob acquired against full payment a given area in the vicinity of Shechem, after which two of his sons conquered the whole region. The parallel is unmistakable.

There is still another parallel, no less manifest. When the children of Israel invaded the country in the days of Joshua and conquered it in actuality, then, too, according to the account of the tradition reflected in the Book of Joshua, the key points seized were precisely those that we have noted in the ideal conquests of Abram and Jacob. The first city to be captured after entering the land by way of Gilgal and Jericho was, we are told in the Book of Joshua (vii 2), *Ai . . .east of Bethel,* and the children of Israel, aiming to take it, stationed themselves, according to the statement in Joshua, *between Bethel and Ai, to the west of Ai* (viii 9; compare *v.* 14) — the very expressions that we find in the story of Abram (Gen. xii 8: *on the east of Bethel, and pitched his tent, with Bethel on the west and Ai on the east*). The repetition of these words is certainly not accidental and undoubtedly has a specific motive. It is clear that the author of the Book of Joshua phrased his account in conformity with what is stated here in the Book of Genesis. This impression grows stronger when we read further on in the Book of Joshua that, immediately after the capture of Ai, Joshua went up to Shechem (viii 30): *Then Joshua built an altar in Mount Ebal to the Lord,* etc., and mount Ebal is, of course, near to Shechem (it should be noted that in Joshua, too, the building of an altar is mentioned). The meaning, therefore, is that to begin with Joshua gained control over the line Ai—Bethel—Shechem. Thence he succeeded in subduing the settlements west or south-west of the line (ch. ix), and in seizing thereby the greater part of the central area of the country. In the continuation of the Book of Joshua it is related how the children of Israel spread southward and north-ward, to the two remaining regions, south of Bethel (ch. x) and north of Shechem — the very threefold division that we found in Genesis.

Now we can understand why the Torah stressed, in all their detail, Abram's journeys on entering the land of Canaan, at first as far as Shechem, and subsequently up to Ai-Bethel. Scripture intended to present us here, through the symbolic conquest of Abram, with a kind of forecast of what would happen to his descendants later. According to this tradition the token was first given to Abram and afterwards repeated to Jacob, and the significance of the duplication is to corroborate and ratify, as the Bible itself makes clear when citing the words of Joseph to Pharaoh (xli 32): *And the doubling of Pharaoh's dream means that the thing is fixed by God, and God will shortly bring it to pass.* In conformity with this, the Book of Joshua portrays for us the actual subjugation in a manner paralleling the ideal conquest by the Patriarchs — even the wording is similar—as though to say, the possession of the land gained in the days of Joshua was already implied, in essence, in the symbolic conquest that the first patriarchs had effected in their time, and that it was all predestined and foretold from the beginning in accordance with the Lord's will.

It remains to add that the two places discussed were not only considered key points geographically, but also as religious centres of the Canaanite population. Hence the proclamation by Abram of the name of 'ה *YHWH* at these places signifies the proclamation of the supremacy of 'ה *YHWH*, the God of Abram, over the gods of Canaan.

§ 6. In this section, as in those preceding, numerical symmetry is discernible. This obtains not only, as we have noted, in the use of the number *ten* (ten generations), which is the basic numeral of the decimal system, but also in the use of the number *seven,* which was considered the number of perfection (compare my remarks above, in § 5 of the general introduction to the Pentateuchal stories about Abraham). The blessing bestowed by the Lord on Abraham in *vv.* 2–3 comprises seven expressions of benison, as we shall explain in detail later, and it is evident that the Bible intended by this formulation to set before us a form of blessing that was perfect in every respect. It should also be observed that each of the key words in this section — *Abraham* and *land* — occurs, as usual, seven times in the section.

§ 7. The exponents of the documentary theory distribute the verses of this section, and even fragments of them, between the two sources J and P, and the editorial work of the Redactor (R). In regard to the details of the analysis the views of the exegetes differ, but generally speaking the majority opinion appears to be that *vv.* 1–4a and *vv.* 6–8 should be assigned to J, *vv.* 4b–5 to P, and *v.* 9 to R. However, the very fact that the section corresponds as a whole and also in its particulars to the tradition relating to the journeys of Jacob and the conquest of the land by Joshua, and the added fact that the form of the section shows distinct signs of numerical harmony, are testimony to its unity. Nor can it be countered that all this is evidence only of the labours of the redactor, for if the redactor gave the narrative a perfected form, he was no ordinary editor but an author, and his work was planned from the start and skilfully put together, and is not the chance product of the mechanical combination of fragments, as the adherents of the documentary hypothesis suppose.

And another point. The reasons advanced for dividing the section between different sources are not only negatived by the clear evidence mentioned above, but even intrinsically they constitute no proof. I examined all these arguments in detail, one by one, in my study 'Studi sulla Genesi', ii (in *Giornale della Società Asiatica Italiana,* New Series, i [1925–1926], pp. 217–220), and I showed that each one fails to prove anything. It is superfluous to repeat here what I wrote in that article; but to two of the contentions, which might at first appear to be weighty, I shall devote a few lines at this stage.

(a) The first is that verse 5 (*And Abram took Sarai his wife, and Lot his brother's son, and all their possessions which they had gathered, and the souls that they had won in Haran; and they set forth to go to the land of Canaan; and into the land of Canaan they came*) repeats what was already stated in *v.* 4a (*So Abram went, as the Lord had told him; and Lot went with him*). It is true that the verse reiterates what was narrated in essence earlier, but when we understand the structure of the section properly, we see at once that this repetition is not only possible but is justified and correct from every point of view. The section is composed of two paragraphs, as I shall show later. The first paragraph (*vv.* 1–4) cites the Divine communication to Abram in detail: *Go your own way, from your country,* etc., and, as is usual in such instances, it adds in the last verse the general observation that Abram did as the Lord had commanded him. We have often read similar remarks at the end of paragraphs in the section of the Flood, and we shall come across such concluding statements many more times in the continuation of the Pentateuchal books. The second paragraph (*vv.* 5–9) describes Abram's journey in detail; the general statement is thus followed by a detailed account. The latter must naturally start at the beginning, relating how Abram set forth on the journey; nor can it confine itself to a simple recapitulation of the story, but must elucidate it further, giving an exact list of the persons and possessions that Abram took with him on his journey. Both verses are thus necessary, each in its own place.

(b) The section contains expressions and deals with topics that are considered to be characteristic of P. All the chronological data are attributed to P; now in *v.* 4b we are given chronological information about Abram's age (*and Abram was five and seventy years old when he departed from Haran*). Similarly, the formulation of *v.* 5 (*And Abram took Sarai his wife . . . and they set forth to go,* etc.) is regarded as peculiar to P. It stands to reason, however, that if we assign to P all verses that include themes and expressions of this kind, they must unquestionably all be found in P and in P only; if now a scholar subsequently uses this fact to prove that a given verse belongs to P because it comprises subjects or phraseology of this nature, he is simply arguing in a circle or begging the question, which is logically an obvious fallacy. Furthermore, in so far as the chronological data are concerned, we have already seen in the previous sections (not only in those that are essentially chronological, but also in narrative sections like that of the Deluge) that this information is an inseparable part of the context; and we shall observe the same in the succeeding sections. How Abram's age is closely linked in this section with the story itself, we shall explain later in the continuation of our commentary. As for the formula used in *v.* 5, *And Abram took,* etc., I have shown earlier, in my annotations to xi 31 (see above, pp. 277 ff.), that it was a common usage already in Canaanite literature, whence it was transmitted as a legacy to the Israelites, and, needless to say, it was not bequeathed to one specific author or group of writers in Israel, but to all Isaelite writers alike.

To sum up: there is no compelling reason for splitting up the section among various sources, but on the contrary there are important arguments that prove its unity.

THE LORD'S COMMAND AND PROMISES

CHAPTER XII

1. *And the Lord said to Abram,*
   'Go your way, / from your country and your kindred
   and your father's house / to the land that I will show you.

2. *And I will make of you a great nation, / and I will bless you,*
   and make your name great, / so that you will be a blessing.

3. *I will bless those who bless you, / and him who curses you*
        I will curse;
   And in you will be blessed / all the families of the earth.'

4. *So Abram went, / as the Lord had told him;*
   And Lot went with him.
   And Abram —
   was five and seventy years old / when he departed from Haran.

1. *And the Lord said unto Abram*] Here speech only is referred
to, whilst in *v.* 7 it is written: *Then the Lord appeared unto Abram.*
Apparently Scripture wishes to tell us that until Abram reached the
Chosen Land he was not granted the privilege that the Lord should
appear to him in a vision; he only heard His voice just as Adam
and Noah before him had heard it.

Go your way [לֶךְ-לְךָ *lekh-lᵉkhā,* literally, 'Go to you']/The word
לְךָ *lᵉkhā* ['to you'], which has been added to the imperative לֵךְ
lekh ['Go'], is not without specific signification. Rashi's explanation, 'for your benefit and good' (compare B. Rosh Hashana 16b,
according to one view: 'It was the merit of the land of Israel that
benefited him') is implausible, for it is not possible to suppose that
the Bible wishes to tell us that it was for his personal advantage
that Abram went to Canaan; moreover, in other passages of
Scripture it is quite impossible to give this interpretation to the
Lāmedh after the verb הָלַךְ *hālakh* ['go']. Most modern commentators pay no attention to this question; Koenig, who does raise
the matter, gives a similar explanation to that of Rashi. In order
to determine the meaning of the phrase we must examine similar

passages. Such an investigation will prove to us that in each case the reference is to someone (or something) who goes alone (or only with those who are specially connected with him) and breaks away from the community or group in whose midst he was till that moment. The most interesting parallel occurs in Gen. xxii 2, at the beginning of the section of the Offering of Isaac (I dealt with this parallel in my aforementioned essay, 'Studi sulla Genesi', 1926; and I was followed by others); the correspondence in the phrasing indicates parallelism of content. Here, in our passage, it is written: לֶךְ לְךָ *lekh-lᵉkhā* . . . TO THE LAND THAT I WILL SHOW YOU, and there, in chapter xxii: *and* לֶךְ־לְךָ *lekh-lᵉkhā to the land of Moriah, and offer him there as a burnt offering upon one of the mountains* OF WHICH I SHALL TELL YOU. In both cases Abram undergoes an ordeal: here he has to leave behind his aged father and his environment and go to a country that is unknown to him; there he has to take leave of his family circle for a little while, and of his cherished son for ever; his son, it is true, will accompany him for the first part of the way, but only so that he might bid him farewell for ever. Thereafter he must go on his way *alone,* the way of absolute discipline and devotion. In both instances the test is made harder by the fact that the destination of the journey is not stated beforehand. Here it says: *to the land that I will show you;* I shall not tell you now to which land you have to go, but you must have faith and hearken and obey; you must journey on until I say to you, 'Enough'. Similarly it is stated there: *upon one of the mountains of which I shall tell you;* I shall not tell you at this stage on which mountain you are to offer him to me for a burnt offering, but you must believe and hearken and obey; you must continue to journey till I say to you: 'This is the place'.

Following are verses containing a similar usage:

Exodus xviii 27: *Then Moses let his father-in-law depart, and* HE WENT HIS WAY [וַיֵּלֶךְ לוֹ *wayyēlekh lō*] *to his own country* (Jethro goes alone, leaving Moses, his family and all Israel).

Joshua xxii 4: *and now turn and* GO ON YOUR WAY [לְכוּ לָכֶם *lᵉkhū lākhem*] *in the land where your possession lies* (so Joshua spoke to the tribes of Transjordan, when they were about to take leave of the other tribes of Israel after they had fought together with them to conquer the country west of the Jordan).

i Sam. xxvi 11–12: *and let us go on our way* [נֵלְכָה לָנוּ *nēlᵉkhā lānū*] (after taking Saul's spear and jar of water, we shall leave this area and get away from Saul and his army; later it is related: *and they went on their way* [וַיֵּלְכוּ לָהֶם *wayyēlᵉkhū lāhem*] (so they left and went away, as David had said).

Jeremiah v 5: I WILL MAKE MY WAY [אֵלְכָה לִי *'ēlᵉkhā lī*] to the great (the prophet prepares to depart from the general populace and to draw near for a moment by himself to the great ones among the people).

The Song of Songs ii 10: *My beloved speaks and says to me: 'Arise, my love, my fair one, and* COME AWAY' [לְכִי לָךְ *lᵉkhī lākh*]; similarly *ibid. v.* 13: *Arise, my love, my fair one, and* COME AWAY (the lover invites his beloved to leave her home and family for a little while and to go alone with him for a stroll in the village).

Ibid. v. 11: *the rain is over and* GONE [הָלַךְ לוֹ *hālakh lō*] (has departed·from us).

Ibid. iv 6: I WILL HIE ME [אֵלֶךְ לִי *'ēlēkh lī*] to *the mountain of myrrh and the hillside of frankincense* (I will go alone, and I will leave behind every other thought and every other companion).

Compare also Gen. xxi 16: THEN SHE WENT, AND SAT HERSELF DOWN [וַתֵּלֶךְ וַתֵּשֶׁב לָהּ *wattēlekh wattēšebh lāh*] *over against him* (she went away from her son and sat down alone).

In the same way the expression לֶךְ־לְךָ *lekh-lᵉkhā* is to be understood here. Go, you by yourself, or only with those who are united to you in unique relationship, go on the way that belongs to you alone, and leave behind your kinsfolk amongst whom you have lived till now and who do not wish or are not able to associate themselves with you in your new way.

From your country and your kindred and your father's house] Koenig has rightly pointed out that there is progression here. The first step is, *from your country*: you must go from the land in which you were born and grew up and were reared. This is followed by a harder test: you must leave *your kindred* [מוֹלֶדֶת *mōledheth*], the family group to which you are bound by ties of blood (in classical Hebrew the word מוֹלֶדֶת *mōledeth* means 'kindred' and not, as in modern Hebrew, 'native land'). Thereafter comes the hardest wrench of all: *and from your father's house*; it is not only the family group in the wider signification [i. e. clan] that

311

you have to forsake, but also the narrower and more cherished circle, your father's house (here, too, the words are not to be understood in their modern connotation, 'from the house of your father, but in the sense of 'from your בֵּית אָב *bēth 'ābh'* [i. e. the family branch within the clan; cf. Exod. xii 3]), the circle of which your father Terah is the head; and consequently you must also leave your aged father behind. According to my interpretation, there is no discrepancy between this verse and the verse above (xi 28), which refers to Ur of the Chaldees as the land of the מוֹלֶדֶת *mōledheth* ['kindred' not 'birth'] of Abram's brother, Haran; on this problem see my annotations to xi 28 (pp. 271 ff.).

To the land that I will show you] The progression continues. As I have already indicated, the journey, without prior knowledge of the final goal, is a most drastic test. Unqualified devotion is required of Abram; and he stands the test.

2–3] This is the Divine promise to Abram regarding the reward that would be given him for his faithfulness. It contains seven expressions of blessing, as the Talmudic sages already noted (Bereshith Rabba, xvii 4); this is not a haggadic exposition but the essential primary intent of the text (I dealt also with this point in my essay 'Studi sulla Genesi', 1926; and other scholars followed my lead). Seven is the number of perfection, and the blessing bestowed upon Abram is perfect and complete.

Following are the seven expressions of benison (each verb constitutes a separate benediction):

1 *And I will make of you a great nation,*
2 *and I will bless you,*
3 *and make your name great,*
4 *so that you will be a blessing.*
5 *I will bless those who bless you,*
6 *and him who curses you I will curse;*
7 *and in you will be blessed all the families of the earth.*

Similarly we find seven expressions of benison in the benedictions bestowed upon Isaac and Jacob. To Isaac God said (Gen. xxvi 3–4; here, too, the verbs, which signify future actions, have to be counted):

1 *and I will be with you,*
2 *and I will bless you;*

312

3 *for to you and to your descendants I will give all these lands,*

4 *and I will fulfil the oath which I swore to Abraham your father.*

5 *I will multiply your descendants as the stars of heaven,*

6 *and will give to your descendants all these lands;*

7 *and by your descendants all the nations of the earth shall bless themselves.*

To Jacob it was said (Gen. xxvii 28–29):

1 *May God give you of the dew of heaven, etc.*

2 *Let peoples serve you,*

3 *and nations bow down to you.*

4 *Be lord over your brothers,*

5 *and may your mother's sons bow down to you.*

6 *Cursed be every one who curses you,*

7 *and blessed be every one who blesses you!*

This is certainly no coincidence, but a preconceived scheme; it follows that all the conjectures that have been advanced regarding the division of these blessings among the sources and the assignment of some of them to one source and of others to another are incorrect.

2. *And I will make of you a great nation*] — the blessing of abundant offspring in wondrous measure. This blessing is particularly important for a man like Abram, who thus far had no son, although he had already reached old age. The very faith he must have in the promise is part of the test itself.

And I will bless you] — that is, I shall give you My blessing. The concept of blessing signifies the bestowal of all good, protection from all evil (in the priestly benediction, Num. vi 24: *The Lord bless you and* KEEP YOU), the granting of grace (*ibid. v.* 25: *and be* GRACIOUS *to you*), and enduring happiness and peace (*ibid. v.* 26: *and give you* PEACE). No ordinary life shall be vouchsafed to you and to your descendants, but life that is blessed of the Lord.

And make your name great] The name is a symbol of one's personality, and is identifiable, according to the ideas of the ancient Orient, with the personality itself. Not only shall a great nation come forth from you, but also your own name, your ideal worth, shall be great in the world.

So that you will be a blessing [וֶהְיֵה בְּרָכָה *weheyē berākhā*] / The precise meaning of the expression does not appear to be clear, and various interpretations of it have been suggested: (1) you will be full of blessing, you will be blessed (so the Septuagint, Targum Onkelos and the Palestinian [Pseudo-Jonathan] Targum A), but this interpretation does not fit the wording of the text; the same applies to explanation (2), namely, that of Rashi (compare Bereshith Rabba, xxxix 18): you will bless whomsoever you please; (3) the exposition of Naḥmanides: you will be the blessing wherewith people will bless themselves, saying, 'God make you like Abram!' (compare Gen. xlviii 20). In modern times certain emendations of the text have been proposed, such as, 'and it shall be [וְהָיָה weḇāyā] a blessing' (Giesebrecht, Gunkel), or 'and it shall be that when I bless' [וְהָיָה אֲבָרְכָה weḇāyā 'ăḇḇārekḫā] (Winckler); but no one with a sound feeling for the Hebrew language could concur in such 'amendments'. The key to the understanding of this verse is to be found in Zech. viii 13: *And as you have been a curse among the nations, O house of Judah and house of Israel, so will I save you and you shall be a blessing*. The expression *among the nations,* which supplements the clause *and as you have been a curse* (an antithetic parallel to the expression under discussion) shows that explanation (1) is unacceptable; the fact that the word has *Bēth* ['among'] and not *Lāmedh* ['to'] disproves interpretation (2); the connection between AND YOU SHALL BE *a blessing* and SO I WILL SAVE YOU, and the entire paragraph in Zechariah, which refers to the happiness of resuscitated Israel, support the exposition of Naḥmanides. The imperative form וֶהְיֵה *weheyē* is also easily explicable in the light of this interpretation: since I shall make a great nation of you and bless you and make your name great, you will become an example of blessing. It is the imperative that particularly expresses the result of preceding action, as in Gen. xx 7: *and he will pray for you,* AND YOU SHALL LIVE [וֶחְיֵה *weheyē*]; or *ibid.* xlii 18: *Do this* AND YOU WILL LIVE [וִחְיוּ *wiheyū*].

3. *And I will bless those who bless you*] Those who bless you — that is to say, those who will show you sympathy and friendship and will seek your welfare — will also receive blessing from Me.

And him who curses you I will curse] Contrariwise, those who are opposed to you and seek to hurt you will receive My curse. The original signification of the verb קָלַל *qālal* was to *despise, degrade,* from which stems the connotation of seeking another person's harm, and of wishing that evil may befall him. Whoever is opposed to you is opposed to the mission that I gave you, and hence it is right that he should be punished.

The difference between the plural *those who bless you* and the singular *him who curses you* was introduced, it seems, for the sake of diversification and variation in the parallelism, for which reason a change was also made in the order of the words of the two clauses. The view that Scripture intends to indicate here that the cursers will be few and those who bless many is a homiletical interpretation and not the actual sense of the text.

And in you will be blessed all the families of the earth] According to some commentators the meaning here is that Abram's name will serve as a classic example in formulating benedictions; but this explanation, which is apparently correct for the words *so that you will be a blessing,* in v. 2, does not accord with the phrasing of this verse. The form of the verb וְנִבְרְכוּ *nibhrekhū* ['be blessed'], which is in the *Niph'al* conjugation, and the emphasis on the word *all* require another interpretation. A similar expression (*and in him all the nations of the earth shall be blessed*) occurs later, in xviii 18, in the section dealing with the people of Sodom and Abraham's prayer for them. Hence it appears preferable to take the meaning to be that the father of the Israelite nation will be privileged to become a source of benison to all peoples of the world, and his merit and prayer will protect them before the Heavenly Court of Justice. We have here the first allusion to the concept of universalism inherent in Israel's faith, which would subsequently be developed in the teaching of the prophets.

This is a beautiful conclusion to the promises of blessing given to Abram.

In the original a poetic rhythm is clearly noticeable in the Divine utterance (compare the arrangement of the verses on p. 309). The rhythm is mainly quaternary, and mostly it is composed of two double beats; at the end it broadens a little and concludes with a series of three beats (*v.* 1b — 2:2; *v.* 2 — 3:1; 2:2; *v.* 3 — 2:2; 2:2; 2:3).

4. *So Abram went, as the Lord had told him*] This verse, the last

of the paragraph, comes to tell us, after the manner of so many paragraph-endings in the section of the Flood, that Abram, like Noah in his day, fulfilled the command given him by the Almighty. The Lord said to him, *'Go'*, and *he went*. The repetition of the verb used in the injunction emphasizes the swiftness and completeness of Abram's obedience. He carried out what he was enjoined to do forthwith, without any hesitation.

And Lot went with him] Our knowledge of Lot goes back to what we were told about him in the final paragraph of chapter xi; already there the Bible mentions him together with Abram and Sarai, as though to inform us that since then the orphan Lot had formed part of the special group of his uncle Abram within the larger family circle of Terah. But the wording of our verse indicates a difference between Abram and Lot: Abram went because thus the Lord had commanded him (*and Abram went*, AS THE LORD HAD TOLD HIM), whereas Lot went only on account of Abram (*and Lot went* WITH HIM). Lot was unable to raise himself to the level of his uncle; and the gulf between them becomes increasingly evident in the continuation of the passage.

And Abram was five and seventy years old when he departed from Haran] Regarding the view that these words are to be detached from the preceding passage, and assigned to P like all other chronological data, and for the counter arguments, see the introduction to this section, §7, pp. 306ff. Here, at the end of the paragraph, it is quite in order, after the manner of so many Pentateuchal narratives, to indicate the age of the hero of the story at the time of the episode described (compare, for example, Gen. xvi 16; xvii 24 f.; xxv 26; xli 46; Exod. vii 7), the purpose being to stress, in keeping with the entire tenor of the paragraph, the great merit of Abram when he stood the test of migration to Canaan. The undertaking of the journey, without prior knowledge of when and where it would end, would have been a severe test even for a young man, how much more so for an old man of seventy-five. Abram's faith in the promise that he would become a great nation was also very meritorious, especially as he was still childless at so advanced an age.

And another point. It is precisely from the information furnished here about the patriarch's age that we learn, at least according to the figures given in the Masoretic text (see my remarks above, pp. 259, 282), that Terah was still alive at the time of his son Abram's departure. Taking leave of his very aged father, without hope of seeing him alive again, was also without doubt very grieving to a loving and devoted son. Notwithstanding, Abram did not hesitate; the Lord said to him, 'Go!', and he went. It is quite clear, therefore, that the mention of his age at the time of trial is not an alien element in the narrative proper. It is alluded to incidentally, and in this form it leaves a deeper impression on the perceptive reader than would an explicit statement about the greatness of Abram's virtue.

There is no need to note that the figure seventy-five is given here for the sake of numerical harmony, which is so common a feature of the Pentateuchal stories. The determination of a person's exact age by reference to his registration with the authorities at the time of birth, which is standard practice in countries where European civilization prevails, was not customary in the ancient East, and to this day it is not universally practised in the Orient. Even in Israel it is still difficult to ascertain the exact age of an old man belonging to one of the eastern communities. He himself does not know precisely the number of his years, and if he is asked about his age he will reply, for example, that he has already reached 'the age of strength' [i.e. eighty; see Psa. xc 10; Ethics of the Fathers, v 21], or that he is even a hundred years old; neither he nor his family imagine for a moment that these figures are accurate. We should not attribute to Scripture the intention of indicating Abram's years with any greater precision.

On the ascending order of the numbers (*five and seventy years* and not *seventy and five years*) see my observations in *The Documentary Hypothesis*, English translation, pp. 51–53.

I have already noted earlier (Part I, pp. 259 ff.) that the time unit of the chronological data given in the narratives of the Book of Genesis is a lustrum — that is, sixty months — in conformity with the sexagesimal system used among the Sumerians and current in the ancient East. Hence the ages recorded in these narratives are mostly multiples of five, to which seven or a multiple of seven is added. Here, in the verse before us, we have an exact multiple of five.

The fixing of Abram's age, at the time of his leaving Haran, at seventy-five establishes the basis for the symmetrical division of his life-span (see p. 282): the first period, consisting of seventy-five years, with his father; the second period, covering twenty-five years (a third of the length of the first), without his father and still without a son by his wife Sarah; and the third stage, comprising seventy-five years like the first, without his father but together with Isaac his son by Sarah.

SECOND PARAGRAPH

ABRAM'S JOURNEYS IN THE LAND OF CANAAN

5. *And Abram took / Sarai his wife / and Lot his brother's son,*
   and all their possessions / which they had gathered,
   and the souls / that they had won in Haran;
   and they set forth / to go to the land of Canaan;
   and they came / into the land of Canaan.

6. *And Abram passed / through the land*
   to the place of Shechem, / to the terebinth of Moreh.
   And the Canaanites / were then in the land.

7. *Then the Lord appeared to Abram, / and said,*
   'To your descendants I will give / this land.'
   So he built there an altar / to the Lord, who had appeared
   to him.

8. *Thence he removed to the mountain / on the east of Bethel,*
   and pitched his tent, / with Bethel on the west and Ai on the
   east;
   and there he built an altar / to the Lord
   and proclaimed / the name of the Lord ['ה YHWH*].*

9. *And Abram journeyed on, / still going toward the Negeb.*

After it has been stated in *v.* 4, in general terms, that Abram went as he had been commanded, this paragraph comes to relate the details of his itinerary. This is a literary device commonly employed by the Torah: commencing with a general statement, it proceeds to give a detailed account. The description of the journey starts with the first moment, the moment of preparation, when the head of the family gathers all his people and possessions in readiness to leave.

5. *And Abram took*, etc.] The travel preparations are described by this stereotyped Biblical formula. The formula is not a particular characteristic of the school of P, as the adherents of the documentary hypothesis believe; the occurrence of similar expressions in the Ugaritic texts (see the introduction to this section, § 8) proves that it is part of the literary tradition of the Israelites, who received it from the Canaanites, the earlier inhabitants of the land.

Sarai his wife] She was mentioned above, xi 29–31; see my note *ad locum*.

And Lot his brother's son] He, too, was mentioned earlier, xi 27, 31, and also in this chapter, *v.* 4. At first glance it is difficult to understand why, after Lot's name has been mentioned in *v.* 4 by itself, implying that he was known to us already, his name is followed, in *v.* 5, by the appositional phrase, 'his brother's son', as though it were necessary to inform the reader who Lot was. But this is only an apparent difficulty. In *v.* 4 Scripture's intention was only to indicate briefly and in general terms the fact of the journey, and for this purpose the Torah was content to mention Lot's name only, that being enough; for we already knew who Lot was. Here, in *v.* 5, the aim is to depict in detail the preparations made for entering Canaan, and to let us know, in terms of the established formula, exactly who were travelling. Now it is precisely in stereotyped expressions of this kind that it is customary to indicate the degree of kinship between each member of the family and the person standing at its head, even if this relationship is already known. Thus we find above (xi 31): *And Terah took Abram his son, and Lot son of Haran, his grandson, and Sarai his daughter-in-law, his son Abram's wife; and they went forth*, etc., although it had previously been explicitly stated that Abram was the son of Terah, and Lot was the son of the latter's son Haran, and Sarai was Abram's wife. Compare also xxxvi 6; Exod. xviii 2–4. There is logic behind this traditional formulation: after the opening statement, *And Abram took,* the Bible explains in detail by what right

319

the head of the family *took* so-and-so and so-and-so, the answer being that he took them because they were his dependants.

Several scholars saw a difficulty also in the fact that the reading here is *his brother's son,* without any mention being made of the brother's name, and they supposed that there was a textual error here, the original wording being, *and Lot the son of Haran, his brother* (so, for example, Gunkel). But these exegetes failed to understand the expression *his brother's son.* This compound term denotes a single concept, like *nephew* in English; the Bible does not mean to refer to Abram's brother as such, but only to the relationship between Lot and Abram.

And all their possessions which they had gathered] They took with them all that they had; they left Haran completely, not intending to return there again.

And the SOULS [נֶפֶשׁ *nepheš*] *that they had* WON [עָשׂוּ *ʿāśū*] *in Haran*] נֶפֶשׁ *nepheš* ['soul', 'person'] as a word can denote male and female slaves, but that does not appear to be the meaning here, for several reasons:

(a) The slaves and handmaids are already included in *all the possessions which they had gathered.*

(b) The verb עָשׂוּ *ʿāśū* [literally, 'made'] is not the correct term for acquiring slaves.

(c) The 'making of the souls' is limited to Haran only, whereas if the reference were to slaves, male and female, there is no reason to exclude those that were acquired in Ur of the Chaldees or in other places. The rabbinic sages explained it as an allusion to proselytes (Abram converted the men, and Sarah the women). In this form it is certainly a homiletical exposition, but it seems that this haggadic interpretation approximates to the actual meaning of the text, and that we have here one of those verses that point to the theme of an ancient tradition that was not indeed incorporated in the Torah in its entirety, but was known to the Israelites, and hence a passing allusion to it sufficed (see above, the general introduction to the Pentateuchal narratives concerning Abraham, §5). Possibly the old tradition related that Abram, since he acknowledged his Maker, and hearkened to His voice, which spoke to him, and attained to the belief that He was the supreme God, the Creator of all things and the Lord of all, began to proclaim in *Haran* the

basic principles of his faith, and succeeded in winning for it a
number of souls. Also the statement in *v.* 8, *and proclaimed the
name of the* LORD ['ה *YHWH*] (see my commentary *ad locum*),
and the title of honour accorded to Abraham by the children of
Heth dwelling in Hebron — *you are a prince of God among us*
(xxiii 6) — allude apparently to a proclamation and missionary
work of this nature. Although it might appear from the section
of the Circumcision (xvii 27) that the people who were drawn to
Abram's faith were only his slaves born in his house or purchased
from strangers, yet if we study the section carefully we shall see
that the meaning is that only these were circumcized because they
alone, since they belonged to Abraham's household, were enjoined
to be circumcized, as it is explicitly stated *ibid., v.* 12, whereas
those who joined the new faith in the spiritual sense only were
not specifically commanded to observe this rite.

And they set forth] — Abram and all those whom he took
with him from Haran.

To go to the land of Canaan] In the Lord's communication to
Abram it is not expressly stated to which land Abram had to direct
his steps; only a general expression is used (*v.* 1): *to the land that
I will show you.* However, any one setting out on a journey, even
if he does not know his final goal, must nevertheless choose a
definite direction in which to go. Now we have already noted
earlier, in our annotations to xi 31, that Abram and his company,
even whilst they were still in Ur of the Chaldees, felt an inner urge
to go to the land of Canaan, and they influenced the whole family
to the extent that they all *went forth with them* with a view to
travelling together to that land. The rest of the family, however, did
not feel that inner compulsion that Abram and his followers experienced, and did not succeed in resisting the lure of idolatry and
abandoning paganism. Although *they went forth with them* — with
Abram and his band — *to go to the land of Canaan,* yet when they
reached Haran, mid-way to their goal, they settled there and did
not continue their journey further. This time, when Abram distinctly
heard the voice of the Lord commanding him to leave his father's
house and to go to the land that He would show him, he realized
that the desired direction was the one for which he had long
yearned. Where he was to stop, he did not know; but this it

321

appeared to him must be the direction. Consequently, he set his face towards the land of Canaan.

And they came into the land of Canaan] They did not stop midway, but came to the land to which Abram had intended to go.

How and by what route they came from Haran to the land of Canaan, the Bible does not tell us. It is probable (see the introduction to this section, § 5), that many tales about Abram's adventures on the way were current among the Israelites, but the Torah refrained from mentioning them in order not to distract the reader's mind from the main theme by referring to details that could not contribute to its didactic purpose. But evidence of the existence of an ancient tradition relative to the journey is still discernible, as I indicated in the aforementioned subsection of the introduction, in the Pentateuchal reference to Damascus-Eliezer, the inheritor [בֶּן מֶשֶׁק *ben mešek*] * of Abram's house (xv 2); apparently the saga told how Eliezer joined Abram when he passed through Damascus. Although Scripture tells us nothing about Abram's occupation in Haran, we may conjecture that already there he was a sheep farmer, for we are informed later that the members of his family who remained in Haran engaged in sheep-rearing. Shepherds coming from Northern Mesopotamia with their flocks were able to pass along the edge of the Fertile Crescent *via* the environs of Carchemish, Aleppo and Qatna as far as Damascus, or by way of the oases, especially Palmyra, which was the most important of them, and from there to Damascus. Be that as it may, before reaching the borders of the land of Canaan they certainly passed through the neighbourhood of Damascus.

6. *And Abram passed through the land*] — Abram and all his company, of course. In order to understand these words correctly, we must bear in mind two other verses: (a) Jos. xxiv 3: *Then I took your father Abraham from beyond the River and led him through all the land of Canaan;* (b) Gen. xli 46: *And Joseph went out from the presence of Pharaoh, and went through all the land of Egypt.* The word *all* in the sentence from Joshua corresponds to what is narrated in our passage, to wit, that Abram entered the land of Canaan *via* the northern border and journeyed southward, at

* See dictionaries s.v.; Encyclopedia Biblica (Hebrew), vol. ii, p. 675 s. *Dammeśeq Eliezer.*

first as far as the place of Shechem, subsequently further south to the district of Bethel, and finally further south still, to the Negeb.

The journey across the land described here included the *whole* country, from the northern to the southern extremities. Similarly it is stated of Joseph that he passed through the entire land of Egypt — through its length, of course, for inhabited Egypt, apart from the Delta, is only a narrow strip along the length of the Nile, which flows from the south to north. The object of Joseph's tour was to show the entire population of Egypt that, after Pharaoh, he was the master of the country; it was as though he took control of the whole of Egypt. In the same way, Abram's passage across the land of Canaan from north to south represents the ideal transfer of the country to his possession for the purpose of the Lord's service. He was like a man who has acquired a field and inspects it from end to end. Compare also xiii 17: *Arise, walk through the length and the breadth of the land, for I will give it to you.*

It should also be noted that the use of the verb עָבַר *ʿābhar* in this verse may be intended as a word-play. In the narratives about Isaac the verb צָחַק *ṣāḥaq* ['laugh', 'sport'] occurs a number of times, not only in the interpretation of the name, but also subsequently as a *leitmotiv* that accompanies Isaac throughout his life; this is also true of the verb עָקַב *ʿāqabh* ['follow at the heel', 'assail insidiously', 'circumvent', 'overreach'] in the stories of Jacob, and of the verb יָסַף *yāsaph* ['add', 'increase', 'do again'] in the Joseph cycle of tales. Likewise in our verse an allusion can be found to the name of Abram *the Hebrew* [הָעִבְרִי *hāʿibhrī* from the root עָבַר *ʿābhar*] (xiv 13). Possibly this was clearer in the ancient narratives that antedate the Torah.

To the place at Shechem] Many commentators are of opinion that the word מָקוֹם *māqōm* ['place'] signifies a sanctuary and that the meaning here is that Abram came to the Canaanite Temple at Shechem. But this view is improbable. It is true that the word מָקוֹם *māqōm* sometimes denotes a hallowed site, for example in the section of the offering of Isaac (xxii 3–4), and in the expression that frequently occurs in the Book of Deuteronomy, *the place that [the Lord] will choose.* But in these passages the sanctity of the place is something necessarily deduced from the context, whereas intrinsically the word מָקוֹם *māqōm* retains its basic meaning of

323

'place'. We must not attribute to it, on the basis of such verses, a sacred connotation, any more than we may assign to it the signification of prison-house in the light of the phrase in xxxix 20: *the place where the king's prisoners were confined,* and subsequently (xl 3): *in the prison, the place where Joseph was confined.* The word מָקוֹם *māqōm* by itself does not indicate the specific character of the place, just as the Latin word *loca* ['places'] does not inherently connote *loca sancta* ['holy places']. Proof is afforded by the expression occurring later (xiii 4), *unto the place of the altar;* since the altar is none other than the sanctuary, it is obvious that Scripture does not intend to say, *unto the sanctuary of the sanctuary,* which would be sheer tautology. Nay more, Abraham, whose primary intention was to keep away from idolatry would surely not have visited specifically the temples of the Canaanite gods. Although it is possible that, after the conquest of the land by the Israelites, the conquerors gradually became accustomed to regard some of the Canaanite sanctuaries as Holy places, and even to link them with the stories of the Patriarchs, yet it is inconceivable that the Torah would relate that Abram intentionally drew near to the pagan shrines. The meaning of the verse is much simpler. Abram and his companions certainly did not enter the city of Shechem. They were nomads — tent-dwellers and herdsmen, as we stated — and they undoubtedly did not pitch their tents in the city but in its environs, in the area that was uninhabited and uncultivated, in the region that could serve, without let or hindrance, as a site for the dwellings of the shepherds. For this reason the Torah does not say that Abram came *to Shechem* but *to the place of Shechem,* that is, to the place in which the city is situated. So, indeed, it is expressly written of Jacob (xxxiii 18): *And Jacob came safely to the city of Shechem* ... AND HE CAMPED BEFORE THE CITY. It is similarly stated later on (*v.* 8) of Abram when he reached Bethel, that he pitched his tent in the neighbourhood of Bethel, mid-way between Bethel and Ai.

Ancient *Shechem* was situated in a place now called Tell Balâṭa, south-east of the present city of Shechem. Thanks to its geographical position in the centre of the land, at the intersection of the roads from north to south and east to west, it became a key-point of the country. As I indicated earlier, in the introduction to this section, mention is made of the conquest of the land of *Skmm*, which is apparently Shechem, by the Egyptians as early as the nineteenth century B.C.E., in the reign of Sen-Usert III; also in the second series of the Egyptian execration texts, which belong to the same century, the name of the city *Skmìmì* occurs. The excavations conducted at the site have proved that, in the period of the Hyksos and after, the city of Shechem was strongly fortified; likewise the El-Amarna Tablets (15th–14th century) show that in their period Shechem was an important royal city. There is no need to dwell here on the subsequent history of the city.

Regarding the parallelism between this verse and the Biblical narratives concerning Jacob and his sons in Shechem and the conquest of the place in the days of Joshua, and on the significance of these parallels for the understanding of the purport of our section, see the introduction to the section, § 5.

To the terebinth [אֵלוֹן *'ēlōn*] *of Moreh*] אֵלוֹן *ēlōn* and אֵלָה *'ēlā,* possibly also אַלָּה *'allā,* are the names of a species of tall trees, apparently *Pistacia terebinthus L.,* whose subspecies *var. palaestina Engl.* (known as *Pistacia palaestina Boiss*) attains to a height of approximately fifteen metres, and to an age of several centuries — even to more than a thousand years. The word אַלּוֹן *'allōn* (with *Pathaḥ* under the *'Aleph* and *Dāgheš* in the *Lāmedh*) denotes, it seems, another tree, of the genus *Quercus.* Possibly the primary signification of all these names was generally speaking a high and sturdy tree; traces of this original sense are sometimes discernible in the language of the Bible.

On account of the size, strength and longevity of these towering trees, people honoured and revered them, and attributed to them a certain sanctity. In Deut. xi 30, the terebinths of Moreh are referred to in connection with the blessings and curses pronounced on Mount Gerizim and Mount Ebal, which were in the neighbourhood of Shechem. There may have been a grove of terebinths there, and the place was called both אֵלוֹנֵי מוֹרֶה *'ēlōnē Mōre* ['terebinths of Moreh'], in the plural, and אֵלוֹן מוֹרֶה *'ēlōn Mōre* ['terebinth of Moreh'], in the singular with collective meaning (the ancient versions translate the word in the singular also in Deut. xi 30). It would seem that the statement in Gen. xxxv 4 that Jacob hid beneath the terebinth that was near Shechem the images of the foreign deities that he had taken away from the members of his family (*v. 2: Put away the foreign gods that are among you*) likewise refers to this place. The same also applies, although the vocalization there is אַלָּה 'allā, to what is narrated in Jos. xxiv with regard to the injunction, similar to that of Jacob, given by Joshua at Shechem (*v. 23: Then put away the foreign gods which are among you*), and in regard to the great stone that he set up there beneath the oak in the sanctuary of the Lord (*v. 26*); the sanctuary is apparently the site of the altar mentioned in Deut. xxvii 5–7. It is doubtful, however, if also *the Diviners' Terebinth* in the vicinity of Shechem (Jud. ix 37), and *the terebinth of the pillar at Shechem*, where Abimelech the son of Gideon was made king (Jud. ix 6), are different names for the *terebinth of Moreh*.

It may well be that from the viewpoint of historic development the sanctity of the terebinth of Moreh in the eyes of the children of Israel was a continuation of the Canaanite tradition regarding the holiness of the terebinth, but according to the Torah's conception the sanctity undoubtedly originated with Abraham; indeed, the place is associated with memories of the destruction, in the days of Jacob and Joshua, of the evidence of heathen worship. The meaning of our verse apparently is that Abraham chanced to select the site of the terebinth for erecting his tent in its shade, and the Lord appeared to him there, and on account of this Divine Revelation the place became sacred to him and to his offspring.

According to the exegesis reflected in Targum Onkelos, the Palestinian Targum [Pseudo-Jonathan] and the translation of Jerome (so, too, Aquila's rendering of Deut. xi 30), the meaning of the word אֵלוֹן 'ēlōn is 'a plain'. Possibly the intention underlying this exposition was to prevent the reader from connecting the narrative with the belief of the Samaritan inhabitants of the district that a certain tree to which they pointed in the locality, and which gave rise, it appears, to the name Tell Balâṭa [*ballûṭ* means 'oak' in Arabic] was sacred. This interpretation seems to be based on the Greek word αὐλῶν which actually denotes 'a plain', and is certainly of late origin. Even if we agree with Ginsberg's conjecture that there existed in ancient Hebrew and in Ugaritic a word like אֵלוֹן 'ēlōn meaning 'a plain', our verse unquestionably alludes to the tree that we have mentioned.

Moreh] Some exegetes have explained the word in the sense of
יוֹרֶה *yōre*, '[early] rain' (this is the meaning of the word in Joel
ii 23, and perhaps also in Psa. lxxxiv 7); but more probably it has
the signification of 'teaching', that is to say, the tree was so called
on account of the oracles [literally, 'teachings'] that the priests
used to deliver in answer to enquirers (compare Hab. ii 18: *a
metal image, a teacher of lies,* and *ibid. v.* 19: *can this give
revelation?*).

Our verse apparently contains a play [in the word Moreh] on
the references (in our paragraph) to 'showing' and 'appearing'
[both verbal forms derive from the stem רָאָה *rā'ā*, 'to see'] (*v.* 1:
I will show you [אַרְאֶךָ *'ar'ekkā*]; *v.* 7: *Then . . . appeared* [וַיֵּרָא
wayyerā'] . . . *who had appeared* [הַנִּרְאֶה *hannir'e*]), and the underlying thought may be explained in one of the following two ways:
(1) the Canaanites already had called the terebinth by the name
Moreh, and what happened there to Abraham proved that this name
was most appropriate to the place, since *the Lord had appeared to
him* there; the Canaanites had in mind a *teacher of lies,* as Habakkuk
phrased it, but Abraham began to hear there the voice of the true
Teacher [מוֹרֶה *mōre*]; (2) the terebinth was given this name by
the Israelites at a later date because the Lord had appeared there
to Abraham, and Scripture called it by this name here in anticipation, in the same way as we find the anachronistic mention of
Dan in xiv 14: *and went in pursuit as far as Dan.*

The Septuagint translates here, 'the high terebinth', just as in
Gen. xxii 2 it renders *the land of Moriah* by 'the high land'.

And the Canaanites were then [אָז *'āz*] *in the land*] Two
explanations of this sentence have been suggested. One, hinted at
already by Ibn Ezra, is the interpretation of most contemporary
expositors: And the Canaanites were *still* in the land. According
to this exposition, the passage must have been written at a late
date, when the Canaanites were no longer in the country. The other
interpretation is: And the Canaanites were *already* in the land, that
is to say, that the Canaanites had already seized it from the hands
of the earlier inhabitants of the region (see Rashi). But the sense
of the verse does not accord with either explanation; the word
אָז *'āz* does not mean 'still' or 'already'. Scripture wishes to inform
us, as I explained in 1926 in the aforementioned essay 'Studi'

(p. 233), that אָז 'āz ['then'], at the time when Abraham immi-
grated, the Canaanites were in the land, thus emphasizing that the
country was not empty, and consequently Abraham was not able to
take possession of it at once. (B. Jacob has rightly drawn attention to
similar verses: *And David was* THEN [אָז 'āz] *in the stronghold,
and the garrison of the Philistines was* THEN [אָז 'āz] *at Bethlehem*
[ii Sam. xxiii 14]; AT THE TIME [אָז 'āz] *the army of the king
of Babylon was besieging Jerusalem* [Jer. xxxii 2]). Nevertheless,
even though the Canaanites were at the time the masters of the
land, the promise was given to Abraham that his descendants would
in future possess it, and he himself, as will be stated in the next
verse, performed an act that was symbolic of his acquisition of the
right of possession.

7. *Then the Lord appeared unto Abram*] There, in the environs
of Shechem, near to the terebinth of Moreh, the Lord appeared to
Abraham. Outside the Land, it was given to Abraham only to hear
the Divine voice (*v.* 1); but here, in the land destined to be
specifically dedicated to the service of the Lord, he was also vouchsafed the privilege of a Divine vision. What he saw is not stated
in detail; we are only told that the Vision was accompanied by a
Voice.

And said, 'To your descendants will I give this land'] I have
already pointed out in 'Studi' that this Divine utterance was
connected with the first one that Abram had heard in Haran,
enjoining him to go *to the land that I will show you*. He went, as
he had been commanded, and on his journey he was hoping that
at some place God would say to him: This is the land that I desired
you to reach, and in which I wish you to stay. And so it was said
to him at Shechem: *This land* is the desired land, and it shall
become the heritage of your descendants. Although it is at present
in the possession of other masters, be assured that I shall give it
to your offspring. We find a parallel to this in what is subsequently
related concerning Jacob and his sons when they came from Aram-
naharaim; not only was Shechem the site of their first encampment
on the western side of the Jordan, but it was there also that the
initial conquest by force of arms took place (Gen. xxxiv).

So he built there an altar to the Lord, who had appeared to him]
This was not actually an 'altar', in the etymological sense of the

term — that is, a place for the offering of sacrifices — for no mention whatsoever is made here of an oblation. The reference is to the building of a monument as a memorial (not for any kind of sacrifice), like the altar referred to in Jos. xxii. Abraham erected this monument in remembrance of the Lord's appearance to him at this place, and it served as a token of the sanctification of the land to the service of the God of Abraham, and the symbolic conquest of the country by the patriarch on behalf of his later descendants; the symbol was both religious and national.

8. *Thence* HE REMOVED [וַיַּעְתֵּק *wayya'tēq*] / The verb is in the *Hiph'îl* conjugation, implying an expression like *his tent* as the object; the meaning is: Thence he removed his tent.

To the mountain] Even though we discount completely the interpretation of the word אֵלוֹן *'ēlôn* as 'a plain', it is at least clear that the אֵלוֹן *'ēlôn* ['terebinth'] was situated in a low-lying place between the hills, in the valley between Mount Ebal and Mount Gerizim; and *thence,* from the site of the terebinth, Abram went up by way of the mountain range and continued his course southward.

On the east of Bethel] He ascended the highlands until he reached a point east of Bethel.

Bethel was situated where the Arabic village Beitīn now stands, north of Jerusalem, about three kilometres north-east of Ramallah. Excavations were conducted in the locality under the direction of W. F. Albright in 1927 and 1934; since his complete report on these excavations has not yet been published, we cannot tell the precise nature of the results. Provisionally, on the basis of the preliminary surveys of Albright, it is possible to state that the urban settlement of Bethel was apparently founded approximately in the twenty-first century B.C.E., after the destruction of the big neighbouring city, the ruins of which are located at a mound called by the Arabs et-Tell, that is, *the* Tell (with the definite article), which is apparently Ai [הָעַי *hā-'Ay* is always written with the definite article]; see the note on it below.

We have already seen in the introduction to this section that Abram's encampment in Shechem and Bethel corresponds to that of Jacob in these two places, when he returned from Paddan-aram, and that there is another parallel in the tradition of the conquest in the days of Joshua. Nor was it without reason that tradition pointed to Shechem and Bethel as essential points for the conquest of the land of Israel. It was precisely these cities that were apparently regarded as key-points of the central area of the country. In the Egyptian Stela of Sebek-khu, dating from Sen-Usert III king of Egypt (approximately 1887–1850 B.C.E., which is the very period of the Patriarchs of Israel), the conquest of the land of *Skmm* and of the land of *Rṯnw* by the Egyptian monarch is mentioned. The first name, *Skmm*, seems to be the ancient form of Shechem (to be pronounced, according to Albright, *Sakmâmi*, that is, 'two shoulders'); although some doubts have been expressed about the identification of *Skmm* with Shechem, most scholars are inclined to accept it today after a nominal form corresponding to this was found in another Egyptian source, as will be explained later. The word *Rṯnw*, which is also used as a general term for the land of Canaan and Southern and Western Syria, has not, judging by the context of the inscription ('*Skmm* fell together with *Rṯnw*') this wider connotation here, but appears to denote a limited area like the district of Shechem. Now Albright has suggested that the general term *Rṯnw* may be connected with the Arabic root لوذ *lwḏ*, signifying 'a refuge'; possibly Luz [לוז *Lūz*], too, the earlier name of Bethel, may be derived from this root. If we accept this view, we may be able to understand the word *Rṯnw* in the Sebek-khu inscription as the name of Luz, that is, Bethel; thus the two cities essential for the acquisition of the land correspond to the two important centres mentioned in its military conquest by the king of Egypt.

Egyptian documents also enable us to understand why just these two centres were considered key-points. The two cities, Shechem and Bethel, are situated on the main road leading from north to south over the mountain range, and they both lie at points where there are cross-roads running east and west. The importance of these road junctions in the patriarchal age is clearly shown by the Egyptian execration texts of that period. The names of the cities of the land of Israel recorded in the second series of these texts (second half of the nineteenth century B.C.E.) are arranged, as S. Yeivin has demonstrated, in groups situated along the length of the important roads. Now in the group belonging

330

to the section of the maritime route that turns towards Transjordan, mention is made of Skmimi, a name resembling Skmm in the Sebek-khu inscription, and all the scholars who have studied the subject are agreed that the reference is to Shechem. In the group appertaining to the road that links the maritime route, further south, to Transjordan, a city is mentioned that may perhaps be identified with Luz, that is, Bethel. The name of this city (listed as E 44 in G. Posener's edition) is written in Egyptian script *Ryti;* now it is known that *Lāmedh* is represented in Egyptian writing by *Rēsh*. There is, however, a certain difficulty in the letter *Tāw*, which cannot indicate the *Zayin*, unless we assume that the transcription was not accurate; but at least from the order of the names of the cities it is clear that the reference, if not to Bethel itself, is to a settlement very near to Bethel. S. Yeivin (in private conversation) considered the possibility that the *Rēsh* in this name stands for the Arabic letter *Gayin* غ and that עָיַת *'Ayyath* [Isa. x 28] or עַיָּה *'Ayyā* [Neh. xi 31; i Chron. vii 28], that is, הָעַי *hā'Ay* ['Ai'], is intended.

And pitched his tent, with Bethel on the west and Ai on the east] He erected his tent mid-way between these two places, at a point on the west of which lies Bethel and on the east Ai. On the parallel to the topographical location of these cities given in the Book of Joshua, see my remarks in the introduction to this section, § 5.

Ai [הָעַי *hā'Ay*] / This refers apparently to the place now occupied by the mound that rises about a mile and a half east of Bethel; it is called by the Arabs, as stated above, et-Tell. The excavations that were carried out on the site under the direction of Judith Marquet-Krause and S. Yeivin in the years 1933–1935, and which were interrupted by the untimely passing of Mme Marquest-Krause, showed that it was a great and flourishing city in the third millenium B.C.E., and contained a magnificent temple. In the twenty-second century B.C.E., approximately, the city was completely destroyed, and in the days of Abraham, it seems, there was nothing there but a desolate mound, already centuries old. The name הָעַי *hā'Ay* may signify 'a heap of ruins'.

This is not the place to enter into a detailed discussion of the complicated and disputed question of the elucidation of the account of the capture of Ai contained in Joshua vii–viii; nor can we hope to find a solution to the problem until the excavations at the site will be completed. So, too, only future excavations will be able to determine with exactitude the place between Bethel and Ai to which the verse here refers, and which was certainly a sacred site to the children of Israel, associated with the memories of the tradition concerning Abraham.

And there he built an altar to the Lord] Here, too, it was a memorial monument, like the altar he built in the neighbourhood of Shechem. Now there are two monuments, and it is on the evidence of two witnesses that a matter is established [compare Deut. xix 15].

And proclaimed [literally, 'called on'] *the name of the Lord* [*YHWH*] / The meaning cannot be, as some have held, that he prayed unto the Lord. Prayer was surely not something exceptional in Abraham's life, that it should be necessary to mention it explicitly on this occasion, and without any indication of what he prayed for. In Exod. xxxiii 19, it is stated that the Lord Himself said: *and I will call on* [E. V. *proclaim*] *the name of the Lord before you;* so, too, *ibid.* xxxiv 5 it is writen, *and called on* [E. V. *proclaimed*] *the name of the Lord,* the subject, apparently, being the Lord. There the reference is certainly not to prayer but to the proclamation and explanation of the Lord's name and the attributes connected therewith. In the same way the words have to be understood here. Beside the altar that Abraham built in honour of the Lord, he made proclamations concerning the religion of the Lord to the inhabitants of the land, and thus he continued in the Chosen Land the work that he had already begun when he was in Haran. In view of this, the local people regarded him as 'a prince of God' [E. V. 'mighty prince'] (xxiii 6).

There is thus a harmonious parallelism between the events at Shechem and Bethel. In Shechem the Lord made His will known to Abraham, and in Bethel Abraham made known his devotion to the Lord; in the former city the Lord gave Abraham His promise for the future; and in the latter the Patriarch began to fulfil his mission in his new habitation.

Above, in § 5 of the introduction to our secion, I have explained how Abraham's second encampment in the land, between Bethel and Ai, corresponds to Jacob's second encampment when he came from Paddan-aram, and to the site of the first battle of the Israelites in the conquest of the western side of the Jordan in the days of Joshua, and I have shown how this parallelism is to be interpreted.

9. *And Abram journeyed on, still going toward the Negeb*] After his first two journeys, from the northern extremity to the vicinity of Shechem, and from there to a point near Bethel, Abram continued on his way and journeyed from the neighbourhood of Bethel southward, in the direction of the Negeb, that is to say, as far as the southern border of the Chosen Land. The expression הָלוֹךְ וְנָסוֹעַ *hālōkh wᵉnāsōʻa* [rendered: 'still going'], means going on his journeys, from place to place, after the manner of those who wander with their flocks (Jer. xxxi 24).

The symmetrical arrangement of the narrative is evidenced in the use of the verb הָלַךְ *hālakh* ['to go'] at the end as well as at the beginning of the account. The recurrence, at the conclusion, of the wording employed in the opening verse is the hall-mark of a fitting ending to the story.

The three series of journeys enabled Abraham to tour the entire country, from its northern to its southern border. Now the face of the land bears, in the vicinity of Shechem and Bethel, the two signs of its consecration to the Lord and of its belonging to the seed of Abraham. Its destiny was sealed for generations to come.

SECTION TWO

ABRAM GOES DOWN TO EGYPT

CHAPTER XII, VERSE 10 — CHAPTER XIII, VERSE 4

INTRODUCTION

§ 1. IMMEDIATELY after Abraham had settled in the Promised Land, he was again subjected to a new trial. A severe famine compelled him to leave the land and go down to Egypt. There his wife Sarai found herself in great jeopardy, but the Lord saved her from the danger, and the whole family returned in peace to the land of Canaan. There, standing beside the altar that he had built in Bethel before he left for Egypt, Abraham again proclaimed the name of the Lord [*YHWH*], his God.

So it is narrated in this section. In the following subsections of our introduction, we shall endeavour to clarify the purpose and significance of this tale both in its general aspect and in its details, and also to elucidate its relationship to the preceding story and the other Pentateuchal narratives.

Clearly verses 1–4 of chapter xiii form the sequel and conclusion of the story that begins in xii 10. The division of the text into chapters, which was carried out, as we know, in the Middle Ages, does not correspond to the original arrangement of the sections.

§ 2. This account of the going down of Abram and Sarai to Egypt presents a striking parallel to what is related subsequently, at the end of the Book of Genesis and the beginning of the Book of Exodus, concerning the migration of the children of Israel to that land. There is hardly a verse or half a verse in this section that does not remind us of a parallel statement in the narratives pertaining to the Israelites. Not only in respect of those expressions on which the rabbinic sages commented haggadically (e. g. Bereshith Rabba xl 8), but down to the smallest details of the section, throughout its entire extent, we find an unmistakable parallelism to our story in the saga of the children of Israel. Here it is related in *v.* 10: *Now there*

334

was a famine in the land . . . for the famine was severe in the land; and in the case of the children of Israel we are told: *Now the famine was severe in the land* (xliii 1); and again: *for the famine is severe in the land of Canaan* (xlvii 4). In our passage it is stated, in the same verse, that Abram went down to Egypt *to sojourn there,* and later on it is recorded that Joseph's brothers said to Pharaoh: *We have come to sojourn in the land* (xlvii 4). Abram's anxiety lest the Egyptians slay him whilst letting his wife live (*vv.* 11–13, especially 12: *then they will kill me, but they will let you live*) recalls Pharaoh's decrees cited in the Book of Exodus: *if it is a son, you shall kill him; but if it is a daughter, she shall live* (Exod. i 16), and subsequently: *Every son that is born you shall cast into the Nile, but you shall let every daugther live* (*ibid. v.* 22). The story narrated in our section of how Abram's wife Sarai was taken into the palace of the king of Egypt to be one of his handmaids (*vv.* 14–15) corresponds to what we are told subsequently of the children of Israel who were likewise made bondmen of Pharaoh. In our narrative, we learn of the gifts that Abram was given (*v.* 16: *And for her sake he dealt well with Abram,* etc.), and that on going forth from Egypt he was *very rich in silver, in cattle and in gold* (xiii 2); and in the story of the Exodus we read of *jewellery of silver and of gold, and clothing* [Exod. xii 35] that the Israelites received from the Egyptians on their departure. In both narratives the Torah tells us that the Lord heard the cry of the oppressed and smote Pharaoh with great plagues in order that he should set them free (the word *plague*[*s*] occurs here in *v.* 17 and also in Exod. xi 1). The initial phase of the liberation is described in like terms in both accounts. In our story it is written: *So Pharaoh called Abram, and said* (*v.* 18); and in the other: *And he summoned Moses and Aaron by night, and said* (xii 31). Here Pharaoh says to Abram: TAKE [קַח *qaḥ*] *her,* AND BE GONE [וָלֵךְ *wālēkh*] (*v.* 19); and there Pharaoh says to Moses and Aaron: TAKE [קְחוּ *qeḥū*] *. . . as you have said* AND BE GONE [וָלֵכוּ *wālēkhū*] (Exod. xii 32; the Septuagint rendering, MSS A and B, presupposes the reading, קְחוּ וּלְכוּ *qeḥū ūlekhū* [the two verbs together] as in our passage). It is further written in regard to Abram: AND THEY SET *him* ON THE WAY [וַיְשַׁלְּחוּ *wayyesalleḥū*, literally, 'sent away', 'let go'],*with his wife and all that he had,* the very verb שָׁלַח *salaḥ* [in

335

the *Pi'ēl*, signifying 'let go'], which occurs so often in Exodus, being used. After leaving Egypt, Abram *went up into the Negeb* (xiii 1), in the same way as the spies whom Moses sent to spy out the land after the exodus of the children of Israel from Egypt went up to the Negeb (Num. xiii 17: *Go up into the Negeb yonder;* ibid. *v.* 22: *They went up into the Negeb*). Just as it is stated here of Abram: *And he went* ON HIS JOURNEYS [לְמַסָּעָיו *lemassā'āw*] (xiii 3), so we are told of the children of Israel: *All the congregation of the children of Israel moved* ... BY STAGES [לְמַסְעֵיהֶם *lemase'ēhem*, literally, 'on their journeys'] (Exod. xvii 1); and similar expressions also occur in many other passages (Exod. xl 36, 38; Num. x 6, 12; xxxiii 1, 2). Finally it is mentioned here that Abram came to the site of the altar that he had built at first, between *Bethel* and *Ai*, which was the very place where the children of Israel who had gone forth from Egypt were destined to fight their first battle for the conquest of the land on the western side of the Jordan. Further details regarding the parallelism between the two narratives we shall note below.

These parallels, which are found throughout the section, verse after verse, cannot be fortuitous. It is evident that the Torah purposely underlined the similarity between the two events. When we bear in mind the implications of the parallels to the preceding section (xii 1–9), it becomes apparent that also in this, the second section, Scripture wished to foreshadow in the tales of the Patriarchs the history of their descendants, and to provide a sequel to the preceding section in conformity with its scheme. In the account of how Abram went down to Egypt, what befell him there and how he went forth from there, the Torah presages, as it were, the migration of the Israelites to Egypt after they had settled in the land of Canaan, their servitude and their liberation. The narrative is so worded as to emphasize the parallelism in all its aspects. The whole course of events experienced by the scions is revealed to us as though depicted from the beginning in the life of their sires.

This story is not told, therefore, out of a romantic love for ancient sagas, nor from a desire to satisfy the curiosity of people who find pleasure in delving into the records of antiquity. Its object, like that of all the Pentateuchal narratives, is to instruct its readers. Following are the main teachings that it inculcates:

(a) The bondage of the children of Israel in Egypt was not an accidental calamity but part of a plan prepared beforehand, in accordance with God's will, already in the days of Abraham (compare also xv 13–16), and harmoniously correlated with the overall Divine plan for the destiny of the people of Israel.

(b) From the deliverance of Abram and Sarai from the dangers that threatened them in Egypt, and the parallel salvation of the children of Israel who were enslaved in the same land, it is possible to learn that the Lord is ever ready to protect his faithful ones and to deliver them from all evil, thus providing a source of consolation and hope for countless generations.

Other specific lessons that the details of the story may teach us we shall discuss later on in the commentary.

§ 3. A difficult problem from the literary viewpoint is created by the two analogous narratives that occur later on in the Book of Genesis: the account in chapter xx of Sarai's peril in the palace of Abimelech, king of the Philistines, in Gerar, and the story in chapter xxvi (vv. 7–11) of Rebekah's danger, also in the house of Abimelech, king of the Philistines, in Gerar.

On the face of it this seems strange. It is surprising to find three such similar stories narrated in one book as three successive episodes; and it is even more astonishing that the characters who act and suffer in the second narrative are the same as in the first, and that those of the third are none other than the son and daughter-in-law of the first pair, as though the four of them had been incapable of learning the moral of the first incident, nor even the lesson of the recurrence of events in the second episode. On account of these strange features, the scholars who support the documentary theory are accustomed to attribute the three narratives to three different sources: as a rule our section is assigned to J, chapter xx to E, and the story in chapter xxvi to another stratum of J. Others distribute them differently (see the details in my book *La Questione della Genesi*, p. 304). Additional reasons for this attribution to different sources are: (a) the variation in the use of the Divine Names (the Tetragrammaton in our section, אֱלֹהִים *'Elōhīm* in chapter xx, and again 'ה *YHWH* in ch. xxvi); (b) a number of characteristics, linguistic or of another kind, that are considered to be specifically typical of each of the documents.

However, this analysis does not solve the principal problem of the triplication of the story. Even if we concede that the three tales were derived from three different documents, there still remains the question: why did the final editor find it necessary to incorporate all three accounts in his book? The difficulty remains unresolved, the responsibility of a redactor not being less than that of an author. As for the supplementary arguments, it is clear that they establish no case. The alleged divergence in the use of the Divine Names is entirely unfactual: in chapter xx there occurs apart from the name '*Elōhīm* also the name *YHWH* in *v.* 18 (although it is argued that this verse is a later interpolation, such exegesis, which obliterates all evidence that does not fit in with its preconceived theory, is undoubtedly invalid); the third story is in truth found in a chapter that uses the Tetragrammaton, but in the narrative itself no Divine Name whatsoever is used even once; and if we consult the Septuagint, we shall not find the name *YHWH* even in the first tale, only '*Elōhīm*. Likewise the linguistic peculiarities attributed to each source are only imaginary; only one devoid of a sound grasp of the Hebrew tongue could assert that simple expressions like הֵיטִיב לְ- *hēṭībh l*- ['he dealt well with' (Gen. xii 16)], נָא *nā'* ['I pray thee, please' (*ibid. v.* 13)], הִנֵּה נָא *hinnē nā'* ['behold now' (*ibid. v.* 11)], בְּגְלַל *bigh*e*lal* ['because of' (*ibid.* 13)], מַה־זֹּאת עָשִׂיתָ *maz-zō'th 'āśīthā* ['what is this you have done' (*ibid. v.* 18)], belong specifically to a given source and may not be used by any other writer; or would deny any author the possibility of employing expression like נִקְיֹון כַּפַּיִם *niqyōn kappayim* ['innocency of hands' (*ibid.* xx 5), or אָמְנָה '*omnā* ['indeed' (*ibid. v.* 12)]. So, too, the differentiation of sources on the basis of the synonyms שִׁפְחָה *šiphḥā* and אָמָה '*āmā* ['handmaid'] is purely arbitrary, as I have shown elsewhere. Also the divergence that scholars have sought to find in the moral views expressed in the three stories does not exist in the passages themselves but only in the imagination of the exegetes; we shall deal with this point fully later on in our commentary.

If we wish to find a satisfactory solution to the problem, our investigations must go deeper than does the superficial and mechanical method of source analysis. In particular we must pay attention to two things: (a) the aim of the Pentateuchal narratives; (b) the way in which books were customarily composed in the ancient East.

It appears that, before the Torah was written, various traditions were current in Israel concerning an episode involving the Matriarchs of the nation. Essentially these traditions were alike, but they differed in particulars: one told of Sarai-Sarah in Egypt; another also spoke of Sarah, but in another place, Gerar; whilst a third referred to Rebekah. Possibly all three flowed from one ancient saga, which assumed variant forms in regard to detail as it was handed down by one generation to another; but this process belongs to the pre-history of the narratives and does not affect our problem. When the Torah came to be written, the three versions already existed, side by side, among the Israelites. The Torah, whose object was not to investigate the annals of the Patriarchs historically but only to use the existing sagas for the purpose of religious and ethical instruction, was not concerned to examine the question of the relationship of these traditions, and certainly did not apply to them the principles of historical criticism, which were not yet known at that period. Seeing that each of the three tales could serve its aim, and that the triplication of the theme enhanced the usefulness of the stories, Scripture did not refrain from including the three of them.

An interesting illustration of this method is found in Latin literature. Roman tradition used to relate that Publius Decius Mus, one of the two Roman consuls in 340 B.C.E., devoted himself, in the battle between the forces of Rome and those of the Latin-Campanian League fought near Mount Vesuvius, as an oblation to the gods in order to assure the triumph of his army, and that as a reward for the sacrifice of his life the Romans succeeded in prevailing over their foes. A similar tale was also current about his son, who bore the same name as his father and was one of the Roman consuls in 295, to wit, that in the battle between the Romans and the Samnites and their allies near the city of Sentinum he, too, offered himself as a sacrifice to the deities and thereby brought victory to the Romans. It seems that only the story concerning the son has any historic value, whereas that about his father was only a legend woven round the action of the younger man. But when at the end of the last century B.C.E., the Roman historian Livy (Titus Livius) came to write his great work on Roman history for the glorification of his country and people, and found before him

339

the two traditions, he did not test them in the crucible of criticism; rather, he saw that both of them were useful to his purpose, which was to raise the prestige of the Romans and to emphasize their heroism and devotion to their motherland, and he decided that the duplication was not a disadvantage but that, on the contrary, the twofold display of self-sacrifice in one family could serve as an example, and consequently he did not hesitate to include both tales in his book. Needless to say, this duplication in no way affects the unity of Livy's history. To this work the theories put forward with regard to the composition of the Pentateuch cannot be applied; the personality of Livy is well known, and the fact that he wrote the history is also established. The unity of authorship and of the work is unchallenged.

Furthermore, even a third legend was created in Rome regarding a third Publius Decius Mus, the grandson of the first, who also offered himself as a votive sacrifice to the gods in the day of battle, like his father and grandfather, for the sake of the victory of his forces; and Cicero bestowed on the three men — father, son and grandson — unstinted praise for the example they set in giving their lives for the good of their people. The threefold account lends still greater glory to the heroic act.

The same is true of the Torah; the thrice-told tale of the deliverance of the Matriarchs greatly magnifies the importance and unfailing character of God's help to his votaries. Hence the three narratives were incorporated in the Torah in the same way as the reiterated accounts of the heroism of the Decii were included in the works of the Roman writers.

The significance of the duplications in the Pentateuch is made clear to us by the explicit evidence of the Torah itself. In the story of the two successive and analogous dreams seen by Pharaoh — the dream of the cows and of the ears of grain — it is related that Joseph, after interpreting the dreams, said to Pharaoh (Gen. xli 32): *And the doubling of Pharaoh's dream means that the thing is fixed by God, and God will shortly bring it to pass*. The same principle applies in our case: by doubling and trebling the assurance, the Torah teaches us that *the thing is fixed by God, and God will shortly bring it to pass*.

Not only do we find repetition here but also progression. We

340

have already noted, in the preceding subsection, what the first story comes to teach us through its relationship to the narratives concerning the migration of the children of Israel to Egypt, their enslavement there, and their liberation from it. The second narrative, dealing with Sarah's rescue from the danger threatening her in the palace of Abimelech king of the Philistines, seeks to enlarge the lesson. It may be that the account of this episode in the lives of the Patriarchs is also intended, like the first, to be an omen to their descendants. In i Sam. iv–vi it is recorded that the Philistines captured the ark of the testimony, the holiest of the sacred objects of the Israelites, and brought it to the temple of their god Dagon in Ashdod; but the ark was saved from any desecration, since the Lord cast the image of Dagon to the ground and smote with grievous diseases the inhabitants of Ashdod and the other cities to which the ark was subsequently brought, until the lords of the Philistines decided to restore the shrine to the Israelites; and after taking counsel with their priests and diviners they returned it together with expiatory gifts. Possibly a parallel is to be seen between this story and that of Gen. xx, which tells us that Sarah, the dearly loved wife of the patriarch Abraham, was delivered into the hand of the king of the Philistines and was taken to his palace; but she was saved by the fact that God warned the king and punished him and his household so that they needed to be healed, and in the end the king restored Sarah to Abraham, adding a gift as vindication. This parallelism is not perhaps as clear as that of the first narrative to the history of the children of Israel in Egypt; hence we shall not attribute to it any special importance. We shall revert to it again, however, in our commentary *ad locum.* * At all events, there is undoubtedly an extension of the teaching here: the Lord saved the ancestors of the people of Israel from the hand of *all* its oppressors, from those as distant as the Egyptians and as near as the Philistines, and the recurring deliverance from the hands of the former and the latter gives the assurance — this is the Torah's message to Israel — that salvation will be wrought again whenever the Israelites find themselves in jeopardy.

---

* This section of the Commentary was never written owing to the demise of the author.

The third tale enlarges the promise still further. There the help does not come at the last moment, when the danger is near and only by a miracle is it possible to be delivered from it; in this story Providence guides the course of events in such a way that the peril is averted before it materializes. Thereby the Torah seeks to teach us that the paternal love of the Lord watches over His children so as not only to rescue them from dangers in which they are already involved, but also to forestall the possibility of the dangers that they are liable to bring upon themselves through their fault or default.

But perchance it may be asked: How can we suppose that the three narratives were included in a unitary book, since it is incredible that Abraham and Sarah did not learn the lesson of what befell them in Egypt and committed the same mistake in Gerar, and that their son Isaac was guilty of a like error? But the answer is not difficult: such a question were warranted if the Pentateuchal books were constructed in accordance with the system of logical thinking that the Greeks created for themselves in the fifth century B.C.E., and which the modern world inherited from them; whereas the Torah, like all the works of this epoch, was composed according to the method of organic thinking, which is unlike the Hellenic mode of thought (on the concept of 'organic thinking' see J. Heinemann, דַּרְכֵי הָאַגָּדָה *Darkhē Hā'aggādhā* ['The Methods of the Haggada'], pp. 8–9.

As we stated earlier, at the beginning of this subsection, if we wish to understand the real significance of the trebling of the story, we must also take a glance outside Israel's borders, and consider the literary methods customarily employed in the ancient East. Now in the narrative compositions of the ancient Orient the occurrence of analogous tales is a not uncommon feature. Thus, for instance, in the Babylonian epic of Creation called *Enūma eliš,* a number of themes occur twice in similar form, once in the saga of Ea-Nudimut [Nudimmud], and again in that of his son Marduk (or, it would seem, according to the original version, of Enlil). Examples are: (a) the story of the birth of Ea and the description of his personality, and the same of Marduk; (b) the preparations of Apsu and Mummu to destroy the gods, and those of Tiamat and her allies to the same end; (c) Ea's combat against Apsu and

342

Mummu, and that of Marduk against Tiamat; and similar parallels. It is impossible, however, to apply to the study of Babylonian literature, as M. Jastrow attempted, the method of source-analysis, which obtains in Biblical scholarship. We also find in the Babylonian epic referred to identical passages reiterated three or four times; thus the portrayal of the monsters formed by Tiamat to help her in her struggle occurs not less than four times (on exact repetitions of this nature see my observations in my Commentary on Exodus, Section Three). Similar instances are to be found in Ugaritic literature, which is nearest to the ancient Hebrew writings. One instructive illustration will suffice: in the epic of Baal and Anath the story is narrated in detail of the delegation that the father of the gods sent to his son *Ktr-wḥss*, to persuade him to stop fighting and come to him to hear what he had to tell him; later on we are informed in like terms of a similar deputation that he sent to Anath; and a third time, again, it is related in similar language of another such delegation that Baal sent to Anath. It is superfluous to add that also in Ugaritic literature literal duplications occur in great numbers (see, for instance, my remarks in my commentary on Exodus, *loc. cit.*).

Since the use of repetition was a customary feature of the narrative literature of the ancient East, it is not surprising that Biblical narratives also show clear traces of this literary device. It may be added that generally speaking, throughout the entire range of the patriarchal stories in Genesis, the three national ancestors are depicted as parallel figures. We are presented with a picture of a single course of life, duplicated and triplicated both in its general outline and in the detailed events, which is strengthened and confirmed by the threefold narration as a message of good tidings and an assurance regarding Israel's future destiny. Each of the three patriarchs separated himself, as the Lord's elect, from his relatives who followed a different path (Abraham first left his father's house and then Lot, his brother's son; likewise Isaac parted from Ishmael, and Jacob from Esau); each one received, as the guerdon of his dedication to the Lord's service, a promise of Divine blessing, of numerous offspring and the possession of the Promised Land; each one took a wife (or wives) from the circle of Mesopotamian relatives; each one waited a long time for children

343

by his wife (or by the wife he loved most), and only after protracted waiting was offspring granted to him by Divine grace; each one was compelled to leave the Promised Land on account of famine; each one found himself in peril in a strange country and was saved by the help of God; each one was subjected to other trials, including grave danger to his favourite son, or separation from him for a long period; each one made a covenant with his neighbours who dwelt in the land; each one acquired an estate in the Promised Land. There are certain features, however, that are not common to the careers of all three, but to that of two only. Thus, for example, both Abraham and Jacob migrate from Mesopotamia to Canaan and encamp at the same sites; both of them marry handmaids in addition to their wives in order to beget by them children; for both Isaac and Jacob a journey has to be made to Mesopotamia to obtain from there a spouse for them; both Isaac and Jacob bless, intentionally or unintentionally, the younger son or grandchild instead of the first-born; and so on. Sometimes the duplication occurs in the generation of Jacob's children; both the story of the birth of Isaac's twin sons and that of Judah's twin sons contain a reference to an attempt, successful or otherwise, on the part of the younger son to precede his brother into the world. At times an episode recurs in the lifetime of the same patriarch; thus Jacob twice takes a handmaid to wife.

All this clearly shows that repetition is a fundamental and constant element of the patriarchal narratives in Genesis, and no form of source analysis can eradicate this basic characteristic.

§ 4. Other questions, such as Sarai's age or the ethical character of the story, we shall discuss fully in our commentary on the passage.

THE JOURNEY DOWN TO EGYPT

10. *Now there was a famine / in the land;*
so Abram went down to Egypt / to sojourn there,
for the famine was severe / in the land.

11. *And it came to pass, when he came near / to enter into Egypt,*
that he said / to Sarai his wife:
'Behold now, I know / that you are a woman of beautiful
appearance.

12. *And it will come to pass —*
when the Egyptians see you / they will say, "This is his wife";
then they will kill me, / but they will let you live.

13. *Say, pray, / you are my sister,*
that it may go well with me / because of you,
and that I may live / on account of you.

10. *Now there was a famine in the land*] Drought in the land of
Canaan caused a lack of food there.

So Abram went down to Egypt] This was the usual practice
of the Semitic nomads; when they had insufficient to eat they went
into Egypt, a land blessed with abundance of produce. Several
scholars take the view that the reference here is not to the land of
the Nile but to a region in northern Arabia called in the Akkadian
documents *Muṣri;* this conjecture is not, however, plausible for the
whole context postulates a country distinguished by its fertility like
the basin of the Nile.

The text has *went down,* for 'going down' is the usual term used
to denote the passage from the land of Canaan, a land of mountains
and hills, to the Nile Valley. Only Abram, as head of the family, is
mentioned, but the meaning is: Abram and all his household and
all the possessions that they brought from Haran (*v.* 5). Immediately afterwards (it will be noted) the Torah speaks of his wife
who was with him, even though she has not been mentioned here
specifically. This proves that the reference to Lot later on (xiii 1)
presents no difficulty; see the commentary *ad locum.*

To sojourn there] without doubt the exodus from Canaan grieved

Abram. It was but a short time ago that he arrived there, and that the Divine promise was given him that this land would be his inheritance and that of his descendants, and that he had carried out its symbolic conquest; and behold now he was compelled to leave it! A hard test. The poignancy of the ordeal, which Abram endures not without bitter anguish, is hinted at by Scripture in the words *to sojourn there* and in the reason for the migration, *for the famine was severe in the land.* 'To sojourn there': not to settle permanently, but to dwell there temporarily for a little while, until the time of distress would pass. He does not wish — Heaven forfend! — to forsake the Promised Land.

For the famine was severe in the land] The emphasis on the adjective *severe* indicates how dire was the need. Only because the famine was severe did Abram decide, against his will and with heartfelt grief, to leave the land.

The use of the expression *in the land* to conclude the last clause of the verse as well as the first gives the sentence a fine symmetrical form, which is clearly brought out in the way I have divided the verse above.

On the parallels in this and the following verses to the account given, at the end of Genesis and the beginning of Exodus, of the migration of the children of Israel into Egypt, their bondage and their liberation, see above, the introduction to this section, § 2.

11. *And it came to pass, when he came near to enter into Egypt, etc.*] At first, when he feels the need to go, Abram is not worried lest they should encounter danger in Egypt, but as he draws near to the Egyptian border the possibility of a terrible peril occurs to him. In Egypt he will find himself in the position of a sojourner (*v.* 10: *to sojourn there*) without protection against the tyranny of the local inhabitants, and if the beauty of his wife should arouse the lust of any Egyptian, it will not be difficult for him to kill the unprotected stranger and to take his wife to himself.

Here a difficulty makes itself felt. According to what we are told later (xvii 17), Sarah was only ten years younger than Abram, and consequently she was already sixty-five years old when she left Haran, her husband being at the time seventy-five (xii 4). It seems strange, therefore, that Abram should have entertained the fears that he did about his wife after she had reached old age, and even more fantastic is the story related subsequently of what happened.

The scholars who accept the documentary hypothesis easily evade this difficulty. In their view, all chronological data, such as those in xii 4, belong to P, and the whole of chapter xvii is likewise assigned to P, whereas the account in our section is attributed to J; hence, the information about the ages of Sarai and Abram does not relate to this narrative. But even according to their exegesis the difficulty remains in so far as the redactor — R — is concerned, in that he combined the excerpts from P and J into their present form.

Let us attempt to solve the problem by our methods. In the ancient tradition handed down in Israel before the Torah came to be written there was no difficulty at all, because the story used to be told independently, unrelated to chronology, after the manner of sagas current orally among the people. It is self-understood that in the narration of the episode of Sarai in Egypt, she was portrayed as a woman in the full bloom of her youth. When, however, the traditional tales were collected into one big, comprehensive work, and were arranged and integrated into a homogeneous composition, it was necessary to establish a unified chronological system. For the reasons that we have already discussed (see above, p. 282), Abram's age on leaving Haran was fixed at seventy-five and Sarah's at sixty-five, although this dating did not fit in well with the incident in Egypt. It was not possible to change the chronological system, which was based on determinative factors; nor could the story be omitted, since it was well known among the people, and was suited to the plan and purpose of the Torah. There was thus no choice in the matter. The Bible included both elements — on the one hand the chronological data, and on the other the story — and hinted, as it were between the lines, how they could be reconciled: Abraham and Sarai are described as persons endowed with unusual qualities, so much so that a son was born to them when he was a hundred years old and she ninety. Now if Sarah at the age of ninety was able to bear a son and to suckle him, one may infer therefrom that when she was sixty-five, and even older (ch. xx), she could still be considered 'beautiful of form and of appearance'.

Behold [הִנֵּה *hinnē*] *now*, I KNOW [יָדַעְתִּי *yādhaʿtī*] etc.] In classical Hebrew it is standard usage for the word הִנֵּה *hinnē* to introduce the premise to the main subject: it is a fact that you are

beautiful, and thence danger threatens. Ehrlich has suggested that
יָדַעְתִּי *yādha‘tī* should be understood as a form of the second person
feminine singular, with the archaic termination תְּי־ *-tī*.

12. *And it will come to pass, when the Egyptians see you*] The verb
see [יִרְאוּ *yir’ū*] refers back to the word *appearance* [מַרְאֶה *mar’e*;
also from the stem רָאָה *rā’ā* 'to see'] in the preceding verse, the
sense being: when the Egyptians see your beautiful appearance, etc.

They will say, 'This is his wife', etc.] They will think, and pay
heed to the fact, that you are the wife of this man.

Then they will kill me, but they will let you live, etc.] Then
there is reason to fear that they will kill me but let you live, so that
you will remain without a protector and they will be able to deal
with you as they see fit.

13. *Say, pray, you are my sister, etc.*] Of course, I too, shall say that
you are my sister; compare *v.* 19: *Why did you say, 'She is my
sister'?*

Two questions are asked with regard to this verse:

(a) What benefit did Abram hope to derive from this declaration?

(b) How is Abram's conduct to be evaluated ethically, and,
more particularly, what is the Torah's moral judgement thereon?

The two questions are closely related; they should, therefore, be
examined together.

Most contemporary commentators, approaching these questions
with lack of sympathy towards Israel and his Torah, and adopting
an exegetical method that it is difficult to regard as scientific,
attribute unworthy motives and actions to Abram, and consequently
conclude that the moral level of the narrative is also very low. They
base their view on the words, *that it may go well with me because
of you,* which they interpret as an expression of hope that he would
receive gifts from the Egyptians as Sarah's brother (see Rashi
already on this point). Holzinger, for instance, writes that the story
teaches us (I am translating his statement literally) that Abraham
'with shameful baseness abandons his wife to the lust of a foreign
potentate, and derives material advantage from this dirty business.'
Gunkel, on the other hand, finds in the text the intention to exalt
the shrewdness of the father of the nation, who is able to think
up such ingenious schemes in order to extricate himself from trouble

in an alien country, and the desire to eulogize Sarai, for sacrificing her honour in order to save the life of her lord, who has no hesitation in accepting gifts in compensation for his wife's honour. He adds that the ancient Israelite, and Abram in particular, was devoid of the sense of 'chivalry', which compels a man to protect the honour of his wife and daughter at the risk of his life. It is clear that these exegetes are wanting in proper scientific objectivity. Other expositors adopt a more moderate attitude. Procksch, for example, holds that the Torah does not absolve Abram but condemns him, and that its words imply a negative judgement of his conduct; but on the actual behaviour of Abram even Procksch places an interpretation similar to that of Holzinger and Gunkel. Koenig also explains Abram's action in this way, but in keeping with his apologetic tendency he calls it 'weakness', and seeks to defend it on the ground that the concept of the 'exclusiveness' of the relationship between man and wife was far different in antiquity from that prevailing today (it is difficult, however, to prove that such was the case in the ancient Orient in the age of the Torah, and especially among the Israelites; on xix 8 see my commentary *ad locum**); and he adds that Scripture was concerned to teach us that Abram's 'weakness' brought retribution upon him in the form of Pharaoh's rebuke and the expulsion from Egypt, and, by recording this punishment, to make us aware of its reprobation of Abram's deeds.

Let us attempt to expound the verse objectively, without any bias one way or the other.

That it may go well with me because of you] The aforementioned interpretation of these words, namely, that Abram intended, as it were, to receive presents for exposing his wife to danger, encounters three difficulties:

(a) If this were his intention, the words, *that my life may be spared on your account,* would have preceded the clause, *that it may be well with me because of you;* for if a man does not remain alive, he can have no benefit from the gifts, on the contrary, he is unable to receive them.

* Owing to the author's demise, this section of the Commentary was not written.

(b) From Abram's initial statement (*vv.* 11–12), it is evident that his object in appearing as Sarai's brother is to be delivered from the danger alluded to in *v.* 12, *then they will kill me but let you live;* if, now, he clearly states at the outset that this is his purpose, it is inconceivable that as he continues speaking (*v.* 13b), he would change his reason, making the gifts his aim, and that at the end (*v.* 13 c) he would revert to his original intent, *that I may live on account of you.*

(c) If Abram was prepared to engage in the vile business with which many commentators charge him, there would have been no need to say that Sarai was his sister, for a man who is concerned to protect his wife's honour may be killed but not one who is prepared to abandon his spouse for the sake of gain. Contrary to what Gunkel states, it is just because Abram feels it his duty to offer his life in defence of his wife's honour that he is afraid that he will be slain, for he could not possibly prevail in every combat that he would be compelled to fight against all those who might covet his wife. It should further be noted that what he fears is not only that he would be killed, but also, and even more so, that she would be spared (*but they will let you live*), alone and unprotected in face of the lust of the Egyptians. It is obvious, therefore, that if he wishes to represent Sarai as his sister, it is only because he thinks that in this way he would be able to protect her honour more successfully than if he had to risk a combat with the local inhabitants in a foreign land, or even a series of combats, which could only result in his death without his wife's honour being saved.

To the question how Abram could protect his wife with greater success if he were considered her brother rather than her husband, the answer is provided by the explanation already given by several medieval commentators (in modern times, by S. D. Luzzatto): If any one desires you, it will not occur to him to kill your brother in order to obtain you, but he will ask him to give you to him in marriage, and then it will not be difficult for your brother to put him off with words for a time, until the famine is over and we shall be able to return to Canaan.

In order to understand aright the words *that it may go well with me because of you,* we must also bear in mind the clause after it, *and that I may live on account of you.*

And that I may live on account of you] — a repetition, in different words, of the preceding sentence, after the manner of poetic parallelism. The utterances of the *dramatis personae* in Genesis are often cast in poetic form. [The literal translation of our clause is: 'and that my soul may live on account of you']. The meaning is: 'and that I may live on account of you', the word נַפְשִׁי *naphŝi* ['soul', 'life'] being used instead of the first person, וְאֶחְיֶה *weʾeḥeye* ['and that I may live'], in order to complete the poetic rhythm. Here, too, as in all verses constructed on the principle of parallelism, it is possible to understand one line from the corresponding line. The parallelism between *because of you* and *on account of you* is clear; and just as the expression *on account of you*, which is linked to *that I may live,* certainly does not mean 'on account of your beauty' but 'because you will say that you are my sister', so the phrase *because of you* signifies 'because you will make this statement.' Similarly the words *that it may go well with me* must connote the same as *that I may live.* Thus the sense of the whole verse is: *Say, pray, you are my sister, that it may go well with me,* that is to say, that I may be delivered from the danger of death; *because of you,* because of these your words; *that my soul may live* [literal rendering], that is, that I may live, not die; *on account of you,* on account of these words that you will say.

But Abram is not free from guilt, as the apologists think. On the contrary, Abram's conduct, the Torah intends us to understand, involves two sins.

The first is lack of faith. Although Abram's status in Egypt was that of a stranger, he should not have considered himself isolated and unprotected; he should have felt himself close to and confident in the help of his God. We have seen, it is true, that his trust in the Lord was great and deep, and even at the beginning of this section the Bible reminds us of his faith through the words *to sojourn there,* which show that he was convinced that he would be enabled to return to Canaan and inherit it in accordance with the Lord's promise; nevertheless, his faith had not yet reached the degree of absolute perfection. It was destined to reach this stage in the course of the various trials by which the Lord would test him; but at present it is still subject at times to moments of weakness. Now, when Abram's spirit is perturbed and he is fearful of possible

351

danger, he does not clearly discern what avenues of deliverance are open to him, and instead of taking the royal road, the way of the King of the universe, the path of complete trust in the Lord's help and protection, he chooses crooked paths that appear to his disturbed spirit as likely to lead to a successful result.

The second sin was this: the crooked way that he decided upon was that of falsehood, or partial falsehood (see xx 12). The Bedouins are accustomed to tell lies in order to extricate themselves from trouble or to achieve their desire, and Abram was still afflicted by one of the faults of the Bedouin character; only in the future would he succeed, little by little, in purifying himself completely.

As the narrative proceeds, it becomes clear to us how the Torah sees, and wishes us to see, these two transgressions in Abram's conduct. This clarfication is brought home to us not only by the fact that Abram was punished, as Koenig had already noted (see above), but by the particular nature of the penalty itself. The Torah is accustomed to depict reward and punishment in accordance with the principle of measure for measure. Hence the type of retribution indicates the character of the iniquity. The punishment for the first backsliding is related in the next paragraph.

SECOND PARAGRAPH
DANGER

14. *When Abram entered / Egypt,*
    the Egyptians saw the woman / that she was very beautiful.

15. *And when the princes of Pharaoh / saw her,*
    they praised her / to Pharaoh.
    And the woman was taken / into Pharaoh's house.

16. *And Abram was well treated / for her sake;*
    and he had / sheep, oxen, he-asses,
    manservants, maidservants, / she-asses and camels.

14. *When Abram entered Egypt*] Now this is what happened when Abram reached Egypt, after he had prepared the plan outlined in the preceding paragraph.

The Egyptians saw the woman that she was very beautiful] — that is, they saw that the woman was very beautiful. To begin with it happened as Abram had foreseen; the Egyptians recognized and admired Sarai's beauty. But the dénouement was different from what he had imagined.

15. *And when the princes of Pharaoh saw her*] In order to escape the danger, Abram had relied on his shrewdness, and did not put his trust in the paternal providence of the Lord. Now the very ruse that he had relied upon became a source of evil to him. The only peril that he had envisaged was that which might emanate from the commoners of Egypt (*v.* 12: *And it shall come to pass when the Egyptians see you*), and he thought it would be easy for him, as Sarai's brother, to put them off with words. It never dawned on him that possibly Sarai might be desired by one who could take her without her brother's consent. Thus not what he had anticipated, but something that he had never envisaged, happened. The peril actually arose as a result of his craftiness, from the statement that he was her brother and not her husband. This was Abram's retribution, the punishment fitting the crime. From this we learn that the Torah considered his sin to consist in the fact that he put his trust in cunning and not in God's help. The common people of Egypt saw that the woman was very beautiful, but they were not tempted and they did not do or say anything that the patriarch had conjectured. But it was not only the Egyptian plebeians who noticed her — *the princes of Pharaoh saw her*; it was from them, to whom Abram had originally paid no heed, that the evil came forth.

They praised her to Pharaoh] The princes of Pharaoh told their master about the beauty of the foreign woman, the sister of the man who came to sojourn in Egypt; and Pharaoh, having heard that she was unmarried (compare *vv.* 18–19) issued a command, *and the woman was taken into Pharaoh's house.*

So Abram learns, and with him the reader of his biography, that a man must have implicit faith in God's help, and that he is forbidden to rely on his cleverness alone; the contravention of this prohibition brings its own punishment, for a shrewd man is liable to err, and when he thinks that he has taken precautions against every possibility, he may overlook the very eventuality that is actually due to occur.

353

And the woman was taken into Pharaoh's house] Abram's wife is now in the hands of the king of Egypt. Against the lord of the land the patriarch had no power to do anything, either by force or by guile, to prevent her being taken from him; nor can he do ought now, be it by violence or by stratagem, to save her from shame and enable her to return to him. There is only One who can deliver her and restore her to him: the One to whom Abram had failed to turn when his fears were first aroused.

From the literary point of view, it should be noted that the name Pharaoh occurs, in the Hebrew, at the end of each of the three clauses of this verse. This threefold mention of the name stresses the fact that opposed to Abram is Pharaoh the king of Egypt himself, and the patriarch can in no way oppose him.

16. *And Abram* WAS WELL TREATED [הֵיטִיב *hēṭībh*] FOR HER SAKE [בַּעֲבוּרָהּ *ba'ăbhūrāh*] / This sentence, which reminds us of Abram's words *that it may* GO WELL [יִיטַב *yīṭabh*] *with me* BECAUSE OF YOU [בַּעֲבוּרֵךְ *ba'ăbhūrēkh*] (*v.* 13), further indicates that events took a quite different course from what Abram had imagined. There is a subtle undercurrent of irony here: Abram did think that he would be well treated because of her, because of the lie that Sarai would tell, and in fact he was treated well, but the kind of treatment he received was wholly different from what he had expected. He had thought that, thanks to the untruth that he had asked Sarai to tell, it would go well with him in that he would be delivered from death, and behold he was well treated in another sense (the verb הֵיטִיב *hēṭībh* is used here impersonally, 'one dealt well with him', and its meaning is equivalent to the passive, 'he was dealt with well'), namely, that Pharaoh gave him presents. The king's intention was only to show friendship to the brother of the woman who was taken into his house, but in Abram's eyes the gesture has a most terrible significance, betokening the loss of his wife and the end of his hopes of having children by her.

Why the Torah tells us about these gifts will become clear later on, in the continuation of our commentary.

And he had sheep, oxen, etc.] — an explanation, in detail, of the expression, *and Abram was well treated*; this is the outcome of the good treatment referred to in the first part of the verse. Many exegetes, from rabbinic sages (see B. Baba Meṣi'a 59a;

Midrash Mishle on Prov. xxxi 11) down to modern expositors, interpret the passage to mean that these gifts were the foundation of Abram's wealth. Although it is possible that this was how the ancient tradition concerning the episode of Abram and Sarai in Egypt, which was current among the people before the Torah came to be written, intended the matter to be understood, yet in the present form of the Pentateuch this cannot be the intention, for it was already stated earlier (*v.* 5): *and all their possessions which they had gathered,* and it is further recorded later on (xiii 2): *Now Abram was very rich in cattle, in silver, and in gold,* whereas here no mention is made of silver and gold: and subsequently it is again stated (*ibid. v.* 5): *And Lot, who went with Abram, also had flocks and herds and tents.* It thus appears that the sense of our verse is that through the presents Abram's wealth in cattle was still further increased.

Sheep, oxen, he-asses] These are mentioned first, since it is of them that cattle are primarily composed; then come the *men-servants and maidservants,* who are needed for the management of the possessions; last in order are the *she-asses and camels,* used for riding and transport.

And camels] The reference here to camels appears strange to those who think that in Abraham's time there were no domesticated camels yet in Egypt. Those who accept this view assume that the references here and in other passages of Genesis to camels are anachronistic. But research during recent years into the history of the domestication of the camel proves that this took place, at least in its initial stages, far earlier than was previously supposed and consequently no surprise need be felt at the mention of camels in the Book of Genesis.

THIRD PARAGRAPH

SALVATION

17. *But the Lord afflicted / Pharaoh*
with great plagues, / and his house,
because of Sarai, / Abram's wife.

18. *So Pharaoh called Abram, / and said,*
'What is this you have done to me? / Why did you not tell me
that she was your wife?

19. *Why did you say, / "She is my sister,"*
so that I took her / for my wife?
Now then, here is your wife, / take her, and be gone.'

20. *And Pharaoh gave men orders / concerning him;*
and they set him on the way, with his wife / and all that
he had.

17. *But the* LORD [*YHWH*] AFFLICTED [וַיְנַגַּע *wayᵉnaggaʿ*]
Pharaoh, etc.] Till now the name of *YHWH* has not been mentioned in this section; it is as though Abram had forgotten him.
But He did not forget Abram, and though he sinned He delivered
him. Although Pharaoh's power was tremendous, for he was
regarded as a god by the Egyptians, the Lord [*YHWH*] on high
was mightier still, and He bent him completely to His will.

Undoubtedly the Bible intends us to understand that these
plagues were inflicted on Pharaoh and his house before the king
was able to approach the patriarch's wife. Most of the commentators,
who take an unfavourable view of the whole incident (see above,
on *v.* 13), assume that the purport of the verse is to tell us that
Sarai was not delivered from the danger threatening her, and that
the plagues did not come until she had been defiled. But the story
cannot bear this interpretation for several reasons:
(a) If the Lord wished to save, He could do so in time, and there
was nothing to hinder Him; had the plagues come after the
woman's honour was sullied, they would have served no purpose.
(b) It is difficult to suppose that a story would have gained
currency among the Israelites impugning the purity of the patri-

archal family and of the whole of Israel; and it is even harder to
believe that the Torah would have incorporated such a tale.

(c) When Pharaoh said to Abram (*v.* 19), *Here is your wife,*
it seems as though he intends to say: Behold I restore to you that
which I took from you; I am returning your wife to you as I took
her. Apparently the Torah did not wish to speak openly of so
delicate a matter, but it made its meaning clear to all who read the
text without prejudice. In the word וַיְנַגַּע *wayᵉnagga',* which comes
after the statement, *and the woman was taken into Pharaoh's house,*
the *Wāw* is antithetic: it is true that the woman was taken into
Pharaoh's house, but the Lord afflicted the king in time, and thereby
He delivered her from jeopardy.

One cannot object that what is narrated in *v.* 16 must have taken
a certain amount of time; for previously it was stated only, *and
the woman was taken into Pharaoh's* HOUSE; but we were not told
that she had already been brought to Pharaoh. Before Pharaoh
asked for her to be brought to him, the Lord smote him with great
plagues.

When we understand the episode in this way, the acceptance of
Pharaoh's largesse by Abraham has not the despicable character with
which it could have been regarded if adultery had actually taken
place. Notwithstanding, even without adultery, the acceptance of
Pharaoh's bounty casts a shadow of doubt on the worthiness of
Abram's conduct; and in particular there arises the question: Why
does the Torah tell us all this in detail?

To find the answer to this question, we must consider one of the
provisos of the Laws of Middle Assyria, which deals with a similar
matter. Since the legal tradition in its general outline was common
to all the countries of the 'Fertile Crescent', it may be assumed that
the provisions of this clause were in force in all the countries of
this region. Now this is what is stated in Tablet A of the Middle
Assyrian Laws, paragraph 22, first part (I give a literal translation,
adding explanatory notes in brackets): 'If in the case of the wife of
a man, (one who is) not her father, nor her brother, nor her son,
but another person, should cause (her) to go on any journey
(apparently with him), without knowing that she is the wife of
a man, he must take an oath, and give two tablets of lead to the
husband of the woman.' The commentators differ as to the nature

of the journey mentioned here, but this at least is clear, that the law refers to a man who conveys to some place the wife of another man without realizing that she is a married woman, and apparently he has no relations with her, for in that event it would be an instance of adultery, and the law would have been different. The statute ordains that the man in question should take an oath (apparently, he must swear that he did not lie with the woman) and pay a fine to her husband. The case is very similar to that of Pharaoh and Sarai. Pharaoh, too, brought Sarai into his house without knowing that she had a husband, but he had no intercourse with her. Hence, the law required, according to the statute, which, as far as we are permitted to assume, was known and in force among the Israelites, that Pharaoh should swear to Abram and pay him a fine. But it was impossible for a human court to mulct the king of Egypt for the benefit of a commoner who had come to sojourn in his land. However, the law is law, and what it enacts must be done. The Judge of the whole earth directs the course of events in such a way that the requirements of the statute are fulfilled. Pharaoh declares to Abram that he did not sin against him and did not touch his wife, and he gives him presents in lieu of the penalty that the law prescribes (the story of Abimelech — xx 14–16 — has to be interpreted in the same way). Consequently — and this it seems is the intention of the passage — Abram is able to accept and retain with a clear conscience what he received at the hand of Pharaoh, since these gifts have not the character of bounty but of a fine that must be paid to him by law. Possibly it was not without reason that the Torah was careful not to say in *v.* 16, 'and Pharaoh gave him', or words to that effect, but employs instead an impersonal verb הֵטִיב *hēṭībh* [literally, 'one dealt well'], and a neutral expression וַיְהִי לוֹ... *wayehī lō* ... [literally, 'and there was to him', etc.; rendered: 'and he had' etc.], as though it wished to avoid using such terms as 'giving gifts', and intended to tell us only that Abram received what was due to him by law and equity.

On the parallelism with what the Israelites received from the Egyptians according to the account given in Exodus, which is to be explained on the same lines as our passage, see the introduction to this section and my Commentary of the Book of Exodus.

358

But the Lord afflicted Pharaoh] Although Pharaoh did not commit a great crime and was not deserving of severe punishment, nevertheless he did wrong. According to the Assyrian statute referred to, a man who acts like Pharaoh is accounted a transgressor in that he did not take the trouble to make sure of the marital status of the woman beforehand. This apart, the analogy to the story of Abimelech, where it is stated (xx 6): *and it was I who kept you from sinning against me,* shows that Scripture intends us to understand that these plagues were an admonition and a warning to Pharaoh that he should not fall into the sin of adultery — an admonition and warning that helped not only Sarai and Abram, but also Pharaoh, who was saved thereby from committing a graver offence.

Great plagues] The Bible does not explain the nature of the plagues since this detail was not of importance to the main theme, and it is superfluous to attempt to guess what Scripture does not detail. Similarly, it is unnecessary to endeavour to determine, as several expositors have attempted, in what way Pharaoh came to know that Sarai was Abram's wife. It would seem that the Torah's aim is to inform us that the plagues with which Pharaoh was afflicted at the very time that he sought to have Sarai brought to him gave him food for thought. He saw therein the finger of God, and carefully investigated the matter and discovered the truth. Apparently Scripture avoided going into details that would have diverted the readers mind from the primary theme.

On the parallelism with the plagues inflicted upon Pharaoh and the Egyptians, which are described in Exodus, see above, the introduction to this section.

And his house] This point is mentioned after the complement, *with great plagues,* at the end of the sentence, as though to say: and also his house with him. We have a parallel here to the statement in *v.* 15: *And the woman was taken into Pharaoh's house.* The members of Pharaoh's household cooperated with him in detaining Sarai within the confines of the palace; now since they were partners in his sin, it follows that they must share in his punishment.

Because of Sarai, Abram's wife] — on account of their behaviour towards Sarai, who was a married woman, the wife of Abram.

18. *So Pharaoh called Abram, and said*] As soon as Pharaoh is made aware of the position, he sends for Abram in order to rebuke him.

What is this you have done to me] — an expression of reprimand. The patriarch could have administered the same rebuke to Pharaoh, for it was Pharaoh who wronged Abram, but after the manner of despots, the king changes the rôles; and from a given viewpoint he is justified, since it was actually the declaration of Abram and Sarai that they were brother and sister that misled him.

Why did you not tell me that she was your wife?] The word לָמָה *lāmā* and likewise מַדּוּעַ *maddūaʿ* [both mean, 'why'] are often used to express reprimand. Compare, for example, Exod. ii 20: *Why have you left the man?*; ibid. i 18 (Pharaoh says to the midwives): *Why have you done this?* (here, too, the rôles are changed; the midwives did not do anything, on the contrary, they refrained from doing what Pharaoh wanted).

19. *Why did you say, 'She is my sister'?*] You were not only silent regarding the fact that she was your wife, but you deliberately stated that she was your sister (see above, my annotation to *v.* 13).

So that I took her for my wife] These words do not prove that adultery occurred (Procksch already pointed this out); the expression *I took* signifies only that the woman was taken into the king's harem. It may be added that it is precisely the verb *take* that is used in *v.* 15, in the sentence, *And the woman was taken into Pharaoh's house,* and there, unquestionably, it has this sense. Similarly, in chapter xx 2 it is said of Abimelech: *And . . . took Sarah,* and in that narrative it is expressly stated (*v.* 4): *Now Abimelech had not approached her.*

Now then, here is your wife] I return her to you as I took her (see above, the introduction to this section).

Take her, and be gone] The verb *take* occurs thrice: I took her from you [*v.* 15 and *v.* 19]; now you come and take her back; but get away from me and my country; I do not wish you to remain any longer in Egypt. On the parallel expression in the story of the Israelites in Egypt (Exod. xii 32: *Take . . . and be gone*) see my remarks in the introduction. Possibly, the meaning here is the same as there, namely, that Pharaoh was afraid of the Deity who protected Abram and his wife, and therefore he wanted to remove them from his vicinity.

Abram makes no reply to Pharaoh's reprimand. He cannot answer; his conscience tells him that he has sinned, and he is silent. By the fact that he is compelled to receive the rebuke in silence, the Bible shows us how Abram was punished for his second transgression, the falsehood he told. This teaches us that untruth is not only ethically reprehensible, bringing retribution in its train, but is also injurious from the practical point of view, since it has no foundation in fact and must sooner or later be exposed and do harm to the person who resorts to it.

However, if on the one hand Abram committed sins, which were already punished and expiated, on the other hand his merits, which had earned him the Divine promise that he would have abundant offspring who would become a great nation (*v.* 2), stood him in good stead, and so the episode ended happily, and Sarai was saved.

20. *And Pharaoh gave men orders concerning him*] Pharaoh, who, as stated, saw in the plagues by which he was afflicted the finger of God, hastens to do what a successor to his throne was to do in similar circumstances in the days of Moses, when visited by plagues: he sends away the beloved of God from his presence and appoints men to take charge of them and see to it that they leave Egypt, whilst taking care, at the same time, that no evil befall them, so that their God should not again avenge their wrong.

AND THEY SET [וַיְשַׁלְּחוּ *wayešalleḥū*] *him on the way, with his wife*] On the parallelism between the use of the verb שִׁלַּח *šillaḥ* here and its frequent occurrence in Exodus, see the introduction above.

And all that he had] The Egyptians were careful not to detain any one of his company or to retain any of his property.

1. *So Abram went up / from Egypt,*
   he and his wife, / and all that he had,
   and Lot with him, / into the Negeb.

2. *Now Abram was very rich / in cattle, / in silver, and in gold.*

3. *And he journeyed on / from the Negeb as far as Bethel,*
   to the place / where his tent had been at the beginning,
   between Bethel / and Ai,

4. *to the place of the altar / which he had made there at the first;*
   and there Abram proclaimed / the name of the Lord [YHWH].

1. *So Abram went up from Egypt*] Here, near the end of the narrative, we have an antithetic parallel to what is stated at the beginning. There we are told (*v.* 10): *so Abram went down to Egypt;* and here, in analogous terms: *So Abram went up from Egypt.*

He and his wife, and all that he had] All those who went forth with him from Egypt and all that they brought out with them from there reached their destination in peace.

And Lot with him] Till now Lot has not been mentioned in this section; hence most commentators are of the opinion that, in the primary form of the section, Lot did not go down to Egypt with Abram; and they regard the words, *And Lot with him,* or even the whole verse, as the addition of a later editor. But according to the literary methods that characterize the Book of Genesis, not only was it unnecessary to mention Lot earlier, but it was essential not to refer to him. We have already observed (see above, pp. 275 f., 280 f.) that each passage mentions the people on whom the reader's attention ought to be focussed, but does not refer to those who, even though they were together with the persons who are specified, remained on the periphery and did not occupy the central position among the *dramatis personae.* Similarly, in the section describing how Abram went up from Haran (xii 1–9) to Canaan, sometimes

362

the patriarch is mentioned alone, as head of the immigrating family, and at other times all the members of the family are detailed, depending on the varying requirements of the episodes concerned. Abram only is mentioned when the primary theme is the migration as such; all are named when the main purpose is to list those who took part therein. The same obtains in our section: at first the principal topic is just the going down to Egypt; hence Abram only, as head of the emigrating family, is referred to by name; later on, when the departure from Egypt is spoken of (xii 20), it was necessary to make express mention of Abram's wife because of what had been narrated concerning her in the preceding verses, whereas the other members of the family, including Lot, were of interest only collectively, in order to show that not one of Abram's household was detained in Egypt, and it sufficed to include them all in the expression, *all that he had*. But here, when we tell the story of the return to Canaan, Lot begins to be personally significant, since it is necessary to prepare the ground for the account of his separation from Abram, which occurs in the next section; consequently it is not enough to repeat the phrases that were already used in connection with their leaving Egypt (xii 20: *he and his wife, and all that he had*), but there is added *and Lot with him*, in order to point out explicitly that Lot was included in the words *all that he had*.

Into the Negeb] — in the direction of the Negeb region, which is in the south of Canaan. Apparently the period of famine had already passed, and it was possible to return there with confidence. The expression *into the Negeb,* which comes near the end of the section, provides a parallel to the conclusion of the preceding section (xii 9). Although the reference there is to a journey towards the Negeb from the north, and here it is to travelling to the Negeb from the south, yet the phrase *into the Negeb* is identical in both verses.

2. *Now Abram was very* RICH [כָּבֵד *kābhēdh*] *in cattle, in silver, and in gold*] *The word* כָּבֵד *kābhēdh* [literally, 'heavy'] is in antithetic parallelism to what is narrated at the commencement of the section (xii 10: *for the famine was* SEVERE [כָּבֵד *kābhēdh*]): then Abram suffered because the famine was כָּבֵד *kābhēdh* ['heavy', 'severe']; now he is very כָּבֵד *kābhēdh* ['heavy', 'laden', 'rich']

363

with possessions. Regarding the parallelism with the destiny of his children, who would leave Egypt with great wealth (xv 14), see the introduction to this section. This verse also serves to prepare us for the story in the following section.

3. *And he journeyed on* [לְמַסָּעָיו וַיֵּלֶךְ *wayyēlekh lᵉmassāʿāw;* literally, 'he went on his journeys'] *from the Negeb as far as Bethel*] When he reached the Negeb, he did not wait there, but continued to go on his way northward — *on his journeys* — journey after journey, in keeping with the pace of the cattle before him, and he came to Bethel. In these words, too, there is a parallel to the conclusion of the preceding section (xii 9: *And Abram journeyed on,* STILL GOING [וְנָסוֹעַ הָלוֹךְ *hālōkh wᵉnāsōaʿ*] *toward the Negeb*).

To the place where his tent had been at the beginning, between Bethel and Ai] The place is indicated here with exactitude, since this is important to establish the parallelism, which we have already noted, between the tradition relative to Abram's journeys and that of the Book of Joshua concerning the site of the first battle. Just as Abram encamped there when he came up from Haran, and also on his return from Egypt, in order to possess himself of the land of Canaan, even so his descendants began there the series of battles for the conquest of the country.

4. *To the place of the altar which he had made there at the first*] Abram came to the very spot where he had built the altar when he went up from Haran, the site that he loved so dearly because on it stood the altar, the second monument (the first that he now encounters on coming from the south) to the symbolic conquest of the land and its consecration to *YHWH,* his God.

And there Abram called upon the name of the Lord [*YHWH*] / As soon as he came back, after the interruption caused by his emigration to Egypt, Abram resumed his work of founding his new religion, and he proclaimed there, next to the altar, the name of *YHWH,* his God (see the annotation to xii 8). His return to Canaan is not just an ordinary migration on the part of a shepherd wandering from place to place; it is the return to the land appointed for his mission, and the mission of the offspring, of a man who had dedicated himself and his descendants to a new faith. Therefore, as soon as he is back unharmed after the severe trial to which he was subjected in Egypt, he renews his work for the fulfilment of his vocation, and he confirms the symbolic acquisition of the land in the name of *YHWH* by going up to the place where he had built his altar at first, and by renewing the proclamation of *YHWH*'s name, which he had already begun at this site (xii 8). The parallelism with the conclusion of the preceding section is not only one of form but also of content. The ending is marked by thematic solemnity and literary grace.

SECTION THREE

LOT PARTS FROM ABRAM

CHAPTER XIII, 5–18

INTRODUCTION

§ 1. THIS SECTION narrates how Abram proposed to Lot for the sake of peace — to avoid contention between his and Lot's herdsmen — that he should part from him. This, too, is a test and trial for Abram: he was hoping to become a great nation (xii 2), yet now, even though he was still childless, he was compelled, out of his love of peace, to separate himself from his brother's son, who was to him as a son.

He lets Lot choose the place he desires, and the latter selects the most fertile area, the region of Sodom and its satellite towns, although it is at the extremity of the territory of Canaan (see my annotation to x 19, pp. 215 f), far from the centre of the Promised Land, and its inhabitants are 'wicked, great sinners against the Lord.' Abram remains faithful to the land of Canaan, which was promised to him by the Lord; he is not eager to secure the fattest land but that to which he was brought by the grace of the Most High. And the Lord confirms the assurance in regard to the acquisition of the land and the numerous descendants that would issue from him. After the test, Abram is consoled by the word of God, which renews for him the promise and the blessing.

§ 2. In this section, too, the deeds of the sires continue to be depicted as though they forecast the fate of the scions. Lot rejects the land of Canaan and settles at the end of its border; in keeping with this attitude, his offspring, the children of Moab and Ammon, are to have no portion in it. Subsequently we are told (xix 30) that Lot departed from the border area, which he had originally chosen, since he was afraid to dwell there, and made his abode in the hill country, that is, on the high plateau on the eastern side of the Jordan, where his descendants would settle in the future. By this act, their destiny, as it were, is determined. Having also rejected the district in which the cities of the plain are situated, he thereby relinquishes his right to them on behalf of himself and his children. When Abram says to Lot, *Is not the whole land before you?* etc., he renounces his claim, generally speaking, to the land that Lot would select for himself, and this concession applies particularly, of course, to the land that Lot ultimately chooses, namely, the highland of Transjordania. This, likewise, is an act of the fathers that foreshadows events in the history of the children. It is recorded in the Book of Deuteronomy that when the Israelites went forth from Egypt, just as Abram and Lot are now going forth from there, God told them that they were forbidden to attempt to conquer the land of Moab (Deut. ii 9): *Then the Lord said to me, 'Do not harass Moab or contend with them in battle, for I will not give you any of their land for a possession, because I have given Ar to the sons of Lot for a possession.'* The parallelism of theme is manifest. The fact that the Moabites are called 'the sons of Lot' lends emphasis to the analogy. The same applies to the sons of Ammon. In the continuation of the passage it is stated (*ibid. v.* 19): *and when you approach the frontier of the sons of Ammon, do not harass them or contend with them, for I will not give you any of the land of the sons of Ammon as a possession, because I have given it to the sons of Lot for a possession.* Here, too, the designation 'the sons of Lot' is stressed, and not without reason. Abram shows by his conduct towards Lot how his descendants must behave towards Lot's descendants.

Although David is destined to impose his rule over the sons of Moab and Ammon, yet even in the days of Israelite dominion the Moabites and Ammonites will continue to dwell in their land; they will not be expelled from it, for it is their heritage, apportioned to them from the beginning.

Herein we also see the connection between this section and the one preceding, which tells of Abram and Lot dwelling in the land of Egypt. The negotiations between them over the division of the land take place after their exodus from Egypt, just as the warnings mentioned earlier were communicated to the Israelites after they had emerged from the Egyptian bondage.

§ 3. The focal point of the section is the corroboration of the promise regarding the acquisition of the land, which is given to Abram in *vv.* 14–17 with an elaboration of detail that is certainly not accidental. Similarly, we cannot regard as fortuitous the fact that the word אֶרֶץ *'eres* ['land', 'earth'] occurs seven times in this section, which is a customary distinction for the key-word of a section in the stylistic technique that I have discussed so often in the course of my annotations.

This promise includes also the region of the cities of the plain. Although Abram was prepared to give it up in favour of Lot, yet the Divine communication confirms to him the promise regarding the possession of the whole land, as far as and including that area. It is stated earlier [xiii 10]: *And Lot lifted up his eyes, and saw that the whole basin of the Jordan* etc., from which we can clearly infer that Abram and Lot at the time of their parting were standing on high ground from which it was possible to *see* the Jordan basin. Now behold, the Lord says to Abram: *Lift up your eyes, and* LOOK [literally, 'see'] *from the place* (the word 'place' is purposely stressed) *where you are, northward and southward and eastward and westward; for all the land which you* SEE *I will give to you and to your descendants forever.* The area chosen by Lot is thus expressly included in this promise.

§ 4. There is another point emphasized by the Bible here as a sign unto the children, to wit, the settlement of Abram in Hebron. Although it is clear that Abram's connection with Hebron was an integral part of the tradition and was based on ancient memories dating back to the days of the Patriarchs, yet the mention of the matter at this stage, immediately after the promise of the possession of the land throughout its length and breadth, is obviously significant. Apparently the sense of the passage is this: since immediately after Abram had been told, *Arise, walk through the length and breadth of the land, for I will give it to you,* Divine providence caused him to settle in Hebron, this presages that it is at Hebron that a kingdom would be established that would have dominion over the whole land. The Divine announcement made to Abram now was fulfilled in David, who founded his monarchy in Hebron. As soon as he had received the Divine promise, Abram made his abode at Hebron, which was eventually to become the centre of action leading to the fulfilment of this promise.

FIRST PARAGRAPH

THE DISPUTES

5. *And Lot also, / who went with Abram,*
   had flocks, and herds, / and tents.

6. *And the land could not support them / that they might dwell*
   together;
   for their possessions were so great, / that they could not dwell
   together.

7. *And there was strife —*
   between the herdsmen of Abram's cattle / and the herdsmen
   of Lot's cattle.
   Now the Canaanite and the Perizzite / dwelt then in the land.

5. *And Lot also,* etc.] The word *also* links this section with the
one preceding, and especially with *v.* 2, which served, as I
explained, to prepare us for the story contained in this section.

Who went with Abram] There is a reason for this clause; it
comes to remind us what we were told earlier (xii[5]) — — — .*

* See Translator's Forword, pp. VII–VIII.

INDEXES*

I. BIBLICAL REFERENCES **

* References are to pages.
** Numbers printed in italic refer to the pages in which the commentary on the verse is given.

1. BIBLICAL REFERENCES

I. BIBLICAL REFERENCES

II. OTHER LITERARY REFERENCES

(Ancient and Modern)

III. Notabilia